HINDUISM
BUDDHISM
ZOROASTRIANISM
JAINISM
SIKHISM
ISLAM

This volume of the basic teachings of Eastern mysticism makes available for the first time the rich variety of thought and vision from India and the Near East. These religious philosophies have as their goals the direct experience of God and the universe—of partaking in the unity of all things and of learning of a level of being beyond mere consciousness. The fundamental writings gathered here are the roots of the Eastern mystical religions and philosophies.

RAYMOND VAN OVER, author of PSYCHOLOGY AND ESP and editor of THE TAOIST TALES and the I CHING (all published in Mentor editions), is a member of the Society for the Scientific Study of Religion. EASTERN MYSTICISM, Volume II, which will cover the religions of the Far East, will also be published in a Mentor edition.

MENTOR Books of Special Interest

EASTERN MYSTICISM

EASTERN MYSTICISM

Volume I: The Near East and India

Edited with an Introduction and Commentary by

Raymond Van Over

A MENTOR BOOK

NEW AMERICAN LIBRARY

TIMES MIRROR
NEW YORK AND SCARBOROUGH, ONTARIO
THE NEW ENGLISH LIBRARY LIMITED, LONDON

Copyright © 1977 by Raymond Van Over

Library of Congress Catalog Card Number: 77-73988

MENTOR TRADEMARK REG. U.S. PAT. OFF. AND FOREIGN COUNTRIES
REGISTERED TRADEMARK—MARCA REGISTRADA
HECHO EN CHICAGO, U.S.A.

SIGNET, SIGNET CLASSICS, MENTOR, PLUME AND MERIDIAN BOOKS
are published *in the United States* by
The New American Library, Inc.,
1301 Avenue of the Americas, New York, New York 10019,
in Canada by The New American Library of Canada Limited,
81 Mack Avenue, Scarborough, 704, Ontario,
in the United Kingdom by The New English Library Limited,
Barnard's Inn, Holborn, London, E.C. 1, England

First Mentor Printing, August, 1977

1 2 3 4 5 6 7 8 9

PRINTED IN THE UNITED STATES OF AMERICA

FOR CAMILLA,
who sustains, nourishes, and
creates an alchemy beyond words or deeds.

ACKNOWLEDGMENTS

When compiling a book like *Eastern Mysticism*, which uses large and varied sources, one accrues extremely large debts. Beyond the direct acknowledgments thankfully given to publishers for reprinting their material, there is an additional debt to the many orientalists and scholars upon whom I relied. It is to their translations, their analyses, their long labors, that I owe the deepest obligation. It is one that I warmly acknowledge, for their works have given me many hours of pleasure and enlightenment that I cannot ever repay.

PART ONE HINDUISM

Rig Veda selections are from *Rig Veda Sanhita, A Collection of Ancient Hindu Hymns*, trans. by H. H. Wilson (London: Trubner & Co., 1888); *The Hymns of the Rig Veda* (two vols.), trans. by R. T. H. Griffith (Benares: E. J. Lazarus Co., 1889, 1896); *Sacred Books of the East* (vols. 32 and 46), trans. by F. Max Muller and H. Oldenburg (Oxford at the Clarendon Press, 1891, 1895).

Bhagavad Gita selections are from *The Song Celestial or Bhagavad Gita*, trans. by Sir Edwin Arnold (London, 1885).

Principal Upanishads selections are from *Sacred Books of the East* (vols. 1 and 15), trans. by F. Max Muller (Oxford at the Clarendon Press, 1879, 1884).

Patanjali's Yoga Sutra is from *Raja Yoga, or Conquering the Internal Nature*, trans. by Swami Vivekananda (Calcutta: Swami Trigunatita, 1901). Reprinted in 1937 by Luzac & Co., London; by Swami Pavitrananda, Mayavati, Almora, Himalayas: Advaita Ashrama, 1944; and a new, revised edition by Ramakrishna-Vivekananda Center, 1956.

The Aphorisms of Sandilya are from *The Aphorisms of Sandilya, or The Hindu Doctrine of Faith*, trans. by E. B. Cowell (Varanasi, U. P.: Indological Book House, 1878, 1965).

The Writings of Sankaracharya are from *The Crest Jewel of Wisdom and other Writings of Sankaracharya*, trans. by Charles Johnston (London: The Path, 1894, 1895, 1896); also reprinted by Theosophical University Press, Covina, Calif., 1946.

The Sacred Hymns of the Saivites are from *The Religion and the Philosophy of Tevaram*, by M. A. Dorai Rangaswamy (Madras, India: University of Madras Press, 1958); *Lalla-Vakyani, or the Wise Sayings of Lal Ded, A Mystic Poetess of Ancient Kashmir*, trans. by Sir George Grierson (London: Royal Asiatic Society, 1920).

PART TWO BUDDHISM

Most of the Buddhist selections are from the *Sacred Books of the East*. Buddha's First Sermon and Last Sermon are from vol. 11 (1881); The Questions of King Milinda is from vol. 35 (1890); If He Should Desire is from vol. 11 (1881), all trans. by T. W. Rhys Davids.

The Way of Purity is from *Buddhism in Translation*, by H. C. Warren (Harvard University Press, 1896); and *The Sacred Books and Early Literature of the East*, ed. by Charles F. Horne, vol. 10 (New York & London: Parke, Austin & Lipscomb, 1911).

Existence and Nirvana in Hinayana Buddhism selections are all from

Buddhism in Translation, by H. C. Warren, and from The Questions of King Milinda, *Sacred Books of the East,* vol. 35.

The Way of Virtue is from vol. 10 of the *Sacred Books of the East,* trans. by F. Max Muller.

PART THREE ZOROASTRIANISM, JAINISM, AND SIKHISM

Zoroastrian Gathas, Yashts, and Hymns are from *The Essential Unity of All Religions,* by Bhagavan Das (Benares, India: Kashi-Vidya-Pitha, 1932, 1939); the *Zend-Avesta,* vol. 31, Part III, *Sacred Books of the East* (1887), trans. by L. H. Mills.

Jaina Sutras are from the *Sacred Books of the East,* vol. 22 (1884), trans. by Hermann Jacobi.

Sikh Scriptures are from *The Sikh Religion* (6 vols.), trans. by M. A. Macauliffe (Oxford, 1909); also from *History of the Sikhs,* trans. by Henry Court (Calcutta, India: Susil Gupta Ltd., 1888, reprinted 1959).

PART FOUR ISLAM: SUFI AND PERSIAN MYSTICS

The Koran selections are from *Sacred Books of the East,* vols. 6 and 9 (1880, 1881), trans. by E. H. Palmer. The Pearls of Faith selection is from *Pearls of Faith or Islam's Rosary,* trans. by Sir Edwin Arnold (London: Routledge and Kegan Paul Ltd., 1882).

Selections from the Sufi mystics are listed below. 1. Al-Ghazali: *Some Moral and Religious Teachings of Al-Ghazzali,* by Syed Nawab Ali, reprinted with the kind permission of Sh. Muhammad Ashraf, Kashmiri Bazar (Lahore, 1920, 1944). 2. Ibn al-Arabi: "The Bezels of Divine Wisdom" is from *Studies in Islamic Mysticism,* trans. by R. A. Nicholson, and reprinted with the kind permission of Cambridge University Press (1921). "A Collection of Mystical Odes" is from the *Oriental Translation Fund, New Series,* Vol. 20, trans. by R. A. Nicholson, and reprinted with the permission of the Royal Asiatic Society (1911). 3. Abdul Qadir: *The Revelations of the Unseen,* trans. by M. Aftub-ud-din Ahmad, and reprinted with the permission of Sh. Muhammad Ashraf (Lahore, 1949, 1967). 4. Sana'i of Ghazna: *The Enclosed Garden of the Truth,* edited and trans. by J. Stephenson, reprinted with the kind permission of Samuel Weiser, Inc. (New York, 1972). 5. Mohammad Iqbal: *The New Rose Garden of Mystery,* trans. by M. Hadi Hussain, and reprinted with the kind permission of Sh. Muhammad Ashraf, Kashmiri Bazar (Lahore, 1969). 6. Omar Khayyam: *Quatrains of Omar Khayyam,* trans. by E. H. Whinfield (London: Trubner & Co., 1883). 7. Kabir: *Songs of Kabir,* trans. by Rabindranath Tagore, and reprinted with the kind permission of Samuel Weiser, Inc. (New York, 1974). 8. Rumi: *Sufi Saints and Shrines in India,* trans. by J. W. Sweetman, reprinted with the permission of Samuel Weiser, Inc. (New York, 1970); also *The Mathnawi,* from *Masnavi* by Jalal-ud-din Rumi, trans. by W. Whinfield (London, 1898). 9. Talib: *Sufism: Its Saints and Shrines,* by John A. Subhan, reprinted with the kind permission of Samuel Weiser, Inc. (New York, 1970). 10. Attar: *Readings from the Mystics of Islam,* trans. by Margaret Smith, and reprinted with the kind permission of Luzac & Co. (London, 1950); also *Sufism: Its Saints and Shrines,* by John A. Subhan, reprinted with permission of Samuel Weiser, Inc. (New York, 1970). 11. Hafiz: *Readings from the Mystics of Islam,* trans. by Margaret Smith, reprinted with permission of Luzac & Co. (London, 1970); also from *Sufism: Its Saints and Shrines,* by John A. Subhan, reprinted with permission of Samuel Weiser, Inc. (New York, 1970). 12. Jami: *Sufism: Its Saints and Shrines,* by John A. Subhan, reprinted with permission of Samuel Weiser, Inc. (New York, 1970); also the *Oriental Translation Fund, New Series,* Vol. 16, trans. by R. A. Nicholson, and reprinted with the permission of the Royal Asiatic Society, London; also *The Persian Mystics: Jami,* by F. Hadland Davis, reprinted with the permission of Sh. Muhammad Ashraf, Kashmiri Bazar (Lahore, 1946).

Who never spent the midnight hours
Weeping and waiting for the morrow,
He knows you not, ye heavenly powers.

—GOETHE

Watchman, what of the night?
The watchman says:
Morning comes and also the night
If you will inquire, inquire:
Return, come back again.
                    —ISAIAH 21

Contents

Part Two
BUDDHISM   *197*

Part Three
ZOROASTRIANISM, JAINISM, AND SIKHISM   *287*

Part Four

ISLAM: SUFI AND PERSIAN
MYSTICISM   339

EASTERN MYSTICISM

General Introduction

The greatest paradox of human existence is precisely that we consciously *are*; we live, yet constantly seek meaning in this fact, and delve deeper and deeper into what we sense lies hidden within us. We continuously remind ourselves that life cannot be only as it appears, that too many disconcerting facts remain unanswered. The eternal question "Why?" is always with us, nagging consciousness into reflection, feeding restlessness of spirit, irritating us even in the midst of plenty to seek beyond our apparent contentment. To call this urge merely a sense of adventure, a need for excitement, is nonsense, for how does labeling this yearning clarify its underlying dynamics? They remain unchanged and the mystery unsolved. As Emerson recognized, "Under each deep another deep opens." We seem caught in a process of living that cannot allow life to simply happen, to simply be; for as long as consciousness exists we seek to expand our understanding, to explore different avenues of meaning. In the end humanity seems one thread woven into a garment guided by the hand of nature and perhaps, who knows, to be worn by God.

Human beings are an obstreperous species and cannot lie long in the sun, as does a cat or a flower. We impose and urge our lives into new patterns, while other forms of life simply *are*; they *respond* to causality. We attempt to make causality, to be the cause creating the effect of our lives, and in this we are akin to gods in our desires. We suffer, perhaps, from a divine discontent. The primary difference is that we usually fail, whereas God by definition cannot. Emerson sensed this feeling of yearning when he wrote that "man is a stream whose source is hidden. Always our being is descending into us from we know not whence." What we sense is that the spark which gave life to the single cell of our being is truly greater than the sum total of what we are at any given moment. But how can this be? If life is created by a spark so great as to give breath to the complexity of us all, then the spark should still be residing within, somewhere, at the core of our being. Perhaps we intuit a greater reality within than we allow ourselves to recognize—for indeed,

1

such recognition implies greater responsibility, and this most of us do not want, for we frequently are not responsible even in the simpler aspects of our personal lives. We sense this intuition of an otherness when we turn quietly inward. It is, as William James described it, that "we are continuous with a *More* of the same quality."

What Jacob Boehme called the "signature" of life is perhaps written within every seed, every cell of the brain, every thought that speeds through our minds. But humanity, as Boehme saw with his special vision, has a unique signet involving their ultimate self-revelation, the conscious understanding of the microcosm within and the universal macrocosm without. This is the signature of divinity that mystics see written within the souls of human beings; it is a higher principle that marks the skein of each life according to the distinctive fabric of each temperament.

In every individual's life questions arise like "Who am I? What is the meaning and purpose of life? What is the purpose of *my* life?" These are religious as well as philosophical questions, for they deal with absolutes and concepts of ultimate value. How the questions are approached determines whether they will be considered in a religious, philosophical, or even perhaps a limited behavioral psychological framework. If one asks "Who am I?" in the context of strict rationalism, the problem will be viewed as philosophical or psychological and an answer will be limited by those categories. One of the central revelations of modern thought has been the realization that how people reason about their world reflects the values that shape the culture to which they belong.[1] In other words, our reasoning processes tend to be self-fulfilling dynamics that create cultural and philosophical values that we then analyze as deriving from the culture itself. How one chooses to perceive the problem of identity is therefore vitally important to the scope and depth of the answer available. If one sees humanity as an insignificant particle in the immensity of space, a cosmic accident, then any importance given the human condition or a concept of "self" becomes an ironical joke. Should we then consider individuals as grains of sand in a huge cosmic desert? Or are we all part of a universal field? Is our destiny personal and circumscribed alone, or is it simultaneously personal and interpersonal? Are we so self-contained in our individual consciousnesses that only functional and mechanical answers are possible? Or do we function within a transcendental existence, living as yet untouched by its deepest significance?

[1] See E. A. Burtt, *In Search of Philosophical Understanding* (New York: Mentor, 1965), p. 83.

Answers that perceive human beings as automatons or sophisticated machines leave us with but a regulated future, a destiny circumscribed by machinelike functions. However, the hypothesis that sees humanity as neither insignificant, nor as the medieval center of a truncated universe, but rather as a force within the overall processes of nature is integrative and retains some value for—or form of—human identity. A theory that allows for human identity reduces contradictory tensions between our *feeling* the reality of an inner self and the ever-present pressures of modern reductionist theories in philosophy and psychology that deny this. The integrative hypothesis places the mind of a human being and its unique faculties of consciousness into part of an immense hierarchy, or active universal principle. An individual then has the option to determine through conscious effort either: (1) alienation from this natural hierarchy of cosmic forces; or (2) identification with its principles, thereby becoming a part of its function. The first is dehumanizing and the second augmenting and integrative. This identification necessarily results in the human being evolving from a limited awareness to a larger vision, a unified, even universal perspective. Humanity thus strives toward an "unthinkable communion" as Michael Polanyi has termed it. It is also a religious construction that states that human life does indeed have meaning and a fuller purpose within the universe, and as such, partakes of the divine. Reinhold Niebuhr is therefore no doubt correct in emphasizing that religious faith is basically trust that life, however difficult and strange, has ultimate meaning.

SCIENCE AND MYSTICISM

A true picture of the universe has always been hidden from our physically limited senses. It is axiomatic that our conscious awareness is not only subject to illusion of the senses, but to the delusions of mind as well. To compensate we have developed logical, rational methods of examining the world around us, hoping that when our natural senses and talents failed us, we could rely on what we call the scientific method.

In medieval times there were two acknowledged ways of gaining knowledge. One was *ratio*, or discursive reasoning, the other was *intellectus*, which involved qualities of creative insight, imagination, or intuition. Intellectus was believed the higher faculty, one involving a more profound understanding of the world. This higher insight provided the artist, philosopher and mystic with inspiration and vision. In modern times scientists are becoming more sensitive to this nondiscursive way of knowing.

The eminent physicist Max Planck wrote in his autobiography: "When the pioneer in science sends forth the groping fingers of his thoughts, he must have a vivid, intuitive imagination, for new ideas are not generated by deduction, but by an artistically creative imagination." Human beings apparently have no purely objective way of uncovering what is "real" or "true." We all suffer, in one degree or another, from selective perceptions, which determine what our mind eventually receives as information. Even the scientist working in a completely mechanized environment does not exclude human error entirely, for the experimenter can unconsciously influence the structure, design or behavior of his instruments, or interpret the machine-derived data according to personal bias. This psychological fact is why repeatability is so vital in scientific method. Viewed strictly as a Cartesian argument between objective and subjective truth, humanity seems eternally trapped: first within the confines of our flesh and ego needs, and second within the limitations of our ingenuity to use machines that extend our knowledge. Science, it appears, is near the limits of objectivism.[2]

Perhaps to compensate for past imbalances, a new orientation, an integration between philosophical, cultural, and scientific principles from the Eastern and Western halves of the globe, is arising. People are even beginning to talk in terms of a new "spiritual dimension" in the philosophy of science. This revolution seems most concentrated in atomic physics and psychology. These disciplines have always included a small number of scientist-philosophers who have theorized about what amounts to a mystical (i.e., unitive) view of the universe. The convergence of science and mysticism has traditionally occurred in the hermetic, occult, or theoretic realm, but it seems that the deeper modern science delves into basic life processes, the closer it comes to describing the world in "real" terms—as well as theoretical—identically to the mystics.[3]

Scientists now emphasize energy fields instead of solid particles or mass, probability relations and indeterminacy instead of mechanical determinants. There is no longer talk of elementary particles as spatially perceptible matter—such particles are ulti-

[2]See "Kafkaphysik," *Science News*, July 12, 1975, p. 29, where D. E. Thomsen writes that "modern physics seems to be presiding over the death throes of objectivity. The ancient philosophical props of physics—causality, determinism, materialism—are being swept overboard by the physicists themselves."

[3]Examples of this movement are numerous. Among the most prominent are cultural philosophers like Jean Gebser and P. J. Saher, biologists Adolf Portmann and Edmund Sinnott, geneticist Theodosius Dobzhansky, and numerous physicists such as Erwin Schrodinger, Albert Einstein, and Werner Heisenberg.

mately of nonmaterial derivation. Hence, the atoms that form matter are nonmaterial, the forms of matter composed of atoms are also derived from a nonmaterial source. In Western scientific terms the description of "reality" is in mathematical and symbolic language. In the East these same observations are equivalent to what the Indians call maya, which generally defines the material world as illusion. Yet it is clear that the physical matter we daily deal with is not illusory. The problem becomes one of reference. By what perspective are we considering the world? When the physicist considers it on a subatomic level, there is a surprising agreement with Eastern philosophy.

Although the fifth-century-B.C. philosopher Heraclitus uttered many mystical sentiments, he nevertheless also possessed the temperament of a scientist. The mystical and scientific could remain comfortably within one breast because Heraclitus consciously kept his categories separate. He did not confuse the mystical absolutes, such as "Good and ill are one," with the relativism of the world we live in. Thus, "To God all things are fair and good and right, but men hold some things wrong and some things right." Heraclitus' empiricism: "You cannot step twice into the same river; for fresh waters are ever flowing in upon you." Heraclitus' mysticism: "We step and do not step into the same rivers; we are and are not."

There are a number of key areas where the world views of the mystic and the scientist agree.[4] Both the mystic and the physicist explore the essential nature of life, and are concerned with the ultimate character of what is "real." The physicist begins the search by examining the physical world; the mystic delves within, exploring aspects of consciousness and the character of inner space. Both often arrive at the same conclusion—the essential unity of all things and events. The physicist must spend years in training to conduct investigations properly. Similarly, the mystic pursues many years of hard discipline—both physical and mental—as the writings in this anthology illustrate.

A basic truth that all mystics accept and that the modern philosopher of science is just now beginning to realize is that our conception of reality depends upon our mode of consciousness. The distinction is grounded in the fact that mystics do not perceive the world as a correlate of their own ego. Western nonmystics regard the ego as the exclusive window through which we are capable of perceiving reality, and our traditional science of psychology is built upon this premise. Indeed, our culture's generally held beliefs about the world allow few alterna-

[4]For a thorough and thoughtful comparison between mystics and physicists, see *The Tao of Physics* by Fritjof Capra, a theoretical physicist (Berkeley, Calif.: Shambala Publications, 1975).

tive views. A healthy individual in our culture is defined by a "strong" ego. The Eastern mystic (along with many Western counterparts) considers identity as always temporary; for depending on the frame of reference, it is transitional and malleable. Form changes, composition of atoms, relationships of properties—such as electrical, time-space, and the differences between observers—determine our temporal world. Recognition of flux and change can be the only reliable picture of reality. This the mystic has long accepted and the physicist is just now beginning to adopt.[5] But the insecurity in this approach to life is so obviously devastating to the isolated psyche that the individual tends to fall into either despair or a rigid determinism. Existentialists have extrapolated from this that life is absurd, further isolating and pressuring the individual. This attitude, which eventually reflects upon our self-image, is a major stumbling block in resolving the contradictions between the reality of the inner and outer worlds we experience.

Like the mystic, the modern physicist has been forced to speak of major paradoxes in his search for a true or accurate description of reality. The paradoxes of physics derive from the peculiar dual aspect of matter. Physicists took a long time to accept the paradoxical fact that matter could have two mutually exclusive aspects: that particles are also waves, waves also particles.[6] Matter does not exist with any certainty at the atomic or subatomic level, but rather has "tendencies to exist." The mathematical forms of energies are not three-dimensional waves like sound, but rather "probability waves," abstract mathematical quantities that manifest as a peculiar kind of physical reality somewhere between existence and nonexistence—a world that cannot be described in normal language. The ineffability of this subatomic world corresponds to the problem mystics have when trying to describe their experiences.

Because the particle exists in between the normal states of reality, it is neither present nor absent at any definite place. The particle does not change its position, nor is it stationary. What alters is the "probability wave, and thus the tendencies of the particle to exist" in specific places.[7]

[5]For the Eastern mystical view of change and the impermanence of reality see especially the sections on Hinduism, Buddhism, Taoism, and the I Ching.

[6]See Niels Bohr, *Atomic Physics and Human Knowledge* (New York: Science Editions, 1961), p. 98, where the famed physicist writes: "We meet analogous features in the well-known dilemma about the nature of life, since optical phenomena require the notion of wave propagation, while the laws of transmission of momentum and energy in atomic photo-effects refer to the mechanical conception of particles."

[7]See F. Capra, *The Tao of Physics*.

In describing the paradoxical dilemma a strict rationalist would encounter, J. Robert Oppenheimer wrote: "If we ask whether the position of the electron remains the same, we must say 'no'; if we ask whether the electron's position changes with time, we must say 'no'; if we ask whether the electron is at rest, we must say 'no'; if we ask whether it is in motion, we must say 'no'."[8]

What were once metaphysical mysteries, such as the paradoxes of time-notime, simultaneous existence-nonexistence, self-fulfillment resulting in self-extinction, have come full circle from the cosmic dreams of ancient Eastern philosophers to the cloud chambers of modern physics laboratories. Even though often unrecognized, the models and images of Eastern philosophy now fill the minds of scientists trying to unlock the very same mysteries of reality and existence.

In his 1954 lectures on the "Unity of Knowledge," Niels Bohr emphasized that by widening one's conceptual framework the scope of objective description is also enlarged. Unsuspected aspects can become clarified, and one's general relationship to the world can be drastically modified. This is exactly what has happened traditionally in science as conceptual frameworks were consistently pushed outward and new facts introduced, new theories built. The religious impulse also can be broadening rather than defining or limiting in its relationship to the contemporary world. Some scientists see the very basis of life as a "mystical" process. A good example is Albert Einstein: "The most beautiful and most profound emotion we can experience is the sensation of the mystical. It is the sower of all true science. He to whom this emotion is a stranger, who can no longer wonder and stand rapt in awe, is as good as dead. To know that what is impenetrable to us really exists, manifesting itself as the highest wisdom and the most radiant beauty which our dull faculties can comprehend only in their primitive forms—this knowledge, this feeling is at the center of true religiousness."[9]

As modern science has extended our perceptions of the world by creating powerful and subtle instruments, Western philosophy has slowly begun to develop alternatives to the classical dualism between dead matter and the ethereal soul. Science now confirms that the world is a vibrating, pulsating, living thing, within which we, puzzled human beings, are an integral and important part. Our human importance is no longer based upon the

[8]See J. Robert Oppenheimer, *Science and the Common Understanding* (New York: Oxford, 1954), pp. 42-43.

[9]Quoted by Philipp Frank, *Einstein, His Life and Times* (New York: Knopf, 1947), p. 340; also quoted in M. Laski, *Ecstasy* (London: Cresset, 1961), p. 201; L. Seelig, *Albert Einstein* (Zurich: Europa Verlag, 1954).

arrogant assumption of medieval times that we are the center of the universe, or even the apex of our own world. This realization initially caused great anxiety and isolation, but we are now beginning to perceive ourselves in a new light—as an important partner in universal life forces. By virtue of our reliance upon our conscious, discursive reasoning, our cause and effect perception of the world, we are set apart from other animal life. But the classical view of matter, nature, and our own internal state is rapidly becoming unacceptable in a universe so electric with life forces.

When Spinoza writes that "the more we know of particular things the more we know of God," he is articulating the idea that as the relationships between human nature and the world become clarified, we perceive life as ever more relative, as intricate patterns of an undivided whole. In such a fashion the developing world view of modern science moves ever closer to that of the mystic.[10]

Mystics may not care that modern science is justifying their metaphysical views, but the fact is important, for it reflects a changing world view by science about the nature of reality. The more meaningful and viable parallels established between science (representing the external, objective world) and the mystic (representing the internal, subjective world), the greater our opportunity to fashion an accurate idea of our selves and the universe we live in.

In its broadest sense science is the reduction of multiplicities into singularities; the taking of disparate facts and their organization into coherent formulae; the transmutation of perceived chaos into consciously understood, rational systems. This movement from multiplicty to singularity is the same process that the mind of the mystic initially moves through as it diminishes its perceptual range to a single unitive point of attention during meditation. It is axiomatic that as we move toward any cause we move ever closer to simplicity. Conversely, as we move from cause toward effect we are inclining toward complexity. Both Planck and Einstein observed that the further we move from the complicating world of the senses, the more the physical world picture becomes perfect, elegant, and basically simpler. Science thus imitates the dynamics of life. However, it is this movement toward causes and an ever greater simplicity that the mystic also avidly follows: toward an ever diminishing number of parts until ultimate simplicity—universal oneness—is

---

[10]This idea has become quite popular in recent years. See Lawrence LeShan, *Toward a General Theory of the Paranormal*, Parapsychological Monographs No. 9 (New York: Parapsychology Foundation, 1969). See also his *The Medium, The Mystics, and The Physicists.*

achieved. As consciousness moves toward singleness, as it diminishes its external involvements, there is eventually only one last
thing to perceive—itself! That consciousness can and does perceive itself, while illogical, is empirically provable according to
mystics. In fact, many mystics describe this empiricism as the
only method of validating their own personal experiences to
nonmystics. In short, the mystic is the only person who can
truly say that God ceases to be an object and becomes an experience.

DEFINING MYSTICISM

In the West mystics are not considered "practical"; they are
"revolutionary," "loners," not amenable to authority. This attitude developed from the natural separation between the early
activist, proselytizing Christian church struggling for survival
and the contemplative nature of the mystic. Later the separation was maintained because any independent acquisition of a
mystical "truth" could potentially undermine the authority of
the established church. This antagonism fueled the myth that
mystics are passive and contemplative rather than active—hence,
they are dreamers and impractical. Individual mystics are in fact
as varied as people in other groups. Some were indeed strictly
quietist in their approach to God (Miguel de Molinos, Madame
Guyon); yet others equally passive in spiritual matters were
nevertheless very active in worldly affairs. Most of the great
mystics have been intensely active, possessing great common
sense, and submissive to church authority. Among many examples is St. Bernard of Clairvaux, a tough, realistic, conservative
abbot who became the most influential churchman of twelfth-
century Europe, his power reaching even to Papal Rome. The
Eastern mystics were generally activists in that they headed
monasteries, were philosophers and even political leaders. Examples include the Buddhist patriarchs, the Indians Sankara and
Ramanuja, and Sufis like al-Ghazali and Muhammad Iqbal.

Mysticism has consequently always been confusing to most
people. To the popular mind mysticism conveys magic, occultism, or any peculiar esoteric phenomena—usually from the
"mysterious East." These are all grave misunderstandings of
the word. The term "mystic" has several origins. It derives
from the Greek *mustes*, an initiate, from the verb *muein*,
to close the eyes or mouth and thus keep secret. Its most frequent use was in the rites and initiations of the Greek Eleusian
mysteries. In this sense it can mean hidden truth, esoteric ritual,
or even the inner meaning of something. A "mystic" who had

been initiated into the mysteries was considered reborn, to have gained enlightenment into divine ideas. In its truest sense, then, it cannot be separated from religious aspiration and spiritual enlightenment.

The word "mysticism" was not even widely used until the Middle Ages, and has had many different connotations since then. Some medieval theologians called the mystic's experience "experimental knowledge of God through unifying love"; or "a stretching out of the soul into God through love." Goethe called it "the scholastic heart, the dialectic of the feelings." A Christian scholar, Dean Inge, writes: "Religious mysticism may be defined as the attempt to realize the presence of the living God in the soul and in nature, or more generally, the attempt to realize in thought and in feeling, the immanence of the temporal in the eternal, and of the eternal in the temporal." [11] Evelyn Underhill, both a scholar and mystic, described mysticism as "the art of union with Reality. The mystic is a person who has attained that union in greater or less degree; or who aims at and believes in such attainment." [12]

A mystic is perhaps best defined as one who attempts to achieve direct communion with God or some unifying principle of life. This is a necessarily broad definition, for while mystics vary within the framework of different religions, there is a great similarity between the language and experience the world over. Some commentators like R.C. Zaehner [13] have attempted to show the differences between Eastern and Western mystical experience; while others like Aldous Huxley [14] and A.J. Arberry emphasized the enormous similarities as evidence of a perennial philosophy underlying all human endeavor. Professor Arberry, a renowned Sufi scholar, summarizes his belief that mystical experiences are universal at their core: "Mysticism is essentially one and the same, whatever may be the religion professed by the individual mystic: [It involves] a constant and unvarying phenomenon of the universal yearning of the human spirit for personal communion with God." [15]

Mystical experiences generally fall into two broad categories: those in which feeling or emotion predominates, and those in which experience is noetic or cognitive-intuitive, and occurs pre-

[11] *Christian Mysticism* (New York: Meridian, 1956), p. 5.
[12] *Practical Mysticism* (New York: Dutton, 1915), p. 3.
[13] See Professor Zaehner's *Mysticism, Sacred and Profane* (London: Oxford at the Clarendon Press, 1957).
[14] See *The Doors of Perception*, and also *The Perennial Philosophy*.
[15] *Sufism, An Account of the Mysticism of Islam* (London: Allen & Unwin, 1950), p. 11.

dominately through the mind.[16] The feeling experience is often described in emotional terms of love, or even sensualism, and is more common to religions that emphasize devotion, love, and submission to God's will, like Sufism, Teveram and other Hindu sects, Christianity, and Pure Land Buddhism. A good example of this type of emotionally overwhelming experience was scribbled on a scrap of paper sewn into Blaise Pascal's jacket, and found after his death.

> From about half past ten in the evening to
> about half an hour after midnight.
>   Fire.
> God of Abraham, God of Isaac, God of Jacob,
> Not the God of philosophers and scholars.
> Absolute Certainty: Beyond reason. Joy. Peace.
> Forgetfulness of the world and everything but God.
> The world has not known thee, but I have known thee.
>   Joy! Joy! Joy! tears of Joy!

The Persian mystic-poet Baba Kuhi of Shiraz (d. 1050 A.D.) describes the same total absorption of the mystic experience.

> In the market, in the cloister—only God I saw.
> I opened mine eyes and by the light of His face
>   around me
> In all the eye discovered—only God I saw.
> Like a candle I was melting in His fire:
> Amidst the flames outflashing—only God I saw.

Fire! Light! Joy! Absolute immersion! A terrible glory overwhelms the feeling mystic,[17] and salvation shapes the awesome power that can only come by nonresistance, by immersion and receptive opening to its infinite deeps. Eastern examples abound in Sufism, Hinduism, Buddhism, where love, devotion, and good works are a common combination. It is natural for the follower of bhakti yoga (devotion) to be involved in karma yoga (divine service), which includes the mystic of action.[18] Even in the more God-reduced mystical systems like Buddhism (Zen, Ch'an) there

[16]The cognitive and feeling categories are similar to W. T. Stace's psychological typology—the introvertive and extrovertive—which will be discussed later.

[17]Emotional, evocative adjectives, like "terrible," "awesome," "blissful," "joyful," are not out of place when describing the feeling mystic, but such terms would completely misrepresent the noetic experience of Taoism, Jainism, Sankara's advaitism, or Dhyana Buddhism.

[18]See Sandilya Sutras, and the Bhagavad Gita.

is the tradition of the Bodhisattva, who follows the ideal of good works, of aiding all life to fulfillment. The mystic of action should in fact put to rest for all time the mistaken but popular impression of the mystic's passive, otherworldly reputation.

The emotional or feeling experience seems more frequently reported in the West and is most common to mystics in theistic religions. The noetic quality is most often found in those religions that stress contemplative disciplines, such as forms of yoga, Dhyana Buddhism, and Taoism. These religions and schools consider emotional responses like joy, peace, or bliss a form of worldly attachment that must also be discarded before union with ultimate reality is possible.

The clearest definition of noetic mysticism I have seen states that "the emphasis [is] on immediate awareness of relation with God, direct and intimate consciousness of Divine Presence. It is religion in its most acute, intense and living stage."[19] I prefer this definition because it emphasizes two very important elements: (1) the *empirical* aspect of direct, intense awareness; and (2) the *full consciousness* of the experience. The emphasis on consciousness is in both Eastern and Western religions. For example, the medieval Christian *contemplatio*, or contemplation, was often used to describe the mystical experience. In Eastern religions the emphasis on contemplation as a surrogate for mystical experience is even stronger. One of the clearest examples is in the Yoga Sutras of Pantanjali, where he distinguishes between three stages of consciousness that lead to enlightenment: concentration, meditation, and contemplation.[20]

1. Concentration is the binding of the mind to one place.
2. Meditation is continued mental effort there.
3. Contemplation is the same when there is the shining of the mere object alone, as if devoid of one's own form.

The twentieth-century philosopher S. Radhakrishnan also emphasizes the noetic quality, which he calls "integrated thought." Radhakrishnan believes that mystical consciousness brings things into a new pattern or perspective; integrates them into a unitive reality instead of breaking them into parts as in analytical or

[19]*Dictionary of Philosophy*, ed. D. Runes (New York: Philosophical Library, 1960).

[20]For the complete Yoga Sutras see vol. 1 of *Eastern Mysticism*. For a detailed, highly simplified and clear commentary on Patanjali's sutras see Dr. Ernest Wood, *Practical Yoga, Ancient and Modern* (New York: E. P. Dutton & Co.., 1948); also in paperback (North Hollywood, California: Wilshire Book Co., 1970).

discursive thought. Mysticism also results, therefore, in an insight that unifies previously disparate elements of life.

THE NATURE OF MYSTICISM

The mystical impulse is usually linked with the sophisticated philosophical system that develops in the later stages of a religion—monism. Monism states that ultimate reality is a unity, in contrast to theism or polytheism, which conceives ultimate reality in terms of a godlike, anthropomorphic being or beings.[21] Earlier religions, like the Vedas and Zoroastrianism, were basically sacrificial and did not have many developed mystical elements, even though they existed sublimated in their sacrificial character. The mystical element in sacrificial religions derives from the pantheistic beliefs of early peoples, and the conviction that a divine principle permeates all things. Mysticism develops fully when this divine element is seen not simply as a magical property that dominates the surrounding world and demands worship and propitiation, but rather when it is perceived as an extension of the divine within oneself as well. The separation between the sacrificer and that which is sacrified to is diminished. When this occurs sacrifice is no longer possible, for then one is sacrificing to the divine within oneself. At this point polytheism and animism are transmuted into pantheism, which in turn evolves into a monistic vision of the universe. Psychologically, thanksgiving and wonder take over from fear, awe, and the need to influence divinity in one's favor. If the divine is within oneself as well as in all nature, it is no longer necessary to pray for deliverance, rain, or a good harvest. For the mystic it be-

---

[21]Some scholars have gone so far as to define monism as a synthesis of worship based upon a numinous awareness within any given religion. This seems unnecessarily broad, yet would probably hold true for Advaitism, the Upanishads, and Buddhist absolutism. The synthesis is one in which the supreme object of worship is ultimately transcended. A distinction between the devotional worship represented by the Gita, Ramanuja, and bhakti mysticism, and the more impersonal absolutism of Sankara, is found in each group's use of contemplation and prayer. The devotional and more personal identifies strongly with a supreme personal Lord or Savior, while the absolute monism of the more impersonal systems like Sankara's identifies with a metaphysical Absolute. Both can be monistic, for the distinction is one of emphasis. These distinctions in approach help clarify why the theist often rejects mystical monism, which does not sufficiently emphasize the differences between the worshipper and the worshipped. The theistic mystic, therefore, often argues not only that such a difference exists, but that his salvation depends on it; for if there is no difference between the worshipper and the worshipped, then salvation cannot be requested of a personal Savior or an all-powerful God.

comes necessary only to make oneself more consciously a part of that divine principle.

If mysticism is indeed the peak of developed religions it may result from combining the religious impulse with refined philosophical analysis. As S. Radhakrishnan has observed, all true religions seem to recognize the immanence of God and are highly mystical (i.e., unitive). The justification for this statement is a simple philosophical equation: There can be only one Absolute, and in order to *be* Absolute, It must exist in all things.

Perhaps the study of religion brings one face to face with the fundamentals of human nature. If so, mystical experience is the basic expression of those fundamentals. Theology, the rational examination of religious doctrine, cannot be considered a basic expression of religious feelings. Only the direct experience of an individual with the divine seems to express the fundamental characteristics of humanity's religious aspirations. This is the core of the mystic's approach to the question of what is real.

There are two general religious tendencies in the West—to regard God as transcendent, outside the soul and to be reached by stages; or to regard God as immanent, dwelling within the soul and to be found by going deeply into one's own inner reality also by stages. The latter best correlates with mysticism. Because of its emphasis on God as transcendent and external, Western religious tradition fosters dependence of the individual upon a higher power, whereas Eastern religions tend continually to force the individual back into the self—into what Rudolf Otto termed "introspective mysticism." The self becomes the matrix, the center of intense activity by which the individual hopes to first understand, and then conquer. To accomplish this the "mind" (and consciousness) becomes the mystic's medium.

The psychological emphasis on mind is apparent in the mystic's cleansing not only the will, but also the intellect and imagination. Consciousness to all mystics is imbued with the qualities of a sacrificial urn; the contents must be sanctified and of a pure nature before the desired union with the divine can be accomplished. This does not imply an exceptional emphasis on the "psychic" or parapsychological aspect of the mind, which mystics find suspicious and diverting. They believe that psychic events must be differentiated from the spiritual. On this single point Eastern and Western mystics agree most strongly.

It is important to remember the Eastern emphasis on mind, for with the exception of devotional schools like bhakti, Teveram, Pure Land Buddhism, and Sufism, the Eastern mystical tradition conceives numinous experiences as cognitive rather than feeling states. But the tendency toward the cognitive is so strong that even some devotional schools like Sufism have sects or individuals that stress the mind. To the Eastern mystic each mind is a light unto itself; yet indistinguishable from its universal source. There is no sanctification of the mind beyond cleansing it through mental disciplines. Practically every major concept in Eastern religions, from karma, meditation, or emptiness, depends somewhat upon the cognitive or mind. In the Dhammapada, for example, Buddha says: "All that is, is the result of thought, it is founded on thought, it is made of thought." The Sufi 'Abd al-Karim Jili (c. 1428) wrote that "thought is the basis of existence and the Essence which is in it, and it is a perfect manifestation of God, for Thought is the life of the spirit of the universe. It is the foundation of that life and its basis is Man. Do not despise the power of Thought, for by it is realized the nature of the Supreme Reality."[22]

The same emphasis on thought occurs in a Biblical verse that is perhaps the foundation of Christian mysticism: "The light of the body is the eye: therefore when thine eye is single, thy whole body is also full of light; but when thine eye is evil, thy body also is full of darkness. Take heed therefore, that the light which is in thee be not darkness."[23] Light here is not simply a spiritual glow to St. Luke, like a halo or aura, but rather in this verse it is tantamount to meditative thought, a metaphysical description of the concentrating mind conquering its wandering, prodigal, undisciplined ways until it perceives only a single point—which is the goal of all meditative techniques.

Both Eckhart and Tauler speak of the "ground of the soul." This ground of the soul is also called scintilla or "spark" and is considered the purest or highest part of the human being, and therefore the fittest medium by which the Godhead communicates itself. Because of its purity there is a natural affinity between the two—the soul and God. The scintilla, or *apex mentis* (intellect or contemplative faculty) as it was sometimes called, is conceived by Ruysbroeck as a mirror in which the Divine Being is reflected. St. John of the Cross calls the same *apex mentis* the "eye of the soul, which is understanding." and hence is the particle of divine illumination within humanity. An enlightening descriptive message from the Christian mystic Jacob Boehme further clarifies St. Luke's "singleness of the eye." The disciple says to the Master in one of Boehme's *Dialogues*, "How am I to seek in the Centre this Fountain of Light which may enlighten me throughout and bring my properties into perfect harmony? I am in Nature, as I said before, and which way shall I pass through Nature and the Light therefore, so that I may

[22]Margaret Smith, *Readings from the Mystics of Islam* (London: Luzac & Co., 1972), p. 117.
[23]St. Luke, 11, 34-35.

come into the supernatural and supersensual ground whence this true Light, which is the Light of Minds, doth arise; and this without the destruction of my nature, or quenching the Light of it, which is my reason?"

The Master replies, "Cease but from thine own activity, steadfastly fixing thine Eye upon *one Point*. . . . For this end, gather in all thy thoughts, and by faith press into the Centre, laying hold upon the Word of God. . . . Be obedient to this call . . . thy mind being centrally united in itself, and attending His Will. So shall thy Light break forth as the morning."

The comparison between Eastern and Western mysticism is even more striking when the Biblical passage is set alongside The Secret of the Golden Flower. Light throughout this Ch'an Buddhist-Taoist book is a term that stands for "thought." The two are synonymous. Pure thought results in a pure, bright light within one. Evil thought results in internal shadows that penetrate one's life, influencing and darkening the mind, ever expanding its nigrescent effectiveness. St. Luke's description of light within the eye, the central point of consciousness (Atman), is a further parallel with the East. Also the phrase "making the eye single" occurs in both Eastern and Western mystical writings. The result is the same: the whole being is filled with concentrated thought (light). As Lord Tennyson perceived it,

> Look how the living pulse of Allah beats
> Through all his world . . .
> There is light in all,
> And light with more or less of shade in all
> Man-modes of worship.

In conversations with the renowned Zen exponent D. T. Suzuki, the German existential philosopher Martin Heidegger uses the word "Being" as synonymous with an "inner light" that illuminates our consciousness and the meaning of existence. Light *is* thought. "The light allows us to know that we are beings. It illumines the ground which makes this knowledge possible. . . . Man must seek himself in the ground of life, the Urgrund, the Being of beings . . . Man is neither explained economically, rationally nor politically, his meaning lies in the ontological structure of his reality." [24]

The illumination of life by divine light is the foundation of mystical experience and development. Sufis, for example, conceive of the universe as a projection, or reflection image of God. The divine light emanates and falls upon every atom of

[24] See the introduction to Martin Heidegger's *What Is Philosophy?*, trans. by W. Klubach and J. Wilde (London, 1958), p. 9.

existence, which thereby reflect divine attributes. A fourteenth-century Sufi, Mahmud Shabistari, writes that "the mystic who has seen the Vision of the Unity, sees at the first the light of Real Existence: even more, as he sees, by his gnosis, the pure light in everything he sees, he sees God first."[25]

The same emphasis on illumination, on divine light, occurs in Hinduism. In a verse from the famous Vedanta poem Hastamalaka, the author (allegedly Sankara) describes the essence of the Indian mystic's perception of consciousness as synonymous with light.

> As the single sun reflects itself
> On the surface of every water-jar
> So are our minds enlivened
> Through that common Cosmic Light;
> That thought-free Awareness itself am I.

This verse metaphorically characterizes the common source of all our individual minds as light, yet does not distinguish between the perceiver and the perceived, between the subject and object. The tenth verse concludes, however, with this resolution.

> That one illuminating power in both Light and Eye;
> That unchanging Awareness is my very essence.

No longer is there any difference between the light and the reflecting water-jars. The light that gives form and existence to individual objects is the same that perceives. All three elements result in a perceptual process that is one and the same: the light that shines, the form or object that is given existence by illumination, and the awareness that perceives through the eye or other senses, are all the same "essence." It is this essence of mind and consciousness that the mystic pursues.

CONSCIOUSNESS EAST AND WEST

In the West the conscious mind is used almost exclusively to explore the external world, whereas by its very nature consciousness should also be used to explore the internal world. The Western world did not become generally sensitive to "inner reality" until the development of psychology—with the outstanding exceptions of early mystical philosophers like Parmenides and Heraclitus.

[25]Margaret Smith, *Readings from the Mystics of Islam*, p. 112.

Many modern psychologists reject the very idea of "mind" as being anything more than an epiphenomenon of the brain. The psychologist T. R. Miles, for example, aggressively advocates eliminating the mind entirely, in order to have "an operational approach" to study human beings.[26] Such opinions are found throughout academic psychological literature and are especially popular with experimental psychologists and behaviorists. Neither Freud nor today's leading behaviorist, Harvard's B. F. Skinner, considered consciousness an important factor when investigating human behavior. The rigid rationalism of Western psychology has created false premises by which we judge mental health generally and subjective religious experiences specifically. As psychiatrist Thomos Szasz has observed, if a person talks to God, he is said to be praying; but if he says that God is talking to him, he is said to be schizophrenic. The mystic, therefore, who claims direct experience of the divine cannot escape being considered neurotic or worse.

Most psychoanalysts still follow Freud when considering the depersonalization of the self and nirvanic experience. It is a return to the oceanic sensations of a cosmic womb. Some biologists have even suggested that the unifying perception is a "reliving" of the "ecstasy" when the sperm unites with the ovum—which is a theory only very learned men could enjoy. This basic misunderstanding of Eastern conceptions of the self, mind, and consciousness confuses what is in fact a "transcending of the ego" with a loss of "ego-strength." What is an augmenting experience for the mystic becomes an infantile regression for the psychotherapist. This is unfortunately the position taken by most medical psychologists today. Some of the confusion probably occurred because the description of the psychotic reality is often similar to transpersonal experiences, including the mystical. An example is the psychotic's experience of time. As R. D. Laing describes the psychotic's "mundane time," it is "merely anecdotal, for only the eternal matters." This is identical to the mystic's description of time, yet there must be a qualitative difference, unless one wishes to establish that both are suffering from the same dysfunction. This is not so, however, because there are too many differences left unaccounted for in the two experiences. A short comparison may be helpful.

The madman is lost and foundering in the void, whereas the mystic experiences profound identifications that are the opposite of feeling a lost "being." As Laing appropriately describes the world of the mad, "He muddles ego with self, inner with outer, natural and supernatural." No such broken boundaries of reality

[26] See *Eliminating the Unconscious* (New York: Pergamon, 1966).

exist for the mystic. The boundaries are indeed breached, and will never possess again the same limiting power they had before the mystical experience. But the distinctions between the two worlds are not completely lost as with the mad. Instead of disintegration or dissonance within himself, the mystic experiences a sense of meaningful union with all aspects of the world. Instead of fragmentation, the mystic experiences complete integration. The madman has lost his place in the world, the mystic has found his and proves it by functioning with greater clarity and purpose than before. The madman founders in his own confused mind, the mystic finds peace and an acute sense of value in all life. The madman is torn asunder by the powers unleashed within and around him; the mystic perceives the energies and great powers of the universe as a unifying principle that resolves all his previous confusions and anxieties. While the madman's anxiety is increased by his "oceanic" experience, the mystic's is decreased. The mad are exiled from any sense of "being," in the integrated sense we understand the word. But on the contrary, the mystic's sense of constant, anxious striving which he felt *before* the mystical experience is resolved and he experiences a fullness of "being" never before felt. The madman is split apart by his experience and the mystic is made whole. Again the theme of unity, but this time regarding the human psyche.

Most of the early great systematizers of the unconscious, from F. W. H. Myers to Jung and Freud, did not emphasize any dualism between the various aspects of the psyche, but rather searched for a psychic synthesis. Numerous psychotherapies had the goal of an integrated "mind": Jung—individuation; Maslow—self-actualization; Allport—functional autonomy; Adler—creative selfhood. All of these holistic themes would find some compatibility with Eastern religious views of the psyche.

Carl Jung, for example, argued that merely identifying the contents of the unconscious was not enough, for true health came when the conscious and unconscious were in harmony and coordination of effort. The greater harmony between the two, the fuller the coordination of the activities, the healthier the individual was. As Jung described it, only a unified personality can fully experience life; a personality split up into partial aspects, though calling itself a human being, cannot be so. Jung's theory, however, could not stand without the proviso that the psyche is a self-regulating system continually striving for equilibrium. This balance is considered delicate, and if any aspect of either the conscious or unconscious is out of balance, the psychic system itself does not function well. A balancing of psychic forces is obviously a dynamic process needing constant attention and modulation. This part of Jung's philosophical psychology agrees with the Eastern mystic, who also perceives the self in terms of energy principles, of equilibrium, of a unified harmony between the conscious and unconscious—and, indeed, between all aspects of life. This unification brings one to the conscious realization (and experience of) a greater self deep beneath the layers of disharmonious confusions.

Both Eastern and Western systems agree that the mind is the arbiter of reality, and it is therefore the key to unlocking the mysteries of the inner self. The primary difference is that the mind is seen as a vehicle for transcendence by many Eastern mystics, instead of a catacomb of instincts, ego, and illness. The mind in its natural, original state is conceived by Eastern mystics as primordial quiescence. In its pure, unmodified state it is equivalent to liberation from worldly attachments, from the impurities of material relationships. These material attachments limit the mind's perception of true reality. To overcome our ordinary egocentric consciousness Eastern religions use a variety of meditative techniques.[27] The same theme occurs in Buddhism and Taoism, where one is constantly advised to dissolve the attachments of the ego-centered mind; of slowly diminishing the power of material delusions and the world. The Indian sage Asvaghosa teaches the same path toward enlightenment. In the Tibetan Book of Great Liberation there is a section called the "Yoga of Knowing the Mind," where liberation is found through truly "knowing" one's own mind.

> While the essence of mind is eternally pure and clean, the influence of ignorance makes possible the existence of a defiled mind. But in spite of the defiled mind the mind (per se) is eternal, clear, pure, and not subject to transformation. Further, as its original nature is free from particularization, it knows in itself no change whatever, though it produces everywhere the various modes of existence. When the oneness of the totality of things is not recognized, then ignorance as well as particularization arises, and all phases of the defiled mind are thus developed.[28]

[27] The goal of all meditation is control of the mind, often by some form of concentration on an object, problem, or aspect of one's psyche; or, alternatively, by relaxed and detached observation of the contents of one's mind. There are techniques that suppress verbal or symbolic thinking, and others using rigorous dialectics to force the thinking process to its origins. In the latter, disciples are asked with relentless precision: Who, why, or what is it they seek? Who is the originator of each thought, feeling, or fleeting mental image? Ch'an Buddhism, among several others, demands delving ever more deeply until one achieves an answer that has no antecedent.

[28] London: Oxford, 1954, p. 210.

The Eastern mystic sees the mind as cluttered by the impressions of worldly existence. As the mind is cleansed of the dross attached to it, it returns to its pure state—natural and unmodified, untouched and all-encompassing.

Milton wrote that "the mind is its own place, and in itself/Can make a Heaven of Hell, a Hell of Heaven." This all-embracing capacity to create its own reality, to be reflective of whatever the eye (brain) perceives because of its original purity (impressionability), makes the mind a simultaneous blessing and devilish thing. As the mind ceases to be absorbed with reflecting the subject-object opposition imposed upon it by the exigencies of physical life and egoic needs, it balances the psyche as Jung described, just as the body maintains its own natural balance and health. As the mind turns away from obsessions, attention is drawn to its natural condition, objectless contemplation; the observation of itself by itself. In such a condition the dross of object orientation is shucked as if by a chrysalis taking to wing as a butterfly. Contemplation of the mind by the mind, of consciousness by itself, brings the mind back to its purer, undirected yet all-encompassing original state.

There are numerous examples in this anthology of such Eastern views of the mind. One example is the Brihadaranyaka Upanishad, where a verse explains the central importance of the mind to Vedanta philosophy. Yagnavalkya, the commentator of the chapter, is questioned by Asvala the priest:

"With how many deities does the Brahman priest on the right protect today this sacrifice?

"By one," replied Yagnavalkya.

"And which is it?"

"The mind alone; for the mind is endless," replied Yagnavalkya.[29]

An excellent Western parallel is from the "Poem of the Gospel of St. John."

In the Beginning was Mind: and Mind was with God.
So Mind was God. This was in Beginning with God.
All kept coming into existence through it; and apart from
    it came into existence not a single (thing).
What had come into existence in it was Life; and
    Life was the Light of the (true) Men.
And the Light shineth in the Darkness; and the
    Darkness did not emprison it. . . .

[29] See *Sacred Books of the East*, vol. 15, p. 124.

It was the True Light, which enlighteneth every Man
who cometh into the world.
It was in the world; and the world kept coming into
existence through it.
And the world did not know it. It came unto its own;
and its own did not receive it.
And as many as received it, to them it gave power
to become children of God,—
To those who have faith in his name,—Who was brought
to birth, not out of (blending of) bloods.
Nor of urge of flesh, nor urge of a male,—but out of God.
So Mind became flesh and tabernacled in us,—
And we beheld its glory,—glory as of an only-begotten
Father,—full of Delight and Truth.[30]

THE CHARACTERISTICS OF MYSTICISM

The Christian description of the mystic way is generally divided into three levels or methods: the Way of Purgation, the
Way of Illumination (or Contemplation), and the Way of
Union. Each path has parallels in Eastern myticism. In *Eastern
Religions and Western Thought*, for example, the Indian philosopher S. Radhakrishnan names three similar stages in Hinduism—purification, concentration, and identification. Such stages,
of course, are only rough guides toward understanding the evolu-
tionary character of the mystic path.

After a careful psychological and philosophical analysis of
mysticism, the American philosopher Walter T. Stace listed
seven basic characteristics common to all cultures, religions, and
social conditions: (1) ineffability; (2) paradoxicality; (3) a
feeling that what is apprehended is holy, sacred, or divine; (4)
feelings of blessedness and joy: (5) a sense of utter reality or
objectivity; (6) a sense of Oneness; and (7) that all things are
expressions of this Unity.[31] The renowned Japanese Zen philosopher and mystic D. T. Suzuki listed eight major characteristics
of Eastern mystics: (1) irrationality; (2) intuitive insight;
(3) authoritativeness; (4) affirmation; (5) sense of the beyond;
(6) impersonal tone; (7) feeling of exaltation; (8) momentariness.[32]

[30]*The Gnostic John the Baptiser*, trans. from the original Greek by G. R. S.
Mead (London: Watkins, 1924), pp. 123-26.
[31]See W. T. Stace, *Mysticism and Philosophy* (London: Macmillan & Co.,
1961).
[32]D. T. Suzuki, *Essays, Second Series* (Boston: Beacon Press, 1952), pp.
28-34.

Irrationality involves the philosophic premise upon which the whole of mystical experience rests. Mystics believe one cannot know oneself completely through discursive reasoning and logical observation. The human being is part of a universal whole. How, the mystic implies, can a creature whose character ultimately rests within a universal context be expected to explain itself in terms limited to the "part" perceived at any given moment? The Chinese called this "no-knowledge" and implied by this term the destruction of "part" knowledge, which entangles the mind by definitions and words. It is what Castaneda's Don Juan called "stopping the dialogue."

Noesis or intuitive insight is not simply abstract knowledge. Basic intuition is "the profound unity which is identified as the Real Self." Similar to Western mysticism, all forms of Eastern mysticism seek "enlightenment" by resolving the distinctions between subject-object opposition. As this occurs the "real self" (and unity of all things) is made manifest. But how then does one achieve this identification with the real self, and thereby directly perceive the unitive way?

In most introvertive mystical experience,[33] when consciousness is dissolved from its dependence upon the physical senses and emptied of all "empirical content," the mind becomes a "void" as pure consciousness emerges. Pure consciousness is a state where all distinctions are lost, all objects or symbols by which we discriminate disappear. This is the rationale behind the Ch'an Buddhist's frequent reference to cleansing the mirror (the mind), for even the slightest speck of dust (i.e., attachment or discriminatory perception) would create a point of reference for the conscious mind, an object which would prevent it from perceiving the clear state of its own surface. But how then does consciousness perceive or gain knowledge? All direct links with the senses are gone and noesis, or a direct intuitive experience, becomes the foundation of knowledge and all "knowing."

Authoritativeness. The question of knowledge, or perceiving what is real, is always central to mystical philosophies. Hence Buddha compared the philosopher content with only theoretical knowledge about the essential questions of life to the herdsman of other people's cows. And Mohammed condemns the "inexperienced" philosopher as simply an ass bearing a bag of books. What then gives the mystic the sense of sureness about his way in contrast to all others? The mystic is reassured because each step of the way rests upon the foundation of a new level of experience. This is not just a simple sensory perception, but carries with it a power that transcends anything experienced before.

[33]Walter Stace breaks the mystical experience into two psychological types—extrovertive and introvertive.

It is more real than reality, and carries with it an even greater conviction than pain or pleasure as when one puts a hand in fire or drinks cool water on a hot day.

Affirmation. D. T. Suzuki describes affirmation as "accepting things as they come along regardless of their moral values . . . Buddhists call this 'patience,' that is, acceptance of things in their suprarelative or transcendental aspect where no dualism of whatever sort avails." The mystic is *totally* involved in the interrelatedness of everything. "Zen (Ch'an) is suchness—a grand affirmation."

One of the most important concepts in Eastern religion is spontaneity, which if followed leads one to the "grand affirmation" Suzuki speaks of. Spontaneity—*tzu-jan* in Chinese means literally "being so of itself"—is more than simply action or acceptance without thought. It is a part of the natural process of life. Acceptance involves ceasing to make distinctions and imposing one's will on nature. *Tzu-jan* is not a blind or inattentive reaction in the sense of English "spontaneity," but rather complete identification with the world around one. If a person is *en rapport* with his surroundings, spontaneity or acceptance is a natural reaction. If not, action is forced and based on discrimination. Taoist, Zen, and Ch'an Buddhists believe that the "way" was lost when reason discriminated between one's self and the world. To return to the natural way is to stop discriminating (*pien*) and perceive (*noesis*) nature itself—not its forms. Similar emphasis can be found in Sufism, Vedanta, Tibetan Buddhism, and even Zoroastrianism.

Sense of the beyond. The mystic's feeling the experience as holy or sacred parallels what early Greek philosophers, like Heraclitus and Anaxagoras, meant when they extolled the "sense of the boundless" in human nature. Heraclitus in particular felt that human nature "had no boundaries" other than those we suffered in lieu of fuller understanding. In apprehending what the mystic would call sacred or holy, there is the same loss of the individual personality and the complete obliteration of the objective world. This is quite common to Western and Eastern mystics. In the West it is considered a process of union or transformation into a new being. In China finding the Tao—"returning to whence we came"—cannot take place without transformation, or what in Christianity is called *metanoia*, a change of heart. The same is true of Buddhism, Hinduism, Islam, and the other major Eastern religions.

Impersonal tone. The single most marked difference between Eastern and Western mysticism is personal identification. Walter Stace, Rudolf Otto, and William James, the major Western commentators on mystical experience, curiously did not emphasize this. Although Stace does not incorporate personal elements in his list of characteristics, the testimony of many Western mystics reveals a great amount of sensual, personal commentary. While in general an impersonal quality exists in most Eastern mysticism, several schools do use strong personal and sensual imagery to evoke and describe their experiences.

The Christian mystic often conceives the soul as longing like a lover for return to God to achieve union. In Western occult and alchemical tradition this is expressed as the *coniunctio or* Chemical Wedding, where the mystic seeks the Divine Ground passionately, even evoking sensuous language as the only effective parallel to mundane experience. The same is true of Sufism, devotional Buddhism, Hinduism, and Bhakti mysticism. Buddhism and Taoism in particular do not speak of an objective deity the soul seeks to unite with. The Buddhist suffers no passionate longings for God, nor waits for death to deliver one's soul after a lifetime of devotion and love. If one speaks of deity at all in Buddhism it is in terms of the individual awakened soul, the Self enlightened through conscious awareness of its true and eternal nature.

Transitoriness or momentariness. The abrupt quality compares with the extrovertive mystical experience that comes upon one suddenly and spontaneously. While this may occur often, the individual has no power to bring it back or make it end. The introvertive experience, on the other hand, is achieved by special techniques of internalizing one's attention—which differ according to various cultures and traditions.

While the extrovertive achieves union by utilizing the senses, and is acutely aware of the multiplicity of the phenomenal world mystically transfigured, ultimate perception is the resolution of this multiplicity—the chair, the house, the tree, the mountain, the sky all become fused into a unity. The introvertive achieves the same experience by consciously and willfully shutting down his senses, by slowly and painstakingly dissolving awareness of the multiplicity of impressions that float into the mind. Thus one plunges into inner depths and thereby unites with what the Buddhists and Vedantists call the Real Self; again, in this darkness and absolute quiet a sense of unity is achieved, devoid of any plurality.

The introvertive experience is usually intermittent and of brief duration, which can give rise to periods of depression and aridity. The individual suffers an acute sense of loss or darkness—what St. John of the Cross calls the "dark night of the soul." Once achieved, the deliberately "acquired" introvertive experience can be induced at will and *sometimes* be retained over long periods of time—so the individual is in effect living in what the Christian calls a "state of grace." But even within the introvertive or acquired tradition, few achieve a lasting or permanent mystical consciousness running concurrently with normal consciousness. This peculiar condition of intermingling is very rare. But some, such as St. Teresa and Ruysbroeck in the West, apparently achieved what has been called the Illuminative Life.

The dichotomy between the sudden and gradual attainment seems common to most of the world's mystical religions. In Vedanta, for example, if nirvana is obtained stage by stage and one obtains the sought-after blissful union with Brahman and the true knowledge of the Self (Atman), it is called *Kramamukti*, or gradual liberation. If this same enlightenment is obtained "in the twinkling of an eye," it is called *Givanmukti*, or life-liberation, and is equivalent to the sudden enlightenment of Japanese, Chinese, and Christian mystics.

A similar development into two schools—the sudden and the gradual—took place in Zen. While the Japanese Soto school emphasizes gradualness in attaining satori, the Rinzai school (which Suzuki followed) stresses its sudden and abrupt nature.

Several other important characteristics of the mystical experience that Suzuki did not describe are timelessness, paradox, and stillness.

Timelessness. Eastern and Western mystics both defy conventional concepts of serial time. The Sufi mystic Rumi writes in his Masnavi: "Past and future are what veil God from our sight. Burn up both of them with fire! How long wilt thou be partitioned by these segments as a reed?" Christ also was unrestricted by any sense of linear time: "I am before Abraham was." For the nonlinear intellect time is aborted, a thing incomplete and not determined casually. The Ch'an Buddhist Sixth Patriarch, Hui-neng, questioned his disciples, "Show me your original face before you were born."

To the mystic time is both *now* and *eternal.* Indeed, time for the mystic is similar to the Australian aborigine who describes both past and future with a word that means "to dream." Time is illusory, a dream, a thing of the mind. To transcend time is to transcend thought. Time then is a mode of consciousness, an aspect of the mind that the mystic modulates into timelessness.

Paradox is expressed in practically all mystical writings, and can be found in Taoism, Vedanta, Buddhism, and Sufism, as well as Judaism and Christianity. The mystic's paradox is a real one, for the senses teach one lesson (separateness and isolation) while altered states of consciousness indicate an expanded, unified world noetically perceived. The Christian mystic Nicholas of Cusa called it the "coincidence of opposites." Others have described it as "identity of opposites," or the "union of contraries." The antinomic principle is not unfamiliar to Western philosophy. Hegel discussed it at great length. In fact, paradoxicality has been a part of mystical philosophies in the West back to Plotinus, Plato, and Parmenides. However, the Western artist has traditionally been closer to the Eastern mystic than the thinker, and has frequently been fascinated by the mind's mirrored complexities. Writers like Jorge Luis Borges, and film maker Sergei Eisenstein, seem particularly sensitive to paradox and its influence. Eisenstein even argued that the whole foundation of art (i.e., creation) is the "constant evolution from the interaction of two contradictory opposites." This is a surprisingly close description of Taoist, Buddhist, and Vedanta cosmology. Perhaps the mystic, medium, shaman, and creative artist are all expressing grades of significance in the human mind. This psychic ladder within our inner space is a platform from which we receive singular moments of evidence of the mind's ultimate range and power. The Eastern mystic's approach to the world is like Wittgenstein's; there are only logical problems, not natural ones. At certain levels of consciousness the mystic perceives that nature or the Tao, simply *is*. Nature suffers no dichotomies, no confusions, no problems. Confusion or paradox is a product of human perception and discursive analysis.

Stillness. Earlier I emphasized the questing spirit that characterizes human nature and that reaches its height with the mystic's passion. Yet even while such a spirit is necessary to evolve, the mystic also states that seeking at a given point must stop. For example, it is asked, "Who can find God by searching? Who can find out the Almighty to perfection?" The Absolute cannot be found by searching, but as we progress along the path toward enlightenment we are advised by mystics to be silent, to be still in mind and spirit. In stillness we become receptive for the influx of the universal. Stillness of body, emotion, mind, and spirit is the entrance to exalted consciousness.

The inscription on the Delphic Temple "Know Thyself" is frequently mentioned as one of the foundations of Socratic and, indeed, of Greek and Western philosophy. But there were two inscriptions on the temple; the other was "nothing in excess." They were complimentary ideas, for if one is overburdened by excess, then it is impossible to know the self. This theme runs throughout religious and mystical scripture; there must be a moral equipoise—what in China has been called "The Golden Mean"—that balances out the elements in an individual's life. Only with a balance that eventually reaches perfect equilibrium, and hence poised quietness within, can the true self be uncovered or the Absolute within be found.

EDITOR'S NOTES

Eastern Mysticism was conceived to introduce Western readers to the major religions of the East and their mystical tradition. To accomplish this, a wide range of sacred writings and complete versions of many significant works are included in these volumes. I make no claim of being definitive, however, for to cover completely the enormous sacred literature of the East would take many volumes and editors, something on the order of producing several series like *Sacred Books of the East,* which comprises fifty volumes.

To create an anthology the size of this one means the editor must take on the role of a generalist, and therefore necessarily rely heavily on accepted scholarship. I freely and thankfully acknowledge my special debt to the exceptional work of men like Max Muller, whose translations and interpretations I turned to so often, and others like Heinrich Zimmer, William Theodore de Bary, Philip Yampolsky, Wing-tsit Chan, Arthur Waley, D.T. Suzuki, Edward Conze, Dwight Goddard, S. Radhakrishnan, R.A. Nicholson, A.J. Arberry, R.D.M. Shaw, D. Snellgrove, P.T. Raju, Joseph Kitagawa, Chang Chung-yuan, and so many more that it is impossible to name them all. I went through well over a thousand books in search of these selections, so the list of scholarly acknowledgments becomes impossibly long. I name those above because I owe them a special acknowledgment, for it is upon them that I relied the most heavily and owe the greatest debt.

The virtue of the generalist or nonspecialist approach is that each religion, each fact, each text is examined freshly and is accompanied by a sense of wonder and appreciation that overly specialized scholars sometimes lose. Of course, the most creative scholars retain, and are marked by, their imagination and originality of approach. The danger for the generalist is in getting facts wrong and in misemphasizing information. Double- and triple-checking became necessary precisely because the anthology covers material with which one is initially not secure. As nothing is free from human error, however, I realize certain flaws and distortions are bound to occur in such a broad collection and accept full responsibility for them.

Notes on the Selections

If literature's highest destiny is to excite reflection or meditation, and to create a greater awareness in readers of their inner and outer worlds, then these writings from the Eastern sacred tradition perform that high service. For they are not only *sruti*, as Hindus call mystically inspired writings, but represent the greatest literary tradition of early Eastern civilizations. Indeed, the sacred literature of every culture contains high literary value too often underestimated and underappreciated in the frequent academic wrangling over interpretations and analysis.

As recently as 1960 Aldous Huxley observed that the enormous literature of Buddhism is still very poorly represented in English translations, and most translations that did exist were either out of print or inaccessibly buried in learned journals. While much more from the vast storehouse of Eastern sacred literature has been translated since Huxley's remark, in comparison to what remains untranslated there is still a paucity of important material readily available for the general public. Of the recent paperback editions now available in better translations, most offer only short extracts from limited selections. Consequently, one book may offer short extracts from the Upanishads, but omit other important material from the enormous Hindu literature. Another book may contain extracts from the Taoist "bible," the Tao Teh Ching, but exclude other important selections from the Taoist tradition. In contrast, I have tried to offer large sections of an important text, as well as many other selections from each religion's sacred writings. While *Eastern Mysticism* suffers the inherent weaknesses of all anthologies, the result of this construction is that many key texts have been included in their entirety, such as the complete eighty-one chapters of the Tao Teh Ching. Vitally important writings, such as the Sutra in Forty-two Chapters, may be read in their entirety alongside other key writings from the same religion. The same reasoning applied to each of the major religions included in *Eastern Mysticism*. The exceptions to this rule were those religions, such as Zoroastrianism, that had less overall importance.

A particular religion's impact upon its culture and time was also an important criteria for inclusion. For example, normally a selection of Hindu scriptures would include a few excerpts from the Gita, the Vedas, and the Upanishads. Yet I have considerably expanded the standard selections not only because of the general editorial rationale described above, but because of Hinduism's early and central influence in world religion. The same reasoning applies to the large collection of Chinese writings, which most other anthologies of Eastern sacred literature would not normally include. These cultures contributed so greatly to mankind's early religious consciousness, to the awakening mystical impulse, and the writings are often so highly original, that they deserve to be read by everyone. In addition, they represent the first attempt of human beings to express their numinous feelings about nature, the paradoxes of life and death, self, consciousness, and extinction. Religious sages like Lao Tzu, Buddha, Zoroaster, Maitreya, and Sankara were men inspired in the highest sense of the word. They conceived and presented to the world philosophical and religious insights of complete originality. Indeed, I have been so moved by the ideas and lives of these exceptional individuals—and the hundreds of others I came across during the research for this book—that if this anthology does no more than introduce their names and writings to those unfamiliar with them, its publication is justified.

In every anthology disagreement inevitably arises over the selections. The problem of selection was complicated here because there are sometimes dozens of translations of particularly important texts, with new scholarly translations being made all the time. The translations chosen here are not necessarily the most recent, however, but I have been guided by two factors in my choices: (1) the translations must be of generally high reputation, and (2) they had to be readable and comprehensible to the general public. This was no simple matter when dealing with ancient Eastern texts, for they are often redundant and obscure, and sometimes replete with misleading interpolations by later translators and compilers.

Often the differences between a translation by a modern scholar and one by a renowned turn-of-the-century master, such as Sir Edwin Arnold, are purely technical. I might have chosen a more technically perfect rendering of the Bhagavad Gita, for example, but I doubt if there is any translation (no matter how accurate or technically perfect) with as much poetry and sense of the spirit underlying the Gita as Sir Edwin's. Conversely, some of the readings—especially the longer Buddhist sutras—may seem tedious and roundabout. In most cases such writings were carefully pared down to emphasize the essential message of the text. Some of the sutras, however, still remain repetitive and obscure. This small amount of difficulty can be overlooked, I think, once the reader gets involved in the mood of the sutra itself. All redundancies could not be taken out without hopelessly obscuring the central theme. Repetition was often a characteristic, even a mnemonic device, of the period.

Another important reason I often preferred older translations to modern ones is that contemporary translations are often done by a single person. The Chinese and Tibetan translations of early Sanskrit Buddhist sutras, for example, were accomplished in many cases by groups of fifteen or so scholars. The ideal balance was to have native speakers on both sides of the languages being translated. In translating a single text some scholars would be familiar with the Chinese or Tibetan but ignorant of Sanskrit.

Others were skilled native scholars of Sanskrit, but had little knowledge of Chinese or Tibetan. And in the middle were scholars who possessed fair understanding of Sanskrit as well as the language the text was being translated into. In this way a far more faithful rendering was possible. The advantage of such translations from ancient and difficult languages cannot be overlooked. Joint efforts with a great deal of scholarly interchange, which occurred with the fifty volumes of translations in the *Sacred Books of the East*, are consequently of inestimable value. This scholarly interchange is why so many of the Sanskrit renderings in *Eastern Mysticism* are from *SBE*, even though the final translations were often by a single person. In effect, a decision was made to sacrifice occasional modern usage for superior, one might even say classical, translations.

Another consideration was the text's relationship to mysticism. This was a difficult problem, for while some scriptures, like the Gita, the Tevaram writings, and the writings of Sufi mystics, were quite clearly mystical because of their strong emphasis on devotion and union, others, such as the Jaina sutras, Zoroastrian Gathas, and The Questions of King Milinda, are more tangentially connected with Eastern mysticism.[34] They were chosen because they elucidated some important aspect of the mystical process or mystical consciousness. The Questions of King Milinda, for example, does not deal directly with mystical consciousness or union, but does discuss *moksha* (freedom), knowledge and nirvana—all important dimensions of the mystical experience specifically from the Buddhist viewpoint. Another reason I chose writings like the King Milinda is that these subjects are brought up by a Western intellect, an individual exploring Eastern religious premises from a typically Grecian, philosophical viewpoint.

A third rationale in making selections was more indirect. A group of writings, like Buddha's First and Last Sermons, and Asvaghosa's Life of Buddha, were included not so much for their direct bearing on questions of mystical importance, but rather to offer a very necessary frame of reference for the reader. Buddhism is one of the most subtle and complex of all mystical religions, and I felt it important to give the Western reader some familiarity with the standard references to Buddha's life and teachings. Buddhism combines mysticism with asceticism, a practical ethos of personal growth and conduct with transcendentalism. Asvaghosa's Life of Buddha is a sacred epic, one of the most important in Buddhism, and is credited with

---

[34]Edward Conze feels that "*all* the basic problems of Buddhist wisdom are touched upon" (my italics) in The Questions of King Milinda. See his *Buddhist Scriptures* (Baltimore: Penguin, 1959), p. 145.

converting thousands through its poetry and preaching. Mixed in
with the events of Buddha's life are numerous hints about Buddha's growth and subsequent enlightenment. The verses have an
impact far beyond that of many sutras: "Thus did he complete
the end of self, as fire goes out for want of grass" says Asvaghosa of Buddha. "Thus he had done what he would have men
do: he first had found the way of perfect knowledge." While
such texts do not offer a clear and direct exposition of Buddhistic mysticism as does, say, The Way of Virtue or Dhammapada,
they are valuable selections for Western readers unfamiliar with
the nuances of Buddha's life and Buddhistic mysticism.

In some cases well-known scriptures were not used. Sometimes
duplication can serve to describe similarities in cultures and
thereby aid comparative reading and analysis, but often it is
simply redundant. This was the situation with the famous Vedanta Sutras and the Commentary of Sankara. Sankara's comments on the sutras are justly respected for their historical and
philosophical value, but the sutras themselves are often merely
variations on other writings where the ideas are expressed better.
Many of the Vedanta Sutras' passages are, for instance, the
same discussion as in the Chandogya Upanishad, which is ex-
cerpted in *Eastern Mysticism*.[35]

Notes on the Translations and Language

A word should be said about language, capitalization, and
spelling. There will no doubt be considerable confusion over capitalization and spelling throughout these writings and even the
part introductions themselves. Because Eastern religious writings
distinguish between the exalted and the mundane aspects of a
continuous reality underlying life, translators frequently distinguish between the two aspects by capitalization. This occurs especially throughout the Upanishads where the self as a mundane
expression of the ego-bound individual is rendered by a small *s*.
The Self as Atman, or the universal impersonal aspect of the individual, is always capitalized. The same is true of terms like
"gods," meaning lesser deities, and "God," or the Absolute and
undefinable. Wherever a term is capitalized it indicates the Absolute aspect rather than the mundane or physically relative.

Spelling is even more difficult and confusing. The same word
can often be transliterated several different ways. The most glaring of several variations have been edited out, but in some cases
that was impossible. It is easy, for example, to alter and make

[35]See, for example, the close analysis of George Thibaut, Introduction to the
Vedanta Sutras of Badarayana, *Sacred Books of the East*, vol. 31, p. xli.

consistent "Chandogya Upanishad" in place of either "Chhan-
dogya" or "Khandogya," two equally valid spellings. It becomes more difficult, however, when differentiating between Pali
and Sanskrit terms in the various translations. For example,
should I have changed all the Pali-language "nibbanas" to the
Sanskrit "nirvana," which is the more familiar term, even when
the word "nibbana" appeared in a Pali text? Hardly! It would
serve no useful purpose to arbitrarily alter spellings in Pali writings to the more familiar Sanskrit forms, for that damages the
integrity of differing traditions in a religion that each considers
valid and meaningful. Even within the same language the complexity of spelling can be great. For example, equally authoritative sources spell the same word (including proper names) in several different ways. The name of the Buddhist teacher Asvaghosa
is a good example. It can be spelled "Asvaghosa" (as in H. Zimmer, C. Luk, S. Radhakrishnan, L. Basham); or "Ashvagosha"
(as in T. Richard's *The Awakening of Faith*); or "Ashvaghosha"
(as in Wm. Theodore de Bary's *Sources of Indian Tradition*);
or "Asvaghosha" (as in Samuel Beal's *Buddhist Records of the
Western World*). I have chosen "Asvaghosa" only because it
seems slightly less complex and slighty more common, even
though I reprinted selections from Richard's translation of
Ashvagosha's (his spelling) Awakening of Faith Sutra.

A further complication is that religious terms often have multiple meanings, much as do philosophical terms in different languages. This is especially true of Sanskrit words for which there
are few equivalents in the Western vocabulary, such as "nirvana," "bodhisattva," "dharma," and even "Buddha," which can
have several different meanings. "Dharma" is a good example, for
it is a particularly ambiguous word and has up to ten frequently
used different meanings. In some cases it is used as "teachings,"
in others as "events," or "true facts." However, the word can
also mean the moral law that sustains the world, and is therefore sometimes translated as "virtue." Dharma is not only important to the Buddhist religion across Asia, but is a key term
in Hindu cultures. In fact, Hinduism is occasionally referred to
as Sanatana Dharma, the Eternal Dharma.

The most difficult terms to get straight in one's mind are those
used to designate the numerous forms of cognition or knowledge
in Sanskrit. There is no easy way to understand or gain insight
into the complicated concepts and ambiguous terminology of
Eastern religions. To be honest, it is a difficult study, for not
only does one need to familiarize oneself with a wide range of
concepts and terms, but, most important, one must become sensitive to the nuances behind the words and ideas. This necessarily
takes a long time and involves wading through many books.

In an anthology this large, with so many overlapping religions, languages, and cultures, there is no alternative but to let the variations stand even though there may be initial confusion. Footnotes will frequently clarify many of the more glaring problems, but beyond that I hesitated to go. The differences in meaning, spelling, and conceptual clothing of these basic terms is then a matter of adjustment and learning for the reader. This may seem irritating at first, but one soon becomes used to the variations, much as one unconsciously accepts the differences between British and American spelling and definition. The differences tend to become lost in the context of story and idea. In short, there is no easy way to conquer Eastern religions, but having the major writings together with commentaries and references as in *Eastern Mysticism*, will, I hope, make the task somewhat easier.

The Part Introductions

My central objective in the part introductions accompanying each religion was to reveal the essential ideas of that particular religion. I did not want to analyze the subtle perceptions of these religions from an alien perspective. In both the selections and my part introductions I have therefore attempted to treat each religion sympathetically, as if I were myself a part of that particular spiritual heritage. I saw no point in critically analyzing the episodes of brutality, the schisms, the inconsistencies or stupidity to which all religions at some time have been led by the whims and egotism of their temporal leaders. Each religion, no matter how exalted in concept, no matter how spiritual in execution or tradition, sooner or later succumbs to men of lesser vision who succeed in corrupting the original teachings. Such flaws in application, precisely because traditions are created by imperfect men, should not detract from the essential spiritual teaching of a religion. In this sense I was biased, for I tried to isolate and comment on the highest aspirations of each religion. Where I did comment on what I considered a "negative" moment in a religion's history, it was because that fact had some important bearing on the religion's growth or change.

I have also tried throughout the part introductions, commentaries, and footnotes to adhere as closely as possible to the conclusions of accepted religious scholarship. In some instances, however, there appeared to be aspects of a religion that seemed to me vitally important to a fuller understanding of the mystical element in that religion. Occasionally standard religious references and textbooks unsympathetic to mystical nuances gave no guidance and I emphasized and interpreted as I saw fit. Examples are the emphases on "action" or "sacrifice," the effect of "thought," and on the Zurvan cosmology in the Zoroastrian commentary. Another would be the emphasis throughout the book on the central role of the mind in Eastern mystical religions. I make no claim of originality here, but simply wish to make it clear that mixed in with the hard, scholarly facts are my own extrapolations, emphases, and interpretations.

I have tried to describe each religion's root ideas in the part introductions. Often a root idea, while not as attractive to dialectically inclined scholars, conveys the essential ingredient of complex concepts. Words are too often relied upon as explanations, when in fact they act merely as costume to the actual intention. As P.J. Saher observed in his exceptional book *Eastern Wisdom and Western Thought*, the translating of mystical terminology is not an exact but a very exacting science. The same is true of root ideas in a religion, or any cosmic vision of human existence. Indeed, the purpose of each section was to present a plateau upon which the writings themselves could be displayed. It was not within the scope of the book to give a definitive outline of each religion's dogma. I aimed rather at conveying the central concepts of each religion that gave life to its mystical elements.

Part One

HINDUISM

Introduction

Ancient Hinduism is extremely difficult to define, categorize, or describe. It has no particular system but is rather composed of many philosophical ideas. Most religions are derived from the revelation or inspired reflection of individuals, such as Christ, Confucius, Mohammed, or the Hebrew prophets. But Hinduism is the great exception, for there is no major single historical revelation, prophet or founder, specific dogma or single book to which one can turn. There is a tradition of sacred writings thousands of years old, but no single Bible. It is actually a construction, an accretion of many centuries that crystallized into religious truths, which added to rather than diminished its complexities. These writings are not considered "revelations" from a god, but rather the process of mankind's intuitive insight and his inevitable progress back to the undifferentiated Godhead.

Hinduism can be traced back to the Mohenjo-daro civilization (4000-3000 B.C.), and yet, as in the study of other ancient civilizations, one is dealing not with a cohesive whole, but rather with a people who were just beginning to create a stable life style. Forms of pantheistic worship had developed, and the pre-Aryan groups attached religious significance to trees, tigers, crocodiles, elephants, and even multi-headed monsters. At this time they had already begun to use symbols like the swastika, as well as animal seals that possessed religious importance.

The Hindu religion is sometimes called "sanatana dharma," the "eternal religion," because it is based upon the eternal principles developed in the ancient Vedas and Upanishads, the Indian sacred scriptures. Hindus regard their religion as the oldest in the world, and they may be right. (The Jains, however, believe that their religion is the ancient form of Hinduism, from which the present-day Hindus have gone astray.) The term "Hindu" itself was created by the Persians to describe the inhabitants on the other side of the River Sindhu (the Sanskrit name for the Indus). The forebears of those people now called Hindus considered themselves Aryans, and their religion was the Aryan Way (arya-dharma). Buddha himself, for example, did not know of Hinduism and called his teachings "Aryan Truths." Mahavira, the founder of Jainism and a contemporary of Buddha's, also thought he was teaching his version of the Aryan Way rather than a variation of Hinduism.

To understand Hinduism and its manifold complexities is like learning to read a complex tapestry with many deeply woven threads, each seemingly as important as the other, each containing subtle and intriguing ideas. Standing back and viewing it objectively does not give the perspective one expects or needs. The best way to study Hinduism is to move up close, and examine it slowly and with great care. For this reason large selections from the principal Upanishads, the Gita, the whole of Patanjali's yoga sutras, and numerous selections from Sankara have been included in this volume. The reader who hopes to approach such complicated writings must be willing to sample a great many of them in large amounts.

THE VEDIC AGE AND SACRIFICIAL MYSTICISM

Sometime around 2000 to 1500 B.C. the Aryan tribes began invading India from the north. The religions of the Aryans and the indigenous peoples became intermingled; non-Aryan gods, such as Siva, became identified with Aryan gods, such as Rudra. At first the Indo-Aryan mixture produced a confusing polytheism. Sacrificial worship developed to gratify and propitiate all the gods of nature, such as the Fire-god, Wind-god, Dawn, Water, and so forth. The Aryan invaders brought with them the sacrificial use of fire, and probably the potent mind-altering plant drug called soma. Most Vedic hymns in Book IX are invocations to soma.[1] Perhaps this powerful drug stimulated the sensual abandon that consumed the Aryan people during the early period of the Vedic Hymns (2000-1500 B.C.), and made them often confuse the intoxicated body with the spiritual one.

Nevertheless, from this involvement with the chemically expanded human senses, an awakening of the spiritual instinct seemed to take hold. The worshippers sipped their soma, saw nature transformed before their eyes into scintillating patterns of color and energy. They experienced sensations of power as if they could reach to the gods themselves—and described these feelings in their hymns. The worshipper exults: "We have drunk the Soma, we have become immortal, we have entered into light, we have known the gods" (VIII.48.3). They clearly felt themselves the possessors of a magical force that filled their trans-

[1]See Rig Veda X.25, and footnote 19, for additional facts about soma, its uses in sacrifice by Brahmanic priests, and its personification as a god.

muted beings. They became a sort of supernatural electricity
that permeated the world, or as gods, mingling as they did with
the magical powers of nature. From this primitive hylozoism
where spirit, matter, nature, and consciousness melded into one
there developed a unique form of sacrificial mysticism. They
seemed to believe that the object of sacrifice and the universe
itself were united during the sacrificial rite. This idea was
probably derived from the expanded cognitive experience of the
ancient Aryan magi as they perceived the world through such
magically tinted chemical lenses. The tribal priest or magician
genuinely believed that he was a specially chosen individual; a
man possessed of magical powers and omniscient insight into the
nature of life. In later Vedic times the priests became Brahmans
and held an exalted place in the caste system.

When the Aryans finally established the supremacy of their
faith, all other objects of worship became subsidiary to their
High God Brahman. This developing monotheism, however, was
imperfect; other gods still held varying power and influence over
the people. Nevertheless, during this Vedic period (1200-500
B.C.), a unitive theme in their religion was developing. The Rig
Veda[2] is a collection of metrical hymns to gods as nature powers, and these hymns contain clear signs of perceiving god in an
impersonal way. In the Hymn to the Unknown God, as well as
other hymns to Purusha and Prajapati, it is indicated that God
cannot be described or treated like a person even though he exists.[3]

Like many ancient peoples the Aryans believed that the
creation of the universe and of human beings resulted from the
sacrifice of a cosmic being.[4] The "idea" of sacrifice to the Aryans was more important than the gods themselves. These sacrifices (yajna) and the mysterious powers they evoked (dharma)
implied a great impersonal force at work in the universe—and
the soma apparently induced visions that united them with this
mysterious power. The Vedic sacrifices took a unique turn, however, and became quite different from the practices of other ancient peoples, who generally attempted to cajole or propitiate

[2]There are four Vedas, of which the Rig Veda is the oldest. Together they
are called Samhitas. The others are Yajur Veda, Sama Veda, and Atharva
Veda, which deal with rituals for sacrifice, chanting, spells, and incantations.
[3]For specific comments on Hindu cosmology, creation myths, the divine male
aspect of Purusha and so forth, see footnotes 1, 5, and 14 in the section
"Selections from the Rig Veda."
[4]This is especially true also of Zoroastrianism. See the introduction to Part
Three for a description of Zoroastrian sacrificial mysticism and its theories.
These hymns are included in this anthology. The example cited here is Rig
Veda X. 129.

their gods. The Aryans tried to harmonize themselves with these great forces rather than simply influence them.[5]

In the later Brahmanas (ritual writings about 800-600 B.C.) the sacrificial altar and the objects to be sacrificed are meditated upon as if they were the universe itself. To Upanishadic philosophers the realization gained by this identification between the sacrificed and the universe contained mystical knowledge of existence. In this process only the soul or spirit performing the sacrifice remained at the conclusion. The meditation instructions indicate that the Indo-Aryans understood the possibility of realizing one's own spirit through sacrifice. This was an amazingly sophisticated idea for people so early in their development. "Thus arose the philosophy of spirit realization, of meditation on Atman (humanity's indwelling spirit)," writes P.T. Raju, which began to engage the Upanishadic thinkers from the ninth century B.C. on.[6]

Fire also played an interesting and extremely important part in both sacrificial mysticism and later Hindu beliefs, for it was not only one of the principal Vedic gods, Agni, but the power of creation as well. It has always played a central role in religious symbolism, even in relatively mature religious philosophies. Buddha discoursed on the power of fire to indicate "the ceaseless flux of becoming called the world."[7] Heraclitus also conceived of fire as a basic, universally powerful element and wrote, "This world is an eternally living fire," thus agreeing with the ancient Vedic ritual sacrificers. Both men used fire to represent the metaphysical principle of becoming. Fire is also used to describe the experience of "pranic" energy during the Hindu mystical ecstasy, an experience considered union between the divine within man (Atman) and the eternal Brahman. Fire symbolically melds the two together in a blissful union, and metaphorically describes the electrically charged cosmic-consciousness that results.

In the Vedas, according to the Hymn to the Unknown God, all powers, both universal and worldly, were conceived as the "Golden Child" or "Golden Germ." This Golden Child (Hiranyagarbha in Sanskrit) is the precursor of the universal egg creation myths (brahmanda), which conceives the whole universe as the result of a single Golden Germ. Another cosmogenic theory in the Vedas, also the precursor of later philosophical concepts in both Hinduism and Buddhism, attempts to show the

[5]See S. N. Dasgupta, *Hindu Mysticism* (New York: Ungar, 1959), pp. 10ff.
[6]See "Religions of India," Part One, in Wing-tsit Chan et al., *The Great Asian Religions* (New York, London: Collier-Macmillan, 1969).
[7]S. Radhakrishnan, *Indian Philosophy*, vol. 1 (London: Allen & Unwin, 1951), p. 368.

universe evolved out of a state of "nonbeing" (asat). In the Vedas, for example, both "nonbeing" (asat, a passive condition) and "being" (sat, an active condition) have their origin in Brahman, who has by 600 B.C. become the supreme cosmic principle.[8] As the cosmological concepts become more subtle only their sages were considered able to fathom their complexities—especially ideas like sat and asat. But even here Hinduism displays a peculiar kind of originality, for at the end of the "Hymn of Creation" (X. 129), there is a questioning tone introduced that indicates the intellectual and skeptical mood of the Upanishadic period (900-300 B.C.) that would follow, and the questioning tone of Vedanta philosophy generally.

Sacrificial mysticism in the Vedas before the ascendancy of Brahman characteristically does not recognize any single god or supreme being who commands the universe or mankind.[9] All laws are considered to have existed from time immemorial and are revealed as mankind progresses in spiritual understanding. The Vedic sacrificial mysticism is unusual in its lack of an identifiable spirit or divine principle within man with which the universal forces can unite. Sacrificial mysticism involves external powers that man must learn to identify with and obey. This identification process has a mystical element and prepared the way for more developed forms of mysticism in the Upanishads and Vedantism and Sankara's Advaita.

The selections for earlier Hindu writings emphasize the Vedas rather than the following Brahmana period (800-600 B.C.), which was principally ritualistic (both were sacrificial and magical). The later Brahmanic writings gave way to a more mystical ideal and taught that the ultimate reality of Brahman, the One, was identical with man's Atman, or True Self. This identification between man and god in a single unifying vision is found most clearly in the final portions of the Vedas, the Upanishads. That this was not an isolated movement, but a part of the Indian Vedic tradition, has been accepted by many writers: "The doctrine of the Upanishads was really only the expression within the Vedic or Brahmanical tradition of a great quietistic movement." [10]

The worship of Brahman did not bring with it an immediate monotheism. Ancient Brahmanism was pantheistic, with Brahman considered as a supreme god by some, but only another

---

[8] For a more detailed description and selections from the Vedas, see also Wm. Theodore de Bary, ed., *Sources of Indian Tradition*, vol. 1 (New York: Columbia, 1958), pp. 13ff.

[9] For a thorough analysis of Hindu mysticism and its sacrificial elements see Dasgupta, *Hindu Mysticism*, pp. 16ff.

[10] See de Bary, *Sources of Indian Tradition*, p. 202.

major god by others. But Brahman's impact is clear in that he is the single great exception of all the ancient gods who retained a major influence and power throughout Indian religious history. Brahman is considered ultimately unknowable, yet has taken on phenomenal clothing so men may come to know aspects of him. In these aspects he is *sat-chit-ananda*—symbolically rendered as the embodiment of reality or being (sat), as knowledge or consciousness (chit), and as bliss (ananda).

After Brahman became the Supreme, Unchanging, and Absolute Being of Hinduism, various other gods became simply aspects of his unchanging source. Brahman manifests in the phenomenal world through a trinity of gods (the Trimurti). The three aspects of this neutral, undefinable spirit are: Brahman (a masculine term, not the neuter Supreme Spirit), who is the Creator or Creative aspect; Vishnu, the Preserver; and Siva, the Destroyer, who is also the generator of new life. These three manifestations each developed a following that considered their particular god as supreme. Each devotee considered his god the only true god, and all others secondary manifestations. Hence, the Saivite considered Siva the one true god, and Vishnu a secondary attribute of Siva—and of course, the same was true of the Vaisnavites (worshippers of Vishnu), and of those who preferred to believe the masculine Brahman was the single true god. The Indian people were highly accommodating by nature, however, and most often preferred to incorporate challenging deities into their own systems of belief rather than deny them existence entirely. Perhaps this temperamental preference gave birth to the concept of Trimurti, or Triple Form. This holy trinity of Hinduism has always been popular in India, even though various groups still preferred their own particular god as primary. Brahman, however, was always either the most powerful or one of the most powerful gods of India. He was the Prajapati mentioned in the later Vedic writings and at the peak of his popularity early in India's religious history. He was also considered the greatest of gods in early Buddhist scriptures; but after Gupta times (fourth to seventh centuries A.D.) Brahman as a single deity suffered a slow decline and was little worshipped.

THE UPANISHADS AND VEDANTA

While the philosophy and metaphysics of Hinduism is intricate and immense, there are six basic philosophical systems (darsana) recognized as orthodox by most Hindus: *Nyaya*, which emphasizes logic; *Vaiseshika*, which relies on analysis and nature; *Sankhya*, a form of realistic pluralism; *Yoga*, which concentrates on physical and mental discipline; *Purva Mimamsa,* whose object is duty; and *Vedanta,* concerned with the consistency and exposition of Upanishadic philosophy.

All these systems existed before the birth of Buddhism in the sixth century B.C., and yet they are orthodox Hinduism because they accept the Vedas and Upanishads, and because they hold two basic premises in common: that all in existence is a particle of the many-aspected Godhead; and that only Brahman is eternal and real—all else in the phenomenal world is illusion or maya, and will inevitably pass away.

It was described earlier how the Vedic sacrifice had the peculiar characteristic of emphasizing the ritual even more than the gods. But the movement from the Vedic age into the Upanishadic period (600-300 B.C.) brought about a rejection of the tyranny of the senses evoked by soma, and a new recognition of the importance of detachment and renunciation developed. A cornerstone of Indian philosophy—asceticism and disciplined meditation—sprang into being. (The asceticism, however, would also eventually be abused in excessive torture of the body.) This emphasis on the symbolic act in sacrificial rites and the knowledge gained from it is the starting point for the later Upanishad philosophy. The Upanishads are thus both the culmination of the Vedic teaching and the beginning of a completely new speculative approach to Indian religion. Yet because there is no consistent unified philosophical system developed in the Upanishads, they are considered speculation rather than actual philosophical doctrines. All important Hindu thought, however, including Buddhism, is rooted in the Upanishads.

"Upanishads" means "esoteric teachings," or "secret doctrines." They are the fourth and concluding part of the Vedic writings (Samhitas) and quite philosophical in character despite their lack of any definitive system. The earliest is probably the Brihadaranyaka Upanishad, about the ninth century B.C. The later Upanishads date from around the fifth century B.C. Of the more than two hundred Upanishads extant, eleven or twelve are generally accepted as the earliest and most important. (Selections from the eleven principal Upanishads are included in this anthology.)

Called the Veda-anta, the "end of the Veda," the Upanishads contained the essence of the Vedic teaching. The many philosophical ideas born of the Vedas are therefore labeled "Vedanta." The Vedanta is grounded in two main groups of writings: Uttara Mimamsa, or "Later Investigation," because it deals with the later Upanishads; and the earlier portions of the Vedic writings, which are called Purva Mimamsa, "Prior Inquiry" or "inquiry into ritual."

The Purva Mimamsa is mainly concerned with the Mantras (chants) and Brahmanas (rituals), and aims to clarify the religious laws of the Vedas. It is not so much a philosophy as an intellectual exercise in Hindu theology and logic. Developed by Jaimini (fourth or fifth century A.D.), it posts no supreme god or highest reality, for the Vedas as a whole are considered the supreme religious teaching. The Veda is believed to have existed throughout eternity, and teaches that the Dharma must be obeyed. The Dharma is obligatory or necessary laws; it embodies concepts of duty and order and encompasses the whole of Indian social aims. It is law or mirror of all moral action in the ideal society.[11] The Purva Mimamsa provided answers or laws that would not be questioned. It specified how the ritual or sacrifice should be performed, and what the proper duties of each individual should be.

The Uttara Mimamsa, on the other hand, is concerned with expounding and clarifying the intellectual foundation underlying the concept of Brahman or Supreme Reality. Traditionally, this system was developed by Badarayana (fourth or fifth century B.C.) and refined by the three great Indian sages Madhva, Ramanuja, and Sankara. It is studied and practiced in its dualistic, qualified-monistic, and monistic aspects. Madhva, who was a dualist, argued that Brahman inescapably possessed attributes, otherwise he could not manifest at all. Brahman is sometimes called Isvara, and also incorporates the three aspects of creator, preserver, and destroyer mentioned earlier. According to Madhva, Isvara (God) controls all aspects of the universe, but the soul is at some point distinct from its creator. Ramanuja championed a qualified monism. He too believed that Brahman with attributes was distinct from the individual soul that was a part of it, but eventually the soul united with the Creator.

Sankara (or with his title of respect, "Acharya," Sankaracharya) is considered by most scholars the greatest of Indian thinkers and mystics. This ninth-century religious reformer was a dedicated monist and the founder of a dominant philosophical system—Advaita. Advaita ("allowing no second") is a monistic or nondualistic system in which the soul is considered identical with all other aspects of the universe, and Brahman *without* attributes is considered the basic and Absolute Reality.[12] Sankara's analysis of Brahman differs little from the "void" (sunyata) or

---

[11] See Heinrich Zimmer, *Philosophies of India* (New York: Pantheon, 1951), pp. 40-41. See also Laws of Manu, *Sacred Books of the East*, vol. 25, trans. by Georg Buhler (Oxford at the Clarendon Press, 1886).

[12] As mysticism is most closely associated with monism in philosophy and religion, Sankara is the Indian thinker given most space and attention in this book.

nirvana of Mahayana Buddhism. This fact has led some critics to call Sankara a crypto-Buddhist.[13]

According to Sankara, whose intellectual comparison with the Catholic Thomas Aquinas is a fair one, the individual soul seemed distinct from the Over-Soul or Absolute Reality of Brahman, because the embodied soul (jiva) is in error about its own true character. The egoic self considers itself bound, captured in the cycle of world experience. But this error, Sankara argues, disappears with the light of self-realization. The embodied soul, or "life monad" as the modern Indian philosopher S. Radhakrishnan calls it, is in essence the True Self (Atman), which is identical with Brahman, the universal and Eternal Reality. The self's bondage is an illusion, it is nonexistent. The idea of liberation is also therefore an illusion, for one not truly in bondage cannot be freed. It is for this reason that one is constantly puzzled by curious and often frustrating statements about "nothingness" in eastern mystical teachings. Sankara states this point in his famous commentary on the Mandukya Upanishad: "There is no dissolution, no beginning, no bondage, and no aspirant; there is neither anyone avid for liberation nor a liberated soul. This is the final truth." The sage or guru therefore uses the term "liberation" only to describe the state of bondage that exists in the pupil's own mind (imagination).[14]

Basically, however, all Vedantists agree that proper understanding of the Upanishads, through the medium of Vedantic philosophy, will lead one to the desired goal—reabsorption of the soul (jiva) in the Supreme Soul or Brahman. The Vedanta approach to reality describes a progression that is a constant part of all religions with a strong mystical element: one moves from simple forms of knowing to ever more complex stages of understanding, until union with Ultimate Reality allows one to have final assurance and knowledge. The Vedantist teaches that there are three stages to ultimate understanding. The first is faith, where the seeker simply accepts the laws of nature as expression of divine existence. The second path is reason, whereby the seeker attempts to understand these laws by rational and logical prosess. Both these paths, however, lack total certainty, for reason contains its own limitations just as faith does. Full conviction can only come when the seeker, after long and disciplined yogic labors, experiences oneness with Ultimate Reality or Brahman. Experience, then, is the third and only sure way.

The religious philosophy of the Vedanta is primarily inward

[13]See A. L. Basham, *The Wonder That Was India* (New York: Grove, 1954), p. 328.

[14]See Zimmer, *Philosophies of India*, pp. 455-59.

and spiritual. It seeks for a deeper and more direct understanding of the ultimately real, and perhaps is the essence of the
mystical in Hinduism. The Vedantists' pursuit of unifying principles by which they can understand the world implies an auto-
matic rejection of dualism. The universe is viewed as an
extension of Vedic ritualistic concepts (meaning Brahman),
which is complemented by the microcosmic nature of the Atman
or the human "True Self." From this melding comes the most
significant concept in the Upanishads, that the macrocosmic
Brahman and the microcosmic Atman are one and the same.
It became the chief concern of the philosophically inclined
Upanishadic sages to explore this essential union between man
and the universe.

The problem was *how* to obtain direct experience of this great
truth and thereby arrive at absolute certainty. The "Self"
described in the Vedanta is not the individual, personal self as
we understand it in English, or even the varieties of "self"
images evoked in psychology. Nor is it the Judeo-Christian
"soul," which is so often seen as a spiritual tinderbox within the
individual waiting to be fired by the grace of God. The "Self" in
most eastern religions generally, and in its earliest expression in
the Upanishads specifically, is considered a universal core within
each human being. This "Universal Self" is closer to the
Western concept of "God within" than any other parallel. The
Upanishads teach that the divine spark that ignited the universe
into being and created all living things is the hidden aspect of our
eternal selves; yet it is an eternal mode that never dies, that
has existed before our worldly present "selves." To uncover this
internal True Self one must diminish the ego and the illusions it
creates. This will augment the True Self and its inner existence
will be made known to our conscious minds. As the Chandogya
Upanishad (III. 14. 3-4) describes it: "This is my Self within
the heart, greater than the earth, greater than the sky, greater
than all worlds. This is Brahman."

The Vedanta teaches that those who pray for personal immortality are basing their prayer on the ultimateness of the individual. Vedantists reject this dependence upon things of the worldly
personality. The reality of the finite world persists within such
persons' consciousnesses as their most important idea. Consequently, nothing of value in their finite world is lost as long as their personal selves survive. A simple transference allows the ego to
achieve the fullest satisfaction for whatever it sought unsatisfac-
torily on earth. Paradise becomes then a place where ungratified
personal needs are finally fulfilled. As the Taittiriya Upanishad
says, the enjoyment we have in the world is only a shadow of
the divine bliss (II.8). For the Vedantist the liberated condi-

tion is where the things of the world are obliterated, where the
creature as creature is abolished and becomes one with the
Creator—or more accurately—finally *realizes* his oneness with
the Creator. This unity of the individual spirit with Brahman
then is the first principle of Upanishadic doctrine. The Atman,
or divine immanence, is its central fact. The relative differences
between the divine condition and humanity are resolved in a
higher unity, an exalted synthesis.

Throughout the Upanishads, Atman and Brahman consume
one's attention. Atman meant in its earliest form "vital breath,"
and came only later to mean "spirit" or one's "Higher Self," the
cosmic principle within man. But both Atman and Brahman are
utterly impersonal realities transcending any "personalizing" limitations. They are both considered ineffable and beyond the
finite. Atman has been described as "pure consciousness," as
"bliss," or even as "intelligence" in Hindu writings, but these
terms should always be read as nonlimiting descriptions. For
even while the Atman resides silently within each of us, it remains a divine principle that transcends each of us individually.
"Concealed in the heart of things lies the Atman" says the Katha Upanishad, "smaller than the smallest atom, greater than
the greatest spaces" (I.2.20). This emphasis on immanence became the core of Upanishadic and later mystical teachings. In
the Svetasvatara Upanishad it says, "The One God is hidden in
all beings. He is the all-pervading, all-filling inner Self of all
beings, the Overseer of all activities" (VI.11). In a continuing
refrain this basically mystical unitive vision of the world
resounds throughout the Upanishads. "All this universe is in
truth Brahman. He is the beginning and end and life of all"
(Chandogya, III.14.1).

The practical method of attaining this unitive vision is
naturally another outstanding preoccupation of the Upanishads.
The realization of God, which is identical to Self-Realization,
involves many factors: a high degree of ethical conduct, self-
discipline, right knowledge, and so forth. It also involves those
universal moral commandments one finds in other developed
religions: charity, mercy, the avoidance of injury to all life
(ahimsa). But special emphasis is given to achieving tranquillity
of spirit. "He who has not ceased from evil-doing, he who is not
tranquil, he who is not composed, whose heart has not gained
peace, cannot reach this Self even by right knowledge," says the
Katha Upanishad (I.2.24).

YOGA AND PATANJALI

Some techniques for self-realization are ancient and go back to the Vedas, while others were the direct result of later philosophers who created their own theories and great systems—like Patanjali and his yogic teachings. Asceticism, however, brought about the initial experimentation that gave birth to yoga. Even though asceticism had existed in early Vedic times, by the Upanishadic age it had become widespread and new teachings had developed that rejected the earlier soma-derived visions of the sacrificial priests. No doubt many of the ascetics were solitary psychopaths inflicting terrible wounds upon their bodies, but some concentrated on mental exercises that seemed to produce spiritual results, and went beyond simple mortification of the body.

In the Upanishads the magical, occult, and mystical were often intricately entwined. The original motive of the ascetics seemed to be the highly nonspiritual pursuit of magical powers, which the Brahmanic priests claimed by virtue of birth and their role in society. In the Samkhya Yoga, for example, meditation was advocated not so much for the "mystical way" by which the individual soul enters the "Highest Light," but rather as a method for the "magical way" of occult powers. Again, as in most early religions, those who accept these magical powers are distinct from those who reject them in favor of a transcendent goal. In yoga the ascetic who succumbs to this temptation of magical powers obtained through meditation is believed to remain a mere "magician" without power to go beyond his own limited desires. Only a renewed vigor at this stage of development, a further renunciation of all the minor virtues acquired along the road to spiritual enrichment, brings the ascetic to his ultimate goal—union with Brahman. The use of the siddhis, or magical powers, acquired by yogic discipline must always be abandoned in order to gain the supreme freedom of samadhi (bliss) and moksha (liberation). In the Svetasvatara Upanishad it is written: "When absorbed in this concentration the yogi sees by the true nature of his own self, which manifests like a light the true nature of Brahman, which is unborn, eternal, free from all effects of nature, he gets released from all bonds."

As the ascetic practiced his meditational and mental arts his mind began to experience realities he could not find words to describe. In effect, he found himself plumbing the cosmic mysteries without soma, without ritual, but by simply delving into his own mind. As one yogi described it, by going "from darkness to darkness deeper yet," he solved all the mysteries of existence. The yogis' metaphysical interpretations of their mystical ecstasies no doubt varied from sect to sect; yet from the fundamental sameness they realized that the sense of freedom, bliss, and triumph of soul and mind could be experienced by all willing to discipline themselves. From these mystical exercises the yogi created elaborate but effective techniques for inducing ecstasy. Slowly a complex metaphysical system for interpreting the experience developed. Because of this concentration on inducing ecstasy, the mystical experience is fundamental to Indian religion, whereas in other religions it has only varying importance.

From this systematizing developed yoga (Sanskrit for "yoke" or "union"), which eventually became a darsana ("orthodox system") and flourished throughout all branches of Hinduism.[15] The aim of yoga, therefore, is to attain complete union with Brahman or Supreme Being, by ceasing of mental activity, development of concentration, and meditational skills. There are eight ways to achieve these goals, which involve hard discipline and training:

1. *Self-control* (yama), or practicing the moral rules of nonviolence, truthfulness, honesty, chastity, and avoiding greed
2. *Observance* (niyama) of the above five moral rules
3. *Posture* (asana), which involves sitting in specific positions essential to good meditation and physical discipline
4. *Control of breath* (pranayama), where it is held and controlled in unusual rhythms thought to be of spiritual and physical value
5. *Restraint* (pratyahara) in which the sense organs are trained to ignore their perceptions
6. *Steadying the mind* (dharana), involving concentration on a single object, e.g., tip of nose, icon, sacred symbol, and so on
7. *Meditation* (dhyana), when the mind is so steadied that the object of concentration fills the whole of one's attention
8. *Deep meditation* (samadhi), when the whole personality is temporarily dissolved in the awareness of a greater reality

The final stage of samadhi is another of those mysterious but specialized ideas one finds in Eastern religions. Samadhi is a Sanskrit word usually translated as "bliss," "ecstasy," "rapture," and so forth; but Patanjali, the founder of the yoga system, meant something quite untranslatable. Patanjali (whose life is

[15]For a more detailed description of this whole period and the life of ancient India, see Basham, *The Wonder That Was India.*

dated between the second and fourth centuries B.C.) taught that
during samadhi everything within the conscious mind vanishes
except the object meditated upon. For example, if one meditates
upon the image of Christ, the reality of the Christ figure becomes the only reality within the concentrating mind (citta).
Patanjali explains in his later sutras that a transformation
within the mind follows a definite progression once one attains a
degree of "mind control": (1) I am *conscious* of the being of
Christ; (2) I *am* the form of Christ; (3) The *Being* of Christ
am. The final, ungrammatical statement represents the loss of
the "I" and total identification, the complete self-transformation
of the meditator into that which he meditates upon. To Patanjali the knowledge gained of the object concentrated upon is utterly real. If it were imaginary the whole experience would be
nothing more than a mental exercise. The transformation is
therefore from the illusory perception of the physical world to
the creation of the utterly real within oneself. This reality has
obvious implications for ethical philosophy: what one holds in
one's mind, one becomes!

There are other yoga systems beside the raja yoga (Royal
Yoga) just outlined. There is also hatha yoga and laya yoga,
which emphasize physical methods for achieving their goals. And
still another form is mantra yoga, or the "yoga of spells," which
uses repetition of magic syllables as a means of dissociating consciousness and inducing ecstatic trance. This emphasis on magic
syllables, on invocation, on the holy word, on the use of sound
to evoke mystical consciousness, already existed in the early
Vedas and was used by the Brahman priests during rituals, but
was crystallized in the Upanishads. The use of sound is a fascinating mystical element in the Upanishads, for it is the same
obsession with sound that one finds throughout religious literature. Its use, however, is much more developed in Hinduism.

Certain sounds are considered identical to Brahman. In the
Katha Upanishad, for example, it is written, "that which all the
Vedas declare, that which all austerities utter, that desiring
which they lead the life of Brahmacharya, that word I will tell
thee briefly is AUM. That word is Brahman; that word is Supreme." In the Prasna Upanishad, AUM is described as Brahman before and after It created the world.[16]

---

[16]See the Fifth Question of the Prasna Upanishad, and the Second Khanda
of the Mundaka Upanishad for a scriptural description of the significance
of AUM. The similarity to the Christian emphasis on the "Word" is striking.
The Gospel of St. John begins: "When all things began, the Word already
was. The Word dwelt with God, and what God was, the Word was. The Word,
then, was with God at the beginning, and through him all things came to be."
(*The New English Bible* translation.)

Sound is both a technique for concentrating the attention and for cleansing the perception. The use of "holy sound" is incorporated into yogic practices in the belief that such chanting helps awaken the dormant spiritual faculties within man. It is metaphorically cleaning the glass through which we perceive reality, and is perhaps similar to William Blake's idea that "If the doors of perception were cleansed, every thing will appear to man as it is, infinity." In the Maitri Upanishad, which contains many yogic meditation techniques, there are parallel descriptions of the importance of the mystical symbol AUM (a variant spelling is OM) in Brahmanism. In the Yogic Upanishads, which are somewhat later chronologically, sound is brought directly into the meditative experience as a guide for certain yogic attainments. The symbolic letters OM, however, also represent Isvara, the god of the yoga school, and therefore take on multiple importance. Yogis believed the OM sound would aid meditation and give insight into the pure soul.

The use of AUM during meditation is common to the middle-period Upanishads, and the Maitri Upanished clarifies the use of mystical sounds and distinguishes between meditations which rely on the use of "word" and those which rely on the "nonword" sounds. The Madabindu Upanishad describes a wide variety of auditory phenomena that manifest themselves during "word' meditation. In the Madabindu a great bird symbolizes the AUM sound itself. The right wing is A, with the following letters extending across its body describing the letters' cosmic value and the different worlds to which they correspond.

The auditory phenomena within one's head during meditation reflect different levels of perception. Internal sounds, such as AUM, are meant initially to drown out all other noises from the external world. The first internal sounds that a meditating yogi actually experiences, according to the Madabindu, are violent as the ocean, thunder, or waterfall. A second stage is reached when the sounds begin to acquire a musical character such as a bell or horn. Finally the sounds become delicate, muted, and extremely fine, as that of a bee or a distant flute. The more subtle the sounds the yogi hears within himself during meditation, the greater is the evidence of his progress. The final stage of meditation, according to the Madabindu Upanishad, is union with the paramatma or universal spirit, and possesses no sound. This is liberation and the yogi has no awareness of any physical sensation—including sound. He is "as a piece of wood, he has cognizance of neither cold nor heat, nor pain nor pleasure."

Sacred song, hymns of praise, mantric syllables chanted in meditation all reveal the dependence of the worshipper upon sound. They purposefully direct conscious attention, exalt the

wandering spirit into a state of religious awe, and eventually
into confrontation with numinous powers. The sounds of mankind's religious yearning seem the key into sacred chambers left
untouched by other forms of devotion. Good actions, for example, may store up good karma according to some schools, but
such actions serve only to make one more aware of the religious
context of our lives and the ethical responsibilities imposed by
that realization. Starvation, flagellation, asceticisms of all sort
beat the flesh into quiescence; but in the process mutilate the
very creation in which divinity has chosen to reside. This music
of the soul, then, that Hinduism utilized—as did later gnostic, Islamic, and Christian mystics—seems to be the sounds of spiritual
yearning that reach beyond ascetic physical disciplines and fill
the supplicant with joy, and finally complete freedom.

SANKHYA

In addition to the Vedanta or Upanishadic doctrines, another
major philosophical school closely related to yoga dominated Indian philosophy—Sankhya. Sankhya ("reasoning"), one of the orthodox systems (darsanas), was founded by the legendary sage
Kapila. The central premise of Kapila's rationalistic approach
was that since something cannot come out of nothing, it is assumed the universe must have always existed. But because there
must be a halt in the succession of causes, there is believed to
be an eternally existing essence lying at the farthest bounds of
human thought.

There are two basic principles in Sankhya: Prakriti (or primeval
matter), that which "evolves, produces, or brings forth"; and
Purusha (primal spirit). Just as in the Chinese eternal energy
principle of chi, within which the interaction between yin-yang
brings the phenomenal world into existence, so there are three
gunas or essences in Prakriti. They are the Sankhya trinity and
basic substances of all that is: goodness (sattva), energy (rajas), and darkness (tamas). Again, as in other ancient religions
(such as Chinese yin-yang), the life energy is considered male
and female. In the Puranas (legends) and the Tantras (textbooks, devotion literature) in particular, Prakriti is considered
female, the mother of the universe, who is married to Purusha
or primal male.

According to Kapila, when the three gunas are in equilibrium
matter is static; but when the perfect balance is disturbed one
or the other becomes dominant and matter begins evolving into
cosmic egoity, intellect, the subtle elements of the universe, and
so on. Purusha or Spirit alone is intelligent, and its characteris-

tics are reflected in both cosmic and individual functions. The spirit's association with matter produces evolution, conscious experience, and the resultant misery of worldly existence. Knowledge and freeing oneself from material bondage consist in realizing the distinctness of spirit from matter, and that material activities are the result of the interplay between the two. Kapila argued that the spirit element became free from all mundane fetters when it realized that all phenomena it was experiencing were only reflections produced by matter.[17]

Sankhya philosophy was highly rationalistic, and yet very close to the philosophy of yoga. The central difference is that yoga followed the Vedanta idea that insentient matter (Prakriti) did not explain creation and that a Supreme Being alone could be the source of the universe and human life. While accepting the general principles of Sankhya ideas the yoga school added God (Isvara) as an omniscient, eternal teacher who was not a creator, but a specially exalted soul that had existed for all eternity without ever having been enmeshed in matter.[18] The lack of a God in Kapila's thinking led many to consider it an atheistic philosophy.[19]

Another central difference berween the yoga school and the Sankhya theories of Kapila involved the yogis' descriptions of mystical ecstasy. The yogis maintained that during the ecstatic moment they were face to face with God. Kapila retorted, much as a modern-day rationalist would: "You have not proved the existence of your Lord, and therefore I see no reason why I should alter my definition of perception in order to accommodate your ecstatic visions." In his attempt to silence the yogis Kapila denied their God, but as Max Muller has pointed out, he himself was far from denying the existence or non existence of a Supreme Being.[20] He took an agnostic position and tended to avoid metaphysical speculation. Some believe that Buddha later followed Kapila's teachings in developing his own skeptical approach to "unanswerable" questions. But the connection between the two is tenuous, for Buddha did not concede the Vedas any independent authority and Kapila did accept the Vedas as "revealed."

[17]See Max Muller, *Selected Essays* (London: Longmans Green, 1881), vol. 2, pp. 218-19.

[18]See Basham, *The Wonder That Was India,* pp. 324ff.

[19]See E. Royston Pike, *Encyclopedia of Religion* (New York: Meridian, 1958); and also Basham, pp. 324ff.

[20]Muller, *Selected Essays,* vol. 2, p. 219.

BHAKTI AND THE BHAGAVAD GITA

The Bhagavad Gita ("Song of the Lord") is the prime exponent of devotional mysticism in Hinduism. A long dramatic theosophical poem, it is a part of the mammoth epic Mahabharata, and is perhaps one of the most famous and loved pieces of Indian religious literature ever created. Its popularity in the West is so great that it has been translated more than forty times into English alone. Along with many Western scholars and philosophers, the skeptical and irascible German philosopher Schopenhauer was an avid devotee. He wrote of the Gita: "It has been the solace of my life, it shall be the solace of my death . . . In the morning I bathe my intellect in the stupendous and the cosmological philosophy of the Bhagavad Gita, since whose composition many years of the gods have elapsed and in comparison with which our modern world and its literature seem puny and trivial and I doubt if that philosophy is not to be referred to a previous state of Existence, so remote is its sublimity from our conceptions."

The Gita's creation was probably between the third and first centuries B.C., and was the work of several hands. Many scholars date the creation of the Gita around the fifth century B.C. More conservative scholars feel that the many hands composing its seven hundred verses did their work over long periods of time and that its final version was set by the third century B.C. For a more detailed description of its origins, see *The Bhagavadgita*, by S. Radhakrishnan (New York: Harper & Brothers, 1948), p. 14. The principal themes are set in a dialogue between Krishna (a manifestation of the god Vishnu) and Arjuna, a young prince and hero of the Mahabharata. The Gita speaks of three paths to salvation, all of which are acceptable in orthodox Hinduism: the way of knowledge (jnana, mainly contemplative); the way of works (karma); and the way of devotion (bhakti).

The term "bhakti" ("devotion") comes from the same root as "Bhagavata," which explains its use in the title. Bhagavatism is a monotheistic concept, as in the Gita, and preaches basically the doctrine of Vishnu's supremacy over other gods, but does not reject any "way" or "path." (There are, in fact, three main deities upon which the bhakti movement as a whole is centered—Vishnu, Siva, and Shakti—with each being considered the single, highest god by its followers.) While the word "bhakti" comes comparatively late in Hindu sacred writings, its implications of devotion to a personal god seem as ancient as the prayers in very early Vedic hymns to the ethical god Varuna.[21] The Upanishads, like

[21]See C. H. Loehlin, *The Sikhs and Their Scriptures* (Lucknow, U.P., India: Lucknow Publishing House, 1964), pp. 55ff.

Vedantism itself, are somewhat intellectual and yet the devotional concept of bhakti can be found in early Upanishads like the Katha (II.23):

> This Soul (Atman) is not to be obtained by instruction,
> Nor by intellect, nor by much learning.
> He is to be obtained only by the one whom He chooses;
> To such a one that Soul reveals His own person.

Also in the Svetasvatara Upanishad (VI.23) the term "bhakti" appears for the first time in Hindu scriptures:

> To one who has the highest devotion (bhakti) for God,
> And for his spiritual teacher (guru) even as for God,
> To him these matters which have been declared
> Become manifest if he be a great soul (mahatman)—
> Yea, become manifest if he be a great soul.

So even though the whole thrust of the Upanishads is salvation by knowledge, the beginning of devotional theism is already apparent. But it is in the epic Mahabharata where bhakti comes into its own. In the sixth book of the Gita, bhakti is claimed to be the supreme way of salvation. Also in the Gita (II.54) the Lord Vishnu says, "Not for the Vedas, not for mortifications, not for almsgiving, and not for sacrifice may I be seen in such guise as thou hast seen me. But through undivided devotion, Arjuna, I may be known and seen in verity, and entered."

The Gita states that one need not be bound to the world if one's labors are performed in the spirit of self-surrender to God. The way of works should, the Gita says, be seen as part of the path of devotion. And while the Gita maintains that the yogi who pursues knowledge (jnana) can indeed become Brahman, it is a lower path than devotion; for knowledge is the lower aspect of the Godhead, and loving service is the higher. But even good words are not equal to devotion, for God loves the meek and eschews those proud of achievement. Thus bhakti yoga is superior to all other forms, for devotion is itself its own fruit.

Although Krishna is frequently described as God transcendent rather than God immanent in the Gita, Krishna admits that he is in the heart of all beings. Bhakti as expressed in the Gita therefore began as respectful adoration, as awe in the face of the numinous—which is a description of theistic mystical confrontation familiar to westerners. As Krishna is revealed in his form as Vishnu for the first time, Arjuna falls on his knees before him and says:

You are the father of the Universe, of all that moves
   and all that moves not, its worshipful, worthy teacher.
You have no equal—what in the three worlds could
   equal you, O power beyond compare?

So, reverently prostrating my body,
   I crave your grace, O Blessed Lord.
As father to son, as friend to friend, as love to
   beloved, bear with me, God.

I rejoice that I have seen what none has seen before,
   but my mind trembles with fear.
Graciously show me again your earthly form,
   Lord of the Gods, Home of the World.

The knowledge doctrine that Krishna teaches Arjuna in the
Gita is similar in parts to Sankara's advaita, even though much
is theistic in the book. Advaita conceives all reality as ultimately One. This singular Reality manifests itself in the forms,
names, and all impermanent phenomena of the world. In addition to the advaitan philosophy, the Gita frequently turns to a
unitive theme as well as devotion: "Those who worship in Me,
regarding Me as the Supreme Goal, meditating on Me with
single-minded devotion, I speedily save from the ocean of
samsara (worldly attachments that cause rebirth)." Nonattachment from the fruits of one's actions is another important idea
in the Gita, and indeed, permeates Hinduism, Buddhism, and
eastern mystical religions generally. If one is weak and cannot
follow the path of complete devotion, or the hard discipline outlined in the Gita, the book advises, "Take refuge in Me, perform all actions with self-control, not for the sake of the
benefits they may bring."

This separation from the results of your action will ultimately
lead to nonattachment and freedom from karmic ties to the
world. The Gita is also highly flexible. Throughout its pages one
gets the impression of practical concerns, of understanding the
necessity of working with the weaknesses inherent in the worldly
bound human personality. The Gita consequently describes (and
allows) many different approaches to union with the Ultimate
Reality that remains the source of all manifested life. "By whatever way men approach Me," the Gita gently advises, "by that
way do I come to them. All paths that men follow lead to Me."
This is a highly mystical phrase, for we are in effect being told
that all paths men follow will ultimately continue our personal
evolution toward a unitive goal. It is apparently each individual's destiny, according to the Gita's message, to ineluctably ful-

fill personal evolution, regardless of the path, methods, or goals chosen.

When Krishna talks of "Me" in the universal sense, he is not speaking of an anthropomorphic godself unto which mankind moves. Krishna's "Me" is the Godhead as the Universal Self. Krishna says clearly that "I am the Self in the heart of all beings." Again the message of the theistic mystic. Within the core of each being there resides sleeping divinity. To find God, or to become united with a Universal Source, it is to the sleeping Higher Self that one travels, it is within oneself that one moves to discover the knowledge of God and to achieve freedom for the enwebbed spiritual center.

The passionate devotionalism of the Gita affected the whole Indian community. By the twelfth century, or medieval period, bhakti had taken a strong hold in southern India or Tamil country, where some of the most beautiful of all devotional literature poured forth from the pens of the Tamil saints and poets. The eleven sacred books (Tirumurai) of the Saivites, who spoke and wrote in the Tamil, were composed between the seventh and tenth centuries. These books are anthologies of hymns composed by the sixty-three Nayanars, or Teachers of the Saivites (worshippers of Siva). And chief among the eleven books are the Tevaram, containing hymns by the three major bhakti poets: Appar (also Apparswami), Sundaramurti (also Sundarar), and the Tiruvasagam of Manikka Vasagar, all of whom are represented in this volume. The Saivites wrote of complete surrender to the Lord (Prapatti), which is the cardinal doctrine of the South Indian School. This group considers the final teaching in the Gita to be where Krishna tells Arjuna: "Giving up all duties, take refuge under Me alone; I shall deliver you from all sins" (18.66).

The bhakti mystic is clearly theistic. He needs a personalized god upon whom he can flood his intense devotion. The intellect and emphasis on knowledge so frequent in Vedanta philosophy is replaced in bhakti by passionate commitment. The emphasis on mind that Sankara had popularized and systematized in the ninth century was altered by another great Indian philosopher who was a bhakti, Ramanuja (c. 1017-1137). Like Sankara, he based his doctrines on the Upanishads and the Brahma Sutras. But Ramanuja developed a qualified monism in his version of devotional mysticism, based in large part on the teachings in the Bhagavad Gita. Sankara argued that any personal god would be less than a Supreme God by definition. This argument didn't influence Ramanuja, whose Supreme Being was indeed a personal one. He accepted the bhakti idea that the best way to salvation was for the worshipper to realize that he was but a particle of God. He argued that if one abandoned one's self entirely and trusted in God's will, His grace would inevitably encompass him. As distinguished from the impersonal World Soul or Supreme God of Sankara, Ramanuja's God needed men as much as mankind needed Him. Ramanuja's qualified monism, and the justification for his philosophy being considered mystical, lies primarily in his belief that the individual soul was made by God out of His own essence and would eventually return and be reunited with Him. The consciousness of the individual would always remain distinct and intact, yet once in full communion and living within God's omniscience, evil could not touch the personal "I" that had become eternal by virtue of its being a part of the Godhead. In other words, the soul or conscious "I" was both at one with God but separate. Ramanuja's emphasis on loving devotion was pure bhakti, and after his death his ideas spread widely, replacing the more distant, impersonal Godhead of Sankara with a personal and accessible Lord who possessed numerous identifiable attributes. Ramanuja's philosophy became the justification for many later bhakti sects. And while Ramanuja was not the philosopher or theorist Sankara was, his system afforded the bhakti movement the philosophical foundation it had lacked.

As we have seen, bhakti is only one part of a vast, complex religious system that gave birth to other, equally great religious visions, like Sikhism, Buddhism, Jainism. But throughout the Hindu system run recurrent mystical themes. As Sir Charles Eliot said years ago. "Hinduism appeals to the soul's immediate knowledge and experience of God. The possibility and truth of this experience is hardly questioned in India, and the task of religion is to bring it about." But one of the most important threads that ties together the complex fabric of Hindu religious thought is that there is allowance for an absolute liberty in the world of thought and intellect. Only in relation to moral codes are there strict demands. Intellectually, all may be Hindus if they are a part of the Hindu culture. As Gandhi described this most intriguing and complex of religions: "A man may not believe in God and still call himself a Hindu. Hinduism is a relentless pursuit after truth. Truth is God."

1. Selections from the Rig Veda

To the Unknown God

In the beginning there arose the Golden Child.[1] As soon as born, he alone was the lord of all that is. He established the earth and this heaven: Who is the God to whom we shall offer sacrifice?

He who gives breath, he who gives strength, whose command all the bright gods revere, whose shadow is immortality, whose shadow is death: Who is the God to whom we shall offer sacrifice?

He who through his might became the sole king of the breathing and twinkling world, who governs all this, man and beast: Who is the God to whom we shall offer sacrifice?

He through whose might these snowy mountains are, and the sea, they say, with the distant river; he of whom these regions are indeed the two arms: Who is the God to whom we shall offer sacrifice?

He through whom the awful heaven and the earth were made fast, he through whom the ether was established, and the firmament; he who measured the air in the sky: Who is the God to whom we shall offer sacrifice?

He to whom heaven and earth, standing firm by his will, look up, trembling in their mind; he over whom the risen sun shines forth: Who is the God to whom we shall offer sacrifice?

When the great waters went everywhere, holding the germ, and generating light, then there arose from them the breath of the gods: Who is the God to whom we shall offer sacrifice?

[1]The Sanskrit word Hiranyagarbha, "Golden Child," needs some explanation. It has been translated in a variety of ways, but Max Muller made his choice here because the word means literally the golden embryo, the golden germ or child, born of a golden womb. It was probably mankind's first attempt to name the god of the sun. Another odd fact about this hymn is the concept of one God, which pervades the whole, written in a culture that was pantheistic and had gods for storms, sky, fire, etc.

He who by his might looked even over the waters which held power and generated the sacrifice, he who alone is God above all gods: Who is the God to whom we shall offer sacrifice?

May he not hurt us, he who is the begetter of the earth, or he, the righteous, who begat the heaven; he who also begat the bright and mighty waters: Who is the God to whom we shall offer sacrifice?

Pragapati, no other than thou embraces all these created things. May that be ours which we desire when sacrificing to thee: may we be lords of wealth!

Rig Veda X.121

Who is our father, our creator, maker,
Who every place doth know and every creature,
By whom alone to gods their names were given,
To him all other creatures go to ask him.

Rig Veda X.82.3

1. The great fire at the beginning of the dawn has sprung aloft, and issuing forth from the darkness has come with radiance. Agni,[2] the bright-bodied, as soon as born, fills all dwellings with shining light.

2. When born, thou, O Agni, art the embryo of heaven and earth, beautiful, borne about in the plants; variegated, infantine, thou dispersest the nocturnal glooms; thou issuest roaring loudly from the maternal sources.

3. May He, who as soon as manifested is vast and wise, and thus universally pervading, defend me, his third manifestation; and when the worshippers ask with their mouths for his own water, animated by one purpose, they praise him in this world.

4. Therefore the genetrices of all things, the herbs, the cherishers of all with food, wait on thee who art the augmenter of food, with sacrificial viands; thou visitest them again, when they have assumed other forms, thou art amongst human beings the invoker of the gods.

5. We worship Agni for prosperity, thee, who art the invoker of the gods, the many-coloured conveyance of the sacrifice, the brilliant banner of every offering, the surpasser of every other deity in might, the guest of men.

6. Arrayed in splendid garments, that Agni abides on the

[2]Agni is second only to Indra in prominence in the Vedic pantheon of ancient India. Agni is personified as fire in all its forms: of the sky, lightning, meteors, stars, comets, and especially the fire of the sacrificial altar. The god functions as a liaison between Brahman priests who perform the sacrifices and the heavenly gods. Agni is invoked more often in the Vedic hymns than any other deity.

navel of the earth;[3] do thou, royal Agni, who art radiant, born
in the footmark of Ila,[4] offer worship here as *Purohita* to the
gods.

7. Thou hast ever sustained, Agni, both heaven and earth, as
a son supports his parents; come, youngest of the gods, to the
presence of those desiring thee; Son of strength, bring hither the
gods.

Rig Veda X.1

1. Purusha,[5] who has a thousand heads, a thousand eyes, a
thousand feet, investing the earth in all directions, exceeds it by
a space measuring ten fingers.

2. Purusha is verily all this visible world all that is and all
that is to be; he is also the lord of immortality; for he mounts
beyond his own condition for the food of living beings.

3. Such is his greatness; and Purusha is greater even than
this; all beings are one-fourth of him; his other three-fourths,
being immortal, abide in heaven.

4. Three-fourths of Purusha ascended; the other fourth that
remained in this world proceeds repeatedly, and, diversified in
various forms, went to all animate and inanimate creation.[6]

5. From him[7] was born Viraj and from Viraj Purusha; he, as
soon as born became manifested, and afterwards created the
earth and then corporeal forms.

6. When the gods performed the sacrifice[8] with Purusha as
the offering, then Spring was its ghi, Summer the fuel, and Au-
tumn the oblation.

[3] The altar of the earth is meant.

[4] The North-altar.

[5] Like many other primitive communities, the ancient Vedic Aryans believed
the creation of the human race, and indeed the whole world, was the result
of the sacrifice, the self-immolation of a great cosmic being. In their case it
was the male element, Purusha. In this hymn the poetic vision is truly mystical in that all anthropomorphism is omitted and Purusha's sacrifice is set
against a great cosmic panorama that makes God, man, and the universal all
the result of a single sacrificial act, and of a single substance. It is the beginning of a highly sophisticated religious philosophy that came to full flower
in the later Upanishads. For further discussion see S. Radhakrishnan, *Indian Philosophy*, vol. 1 (New York: The Macmillan Co.; London: Allen &
Unwin Ltd., 1923, 1951). See also *Sources of Indian Tradition*, vol. 1, General Editor, Wm. Theodore de Bary (New York: Columbia, 1958).

[6] That is, by individuals in death and birth, or in the world by its temporary
dissolution and renovation.

[7] The presiding male or spirit, "life," the "first man." Viraj: primeval germ,
the female counterpart of the male principle Purusha.

[8] This sacrifice is supposedly imaginary, or mental (manasam).

7. They immolated as the victim upon the sacred grass Purusha, born before creation; with him the deities who were Sadhyas[9] and those who were Rishis sacrificed.

8. From that victim, in whom the universal oblation was offered, the mixture of curds and butter was produced, then he made those animals over whom Vayu presides, those that are wild, and those that are tame.

9. From that victim,[10] in whom the universal oblation was offered, the Richas[11] and Sama-hymns were produced; from him the metres were born; from him the Yajush[12] was born.

10. From him were born horses and whatsoever animals have two rows of teeth; yea, cows were born from him; from him were born goats and sheep.

11. When they immolated Purusha, into how many portions did they divide him? What was his mouth called, what his arms, what his thighs, what were his feet called?

12. His mouth became the Brahmana, his arms became the Rajanya, his thighs become the Vaisya, the Sudra was born from his feet.[13]

13. The moon was born from his mind; the sun was born from his eye; Indra and Agni were born from his mouth, Vayu from his breath.

14. From his navel came the firmament, from his head the heaven was produced, the earth from his feet, the quarters of space from his ear, so they constituted the world.

15. Seven were the enclosures of the sacrifice, thrice seven logs of fuel were prepared, when the gods, celebrating the rites, bound Purusha as the victim.

16. By sacrifice the gods worshipped him who is also the sacrifice; those were the first duties. Those great ones became partakers of the heaven where the ancient deities the Sadyas abide.

Rig Veda X.90

[9]Sadhya meaning those competent to create.

[10]Victim in the sense of materials for sacrifice.

[11]Stanzas of the Rig Veda.

[12]Yajush refers to the Yajur Veda, and the spells and charms noted there.

[13]That is, the Brahmins are like speech from the mouth, which in turn reflects thought, and hence the thinking man, the superior and legislating capacity. The Rajanja is like the arms that defend the ruling group of society. The Vaisyas are the artisans and craftsmen who are like thighs in that they support and sustain. The feet provide the labor, the movement and activity of society; and so the Sudras are the workers. It can be seen that this hymn conceives of the human organism in grades of significance. This hymn was perhaps the earliest expression of the Indian caste system, which started out as an occupational grading and later became hereditary.

1. The non-existent was not, the existent was not;[14] then the world was not, nor the firmament, nor that which is above the firmament. How could there be any investing envelope,[15] and where? Of what could there be felicity? How could there be the deep unfathomable water?

2. Death was not, nor at that period immortality, there was no indication of day or night; That One unbreathed upon breathed of his own strength, other than That there was nothing else whatever.

3. There was darkness covered by darkness in the beginning, all this world was indistinguishable water; that empty united world which was covered by a mere nothing, was produced through the power of austerity.[16]

4. In the beginning there was desire,[17] which was the first seed of mind; sages having meditated in their hearts have discovered by their wisdom the connexion of the existent with the non-existent.

5. Their ray[18] was stretched out, whether across, or below, or above; some were shedders of seed, others were mighty; food was inferior, the eater was superior.

6. Who really knows? who in this world may declare it? when was this creation, whence was it engendered? The gods were subsequent to the world's creation; so who knows whence it arose?

7. He from whom this creation arose, he may uphold it, or if he may not no one else can; he who is its superintendent in the

---

[14]In Hindu cosmology "sat" and "asat" mean visible and invisible existence and can relate, as they do here, to matter and spirit (purusha and prakriti). Indra in early creation myth slew the demon Vritra, and thereby brought the existent (sat) out of the nonexistent (asat). Even while Indra is thought of as the personal creator, and is the One God (eka deva), there is another aspect conceived of as impersonal creative impulse called That One (tad ekam). In later cosmological speculation the distinctions between purusha and prakriti are blended and become one immaterial, incomprehensible First Cause, or Brahman. The First Cause was undeveloped in the beginning, yet existed before inactive matter or active spirit. Nothing else existed, neither matter nor spirit before creation, until Brahman, who is eternally existing essence, differentiated and brought about the First Cause. It was believed that only the sages were able to grasp the meaning of the relationships between "being" (sat) and "nonbeing" (asat).

[15]What living being could exist, there being no life?

[16]This does not mean penance, but rather the contemplation of things that were to be created.

[17]That is, in the mind of the Supreme Being.

[18]The ray of creation, which developed like the flash of the sun's rays. The suddenness of creation was so quick that creation took place simultaneously in all three portions of the universe: those in the central space, those above and those below.

highest heaven, he assuredly knows, or if he knows not no one else does.

Rig Veda X.129

1. Sanctify Soma[19] our mind, our heart, our intellect; and may thy worshippers delight in thy friendship, like cattle in fresh pasture, in thine exhilaration produced by the sacrificial food; for thou art mighty.

2. They who seek to touch thy heart, Soma, worship thee in all places; and these desires for wealth rise from my heart at thine exhilaration; for thou art mighty.

3. Verily, Soma, I practise all thy observances with fullness; and as a father to his son, so do thou in thy exhilaration make us happy; protect us from being killed by our enemies; for thou art mighty.

4. Our praises converge Soma towards thee, as herds towards a well; establish our pious acts, Soma, for us to live long, as the priest sets up the cups for thine exhilaration; for thou art mighty.

5. The intelligent priests, whose desires are fixed on the fruit of good works, with sacred rites show forth the praises of thee, Soma, who art wise and powerful; do thou, in thy exhilaration, grant us pastures, abounding with cattle, and with horses; for thou art mighty.

6. Thou protectest our cattle, Soma, and the variously occupied world, contemplating all existing beings; thou preparest the

[19]Nearly all the hymns in Book IX are invocations to soma, which is a juice extracted from a type of milkweed, *Asclepias acida*. The juice was prepared with elaborate ritual, and energized the priests, opening their perceptions to the grandeur of the universe. Soma allowed early man to be in personal touch with the gods they so yearned for. The soma was such an important part of the Vedic sacrificial rituals that it was thought to convey mystical qualities to the hymns themselves (see Rig Veda IX.6.9). Soma as a plant was viewed as a drink of the gods. In this sense it became an aesthetically important part of Aryan culture, for it imparted indescribable beauty to life. Soma was also eventually a god itself, and as such was perceived as mystical consciousness in the making; beauty and wonder became divine expressions provable by ritualistic drinking and use of soma. Initially soma juice created a perception of divinity, but through habit and training of the mind, the ancient Aryans became entranced with not just beauty, a sense of an awesome power beyond the sensual experience. At this stage the plant was raised to the status of a god and was symbolic of the Highest Reality. Soma was frequently mentioned in the Zendavesta as Haoma, and was also freely used by Zoroastrian priests. For further discussion see T.G. Mainkar, *Mysticism in the Rig Veda*. (Bombay, India: Popular Book Depot, 1961). Also S. Radhakrishnan, *Indian Philosophy*, p. 83ff. See also Soma: Divine Mushroom of Immortality (New York: Harcourt Brace Jovanovich, 1968), where R. Gordon Wasson argues that soma was a hallucinogenic mushroom, the Amanita muscaria.

world for them to live in for thy exhilaration; for thou art
mighty.

7. Be on all sides our preserver, Soma, thou, who art unassail-
able; drive away, monarch, our adversaries in thine exhilaration,
and let no calumniator rule over us; for thou art mighty.

8. Soma, author of good works, liberal granter of fields, be
vigilant in supplying us with food; and in thy exhilaration
preserve us from oppressive men, and from sin; for thou art
mighty.

9. Utter destroyer of enemies, Soma, who art the auspicious
friend of Indra, protect us, when hostile warriors everywhere
call us to the combat that bestows offspring; by thine exhilaration preserve us; for thou art mighty.

10. Such is the Soma which, swiftly moving, exhilarating, acceptable to Indra, has given increase to our understanding; it
has increased in intelligence of the great and pious Kakshivat in
thine exhilaration; for thou art mighty.

11. This Soma bestows, upon the pious donor of the libation,
food with cattle; it gives wealth to the seven priests in the
manifold exhilaration; it has restored their faculties to the blind,
and the lame.[20]

Rig Veda X.25

To Vayu[21]

Come hither, O Vayu, thou beautiful one! These Somas are
ready, drink of them, hear our call! O Vayu, the praisers
celebrate thee with hymns, they who know the feast-days, and
have prepared the Soma. O Vayu, thy satisfying stream goes to
the worshipper, wide-reaching, to the Soma-draught. O Indra and
Vayu, these libations of Soma are poured out; come hither for
the sake of our offerings, for the drops of Soma long for you.
O Indra and Vayu, you perceive the libations, you who are rich
in booty; come then quickly hither! O Vayu and Indra, come
near to the work of the sacrificer, quick; thus is my prayer, O ye
men! I call Mitra, endowed with holy strength, and Varuna, who
destroys all enemies; who both fulfill a prayer accompanied by

---

[20]Soma also possessed curative powers; and as a plant-god associated both
with spirit and body no doubt carried a potent medicinal effect. Illness could
be obliterated from consciousness: "We have drunk the Soma, we have become immortal, we have entered into light, we have known the gods."

[21]Vayu is the god of wind. The Maruts are the storm gods.

fat offerings. On the right way, O Mitra and Varuna, you have obtained great wisdom, you who increase the right and adhere to the right; These two sages, Mitra and Varuna, the mighty, wide-ruling, give us efficient strength.

Rig Veda I.2

To Vayu

O Vayu, may the quick racers bring thee towards the offerings, to the early drink here, to the early drink of Soma! May the Dawn stand erect, approving thy mind! Come near on thy harnessed chariot to share, O Vayu, to share in the sacrifice! May the delightful drops of Soma delight thee, the drops made by us, well-made, and heaven-directed, yes, made with milk, and heaven-directed. When his performed aids assume strength for achievement, our prayers implore the assembled steeds for gifts, yes, the prayers implore them. Vayu yokes the two ruddy, Vayu yokes the two red horses, Vayu yokes to the chariot the two swift horses to draw in the yoke, the strongest to draw in the yoke. Awake Purandhi (the morning) as a lover wakes a sleeping maid, reveal heaven and earth, brighten the dawn, yes, for glory brighten the dawn. For thee the bright dawns spread out in the distance beautiful garments, in their houses, in their rays, beautiful in their new rays. To thee the juice-yielding cow pours out all treasures. Thou hast brought forth the Maruts from the flanks, yes, from the flanks of heaven. For thee the white, bright, rushing Somas, strong in raptures, have rushed to the whirl, they have rushed to the whirl of the waters. The tired hunter asks luck of thee in the chase; thou shieldest by thy power from every being, yes, thou shieldest by thy power from powerful spirits. Thou, O Vayu, art worthy as the first before all others to drink these our Somas, thou art worthy to drink these poured-out Somas. Among the people also who invoke thee and have turned to thee, all the cows pour out the milk, they pour out butter and milk for the Soma.

Manu has established thee, O Agni, as a light for all people. Thou hast shone forth with Kanva, born from Rita, grown strong, thou whom the human races worship. Agni's flames are impetuous and violent; they are terrible and not to be withstood. Always burn down the sorcerers, and the allies of the Yatus, every ghoul.

Rig Veda I.134

Bright, flaming, like the lover of the Dawn,[22] he has, like the light of the sky, filled the two worlds of Heaven and Earth which are turned towards each other. As soon as thou wert born thou hast excelled by thy power of mind; being the son of the gods thou hast become their father. Agni is a worshipper of the gods, never foolish, always discriminating; he is like the udder of the cows; he is the sweetness of food. Like a kind friend to men, not to be led astray, sitting in the midst, the lovely one, in the house; like a child when born, he is delightful in the house; like a race-horse which is well cared for, he has wandered across the clans. When I call to the sacrifice the clans who dwell in the same nest with the heroes, may Agni then attain all divine powers. When thou hast listened to these heroes, no one breaks those laws of thine. That verily is thy wonderful deed that thou hast killed, with thy companions, all foes; that, joined by the heroes, thou hast accomplished thy works. Like the lover of the Dawn, resplendent and bright, of familiar form: may he thus pay attention to this sacrificer. Carrying him they opened by themselves the doors of heaven. They all shouted at the aspect of the sun.

Like unto excellent wealth, like unto the shine of the sun, like unto living breath, like unto one's own son, like unto a quick takvan Agni holds the wood, like milk, like a milch cow, bright and shining. He holds safety, pleasant like a homestead, like ripe barley, a conqueror of men; like a Rishi uttering sacred shouts, praised among the clans; like a well-cared-for race-horse, Agni bestows vigor. He to whose flame men do not grow accustomed, who is like one's own mind, like a wife on a couch, enough for all happiness. When the bright Agni has shone forth, he is like a white horse among people, like a chariot with golden ornaments, impetuous in fights. Like an army which is sent forward he shows his vehemence, like an archer's shaft with sharp point. He who is born is one twin; he who will be born is the other twin—the lover of maidens, the husband of wives. As cows go to their stalls, all that moves and we, for the sake of a dwelling, reach him who has been kindled. Like the flood of the Sindhu he has driven forward the downward-flowing waters. The cows lowed at the sight of the sun.

                                                        Rig Veda X.186

---

[22] The sun.

2. *Selections from the Bhagavad Gita*

Chapter VI

The Book of Religion by Self-Restraint

Krishna. Therefore, who doeth work rightful to do,
Not seeking gain from work, that man, O Prince!
Is Sanyasi and Yogi—both in one
And he is neither who lights not the flame
Of sacrifice, nor setteth hand to task.

Regard as true Renouncer him that makes
Worship by work, for who renounceth not
Works not as Yogin. So is that well said:
"By works the votary doth rise to faith,
And saintship is the ceasing from all works;"
Because the perfect Yogin acts—but acts
Unmoved by passions and unbounded by deeds,
Setting result aside.

Let each man raise
The Self by Soul, not trample down his Self,
Since Soul that is Self's friend may grow
  Self's foe.

Soul is Self's friend when Self doth rule o'er Self,
But Self turns enemy if Soul's own self
Hates Self as not itself.[1]

The sovereign soul
Of him who lives self-governed and at peace
Is centred in itself, taking alike

[1] The Sanskrit has this play on the double meaning of *Atman*.

Pleasure and pain; heat, cold; glory and shame.
He is the Yogi, he is *Yukta*, glad
With joy of light and truth; dwelling apart
Upon a peak, with senses subjugate
Whereto the clod, the rock, the glistering gold
Show all as one. By this sign is he known
Being of equal grace to comrades, friends,
   Chance-comers, strangers, lovers, enemies,
Aliens and kinsmen; loving all alike,
Evil or good.

    Sequestered should he sit,
Steadfastly meditating, solitary,
His thoughts controlled, his passions laid away,
Quit of belongings. In a fair, still spot
Having his fixed abode,—not too much raised,
Nor yet too low,—let him abide, his goods
A cloth, a deerskin, and the Kusa-grass.
There, setting hard his mind upon The One,
Restraining heart and senses, silent, calm,
Let him accomplish Yoga, and achieve
Pureness of soul, holding immovable
Body and neck and head, his gaze absorbed
Upon his nose-end,[2] rapt from all around,
Tranquil in spirit, free of fear, intent
Upon his Brahmacharya vow, devout,
Musing on Me, lost in the thought of Me.
That Yogin, so devoted, so controlled,
Comes to the peace beyond,—My peace, the
   peace
Of high Nirvana!

    But for earthly needs
Religion is not his who too much fasts
Or too much feasts, nor his who sleeps away
An idle mind; nor his who wears to waste
His strength in vigils. Nay, Arjuna! call
That the true piety which most removes
Earth-aches and ills, where one is moderate
In eating and in resting, and in sport;
Measured in wish and act; sleeping betimes,
Waking betimes for duty.
    When the man,
So living, centres on his soul that thought

---

[2] Literally, as it is in the original.

Straitly restrained—untouched internally
By stress of sense—then is he Yukta. See!
Steadfast a lamp burns sheltered from the wind;
Such is the likeness of the Yogi's mind
Shut from sense-storms and burning bright to Heaven.
When mind broods placid, soothed with holy wont;
When Self contemplates self, and in itself
Hath comfort; when it knows the nameless joy
Beyond all scope of sense, revealed to soul—
Only to soul! and, knowing, wavers not,
True to the farther Truth; when, holding this,
It deems no other treasure comparable,
But, harboured there, cannot be stirred or shook
By any gravest grief, call that state "peace",
That happy severance Yoga; call that man
The perfect Yogin!
   Steadfastly the will
Must toil thereto, till efforts end in ease,
And thought has passed from thinking.
   Shaking off
All longings bred by dreams of fame and gain,
Shutting the doorways of the senses close
With watchful ward; so, step by step, it comes
To gift of peace assured and heart assuaged,
When the mind dwells self-wrapped, and the soul broods
Cumberless. But, as often as the heart
Breaks—wild and wavering—from control, so oft
Let him re-curb it, let him rein it back
To the soul's governance; for perfect bliss
Grows only in the bosom tranquillised,
The spirit passionless, purged from offence,
Vowed to the Infinite. He who thus vows
His soul to the Supreme Soul, quitting sin,
Passes unhindered to the endless bliss
Of unity with Brahma. He so vowed,
So blended, sees the Life-Soul resident
In all things living, and all living things
In that Life-Soul contained. And whoso thus
Discerneth Me in all, and all in Me,
I never let him go; nor looseneth he
Hold upon Me; but, dwell he where he may,
Whate'er his life, in Me he swells and lives,
Because he knows and worships Me, Who dwell
In all which lives, and cleaves to Me in all.
Arjuna! if a man sees everywhere—
Taught by his own similitude—one Life,

One Essence in the Evil and the Good,
Hold him a Yogi, yea! well-perfected!

Arjuna. Slayer of Madhu! yet again, this Yog,
This Peace, derived from equanimity,
Made known by thee—I see no fixity
Therein, no rest, because the heart of men
Is unfixed, Krishna! rash, tumultuous,
Wilful and strong. It were all one, I think,
To hold the wayward wind, as tame man's heart.

Krishna. Hero long-armed! beyond denial, hard
Man's heart is to restrain, and wavering;
Yet may it grow restrained by habit, Prince!
By wont of self-command. This Yog, I say,
Cometh not lightly to th' ungoverned ones;
But he who will be master of himself
Shall win it, if he stoutly strive thereto.

Arjuna. And what road goeth he who, having faith
Fails, Krishna! in the striving; falling, back
From holiness, missing the perfect rule?
Is he not lost, straying from Brahma's light,
Like the vain cloud, which floats 'twixt earth and heaven
When lightning splits it, and it vanisheth?
Fain would I hear thee answer me herein,
Since, Krishna! none save thou can clear the doubt.

Krishna. He is not lost, thou Son of Pritha!
No!
Nor earth, nor heaven is forfeit, even for him,
Because no heart that holds one right desire
Treadeth the road of loss! He who should fail,
Desiring righteousness, cometh at death
Unto the Region of the Just; dwells there
Measureless years, and being born anew,
Beginneth life again in some fair home
Amid the mild and happy. It may chance
He doth descend into a Yogin house
On Virtue's breast; but that is rare! Such birth
Is hard to be obtained on this earth, Chief!
So hath he back again what heights of heart
He did achieve, and so he strives anew
To perfectness, with better hope, dear Prince!
For by the old desire he is drawn on
Unwittingly; and only to desire
The purity of Yog is to pass
Beyond the Sabdabrahm, the spoken Ved.
But, being Yogi, striving strong and long,

Purged from transgressions, perfected by births
Following on births, he plants his feet at last
Upon the farther path. Such as one ranks
Above ascetics, higher than the wise,
Beyond achievers of vast deeds! Be thou
Yogi Arjuna! And of such believe.
Truest and best is he who worships Me
With inmost soul, stayed on My Mystery!

HERE ENDETH CHAPTER VI OF THE
BHAGAVAD GITA

Chapter VII

The Book of Religion by Discernment

Krishna. Learn now, dear Prince! How, if thy soul be set
Ever on Me—still exercising Yog,
Still making Me thy Refuge—thou shalt come
Most surely unto perfect hold of Me.
I will declare to thee that utmost lore,
Whole and particular, which, when thou knowest,
Leaveth no more to know here in this world.

Of many thousand mortals, one, perchance,
Striveth for Truth; and of those few that strive—
Nay, and rise high—one only—here and there—
Knoweth Me, as I am, the very Truth.

Earth, water, flame, air, ether, life, and mind,
And individuality—those eight
Make up the showing of Me, Manifest.
These be my lower Nature; learn the higher,
Whereby, thou Valiant One! this Universe
Is, by its principle of life, produced;
Whereby the worlds of visible things are born
As from a Yoni. Know! I am that womb:
I make and I unmake this Universe:
Than me there is no other Master, Prince!
No other Maker! All these hang on me
As hangs a row of pearls upon its string.
I am the fresh taste of the water; I
The silver of the moon, the gold o' the sun,
The word of worship in the Veds, the thrill

That passeth in the ether, and the strength
Of man's shed seed. I am the good sweet smell
Of the moistened earth, I am the fire's red light,
The vital air moving in all which moves,
The holiness of hallowed souls, the root
Undying, whence hath sprung whatever is;
The wisdom of the wise, the intellect
Of the informed, the greatness of the great,
The splendour of the splendid. Kunti's Son!
These am I, free from passion and desire;
Yet am I right desire in all who yearn,
Chief of the Bharatas! for all those moods,
Soothfast, or passionate, or ignorant,
Which Nature frames, deduce from me; but all
Are merged in me—not I in them! The world—
Deceived by those three qualities of being—
Wotteth not Me Who am outside them all,
Above them all, Eternal! Hard it is
To pierce that veil divine of various shows
Which hideth Me; yet they who worship Me
Pierce it and pass beyond.

    I am not known
To evil-doers, nor to foolish ones,
Nor to the base and churlish; nor to those
Whose mind is cheated by the show of things,
Nor those that take the way of Asuras.[3]

    Four sorts of mortals know me: he who weeps,
Arjuna! and the man who yearns to know;
And he who toils to help; and he who sits
Certain of me, enlightened.

    Of these four,
O Prince of India! highest, nearest, best
That last is, the devout soul, wise, intent
Upon "The One." Dear, above all, am I
To him; and he is dearest unto me!
All four are good, and seek me; but mine own,
The true of heart, the faithful—stayed on me,
Taking me as their utmost blessedness,
They are not "mine", but I—even I myself!
At end of many births to Me they come!
Yet hard the wise Mahatma is to find,
That man who sayeth, "All is Vasudev!"[4]
    There be those, too, whose knowledge, turned aside

[3]Beings of low and devilish nature.
[4]Krishna.

By this desire or that, gives them to serve
Some lower gods, with various rites, constrained
By that which mouldeth them. Unto all such—
Worship what shrine they will, what shapes, in faith—
'Tis I who give them faith! I am content!
The heart thus asking favour from its God,
Darkened but ardent, hath the end it craves,
The lesser blessing—but 'tis I who give!
Yet soon is withered what small fruit they reap.
Those men of little minds, who worship so,
Go where they worship, passing with their gods.
But Mine come unto me! Blind are the eyes
Which deem th' Unmanifested manifest,
Not comprehending Me in my true Self!
Imperishable, viewless, undeclared,
Hidden behind my magic veil of shows,
I am not seen by all; I am not known—
Unborn and changeless—to the idle world.
But I, Arjuna! know all things which were,
And all which are, and all which are to be,
Albeit not one among them knoweth Me!
   By passion for the "pairs of opposites",
By those twain snares of Like and Dislike,
   Prince,
All creatures live bewildered, save some few
Who, quit of sins, holy in act, informed,
Freed from the "opposites", and fixed in faith,
Cleave unto Me.
   Who cleave, who seek in Me
Refuge from birth[5] and death, those have the Truth!
Those know Me Brahma; know Me Soul of Souls,
The Adhyatman; know Karma, my work;
Know I am Adhibhuta, Lord of Life
And Adhidaiva, Lord of all the Gods,
And Adhiyajna, Lord of Sacrifice;
Worship Me well, with hearts of love and faith,
And find and hold me in the hour of death.

HERE ENDETH CHAPTER VII OF THE
BHAGAVAD GITA

---

[5] I read here janma, "birth;" not jara, "age."—E. Arnold

Chapter VIII

The Book of Religion by Devotion to the One Supreme God

Arjuna. Who is that Brahma? What that Soul of Souls,
The Adhyatman? What, Thou Best of All!
Thy work, the Karma? Tell me what it is
Thou namest Adhibhuta? What again
Means Adhidaiva? Yea, and how it comes
Thou canst be Adhiyajna in thy flesh?
Slayer of Madhu! Further, make me know
How good men find thee in the hour of death?
  Krishna. I Braham am! the One Eternal God,
And Adhyatman is My Being's name,
The Soul of Souls! What goeth forth from Me,
Causing all life to live, is Karma called:
And, Manifested in divided forms,
I am the Adhibhuta, Lord of Lives;
And Adhidaiva, Lord of all the Gods,
Because I am Purusha, who begets.
And Adhiyajna, Lord of Sacrifice,
I—speaking with thee in this body here—
Am, thou embodied one! (for all the shrines
Flame unto Me!) And, at the hour of death,
He that hath meditated Me alone,
In putting off his flesh, comes forth to Me,
Enters into My Being—doubt thou not!
But, if he meditated otherwise
At hour of death, in putting off the flesh,
He goes to what he looked for, Kunti's Son!
Because the Soul is fashioned to its like.

Have Me, then, in thy heart always! and fight!
Thou too, when heart and mind are fixed on Me,
Shalt surely come to Me! All come who cleave
With never-wavering will of firmest faith,
Owning none other Gods: all come to Me,
The Uttermost, Purusha, Holiest!

Whoso hath known Me, Lord of sage and singer,
  Ancient of days; of all the Three Worlds Stay,
Boundless,—but unto every atom Bringer
  Of that which quickens it: whoso, I say,

Hath known My form, which passeth mortal knowing;
  Seen my effulgence—which no eye hath seen—
Than the sun's burning gold more brightly glowing,
  Dispersing darkness,—unto him hath been
Right life! And, in the hour when life is ending,
  With mind set fast and trustful piety,
Drawing still breath beneath calm brows unbending,
  In happy peace that faithful one doth die,—
In glad peace passeth to Purusha's heaven.
  The place which they who read the Vedas name
Aksharam, "Ultimate;" whereto have striven
  Saints and ascetics—their road is the same.
  That way—the highest way—goes he who shuts
The gates of all his sense, locks desire
Safe in his heart, centres the vital airs
Upon his parting thought, steadfastly set;
And, murmuring Om, the sacred syllable—
Emblem of Brahm—dies, meditating Me.

  For who, none other Gods regarding, looks
Ever to Me, easily am I gained
By such a Yogi; and, attaining Me,
They fall not—those Mahatmas—back to birth,
To life, which is the place of pain, which ends,
But take the way of utmost blessedness.

  The worlds, Arjuna!—even Brahma's world—
Roll back again from Death to Life's unrest;
But they, O Kunti's Son! that reach to Me,
Taste birth no more. If ye know Brahma's Day
Which is a thousand Yugas; if ye know
The thousand Yugas making Brahma's Night,
Then know ye Day and Night as He doth know!
When that vast Dawn doth break, th' Invisible
Is brought anew into the Visible;
When that deep Night doth darken, all which is
Fades back again to Him Who sent it forth;
Yea! this vast company of living things—
Again and yet again produced—expires
At Brahma's Nightfall; and, at Brahma's Dawn,
Riseth, without its will, to life new-born.
But—higher, deeper, innermost—abides
Another Life, not like the life of sense,
Escaping sight, unchanging. This endures
When all created things have passed away:
This is that Life named the Unmanifest,
The Infinite! the All! the Uttermost.

Thither arriving none return. That Life
Is Mine, and I am there! and, Prince! by faith
Which wanders not, there is a way to come
Thither. I, the Purusha, I Who spread
The Universe around me—in Whom dwell
All living Things—may so be reached and seen![6]
Richer than holy fruit on Vedas growing,
　Greater than gifts, better than prayer or fast
Such wisdom is! The Yogi, this way knowing
　Comes to the Utmost Perfect Peace at last.

HERE ENDETH CHAPTER VIII OF THE
BHAGAVAD GITA

Chapter IX

The Book of Religion by the Kingly Knowledge and the Kingly Mystery

Krishna. Now will I open unto thee—whose heart
Rejects not—that last lore, deepest-concealed,
That farthest secret of My Heavens and Earths,
Which but to know shall set thee free from ills,—
A royal lore! A Kingly mystery!
Yea! for the soul such light as purgeth it
From every sin; a light of holiness
With inmost splendour shining; plain to see;
Easy to walk by, inexhaustible!

　They that receive not this, failing in faith
To grasp the greater wisdom, reach not Me,
Destroyer of thy foes! They sink anew
Into the realm of Flesh, where all things change!

　By Me the whole vast Universe of things
Is spread abroad;—by Me, the Unmanifest!
In Me are all existences contained;
Not I in them!
　Yet they are not contained,
Those visible things! Receive and strive to embrace
The mystery majestical! My Being—
Creating all, sustaining all—still dwells
Outside of all!

[6] I have discarded ten lines of Sanskrit text here as an undoubted interpolation by some Vedantist—E. Arnold.

See! as the shoreless airs
Move in the measureless space, but are not space,
(And space were space without the moving airs);
So all things are in Me, but are not I.

At closing of each Kalpa, Indian Prince!
All things which be back to My Being come:
At the beginning of each Kalpa, all
Issue new-born from Me.

By Energy
And help of Prakriti, my outer Self,
Again, and yet again, I make go forth
The realms of visible things—without their will—
All of them—by the power of Prakriti.
    Yet these great makings, Prince! involve
        Me not
Enchain Me not! I sit apart from them,
Other, and Higher, and Free; nowise attached!

Thus doth the stuff of worlds, moulded by Me,
Bring forth all that which is, moving or still,
Living or lifeless! Thus the worlds go on!
    The minds untaught mistake Me, veiled in form;—
Naught see they of My secret Presence, nought
Of My hid Nature, ruling all which lives.
Vain hopes pursuing, vain deeds doing; fed
On vainest knowledge, senselessly they seek
An evil way, the way of brutes and fiends.
But My Mahatmas, those of noble soul
Who tread the path celestial, worship Me
With hearts unwandering,—knowing Me the Source,
Th' Eternal Source, of Life. Unendingly
They glorify Me; seek Me; keep their vows
Of reverence and love, with changeless faith
Adoring Me. Yea, and those too adore,
Who, offering sacrifice of wakened hearts,
Have sense of one pervading Spirit's stress,
One Force in every place, though manifold!
I am the Sacrifice! I am the Prayer!
I am the Funeral-Cake set for the dead!
I am the healing herb! I am the ghee,
The Mantra, and the flame, and that which burns!
I am—of all this boundless Universe—
The Father, Mother, Ancestor, and Guard!
The end of Learning! That which purifies
In lustral water! I am OM! I am

Rig-Veda, Sama-Veda, Yajur-Ved;
The Way, the Fosterer, the Lord, the Judge,
The Witness; the Abode, the Refuge-House,
The Friend, the Fountain and the Sea of Life
Which sends, and swallows up; Treasure of Worlds
And Treasure-Chamber! Seed and Seed-Sower,
Whence endless harvests spring! Sun's heat is mine;
Heaven's rain is mine to grant or to withhold;
Death am I, and Immortal Life I am,
Arjuna! Sat and Asat, Visible Life,
And Life Invisible!

   Yea! those who learn
    The threefold Veds, who drink the Soma-wine,
Purge sins, pay sacrifice—from Me they earn
    Passage to Swarga; where the meats divine

Of great gods feed them in high Indra's heaven,
    Yet they, when that prodigious joy is o'er,
Paradise spent, and wage for merits given,
    Come to the world of death and change once more.

They had their recompense! they stored their treasure,
    Following the threefold Scripture and its writ;
Who seeketh such gaineth the fleeting pleasure
    Of joy which comes and goes! I grant
      them it!

   But to those blessed ones who worship Me,
Turning not otherwhere, with minds set fast,
I bring assurance of full bliss beyond.
Nay, and of hearts which follow other gods
In simple faith, their prayers arise to me,
O Kunti's Son! though they pray wrongfully;
For I am the Receiver and the Lord
Of every sacrifice, which these know not
Rightfully; so they fall to earth again!
Who follow gods go to their gods; who vow
Their souls to Pitris go to Pitris; minds
To evil Bhuts given o'er sink to the Bhuts;
And whoso loveth Me cometh to Me.
Whoso shall offer Me in faith and love
A leaf, a flower, a fruit, water poured forth,
That offering I accept, lovingly made
With pious will. Whate'er thou doest, Prince!
Eating or sacrificing, giving gifts,
Praying or fasting, let it all be done
For Me, as Mine. So shalt thou free thyself

From Karmabandh, the chain which holdeth men
To good and evil issue, so shalt come
Safe unto Me—when thou art quit of flesh—
By faith and abdication joined to Me!
   I am alike for all! I know not hate,
I know not favour! What is made is Mine!
But then that worship Me with love, I love;
They are in Me, and I in them!

   Nay, Prince!
If one of evil life turn in his thought
Straightly to Me, count him amidst the good;
He hath the high way chosen; he shall grow
Righteous ere long; he shall attain that peace
Which changes not. Thou Prince of India!
Be certain none can perish, trusting Me!
O Pritha's Son! whoso will turn to Me,
Though they be born from the very womb of Sin,
Woman or man; sprung of the Vaisya caste
Or lowly disregarded Sudra,—all
Plant foot upon the highest path; how then
The holy Brahmans and My Royal Saints?
Ah! ye who into this ill world are come—
Fleeting and false—set your faith fast on Me!
Fix heart and thought on Me! Adore Me!
   Bring
Offerings to Me! Make Me prostrations! Make
Me your supremest joy! and, undivided,
Unto My rest your spirits shall be guided.

HERE ENDETH CHAPTER IX OF THE
BHAGAVAD GITA

Chapter XI

The Book of the Manifesting of the One and Manifold

   Arjuna. This, for my soul's peace, have I heard from Thee,
The unfolding of the Mystery Supreme
Named Adhyatman; comprehending which,
My darkness is dispelled; for now I know—
O Lotus-eyed!—whence is the birth of men,
And whence their death, and what the majesties
Of Thine immortal rule. Fain would I see,

As thou Thyself declar'st it, Sovereign Lord!
The likeness of that glory of Thy Form
Wholly revealed. O Thou Divinest One!
If this can be, if I may bear the sight,
Make Thyself visible, Lord of all prayers;
Show me Thy very self, the Eternal God!

   Krishna. Gaze, then, thou Son of Pritha! I manifest for thee
Those hundred thousand thousand shapes that clothe my Mystery:
I show thee all my semblances, infinite, rich, divine,
My changeful hues, my countless forms. See! in this face of mine,
Adityas, Vasus, Rudras, Aswins, and Maruts! see
Wonders unnumbered, Indian Prince! revealed to none save thee.
Behold! this is the Universe!—Look! what is live and dead
I gather all in one—in Me! Gaze, as thy lips have said,
On God Eternal, Very God! See Me! see what thou prayest!

                       . . .

Thou canst not!—nor, with human eyes, Arjuna! ever mayest
Therefore I give thee sense divine. Have other eyes, new light!
And, look! This is My glory, unveiled to mortal sight!
   Sanjaya. Then, O King! The God, so saying,
      Stood, to Pritha's Son displaying
      All the splendour, wonder, dread
      Of His vast Almighty-head.
      Out of countless eyes beholding,
      Out of countless mouths commanding,
      Countless mystic forms enfolding
      In one Form: supremely standing
      Countless radiant glories wearing,
      Countless heavenly weapons bearing,
      Crowned with garlands of star-clusters,
      Robed in garb of woven lustres,
      Breathing from His perfect Presence
      Breaths of every subtle essence
      Of all heavenly odours; shedding
      Blinding brilliance; overspreading—
      Boundless, beautiful—all spaces
      With His all-regarding faces;
      So He showed! If there should rise
      Suddenly within the skies
      Sunburst of a thousand suns
      Flooding earth with beams undeemed-of,
      Then might be that Holy One's
      Majesty and radiance dreamed of!

So did Pandu's Son behold
All this universe enfold
All its huge diversity
Into one vast shape, and be
Visible, and viewed, and blended
In one Body—subtle, splendid,
Nameless—th' All-comprehending
God of Gods, the Never-Ending
Deity!

           But, sore amazed,
Thrilled, o'erfilled, dazzled, and dazed,
Arjuna knelt; and bowed his head,
And clasped his palms; and cried, and said:
  Arjuna. Yea! I have seen! I see!
  Lord! all is wrapped in Thee!
The gods are in Thy glorious frame the creatures
    Of earth, and heaven, and hell
    In Thy Divine form dwell,
And in Thy countenance shine all the features

    Of Brahma, sitting lone
    Upon His lotus-throne;
Of saints and sages, and the serpent races
    Ananta, Vasuki;
    Yea! mightiest Lord! I see
Thy thousand thousand arms, and breasts, and faces,

    And eyes,—on every side
    Perfect, diversified;
And nowhere end of Thee, nowhere beginning
    Nowhere a centre! Shifts—
    Wherever soul's gaze lifts—
Thy central Self, all-wielding, and all-winning!

              • • •
    Darkness to dazzling day,
    Look I whichever way;
Ah, Lord! I worship Thee, the Undivided,
    The Uttermost of thought,
    The Treasure-Palace wrought
To hold the wealth of the worlds; the Shield provided

    To shelter Virtue's laws;
    The Fount whence Life's stream draws
All waters of all rivers of all being:
    The One Unborn, Unending:
    Unchanging and Unblending!
With might and majesty, past thought, past seeing!

. . .

Of Thy perfections! Space
Star-sprinkled, and void place
From pole to pole to the Blue, from bound to bound,
    Hath Thee in every spot,
    Thee, Thee!—Where Thou art not,
O Holy, Marvellous Form! is nowhere found!

O Mystic, Awful One!
At sight of Thee, made known,
The Three Worlds quake; the lower gods draw nigh Thee;
    They fold their palms, and bow
    Body, and breast, and brow,
And, whispering worship, laud and magnify Thee!
    Rishis and Siddhas cry
    "Hail! Highest Majesty!"
From sage and singer breaks the hymn of glory
    In dulcet harmony,
    Sounding the praise of Thee;
While countless companies take up the story,

    Rudras, who ride the storms,
    Th' Adityas! shining forms,
Vasus and Sadhyas, Viswas, Ushmapas;
    Maruts, and those great Twins
    The heavenly, fair, Aswins,
Gandharvas, Rakshasas, Siddhas, and Asuras,[7]

O Eyes of God! O Head!
My strength of soul is fled,
Gone is heart's force, rebuked is mind's desire!
    When I behold Thee so,
    With awful brows a-glow,
With burning glance, and lips lighted by fire
    Fierce as those flames which shall
    Consume, at close of all,
Earth, Heaven! Ah me! I see no Earth and Heaven!
    Thee, Lord of Lords! I see,
    Thee only—only Thee!
Now let Thy mercy unto me be given,

    Thou, that hast fashioned men,
    Devourest them again,
One with another, great and small, alike!
    The creatures whom Thou mak'st,
    With flaming jaws Thou tak'st,

[7]These are all divine or deified orders of the Hindu Pantheon.

Lapping them up! Lord God! Thy terrors strike
  From end to end of earth,
  Filling life full, from birth
To death, with deadly, burning, lurid dread!
  Ah, Vishnu! make me know
  Why is Thy visage so?
Who art Thou, feasting thus upon Thy dead?
  Who? awful Deity!
  I bow myself to Thee,
Namostu Te, Devarara! Prasid![8]
  O Mightiest Lord! rehearse
  Why hast Thou face so fierce?
Whence doth this aspect horrible proceed?
  Krishna. Thou seest Me as Time who kills, Time who brings
    all to doom,
The Slayer Time, Ancient of Days, come hither to consume;
Excepting thee, of all these hosts of hostile chiefs arrayed,
There stands not one shall leave alive the battle-field! Dismayed
No longer be! Arise! obtain renown! destroy thy foes!
Fight for the kingdom waiting thee when thou hast vanquished
  those.
By Me they fall—not thee! the stroke of death is dealt them
  now,
Even as they show thus gallantly; My instrument art thou!
Strike, strong-armed Prince, at Drona! at Bhishma strike! deal
  death
On Karna, Jayadratha; stay all their warlike breath!
'Tis I who bid them perish! Thou wilt but slay the slain;
Fight! they must fall, and thou must live, victor upon this
  plain!
  Sanjaya. Hearing mighty Keshav's word,
    Tremblingly that helmed Lord
    Clasped his lifted palms, and—praying
    Grace of Krishna—stood there, saying,
    With bowed brow and accents broken,
    These words timorously spoken:
  Arjuna. Worthily, Lord of Might!
    The whole world hath delight
In Thy surpassing power, obeying Thee;
    The Rakshasas, in dread
    At sight of Thee, are sped
To all four quarters; and the company

    Of Siddhas sound Thy name.
    How should they not proclaim

[8]"Hail to Thee, God of Gods, Be favourable!"

Thy Majesties, Divinest, Mightiest?
    Thou Brahm, than Brahma greater!
    Thou Infinite Creator!
Thou God of gods, Life's Dwelling-place and Rest.

    Thou, of all souls the Soul!
    The Comprehending Whole!
Of being formed, and formless being the Framer;
    O Utmost One! O Lord!
    Older than eld, Who stored
The worlds with wealth of life! O Treasure-Claimer,

    Who wottest all, and art
    Wisdom Thyself! O Part
In all, and All; for all from Thee have risen
    Numberless now I see
    The aspects are of Thee!

    For Thou art all! Yea, Thou!
    Ah! if in anger now
Thou shouldst remember I did think Thee Friend,
    Speaking with easy speech,
    As men use each to each;
Did call Thee "Krishna," "Prince," nor comprehend

    Thy hidden majesty,
    The might, the awe of Thee;
Did, in my heedlessness, or in my love,
    On journey, or in jest,
    Or when we lay at rest,
Sitting at council, straying in the grove,

    Alone, or in the throng,
    Do Thee, most Holy! wrong,
Be Thy grace granted for that witless sin
    For Thou art, now I know,
    Father of all below,
Of all above, of all the worlds within

    Guru of Gurus; more
    To reverence and adore
Than all which is adorable and high!
    How, in the wide worlds three
    Should any equal be?
Should any other share Thy Majesty?

    Therefore, with body bent
    And reverent intent,

I praise, and serve, and seek Thee, asking grace.
        As father to a son,
        As friend to friend, as one
Who loveth to his lover, turn Thy face

        In gentleness on me!
        Good is it I did see
This unknown marvel of Thy Form! But fear
        Mingles with joy! Retake,
        Dear Lord! for pity's sake
Thine earthly shape, which earthly eyes may bear

        Be merciful, and show
        The visage that I know;
Let me regard Thee, as of yore, arrayed
        With disc and forehead-gem,
        With mace and anadem,
Thou that sustainest all things! Undismayed

        Let me once more behold
        The form I loved of old,
Thou of the thousand arms and countless eyes!
        This frightened heart is fain

        To see restored again
My Charioteer, in Krishna's kind disguise.
    Krishna. Yea! thou hast seen, Arjuna! because I loved thee
        well,
The secret countenance of Me, revealed by mystic spell,
Shining, and wonderful, and vast, majestic, manifold,
Which none save thou in all the years had favour to behold;
For not by Vedas cometh this, nor sacrifice, nor alms,
Nor works well-done, nor penance long, nor prayers, nor chaun-
    ted psalms,
That mortal eyes should bear to view the Immortal Soul unclad,
Prince of the Kurus! This was kept for thee alone! Be glad!
Let no more trouble shake thy heart, because thine eyes have
    seen
My terror with My glory. As I before have been
So will I be again for thee; with lightened heart behold!
Once more I am thy Krishna, the form thou knew'st of old!
    Sanjaya. These words to Arjuna spake
        Vasudev, and straight did take
        Back again the semblance dear
        Of the well-loved charioteer;
        Peace and joy it did restore
        When the Prince beheld once more

Mighty Brahma's form and face
Clothed in Krishna's gentle grace.

Arjuna. Now that I see come back,
　　Janardana!
This friendly human frame, my mind can think
Calm thoughts once more; my heart beats still again!
　　Krishna. Yea! it was wonderful and terrible
To view me as thou didst, dear Prince! The gods
Dread and desire continually to view!
Yet not by Vedas, nor from sacrifice,
Nor penance, nor gift-giving, nor with prayer
Shall any so behold, as thou hast seen!
Only by fullest service, perfect faith,
And uttermost surrender am I known
And seen, and entered into, Indian Prince!
Who doeth all for Me; who findeth Me
In all; adoreth always; loveth all
Which I have made, and Me, for Love's sole end,
That man, Arjuna! unto Me doth wend.

HERE ENDETH CHAPTER XI OF THE
BHAGAVAD GITA

Chapter XII

The Book of the Religion of Faith

Arjuna. Lord! of the men who serve Thee—
　　true in heart—
As God revealed; and of the men who serve,
Worshipping Thee Unrevealed, Unbodied, Far,
Which take the better way of faith and life?
　　Krishna. Whoever serve Me—as I show
　　　　Myself—
Constantly true, in full devotion fixed,
Those hold I very holy. But who serve—
Worshipping Me The One, The Invisible,
The Unrevealed, Unnamed, Unthinkable,
Uttermost, All-pervading, Highest, Sure—
Who thus adore Me, mastering their sense,
Of one set mind to all, glad in all good,
These blessed souls come unto Me.
　　Yet, hard
The travail is for such as bend their minds
To reach th' Unmanifest. That viewless path

Shall scarce be trod by man bearing the flesh!
But whereso any doeth all his deeds
Renouncing self for Me, full of Me, fixed
To serve only the Highest, night and day
Musing on Me—him will I swiftly lift
Forth from life's ocean of distress and death,
Whose soul clings fast to Me. Cling thou to Me!
Clasp Me with heart and mind! so shalt thou dwell
Surely with Me on high. But if thy thought
Droops from such height; if thou be'st weak to set
Body and soul upon Me constantly,
Despair not! give Me lower service! seek
To reach Me, worshipping with steadfast will;
And, if thou canst not worship steadfastly,
Work for Me, toil in works pleasing to Me!
For he that laboureth right for love of Me
Shall finally attain! But, if in this
Thy faint heart fails, bring Me thy failure! find
Refuge in Me! let fruits of labour go
Renouncing hope for Me, with lowliest heart,
So shalt thou come; for, though to know is more
Than diligence, yet worship better is
Than knowing, and renouncing better still.
Near to renunciation—very near—
Dwelleth Eternal Peace!
    Who hateth nought
Of all which lives, living himself benign,
Compassionate, from arrogance exempt,
Exempt from love of self, unchangeable
By good or ill; patient, contented, firm
In faith, mastering himself, true to his word,
Seeking Me, heart and soul; vowed unto Me,—
That man I love! Who troubleth not his kind,
And is not troubled by them; clear of wrath,
Living too high for gladness, grief, or fear,
That man I love! Who, dwelling quiet-eyed,[9]

Stainless, serene, well-balanced, unperplexed,
Working with Me, yet from all works detached,
That man I love! Who, fixed in faith on Me,
Dotes upon none, scorns none; rejoices not,
And grieves not, letting good or evil hap
Light when it will, and when it will depart,
That man I love! Who, unto friend and foe
Keeping an equal heart, with equal mind

[9]"Not peering about," *anapeksha.*—E. Arnold.

Bears shame and glory; with an equal peace
Takes heat and cold, pleasure and pain; abides
Quit of desires, hears praise or calumny
In passionless restraint, unmoved by each;
Linked by no ties to earth, steadfast in Me,
That man I love! But most of all I love
Those happy ones to whom 'tis life to live
In single fervid faith and love unseeing,
Drinking the blessed Amrit of my Being!

HERE ENDETH CHAPTER XII OF THE
BHAGAVAD GITA

3. Selections from the Principal Upanishads

Isa Upanishad[1]

1. All this, whatsoever moves on earth, is to be hidden in the Lord, the Self. When thou hast surrendered all this, then thou mayest enjoy. Do not covet the wealth of any man!

2. Though a man may wish to live a hundred years, performing works, it will be thus with him; but not in any other way: work will thus not cling to a man.

3. There are the worlds without sun covered with blind darkness. Those who have destroyed their self, who perform works without having arrived at a knowledge of the true Self, go after death to those worlds.

[1] The *Isa Upanishad* is considered by Max Muller to be deceptively simple, while in reality one of the most difficult to understand. In an age of sacrificial religion, the Isa teaches the uselessness of all good works; while at the same time advocating good works performed without any selfish motives, without any desire of reward. Such detachment is a preparation for higher knowledge and a means of subduing passions. This detachment produces serenity of mind, without which a man is incapable of receiving higher understanding, and eventually imparts to the wise complete freedom (moksha) from further births. It can be seen that this short Upanishad contains within it the germ of many of the most complex Indian teachings.

4. The Self is one, though never stirring, and is swifter than thought. The Devas (senses) never reached it, it walked before them. Though standing still, it overtakes the others who are running. Matarisvan, the wind, the moving spirit, bestows powers on it.

5. It stirs and it stirs not; it is far, and likewise near. It is inside of all this, and it is outside of all this.

6. And he who beholds all beings in the Self, and the Self in all beings, he never turns away from it.

7. When to a man who understands, the Self has become all things, what sorrow, what trouble can there be to him who once beheld that unity?

8. He, the Self, encircled all, bright incorporeal, scatheless, without muscles, pure, untouched by evil; a seer, wise, omnipresent, self-existent, he disposed all things rightly for eternal years.

9. All who worship what is not real knowledge (good works), enter into blind darkness: those who delight in real knowledge, enter, as it were, into greater darkness.

10. One thing, they say, is obtained from real knowledge; another, they say, from what is not knowledge. Thus we have heard from the wise who taught us this.

11. He who knows at the same time both knowledge and not-knowledge, overcomes death through not-knowledge, and obtains immortality through knowledge.

12. All who worship what is not the true cause, enter into blind darkness: those who delight in the true cause, enter, as it were, into greater darkness.

13. One thing, they say, is obtained from knowledge of the cause; another, they say, from knowledge of what is not the cause. Thus we have heard from the wise who taught us this.

14. He who knows at the same time both the cause and the destruction of the perishable body, overcomes death by destruction of the perishable body, and obtains immortality through knowledge of the true cause.

15. The door of the True is covered with a golden disk.[2] Open that, O Pushan, that we may see the nature of the True.

16. O Pushan, only seer, Yama (judge), Surya (sun), son of Pragapati, spread thy rays and gather them! The light which is thy fairest form, I see it. I am what He is, the person in the sun.

17. Breath to air, and to the immortal![3] Then this my body

[2] The face of the true (Purusha in the sun) is covered by a golden disk.
[3] These lines are to be uttered by a man in the hour of death.

ends in ashes. Om!⁴ Mind, remember! Remember thy deeds! Mind, remember! Remember thy deeds!

18. Agni, lead us on to wealth (beatitude) by a good path, thou, O God, who knowest all things! Keep far from us crooked evil, and we shall offer thee the fullest praise!

Kena Upanishad

First Khanda

1. The Pupil asks: "At whose wish does the mind sent forth proceed on its errand? At whose command does the first breath go forth? At whose wish do we utter this speech! What god directs the eye, or the ear?"

2. The Teacher replies: "It is the ear of the ear, the mind of the mind, the speech of speech, the breath of breath, and the eye of the eye. When freed from the senses the wise, on departing from this world, become immortal.[1]

3. "The eye does not go thither, nor speech, nor mind. We do not know, we do not understand, how any one can teach it.

4. "It is different from the known, it is also above the unknown, thus we have heard from those of old, who taught us this.

5. "That which is not expressed by speech and by which speech is expressed, that alone know as Brahman, not that which people here adore.

6. "That which does not think by mind, and by which, they say, mind is thought, that alone know as Brahman, not that which people here adore.

7. "That which does not see by the eye, and by which one

---

[4]OM is a word of sacred and solemn invocation in Hinduism. A compound of the three main letters a,u,m, it is a mystical syllable symbolizing the essence of the universe and all knowledge. And while it is the symbol of the manifested and unmanifested Brahman, it also became the monosyllabic symbol of the Trimurti—the Hindu triad of Brahma, Vishnu, and Siva, who represent the union of the three powers of creation, preservation, and destruction. All Hindus worship the Trimurti except the Jains.

[1]This verse is obscure unless one is familiar with Upanishadic thinking. The ear of the ear, and the eye of the eye, etc., should be understood as referring to him who directs the ear, the eye, i.e., the Self or Brahman, who is the source of all perception and insight.

sees the work of the eyes, that alone know as Brahman, not that which people here adore.

8. "That which does not hear by the ear, and by which the ear is heard, that alone know as Brahman, not that which people here adore.

9. "That which does not breathe by breath, and by which breath is drawn, that alone know as Brahman, not that which people here adore."

Second Khanda

1. The Teacher says: "If thou thinkest I know it well, then thou knowest surely but little, what is that form of Brahman known, it may be, to thee?"

2. The Pupil says: "I do not think I know it well, nor do I know that I do not know it. He among us who knows this, he knows it, nor does he know that he does not know it.[2]

3. "He by whom it (Brahman) is not thought, by him it is thought; he by whom it is thought, knows it not. It is not understood by those who understand it, it is understood by those who do not understand it.

4. "It is thought to be known as if by awakening, and then we obtain immortality indeed. By the Self we obtain strength, by knowledge we obtain immortality.

5. "If a man know this here, that is the true end of life; if he does not know this here, then there is great destruction and new births. The wise who have thought on all things and recognised the Self in them become immortal, when they have departed from this world."

Fourth Khanda

1. She replied: "It is Brahman. It is through the victory of Brahman that you have thus become great." After that he knew that it was Brahman.

2. Therefore these Devas—Agni, Vayu, and Indra—are, as it were, above the other gods, for they touched it (the Brahman) nearest.

[2]This again is one of those obscure phrases. Muller interprets its meaning as: We cannot know Brahman as we know other objects, by referring them to a class or isolating differences. But, on the other hand, we cannot be sure that we know him not; that is, no one can assert that we know him not, for we need Brahman in order to know anything. Those, therefore, who know this double peculiarity of the knowledge of Brahman, they surely know Brahman as much as it can be known.

3. And therefore Indra is, as it were, above the other gods, for he touched it nearest, he first knew it.

4. This is the teaching of Brahman, with regard to the mythological gods: It is that which now flashes forth in the lightning, and now vanishes again.[3]

5. And this is the teaching of Brahman, with regard to the psychological body: It is that which seems to move as mind, and by it imagination remembers again and again.[4]

6. That Brahman is called Tadvana,[5] by the name of Tadvana it is to be meditated on. All beings have a desire for him who knows this.

7. The Teacher: "As you have asked me to tell you the Upanishad, the Upanishad has now been told you. We have told you the Brahmi Upanishad.

8. "The feet on which that Upanishad stands are penance, restraint, sacrifice; the Vedas are all its limbs, the True is its abode.

9. "He who knows this Upanishad, and has shaken off all evil, stands in the endless, unconquerable world of heaven, yea, in the world of heaven."

Katha Upanishad

First Adhyaya

SECOND VALLI

1. Death said: "The good is one thing, the pleasant another; these two, having different objects, chain a man. It is well with him who clings to the good; he who chooses the pleasant, misses his end.

---

[3] In this comparison, and illustrating the relationship between other gods and Brahman, is seen that Brahman shines forth suddenly like lightning. Brahman is seen for only a moment in the lightning and then vanishes from sight, yet having touched the phenomenal world it is easier to conceive of the reality of things as distinct from their mere perceptibility.

[4] This illustration of Brahman's movement is psychological. Brahman is proved to exist because our minds move toward things, because there is something in us that moves and perceives, there is something in us that holds our perceptions together (sankalpa) and forms them again by memory and a conceptual gestalt.

[5] Tadvana is one of Brahman's names because of its meaning "desiring of" something; that is, desiring of Brahman.

2. "The good and pleasant approach man: the wise goes round about them and distinguishes them. Yea, the wise prefers the good to the pleasant, but the fool chooses the pleasant through greed and avarice.

3. "Thou, O Nachiketas,[1] after pondering all pleasures that are or seem delightful, hast dismissed them all. Thou hast not gone into the road that leadeth to wealth, in which many men perish.

4. "Wide apart and leading to different points are these two, ignorance, and what is known as wisdom. I believe Nachiketas to be one who desires knowledge, for even many pleasures did not tear thee away.

5. "Fools dwelling in darkness, wise in their own conceit, and puffed up with vain knowledge, go round and round, staggering to and fro, like blind men led by the blind.

6. "The hereafter never rises before the eyes of the careless child, deluded by the delusion of wealth, "This is the world," he thinks, "there is no other"—thus he falls again and again under my sway.

7. "He (the Self) of whom many are not even able to hear, whom many, even when they hear of him, do not comprehend; wonderful is a man, when found, who is able to teach him (the Self); wonderful is he who comprehends him, when taught by an able teacher.

8. "That Self, when taught by an inferior man, is not easy to be known, even though often thought upon; unless it be taught by another, there is no way to it, for it is inconceivably smaller than what is small.[2]

9. "That doctrine is not to be obtained by argument, but when it is declared by another, then, O dearest, it is easy to understand. Thou hast obtained it now; thou art truly a man of true resolve. May we have always an inquirer like thee!"

10. Nachiketas said: "I know that what is called a treasure is transient, for that eternal is not obtained by things which are not eternal. Hence the Nachiketa fire sacrifice has been laid by me first; then, by means of transient things, I have obtained what is not transient (the teaching of Yama)."

11. Yama said: "Though thou hadst seen the fulfillment of all desires, the foundation of the world, the endless rewards of good deeds, the shore where there is no fear, that which is mag-

---

[1]Nachiketas symbolizes the seeker after knowledge or spiritual understanding. The name is formed from "Na" and "chiketa," one who has no knowledge.

[2]An alternative translation may help the reader understand this paragraph better: If it is taught by one who is identified with the Self, then there is no uncertainty. If it has been taught as identical with ourselves, then there is no perception of anything else. If it has been taught by one who is identified with it, then there is no failure in understanding it (agati).

nified by praise, the wide abode, the rest, yet being wise thou hast with firm resolve dismissed it all.

12. "The wise who, by means of meditation on his Self, recognises the Ancient, who is difficult to be seen, who has entered into the dark, who is hidden in the cave, who dwells in the abyss, as God, he indeed leaves joy and sorrow far behind.[3]

13. "A mortal who has heard this and embraced it, who has separated from it all qualities, and has thus reached the subtle Being, rejoices, because he has obtained what is a cause for rejoicing. The house of Brahman is open, I believe, O Nachiketas."

14. Nachiketas said: "That which thou seest as neither this nor that, as neither effect nor cause, as neither past nor future, tell me that."

15. Yama said: "That word or place which all the Vedas record, which all penances proclaim, which men desire when they live as religious students, that word I tell thee briefly, it is Om."

16. "That imperishable syllable means Brahman, that syllable means the highest Brahman; he who knows that syllable, whatever he desires, is his.

17. "This is the best support, this is the highest support; he who knows that support is magnified in the world of Brahma.

18. "The knowing Self is not born, it dies not; it sprang from nothing, nothing sprang from it. The Ancient is unborn, eternal, everlasting; he is not killed, though the body is killed.

19. "If the killer thinks that he kills, if the killed thinks that he is killed, they do not understand; for this one does not kill, nor is that one killed.

20. "The Self, smaller than small, greater than great, is hidden in the heart of that creature. A man who is free from desires and free from grief, sees the majesty of the Self by the grace of the Creator.[4]

21. "Though sitting still, he walks far; though lying down, he goes everywhere. Who, save myself is able to know that God who rejoices and rejoices not?

22. "The wise who knows the Self as bodiless within the bodies, as unchanging among changing things, as great and omnipresent, does never grieve.

23. "That Self cannot be gained by the Veda, nor by understanding, nor by much learning. He whom the Self chooses, by

[3]Yama is here speaking only of the lower Brahmán, not yet the highest. As Max Muller translates this thought, Deva (God) can only be that as what the Old, i.e. the Self in the heart, is to be recognized. It would therefore mean, he who finds God or the Self in his heart.

[4]This can be translated as "through the tranquillity of the senses."

him the Self can be gained. The Self chooses him (his body) as his own.

24. "But he who has not first turned away from his wickedness, who is not tranquil, and subdued, or whose mind is not at rest, he can never obtain the Self even by knowledge.

25. "Who then knows where He is. He to whom the Brahmans and Kshatriyas are as it were but food, and death itself a condiment?"[5]

THIRD VALLI

1. "There are the two,[6] drinking their reward in the world of their own works, entered into the cave of the heart, dwelling on the highest summit (the ether in the heart). Those who know Brahman call them shade and light; likewise, those householders who perform the Trinachiketa sacrifice.

2. "May we be able to master that Nachiketa rite which is a bridge for sacrificers; also that which is the highest, imperishable Brahman for those who wish to cross over to the fearless shore.

3. "Know the Self to be sitting in the chariot, the body to be the chariot, the intellect (buddhi) the charioteer, and the mind the reins.[7]

4. "The senses they call the horses, the objects of the senses their roads. When he (the Highest Self) is in union with the body, the senses, and the mind, then wise people call him the Enjoyer.

5. "He who has no understanding and whose mind (the reins) is never firmly held, his senses (horses) are unmanageable, like vicious horses of a charioteer.

6. "But he who has understanding and whose mind is always firmly held, his senses are under control, like good horses of a charioteer.

7. "He who has no understanding, who is unmindful and always impure, never reaches that place, but enters into the round of births.

8. "But he who has understanding, who is mindful and always pure, reaches indeed that place, from whence he is not born again.

9. "But he who has understanding for his charioteer, and who

[5] In whom all disappears, and in whom even death is swallowed up.

[6] The two are explained as the higher and lower Brahman, the former being the light, the latter the shadow.

[7] The image of a chariot has counterparts in other cultures, notably Plato in the *Phaedrus* and the *Phaedo*. The ruling power of the self in Plato is named *nous* by Plato; in the Upanishads it is called *buddhi*. The chariot has another important function in this passage, especially for yoga, which comes from "to yoke together," to harness the senses.

holds the reins of the mind, he reaches the end of his journey, and that is the highest place of Vishnu.

10. "Beyond the senses there are the objects, beyond the objects there is the mind, beyond the mind there is the intellect, the Great Self is beyond the intellect.

11. "Beyond the Great there is the Undeveloped, beyond the Undeveloped there is the Person (purusha). Beyond the Person there is nothing—this is the goal, the highest road.

12. "That Self is hidden in all beings and does not shine forth, but it is seen by subtle seers through their sharp and subtle intellect.

13. "A wise man should keep down speech and mind;[8] he should keep them within the Self which is knowledge; he should keep knowledge within the Self which is the Great; and he should keep that (the Great) within the Self which is the Quiet.

14. "Rise, awake! having obtained your boons, understand them! The sharp edge of a razor is difficult to pass over; thus the wise say the path (to the Self) is hard.

15. "He who has perceived that which is without sound, without touch, without form, without decay, without taste, eternal, without smell, without beginning, without end, beyond the Great, and unchangeable, is freed from the jaws of death.

16. "A wise man who has repeated or heard the ancient story of Nachiketas told by Death, is magnified in the world of Brahman.

17. "And he who repeats this greatest mystery in an assembly of Brahmans, or full of devotion at the time of the Sraddha sacrifice, obtains thereby infinite rewards."

Second Adhyaya

FOURTH VALLI

1. Death said: "The Self-existent pierced the openings of the senses so that they turn forward: therefore man looks forward, not backward into himself. Some wise man, however, with his eyes closed and wishing for immortality, saw the Self behind.

2. "Children follow after outward pleasures, and fall into the snare of wide-spread death. Wise men only, knowing the nature of what is immortal, do not look for anything stable here among things unstable.

3. "That by which we know form, taste, smell, sound, and loving touches, by that also we know what exists besides. This is that which thou hast asked for.

[8]That is, he should keep down speech in the mind; keep the mind quiet.

4. "The wise, when he knows that that by which he perceives all objects in sleep or in waking is the great omnipresent Self, grieves no more.

5. "He who knows this living soul which eats honey (perceives objects) as being the Self, always near, the Lord of the past and the future, henceforward fears no more. This is that.

6. "He who knows him who was born first from the brooding heat (for he was born before the water), who, entering into the heart, abides therein, and was perceived from the elements. This is that.

7. "He who knows Aditi also, who is one with all deities, who arises with Prana (breath or Hiranyagarbha), who, entering into the heart, abides therein, and was born from the elements. This is that.[9]

8. "There is Agni (fire), the all-seeing, hidden in the two fire-sticks, well-guarded like a child in the womb by the mother, day after day to be adored by men when they awake and bring oblations. This is that.

9. "And that whence the sun rises, and whither it goes to set, there all the Devas are contained, and no one goes beyond. This is that.

10. "What is here visible in the world, the same is there invisible in Brahman; and what is there, the same is here. He who sees any difference here between Brahman and the world, goes from death to death.

11. "Even by the mind this Brahman is to be obtained, and then there is no difference whatsoever. He goes from death to death who sees any difference here.

12. "The person (purusha), of the size of a thumb, stands in the middle of the Self (body?), as lord of the past and the future, and henceforward fears no more. This is that.

13. "That person, of the size of a thumb, is like a light without smoke, lord of the past and the future, he is the same today and to-morrow. This is that.

14. "As rain-water that has fallen on a mountainridge runs down the rocks on all sides, thus does he, who sees a difference between qualities, run after them on all sides.

15. "As pure water poured into pure water remains the same, thus, O Gautama, is the Self of a thinker who knows."

[9]Paragraphs 6 and 7 should be read with the knowledge that the first manifestation of Brahman, commonly called Hiranyagarbha, springs from the tapas of Brahman. Tapas are mentioned in the Upanishads as a means of asceticism, a development of "soul force" to achieve spiritual realization. This freeing of the mind from the body, and thereby energizing thought itself is, in the case of Brahman, the prelude to creation of life itself. Afterward the water and the rest of the elements become manifested. See S. Radhakrishnan, *Indian Philosophy*, pp. 215-16.

SIXTH VALLI

1. "There is that ancient tree, whose roots grow upward and whose branches grow downward;—that indeed is called the Bright, that is called Brahman, that alone is called the Immortal. All worlds are contained in it, and no one goes beyond. This is that.[10]

2. "Whatever there is, the whole world, when gone forth from the Brahman, trembles in its breath. That Brahman is a great terror, like a drawn sword. Those who know it become immortal.

3. "From terror of Brahman fire burns, from terror the sun burns, from terror Indra and Vayu, and Death, as the fifth, run away.

4. "If a man could not understand it before the falling asunder of his body, then he has to take body again in the worlds of creation.[11]

5. "As in a mirror, so Brahman may be seen clearly here in this body; as in a dream, in the world of the Fathers; as in the water, he is seen about in the world of the Gandharvas; as in light and shade, in the world of Brahma.

6. "Having understood that the senses are distinct from the Atman,[12] and that their rising and setting (their waking and sleeping) belongs to them in their distinct existence and not to the Atman, a wise man grieves no more.

7. "Beyond the senses is the mind, beyond the mind is the highest created Being,[13] higher than that Being is the Great Self, higher than the Great, the highest Undeveloped.

8. "Beyond the Undeveloped is the Person, the all-pervading and entirely imperceptible. Every creature that knows him is liberated, and obtains immortality.

9. "His form is not to be seen, no one holds him with the eye. He is imagined by the heart, by wisdom, by the mind. Those who know this, are immortal.[14]

[10] The ancient tree is the fig tree which sends its branches so that they strike the ground and form new stems. In such a fashion one tree grows into a complete forest. In the Bhagavad Gita (XV. 3) the tree of life with its unseen roots is Brahman. Some commentators say the tree is the world, the roots Brahman; others that the tree, roots, and branches should be taken together to represent Brahman in its various manifestations.

[11] A commentator on this text translates it as: "If a man is able to understand Brahman, then even before the decay of his body, he is liberated. If he is not able to understand it, then he has to take body again in the created worlds." That is, of course, rebirth.

[12] That is, the senses are distinct from the Higher Self.

[13] That is, the intellect or buddhi.

[14] The same point is made, and perhaps better said, in the Svetasvatara

10. "When the five instruments of knowledge stand still together with the mind, and when the intellect does not move, that is called the highest state.

11. "This, the firm holding back of the senses, is what is called Yoga. He must be free from thoughtlessness then, for Yoga comes and goes.[15]

12. "He (the Self) cannot be reached by speech, by mind, or by the eye. How can it be apprehended except by him who says: 'He is?'

13. "By the words 'He is,' is he to be apprehended, and by admitting the reality of both the invisible Brahman and the visible world, as coming from Brahman. When he has been apprehended by the words 'He is,' then his reality reveals itself.

14. "When all desires that dwell in his heart cease, then the mortal becomes immortal, and obtains Brahman.

15. "When all the ties of the heart are severed[16] here on earth, then the mortal becomes immortal—here ends the teaching.

16. "There are a hundred and one arteries of the heart, one of them penetrates the crown of the head.[17] Moving upwards by it, a man at his death reaches the Immortal; the other arteries serve for departing in different directions.

17. "The Person not larger than a thumb, the inner Self, is always settled in the heart of men. Let a man draw that Self forth from his body with steadiness, as one draws the pith from a reed.[18] Let him know that Self as the Bright, as the Immortal; yes, as the Bright, as the Immortal."

18. Having received this knowledge taught by Death and the whole rule of Yoga (meditation), Nachiketa became free from passion[19] and death, and obtained Brahman. Thus it will be with another also who knows thus what relates to the Self.

19. May He protect us both! May He enjoy us both! May we acquire strength together! May our knowledge become bright! May we never quarrel! Om! Peace! peace! peace Hari, Om!

---

[15]Compare Patanjali's Yoga Sutra where he says that one requires vigilant earnestness to realize self is Self; This is That.

[16]That is, ignorance, passion, attachments, etc.

[17]Each person has many choices to make during his life; and of all the directions available one of them leads to Brahman.

[18]Or, as another translation has it, "As from a painter's brush a fibre." Radhakrishnan writes: "As one draws the wind from the reed." The wind is always there within the reed, but it must be blown to make sound.

[19]Free from vice and/or virtue.

Upanishad (IV. 20): "Those who know him by the heart as being in the heart, and by the mind, are immortal."

Prasna Upanishad

THIRD QUESTION

1. Then Kausalya Asvalayana asked: "Sir, whence is that Prana (spirit) born? How does it come into this body? And how does it abide, after it has divided itself? How does it go out? How does it support what is without, and how what is within?"

2. He replied: "You ask questions more difficult, but you are very fond of Brahman, therefore I shall tell it you.

3."This Prana (spirit) is born of the Self. Like the shadow thrown on a man, this prana is spread out over it (the Brahman).[1] By the work of the mind[2] does it come into this body.

4. "As a king commands officials, saying to them: Rule these villages or those, so does that Prana (spirit) dispose the other pranas. each for their separate work.

5. "The Apana (the down-breathing) in the organs of excretion and generation; the Prana himself dwells in eye and ear, passing through mouth and nose. In the middle is the Samana (the on-breathing); it carries what has been sacrificed as food equally over the body, and the seven lights proceed from it.[3]

6. "The Self is in the heart. There are the 101 arteries, and in each of them there are a hundred smaller veins, and for each of these branches there are 72,000. In these the Vyana (the back-breathing) moves.

7. "Through one of them, the Udana (the out-breathing) leads us upwards to the good world by good work, to the bad world by bad work, to the world of men by both.

8. "The sun rises as the external Prana, for it assists the Prana in the eye[4] The deity that exists in the earth. is there in support of man's Apana (down-breathing). The ether between sun and earth is the Samana (on-breathing), the air is Vyana (back-breathing).

[1] Over Brahman, that is, the Self.
[2] The work of the mind involves either good or evil deeds.
[3] The seven lights are the organs of sense, the two eyes, the two ears, the two nostrils, and the mouth.
[4] Without the sun the eye could not see.

9. "Light is the Udana (out-breathing), and therefore he whose light has gone out comes to a new birth with his senses absorbed in the mind.

10. "Whatever his thought at the time of death, with that he goes back to Prana, and the Prana, united with light,[5] together with the self (the givatma) leads on to the world, as deserved.

11. "He who, thus knowing, knows Prana, his offspring does not perish, and he becomes immortal. Thus says the Sloka:

12. "He who has known the origin, the entry, the place, the fivefold distribution, and the internal state of the Prana, obtains immortality, yes, obtains immortality."

FOURTH QUESTION

1. Then Sauryayanin Gargya asked: "Sir, what are they that sleep in this man, and what are they that are awake in him? What power (deva) is it that sees dreams? Whose is the happiness? On what do all these depend?"

2. He replied: "O Gargya, As all the rays of the sun, when it sets, are gathered up in that disc of light, and as they, when the sun rises again and again, come forth, so is all this (all the senses) gathered up in the highest faculty (deva), the mind. Therefore at that time that man does not hear, see, smell, taste, touch, he does not speak, he does not take, does not enjoy, does not evacuate, does not move about. He sleeps, that is what people say.

3. "The fires of the pranas are, as it were, awake in that town (the body). The Apana is the Garhapatya fire, the Vyana the Anvaharyapakana fire; and because it is taken out of the Garhapatya fire, which is fire for taking out, therefore the Prana is the Ahavaniya fire.[6]

4. "Because it carries equally these two oblations, the outbreathing and the in-breathing, the Samana is he (the Hotri priest).[7] The mind is the sacrificer, the Udana is the reward of the sacrifice, and it leads the sacrificer every day (in deep sleep) to Brahman.

[5]That is, with Udana, the out-breathing force.

[6]This description of the fires and altars is not clear. The Garhapatya fires and altars are placed in the southwest. These are the household fires, which are always kept burning, and from which fire is taken to other altars. The Anvaharyapakana, commonly called the Dakshina fire, is placed in the south and used chiefly for oblations to the ancestors. The Ahavaniya fire is placed in the east and is used for sacrifices to the Gods.

[7]The Hotri priest is supposed to carry on two oblations (equivalent to the Ahavaniya), and combines the two breathings, the in and out breathings in the same way as the Vyana.

5. "There that god[8] (the mind) enjoys in sleep greatness. What has been seen, he sees again; what has been heard, he hears again; what has been enjoyed in different countries and quarters, he enjoys again; what has been seen and not seen, heard and not heard, enjoyed and not enjoyed, he sees it all; he, being all, sees.

6. "And when he is overpowered by light,[9] then that god sees no dreams, and at that time that happiness arises in his body.

. . .

9. "For he it is who sees, hears, smells, tastes, perceives, conceives, acts, he whose essence is knowledge, the person, and he dwells in the highest, indestructible Self.[10]

10. "He who knows that indestructible being, obtains what is the highest and indestructible, he without a shadow, without a body, without colour, bright.—yes. O friend, he who knows it, becomes all-knowing, becomes all. On this there is this Sloka:

11. "He, O friend, who knows that indestructible being wherein the true knower, the vital spirits (pranas), together with all the powers (deva), and the elements rest, he, being all-knowing, has penetrated all."

FIFTH QUESTION

1. Then Saivya Satyakama asked him: "Sir, if some one among men should meditate here until death on the syllable Om, what would he obtain by it?"

2. He replied: "O Satyakama, the syllable Om (AUM) is the highest and also the other Brahman; therefore he who knows it arrives by the same means at one of the two.

3. "If he meditate on one Matra (the A), then, being enlightened by that only, he arrives quickly at the earth. The Rik-verses lead him to the world of men, and being endowed there with penance, abstinence, and faith, he enjoys greatness.

4. "If he meditate with two Matras (A + U) he arrives at the Manas,[11] and is led up by the Yagus-verses to the sky, to the Soma-world. Having enjoyed greatness in the Soma-world, he returns again.

[8]The Sanskrit word for god here is deva, and is used in the sense of an invisible power, but with a masculine gender. Max Muller generally translates this deva to indicate a special faculty.

[9]That is, in a state of profound sleep or sushupti.

[10]Buddhi and the rest are instruments of knowledge. But there is in addition the knower himself, the person behind the knowing, within the Highest Self.

[11]Literally the mind, but here the moon is meant. The moon is a part of the Brahma-world, reached by the path of the Fathers. (Compare Question I, 15, Prasna Upanishad.)

5. "Again, he who meditates with this syllable AUM of three Matras, on the Highest Person, he comes to light and to the sun. And as a snake is freed from its skin, so is he freed from evil. He is led up by the Saman-verses to the Brahma-world; and from him, full of life (Hiranyagarbha, the lord of the Satya-loka),[12] he learns to see the all-pervading, the Highest Person. And there are these two Slokas:

6. "The three Matras (A + U + M), if employed separate, and only joined one to another, are mortal;[13] but in acts, external, internal, or intermediate, if well performed, the sage trembles not.[14]

7. "Through the Rik-verses he arrives at this world, through the Yagus-verses at the sky, through the Saman-verses at that which the poets teach,—he arrives at this by means of the On-kara; the wise arrives at that which is at rest, free from decay, from death, from fear—the Highest."

SIXTH QUESTION

1. Then Sukesas Bharadvaga asked him, saying: "Sir, Hiran-yanabha, the prince of Kosala, came to me and asked this question: Do you know the person of sixteen parts, O Bharadvaga? I said to the prince: I do not know him; if I knew him, how should I not tell you? Surely, he who speaks what is untrue withers away to the very root; therefore I will not say what is untrue. Then he mounted his chariot and went away silently. Now I ask you, where is that person?"

2. He replied: "Friend, that person is here within the body, he in whom these sixteen parts arise.

3. "He reflected: What is it by whose departure I shall depart, and by whose staying I shall stay?

4. "He sent forth (created) Prana (spirit); from Prana Srad-dha (faith),[15] either, air, light, water, earth, sense, mind, food; from food came vigour, penance, hymns, sacrifice, the worlds, and in the worlds the name also.[16]

5. "As these flowing rivers that go towards the ocean, when they have reached the ocean, sink into it, their name and form

[12]The world of Hiranyagarbha, Brahman, the Golden Child, is also called Satyaloka.

[13]The three Matras when separate are mortal because AUM does not mean the Highest Brahman until they are joined.

[14]The three acts described here are waking, slumbering, and deep sleep. They are meant for Yoga exercises in which the three Matras of OM are joined and used as one word, and also as an emblem of the Highest Brahman.

[15]Faith is supposed to make all beings act rightly.

[16]The Sanskrit word here, nama, stands for name (concept) and form.

are broken, and people speak of the ocean only, exactly thus these sixteen parts of the spectator that go towards the person (purusha), when they have reached the person, sink into him, their name and form are broken, and people speak of the person only, and he becomes without parts and immortal. On this there is this verse:

6. "That person who is to be known, he in whom these parts rest, like spokes in the nave of a wheel, you know him, lest death should hurt you."

7. Then he said to them: "So far do I know this Highest Brahman, there is nothing higher than it."

Mundaka Upanishad

Second Mundaka

FIRST KHANDA

1. This is the truth. As from a blazing fire sparks, being like unto fire, fly forth a thousandfold, thus are various beings brought forth from the Imperishable, my friend, and return thither also.

2. That heavenly Person is without body, he is both without and within, not produced, without breath and without mind, pure, higher than the high Imperishable.[1]

3. From him when entering on creation is born breath, mind, and all organs of sense, ether, air, light, water, and the earth, the support of all.

4. Fire (the sky) is his head, his eyes the sun and the moon, the quarters his ears, his speech the Vedas disclosed, the wind his breath, his heart the universe; from his feet came the earth; he is indeed the inner Self of all things.

5. From him comes Agni (fire),[2] the sun being the fuel; from the moon (Soma) comes rain (Parganya); from the earth herbs; and man gives seed unto the woman. Thus many beings are begotten from the Person (purusha).

6. From him come the Rik, the Saman, the Yagush, the Diksha (initiatory rites), all sacrifices and offerings of animals,

---

[1] The high imperishable here is the creative, but the higher is the noncreative Brahman.

[2] There are five fires, those of heaven, rain, earth, man, and woman.

and the fees bestowed on priests, the year too, the sacrificer, and the worlds, in which the moon shines brightly and the sun.

7. From him the many Devas too are begotten, the Sadhyas (genii), men, cattle, birds, the up and down breathings, rice and corn (for sacrifices), penance, faith, truth, abstinence, and law.

8. The seven senses (prana) also spring from him, the seven lights (acts of sensation), the seven kinds of fuel (objects by which the senses are lighted), the seven sacrifices (results of sensation), these seven worlds (the places of the senses, the worlds determined by the senses) in which the senses move, which rest in the cave of the heart, and are placed there seven and seven.

9. Hence come the seas and all the mountains, from him flow the rivers of every kind; hence come all herbs and the juice through which the inner Self subsists with the elements.

10. The Person is all this, sacrifice, penance, Brahman, the highest immortal; he who knows this hidden in the cave of the heart, he, O friend, scatters the knot of ignorance here on earth.

SECOND KHANDA

1. Manifest, near, moving in the cave of the heart is the great Being. In it everything is centred which ye know as moving, breathing, and blinking, as being and not-being, as adorable, as the best, that is beyond the understanding of creatures.

2. That which is brilliant, smaller than small, that on which the worlds are founded and their inhabitants, that is the indestructible Brahman, that is the breath, speech, mind; that is the true, that is the immortal. That is to be hit. Hit it, O friend!

3. Having taken the Upanishad as the bow, as the great weapon, let him place on it the arrow, sharpened by devotion! Then having drawn it with a thought directed to that which is, hit the mark, O friend, viz. that which is the Indestructible!

4. Om is the bow, the Self is the arrow, Brahman is called its aim. It is to be hit by a man who is not thoughtless; and then, as the arrow becomes one with the target, he will become one with Brahman.

5. In him the heaven, the earth, and the sky are woven, the mind also with all the senses. Know him alone as the Self, and leave off other words! He is the bridge of the Immortal.

6. He moves about becoming manifold within the heart where the arteries meet, like spokes fastened to the nave. Meditate on the Self as Om! Hail to you, that you may cross beyond the sea of darkness!

7. He who understands all and who knows all, he to whom all this glory in the world belongs, the Self, is placed in the ether,

in the heavenly city of Brahman (the heart). He assumes the nature of mind, and becomes the guide of the body of the senses. He subsists in food, in close proximity to the heart. The wise who understand this, behold the Immortal which shines forth full of bliss.

8. The fetter of the heart is broken, all doubts are solved, all his works and their effects perish when He has been beheld who is high and low (cause and effect).

9. In the highest golden sheath there is the Brahman without passions and without parts. That is pure, that is the light of lights, that is it which they know who know the Self.

10. The sun does not shine there, nor the moon and the stars, nor these lightnings, and much less this fire. When he shines, everything shines after him; by his light all this is lighted.

11. That immortal Brahman is before, that Brahman is behind, that Brahman is right and left. It has gone forth below and above; Brahman alone is all this, it is the best.

Third Mundaka

SECOND KHANDA

1. He (the knower of the Self) knows that highest home of Brahman, in which all is contained and shines brightly. The wise who, without desiring happiness, worship that Person, transcend this seed, they are not born again.

2. He who forms desires in his mind, is born again through his desires here and there. But to him whose desires are fulfilled and who is conscious of the true Self within himself all desires vanish, even here on earth.

3. That Self cannot be gained by the Veda, nor by understanding, nor by much learning. He whom the Self chooses, by him the Self can be gained. The Self chooses him (his body) as his own.

4. Nor is that Self to be gained by one who is destitute of strength, or without earnestness, or without right meditation. But if a wise man strives after it by those means (by strength, earnestness, and right meditation), then his Self enters the home of Brahman.

5. When they have reached him (the Self), the sages become satisfied through knowledge, they are conscious of their Self, their passions have passed away, and they are tranquil. The wise, having reached Him who is omnipresent everywhere, devoted to the Self, enter into him wholly.

6. Having well ascertained the object of the knowledge of the Vedanta and having purified their nature by the Yoga of renunciation,[3] all anchorites, enjoying the highest immortality, become free at the time of the great end (death) in the worlds of Brahma.

7. Their fifteen parts enter into their elements, their Devas (the senses) into their (corresponding) Devas.[4] Their deeds and their Self with all his knowledge become all one in the highest Imperishable.

8. As the flowing rivers disappear in the sea, losing their name and their form, thus a wise man, freed from name and form, goes to the divine Person, who is greater than the great.[5]

9. He who knows that highest Brahman, becomes even Brahman. In his race no one is born ignorant of Brahman. He overcomes grief, he overcomes evil; free from the fetters of the heart, he becomes immortal.

Taittiriya Upanishad

Second Valli

FIFTH ANUVAKA

"Understanding performs the sacrifice, it performs all sacred acts. All Devas worship understanding as Brahman, as the oldest. If a man knows understanding as Brahman, and if he does not swerve from it, he leaves all evils behind in the body, and attains all his wishes." The embodied Self of this (consisting of understanding) is the same as that of the former (consisting of mind).

Different from this, which consists of understanding, is the other inner Self, which consists of bliss. The former is filled by this. It also has the shape of man. Like the human shape of the former is the human shape of the latter. Joy is its head. Satisfaction its right arm. Great satisfaction is its left arm. Bliss is its trunk. Brahman is the seat (the support).

[3] The Yoga system, which through restraint (yoga) leads a man to true knowledge.

[4] The eye into the sun, etc.

[5] That is, greater than the conditioned Brahman.

SIXTH ANUVAKA

"He who knows the Brahman as non-existing, becomes himself non-existing. He who knows the Brahman as existing, him we know himself as existing." The embodied Self of this bliss is the same as that of the former understanding.

Thereupon follow the questions of the pupil:

"Does any one who knows not, after he has departed this life, ever go to that world? Or does he who knows, after he has departed, go to that world?"[1]

The answer is: He wished, may I be many, may I grow forth.[2] He brooded over himself like a man performing penance. After he had thus brooded, he sent forth (created) all, whatever there is. Having sent forth, he entered into it. Having entered it, he became sat (what is manifest) and asat (what is not manifest), defined and undefined, supported and not supported, endowed with knowledge and without knowledge (as stones), real and unreal.[3] The Sattya (true) became all this whatsoever, and therefore the wise call it the Brahman Sattya (the true).

SEVENTH ANUVAKA

"In the beginning this was non-existent (not yet defined by form and name). From it was born what exists. That made itself its Self, therefore it is called the Self-made." That which is Self-made is a flavour (can be tasted), for only after perceiving a flavour can any one perceive pleasure.[4] Who could breathe, who could breathe forth, if that bliss (Brahman) existed not in the ether (in the heart)? For he alone causes blessedness.

When he finds freedom from fear and rest in that which is invisible, incorporeal, indefined, unsupported, then he has obtained the fearless. For if he makes but the smallest distinction in it, there is fear for him. But that fear exists only for one who thinks himself wise, not for the true sage.[5]

[1] Muller analizes this phrase to mean: "As he who knows and he who knows not, are both sprung from Brahman, the question is supposed to be asked by the pupil, whether both will equally attain Brahman."

[2] A similar account of the creation is given in the Chandogya Upanishad (VI.2.1): "In the beginning there was that only which is, one only, without a second. It willed, may I be many . . . "

[3] What appears as real and unreal to the senses, not the truly real and unreal.

[4] As flavor is the cause of pleasure, so Brahman is the cause of all things. The wise taste the flavor of existence, and know that it proceeds from Brahman, the Self-made.

[5] Fear arises only from what is not ourselves. There is a possibility of fear, therefore, as soon as there is even the smallest distinction made between our self and the real Self.

"He who knows the bliss of that Brahman, from whence all speech, with the mind, turns away unable to reach it, he fears nothing."[6]

He does not distress himself with the thought, Why did I not do what is good? Why did I do what is bad? He who thus knows these two (good and bad), frees himself. He who knows both, frees himself. This is the Upanishad.

Chandogya Upanishad

Seventh Prapathaka

SEVENTEENTH KHANDA

1. "When one understands the True, then one declares the True. One who does not understand it, does not declare the True. Only he who understands it, declares the True. This understanding, however, we must desire to understand."[1]

"Sir, I desire to understand it."

EIGHTEENTH KHANDA

1. "When one perceives, then one understands. One who does not perceive, does not understand. Only he who perceives, understands. This perception, however, we must desire to understand."

"Sir, I desire to understand it."

NINETEENTH KHANDA

1. "When one believes, then one perceives. One who does not believe, does not perceive. Only he who believes, perceives. This belief, however, we must desire to understand."

"Sir, I desire to understand it."

TWENTIETH KHANDA

1. "When one attends on a tutor (spiritual guide), then one

---

[6]Even if there is no fear from anything else, after the knowledge of Self and Brahman has been obtained, fear might still arise from the commission of evil deeds, and the omission of good works.

[1]One would, for instance, call fire real, not knowing that fire is only a mixture of other, more basic realities.

believes. One who does not attend on a tutor, does not believe. Only he who attends, believes. This attention on a tutor, however, we must desire to understand."

"Sir, I desire to understand it."

TWENTY-FIRST KHANDA

1. "When one performs all sacred duties,[2] then one attends really on a tutor. One who does not perform his duties, does not really attend on a tutor. Only he who performs his duties attends on his tutor. This performance of duties, however, we must desire to understand."

"Sir, I desire to understand it."

TWENTY-SECOND KHANDA

1. "When one obtains bliss in oneself, then one performs duties. One who does not obtain bliss, does not perform duties. Only he who obtains bliss, performs duties. This bliss, however, we must desire to understand."

"Sir, I desire to understand it."

TWENTY-THIRD KHANDA

1. "The Infinite (bhuman)[3] is bliss. There is no bliss in anything finite. Infinity only is bliss. This Infinity, however, we must desire to understand."

"Sir, I desire to understand it."

TWENTY-FOURTH KHANDA

1. "Where one sees nothing else, hears nothing else, understands nothing else, that is the Infinite. Where one sees something else, hears something else, understands something else, that is the finite. The Infinite is immortal, the finite is mortal."

"Sir, in what does the Infinite rest?"

"In its own greatness—or not even in greatness.[4]

2. "In the world they call cows and horses, elephants and

---

[2]The duties of the student include restraint of the senses, concentration of the mind, etc.

[3]Bhuman is sometimes translated as grandeur. It is the highest point that can be reached—the infinite and the true.

[4]In the Upanishads the expression of highest certainty is sometimes followed by a misgiving that it may be otherwise after all: "If you ask in the highest sense, then I say no; for the Infinite cannot rest in anything, not even in greatness."

gold, slaves, wives, fields and houses greatness. I do not mean this," thus he spoke; "for in that case one being (the possessor) rests in something else, but the Infinite cannot rest in something different from itself."

TWENTY-FIFTH KHANDA

1. "The Infinite indeed is below, above, behind, before, right and left—it is indeed all this.

"Now follows the explanation of the Infinite as the I: I am below, I am above, I am behind, before, right and left—I am all this.

2. "Next follows the explanation of the Infinite as the Self: Self is below, above, behind, before, right and left—Self is all this.

"He who sees, perceives, and understands this, loves the Self, delights in the Self, revels in the Self, rejoices in the Self—he becomes a Svarag, (autocrat or self-ruler); he is lord and master in all the worlds.

"But those who think differently from this, live in perishable worlds, and have other beings for their rulers.

TWENTY-SIXTH KHANDA

1. "To him who sees, perceives, and understands this, the spirit (prana) springs from the Self, hope springs from the Self, memory springs from the Self;[5] so do ether, fire, water, appearance and disappearance, food, power, understanding, reflection, consideration, will, mind, speech, names, sacred hymns, and sacrifices—aye, all this springs from the Self.

2. "There is this verse, 'He who sees this, does not see death, nor illness, nor pain; he who sees this, sees everything, and obtains everything everywhere.

" 'He is one before creation, he becomes three (fire, water, earth), he becomes five, he becomes seven, he becomes nine; then again he is called the eleventh, and hundred and ten and one thousand and twenty.'[6]

"When the intellectual aliment has been purified, the whole nature becomes purified. When the whole nature has been purified, the memory becomes firm. And when the memory of the Highest

[5]Before the acquirement of true knowledge, all that has been mentioned before, such as spirit, hope, memory, was supposed to spring from sat; that is, as something different from oneself. Now he is to know that the Sat is the True Self.

[6]These various numbers are meant to show the endless variety of forms of the Self after creation.

Self remains firm, then all the ties which bind us to a belief in anything but the Self are loosened."

Eighth Prapathaka

FIRST KHANDA

1. Hari, Om. There is this city of Brahman[7] (the body), and in it the palace, the small lotus (of the heart), and in it that small ether. Now what exists within that small ether, that is to be sought for, that is to be understood.

2. And if they should say to him: "Now with regard to that city of Brahman, and the palace in it, i.e. the small lotus of the heart, and the small ether within the heart, what is there within it that deserves to be sought for, or that is to be undersood?"

3. Then he should say: "As large as this ether (all space) is, so large is that ether within the heart. Both heaven and earth are contained within it, both fire and air, both sun and moon, both lightning and stars; and whatever there is of him (the Self) here in the world, and whatever is not (i.e. whatever has been or will be), all that is contained within it."[8]

4. And if they should say to him: "If everything that exists is contained in that city of Brahman, all beings and all desires (whatever can be imagined or desired), then what is left of it, when old age reaches it and scatters it, or when it falls to pieces?"

5. Then he should say: "By the old age of the body, the ether, or Brahman within it, does not age; by the death of the

[7]The eighth Prapathaka is a kind of appendix to this Upanishad. The highest point of learning that can be reached by speculation was attained in the seventh Prapathaka—the identity of our self and of everything else with the Highest Self. Such speculation, however, was believed too much for ordinary people. They cannot conceive the Sat or Brahman as out of space and time, as free from all qualities, and in order to help them grasp this reality in stages, they are taught to adore Brahman as it appears in space and time, as an object endowed with recognizable qualities such as living in nature and in the human heart. To ordinary minds the Highest Brahman, besides which there is nothing, and which can neither be reached as an object, nor be considered as an effect, seems like a thing which is not. While the true philosopher after acquiring knowledge of the Highest Sat becomes identified with it suddenly, like lightning, the ordinary mortal must reach it by slow degrees. As a preparation for that higher knowledge (after we have absorbed the seventh Prapathaka), we have the eighth Prapathaka.

[8]The ether in the heart is thought to be a name of Brahman. He is there, and therefore all that comes of him when he assumes bodily shapes exists, both what is and what is not, what is no longer or not yet. In this case the absolute nothingness aspect of Brahman is not intended.

body, the ether, or Brahman within it, is not killed. That (the Brahman) is the true Brahma-city (not the body). In it all desires are contained. It is the Self, free from sin, free from old age, from death and grief, from hunger and thirst, which desires nothing but what it ought to desire, and imagines nothing but what it ought to imagine. Now as here on earth people follow as they are commanded, and depend on the object which they are attached to, be it a country or a piece of land.

6. "And as here on earth, whatever has been acquired by exertion, perishes, so perishes whatever is acquired for the next world by sacrifices and other good actions performed on earth. Those who depart from hence without having discovered the Self and those true desires, for them there is no freedom in all the worlds. But those who depart from hence, after having discovered the Self and those true desires, for them there is freedom in all the worlds."[9]

SECOND KHANDA

1. "Thus he who desires the world of the fathers,[10] by his mere will the fathers come to receive him, and having obtained the world of the fathers, he is happy.

2. "And he who desires the world of the mothers, by his mere will the mothers come to receive him, and having obtained the world of the mothers, he is happy.

3. "And he who desires the world of the brothers, by his mere will the brothers come to receive him, and having obtained the world of the brothers, he is happy.

4. "And he who desires the world of the sisters, by his mere will the sisters come to receive him, and having obtained the world of the sisters, he is happy.

5. "And he who desires the world of the friends, by his mere will the friends come to receive him, and having obtained the world of the friends, he is happy.

. . .

7. "And he who desires the world of food and drink, by his mere will food and drink come to him, and having obtained the world of food and drink, he is happy.

[9]True desires are those which we ought to desire, and the fulfillment of which depends on ourselves, assuming we have acquired the knowledge that enables us to fulfill them.

[10]Max Muller notes that the word for world, loka, while not exact, is the closest in meaning here, for it does convey *enjoying* the company of the fathers.

8. "And he who desires the world of song and music, by his mere will song and music come to him, and having obtained the world of song and music, he is happy.

9. "And he who desires the world of women, by his mere will women come to receive him, and having obtained the world of women, he is happy.

"Whatever object he is attached to, whatever object he desires, by his mere will it comes to him, and having obtained it, he is happy."

THIRD KHANDA

1. "These true desires, however, are hidden by what is false; though the desires be true, they have a covering which is false. Thus, whoever belonging to us has departed this life, him we cannot gain back, so that we should see him with our eyes.

2. "Those who belong to us, whether living or departed, and whatever else there is which we wish for and do not obtain, all that we find there if we descend into our heart, where Brahman dwells, in the ether of the heart. There are all our true desires, but hidden by what is false.[11] As people who do not know the country, walk again and again over a gold treasure that has been hidden somewhere in the earth and do not discover it, thus do all these creatures day after day go into the Brahma-world (they are merged in Brahman, while asleep), and yet do not discover it, because they are carried away by untruth (they do not come to themselves, i.e. they do not discover the true Self in Brahman, dwelling in the heart).

3. "That Self abides in the heart. And this is the etymological explanation. The heart is called hridayam, instead of hridy-ayam, i.e. He who is in the heart. He who knows this, that He is in the heart, goes day by day (when in sushupti, deep sleep) into heaven (svarga), i.e. into the Brahman of the heart.

4. "Now that serene being which, after having risen from out this earthly body, and having reached the highest light (self-knowledge), appears in its true form, that is the Self," thus he spoke (when asked by his pupils). This is the immortal, the fearless, this is Brahman. And of that Brahman the name is the True, Satyam,

5. This name Sattyam consists of three syllables, sat-ti-yam. Sat signifies the immortal, t, the mortal, and with yam he binds both. Because he binds both, the immortal and the mortal,

[11] All the desires mentioned before are fulfilled if we find their fulfillment in our Self, in the city of Brahman within our heart. There we always can possess those whom we have loved, only we must not wish to see them with our eyes; that would be a false covering to a true desire.

therefore it is yam. He who knows this goes day by day into heaven (svarga).

FOURTH KHANDA

1. That Self is a bank, a boundary, so that these worlds may not be confounded.[12] Day and night do not pass that bank, nor old age, death, and grief; neither good nor evil deeds. All evil-doers turn back from it, for the world of Brahman is free from all evil.

2. Therefore he who has crossed that bank, if blind, ceases to be blind; if wounded, ceases to be wounded; if afflicted ceases to be afflicted. Therefore when that bank has been crossed, night becomes day indeed, for the world of Brahman is lighted up once for all.

3. And that world of Brahman belongs to those only who find it by abstinence—for them there is freedom in all the worlds.

FIFTH KHANDA

1. What people call sacrifice (yagna), that is really abstinence (brahmacharya).[13] For he who knows, obtains that world of Brahman, which others obtain by sacrifice, by means of abstinence.

What people call sacrifice (ishta), that is really abstinence, for by abstinence, having searched (ishtva), he obtains the Self.

2. What people call sacrifice (sattrayana), that is really abstinence, for my abstinence he obtains from the Sat the true, the safety (trana) of the Self.

[12]Setu, a Sanskrit word generally translated by "bridge," Max Muller tells us, was originally a bank of earth thrown up to serve as a pathway through water or a swamp. It also served at the same time as boundaries between fields and different properties.

[13]The fifth khanda is chiefly to teach and recommend brahmacharya, or abstinence from all worldly pleasures. This is requested of the student so he may obtain a knowledge of Brahman; for the city of Brahman can be conquered by no one except those who have practiced abstinence. All the fulfilled desires noted in khandas 2-5, whether finding again of fathers and mothers, or entering Brahmaloka (the city of Brahman) with its beauteous palaces and lakes, must be considered as mental only (manasa), and never material (sthula). Considered mentally only they are not false or unreal, even as little as dreams. Dreams, the Upanishads argue, are false and unreal only relatively. That is, they are relative to what we see when we awake but are not real in themselves. Whatever we see in waking has also been shown to be false because it consists of forms and names only. Yet these forms and names possess an element of truth in them—the Sat. Before we realize Sat, all the objects we see in waking seem true, as dreams seem true in dreaming. But once we awaken from this state by true knowledge, we see that nothing is true but the Sat.

What people call the vow of silence (mauna), that is really abstinence, for he who by abstinence has found out the Self meditates (manute).

3. What people call fasting (anasakayana), that is really abstinence, for that Self does not perish (na nasyati), which we find out by abstinence.

What people call a hermit's life (aranyayana), that is really abstinence. Ara and Nya are two lakes in the world of Brahman, in the third heaven from hence; and there is the lake Airammadiya, and the Asvattha tree, showering down Soma, and the city of Brahman (Hiranyagarbha) Aparagita, and the golden Prabhuvimita (the hall built by Prabhu, Brahman).

Now that world of Brahman belongs to those who find the lakes Ara and Nya in the world of Brahman by means of abstinence; for them there is freedom in all the worlds.

SIXTH KHANDA

1. Now those arteries of the heart consist of a brown substance, of a white, blue, yellow, and red substance, and so is the sun brown, white, blue, yellow, and red.

2. As a very long highway goes to two places, to one at the beginning, and to another at the end, so do the rays of the sun go to both worlds, to this one and to the other. They start from the sun, and enter into those arteries; they start from those arteries, and enter into the sun.

3. And when a man is asleep, reposing, and at perfect rest, so that he sees no dream, then he has entered into those arteries. Then no evil touches him, for he has obtained the light of the sun.

4. And when a man falls ill, then those who sit round him, say, "Do you know me? Do you know me?" As long as he has not departed from this body, he knows them.

5. But when he departs from this body, then he departs upwards by those very rays towards the worlds which he has gained by merit, not by knowledge; or he goes out while meditating on Om and thus securing an entrance into the Brahmaloka. And while his mind is failing, he is going to the sun. For the sun is the door of the world of Brahman. Those who know, walk in; those who do not know, are shut out. There is this verse: "There are a hundred and one arteries of the heart; one of them penetrates the crown of the head; moving upwards by it a man reaches the immortal; the others serve for departing in different directions, yea, in different directions."

SEVENTH KHANDA

1. Pragapati said: "The Self which is free from sin, free from old age, from death and grief, from hunger and thirst, which desires nothing but what it ought to desire, and imagines nothing but what it ought to imagine, that it is which we must search out, that it is which we must try to understand. He who has searched out that Self and understands it, obtains all worlds and all desires."

2. The Devas (gods) and Asuras (demons) both heard these words, and said: "Well, let us search for that Self by which, if one has searched it out, all worlds and all desires are obtained."

Thus saying Indra went from the Devas, Virokana from the Asuras, and both, without having communicated with each other, approached Pragapati, holding fuel in their hands, as is the custom for pupils approaching their master.

3. They dwelt there as pupils for thirty-two years. Then Pragapati asked them: "For what purpose have you both dwelt here?"

They replied: "A saying of yours is being repeated, viz. 'the Self which is free from sin, free from old age, from death and grief, from hunger and thirst, which desires nothing but what it ought to desire, and imagines nothing but what it ought to imagine, that it is which we must search out, that it is which we must try to understand. He who has searched out that Self and understands it, obtains all worlds and all desires.' Now we both have dwelt here because we wish for that Self."

Pragapati said to them: "The person that is seen in the eye, that is the Self.[14] This is what I have said. This is the immortal, the fearless, this is Brahman."

They asked: "Sir, he who is perceived in the water, and he who is perceived in a mirror, who is he?"

He replied: "He himself indeed is seen in all these."

ELEVENTH KHANDA

1. "When a man being asleep, reposing, and at perfect rest, sees no dreams, that is the Self, this is the immortal, the fearless, this is Brahman."

Then Indra went away satisfied in his heart. But before he had returned to the Devas, he saw this difficulty. In truth he

[14] The teacher Pragapati means here that the person that is seen in the eye is not the real agent of seeing. This real agent of seeing is perceived by the sages only. The students, however, misunderstand, and think of the person that is seen, and not of the person that sees. To them the person seen in the eye is the small figure imaged in the eye itself. They go on to ask, therefore, whether the image in the water or in a mirror is not the Self.

thus does not know himself (his Self) that he is I, nor does he know anything that exists. He is gone to utter annihilation. I see no good in this.

2. Taking fuel in his hand he went again as a pupil to Pragapati. Pragapati said to him: "Maghavat, as you went away satisfied in your heart, for what purpose did you come back?"

He said: "Sir, in that way he does not know himself (his Self) that he is I, nor does he know anything that exists. He is gone to utter annihilation. I see no good in this."

3. "So it is indeed, Maghavat," replied Pragapati; "but I shall explain him (the true Self) further to you, and nothing more than this.[15] Live here other five years."

He lived there other five years. This made in all one hundred and one years, and therefore it is said that Indra Maghavat lived one hundred and one years as a pupil with Pragapati. Pragapati said to him:

TWELFTH KHANDA

1. "Maghavat, this body is mortal and always held by death. It is the abode of that Self which is immortal and without body.[16] When in the body (by thinking this body is I and I am this body) the Self is held by pleasure and pain. So long as he is in the body, he cannot get free from pleasure and pain. But when he is free of the body (when he knows himself different from the body), then neither pleasure nor pain touches him.[17]

2. "The wind is without body, the cloud, lightning, and thunder are without body, without hands, feet, etc. Now as these, arising from this heavenly ether (space), appear in their own form as soon as they have approached the highest light,

3. "Thus does that serene being, arising from this body, appear in its own form, as soon as it has approached the highest light (the knowledge of Self).[18] He (in that state) is the highest person (uttama purusha). He moves about there laughing (or eating), playing, and rejoicing (in his mind), be it with women,

---

[15]Sankara has explained this as meaning the real Self, not anything different from the Self.

[16]According to some the body is the result of the Self, the elements of the body, fire, water, and earth springing from the Self, and the Self afterwards entering them.

[17]This means ordinary, worldly pleasures.

[18]The wind is here compared with the Self, because it is lost in the ether (space) for a time, as the Self is lost in the body, and then rises again out of the ether and assumes its own form as wind. The stress laid on the highest light is, in one case, the sun of summer, and in the other the light of knowledge.

carriages, or relatives, never minding that body into which he was born.[19]

"Like as a horse attached to a cart, so is the spirit (prana, pragnatman) attached to this body.[20]

4. "Now where the sight has entered into the void (the open space, the black pupil of the eye), there is the person of the eye, the eye itself is the instrument of seeing. He who knows, let me smell this, he is the Self, the nose is the instrument of smelling. He who knows, let me say this, he is the Self, the tongue is the instrument of saying. He who knows, let me hear this, he is the Self, the ear is the instrument of hearing.

5. "He who knows, let me think this, he is the Self, the mind is his divine eye.[21] He, the Self, seeing these pleasures, which to others are hidden like a buried treasure of gold, through his divine eye, i.e. the mind, rejoices.

"The Devas who are in the world of Brahman meditate on that Self (as taught by Pragapati to Indra, and by Indra to the Devas). Therefore all worlds belong to them, and all desires. He who knows that Self and understands it, obtains all worlds and all desires." Thus said Pragapati, yea, thus said Pragapati.

THIRTEENTH KHANDA

1. From the dark (the Brahman of the heart) I come to the nebulous (the world of Brahman), from the nebulous to the dark, shaking off all evil, as a horse shakes his hairs, and as the moon frees herself from the mouth of Rahu.[22] Having shaken off the body, I obtain, self made and satisfied, the uncreated world of Brahman, yea, I obtain it.

---

[19]This passage should be interpreted as the Self enjoying such pleasures only as an inward spectator, without identifying himself with either the pleasure or pain. He sees them, as he says later, with his divine eye. The Self perceives in all things his Self only, nothing else. Sankara refers this passage to Brahman as an effect, not to Brahman as a cause.

[20]The spirit or the conscious self is not identical with the body but only joined to it like a horse, or driving it like a charioteer.

[21]It is divine because it perceives not only what is present, but also what is past and future.

[22]Rahu was a monster who was supposed to swallow the sun and moon at every solar or lunar eclipse. In early legends one hears only of the devouring head or mouth of Rahu. But a body was given him, only to be destroyed by Vishnu, so that again nothing remained of him but his head.

FOURTEENTH KHANDA

1. He who is called ether (akasa) is the revealer of all forms and names.[23] That within which these forms and names are contained is the Brahman, the Immortal, the Self.

I come to the hall of Pragapati, to the house; I am the glorious among Brahmans, glorious among princes, glorious among men. I obtained that glory, I am glorious among the glorious. May I never go to the white, toothless, yet devouring, white abode; may I never go to it.

FIFTEENTH KHANDA

1. Brahma (Hiranyagarbha or Paramesvara) told this to Pragapati (Kasyapa), Pragapati to Manu (his son), Manu to mankind. He who has learnt the Veda from a family of teachers, according to the sacred rule, in the leisure time left from the duties to be performed for the Guru, who, after receiving his discharge, has settled in his own house, keeping up the memory of what he has learnt by repeating it regularly in some sacred spot, who has begotten virtuous sons, and concentrated all his senses on the Self, never giving pain to any creature, except at the tirthas (sacrifices, etc.),[24] he who behaves thus all his life, reaches the world of Brahman, and does not return, yea, he does not return.

[23] Akasa is a name of Brahman because, like ether, Brahman has no body and is infinitely small like the ether or space.
[24] Some say that even a mendicant can give pain when traveling about and importuning people for alms. But the beggar is allowed to seek alms at tirthas or sacred places. He must conduct his begging according to strict rules and only in special areas, and at special times.

Brihadaranyaka Upanishad

Second Adhyaha

FIFTH BRAHMANA[1]

1. This earth is the honey (madhu, the effect) of all beings, and all beings are the honey (madhu, the effect) of this earth. Likewise this bright, immortal person in this earth, and that bright immortal person incorporated in the body (both are madhu). He indeed is the same as that Self, that Immortal, that Brahman, that All.

2. This water is the honey of all beings, and all beings are the honey of this water. Likewise this bright, immortal person in this water, and that bright, immortal person, existing as seed in the body (both are madhu). He indeed is the same as that Self, that Immortal, that Brahman, that All.

3. This fire is the honey of all beings, and all beings are the honey of this fire. Likewise this bright, immortal person in this fire, and that bright, immortal person, existing as speech in the body (both are madhu). He indeed is the same as that Self, that Immortal, that Brahman, that All.

4. This air is the honey of all beings, and all beings are the honey of this air. Likewise this bright, immortal person in this air, and that bright, immortal person existing as breath in the body (both are madhu). He indeed is the same as that Self, that Immortal, that Brahman, that All.

5. This sun is the honey of all beings, and all beings are the honey of this sun. Likewise this bright, immortal person in this sun, and that bright, immortal person existing as the eye in the body (both are madhu). He indeed is the same as that Self, that Immortal, that Brahman, that All.

[1]This brahmana cannot be understood easily without first understanding the symbolic use of "honey," or madhu, which is used throughout it. Madhu, or honey, is used here as something which is both the cause and the effect; as an instance of things which are mutually dependent on each other, or cannot exist without one another. As the bees make the honey, and the honey makes or supports the bees, bees and honey become both cause and effect and are mutually dependent on each other. The argument extends to earth and all living beings who, in the eyes of the Upanishads, are mutually dependent living beings presupposing the earth, and the earth presupposing living beings. The comparison with contemporary attitudes evolving toward similar views about our ecosystem is startling.

6. This space (disah, the quarters) is the honey of all beings, and all beings are the honey of this space. Likewise this bright, immortal person in this space, and that bright, immortal person existing as the ear in the body (both are madhu). He indeed is the same as that Self, that Immortal, that Brahman, that All.

7. This moon is the honey of all beings, and all beings are the honey of this moon. Likewise this bright, immortal person in this moon, and that bright, immortal person existing as mind in the body (both are madhu). He indeed is the same as that Self, that Immortal, that Brahman, that All.

8. This lightning is the honey of all beings, and all beings are the honey of this lightning. Likewise this bright, immortal person in this lightning and that bright, immortal person existing as light in the body (both are madhu). He indeed is the same as that Self, that Immortal, that Brahman, that All.

9. This thunder is the honey of all beings, and all beings are the honey of this thunder. Likewise this bright, immortal person in this thunder, and that bright, immortal persons existing as sound and voice in the body (both are madhu). He indeed is the same as that Self, that Immortal, that Brahman, that All.

10. This ether is the honey of all beings, and all beings are the honey of this ether. Likewise this bright immortal person in this ether, and that bright, immortal person existing as heart-ether in the body (both are madhu). He indeed is the same as that Self, that Immortal, that Brahman, that All.

11. This law (dharma) is the honey of all beings, and all beings are the honey of this law. Likewise this bright, immortal person in this law, and that bright, immortal person existing as law in the body (both are madhu). He indeed is the same as that Self, that Immortal, that Brahman, that All.

12. This true[2] (satyam) is the honey of all beings, and all beings are the honey of this true. Likewise this bright, immortal person in what is true, and that bright, immortal person existing as the true in the body (both are manhu). He indeed is the same as that Self, that Immortal, that Brahman, that All.

13. This mankind is the honey of all beings, and all beings are the honey of this mankind. Likewise this bright, immortal person is mankind, and that bright, immortal person existing as man in the body (both are madhu). He indeed is the same as that Self, that Immortal, that Brahman, that All.

14. This Self is the honey of all beings, and all beings are the honey of this Self. Likewise this bright immortal person is this Self, and that bright, immortal person, the Self (both are

[2]This is often translated, Muller tells us, as truth. But satyam means the true in the sense of the real, not truth.

madhu). He indeed is the same as that Self, that Immortal, that Brahman, that All.

15. And verily this Self is the lord of all beings, the king of all beings. And as all spokes are contained in the axle and in the felly of a wheel, all beings, and all those selfs of the earth, water, etc. are contained in that Self.

Svetasvatara Upanishad

First Adhyaya

1. The Brahma-students say: Is Brahman the cause? Whence are we born? Whereby do we live, and whither do we go? O ye who know Brahman, tell us at whose command we abide, whether in pain or in pleasure?

2. Should time, or nature,[1] or necessity, or chance, or the elements be considered as the cause, or he who is called the person (purusha, vignanatma)? It cannot be their union either, because that is not self-dependent,[2] and the self also is powerless, because there is independent of him a cause of good and evil.[3]

3. The sages, devoted to meditation and concentration, have seen the power belonging to God himself, hidden in its own qualities (guna). He, being one, superintends all those causes, time, self, and the rest.

4. We meditate on him who like a wheel has one felly with three tires, sixteen ends, fifty spokes, with twenty counterspokes, and six sets of eight; whose one rope is manifold, who proceeds on three different roads, and whose illusion arises from two causes.[4]

[1] This means their own nature or independent character.

[2] This is because a union presupposes a uniter.

[3] The self is atman, and is explained in this instance by Sankara as the living self existing in a state determined by karma; that is, work and deeds belonging to a former existence. In the karmic sense the self cannot yet be considered an independent cause.

[4] The Isvara, or Brahman with attributes, is represented here as a wheel with one felly, which is the phenomenal world of appearances. It has three aspects (trivrit), or rather three bands or hoops to bind the felly: these bands symbolizing the three gunas (essences) of the prakriti (an energy principle, "that which brings forth"): the goodness (sattva), energy (rajas), and darkness (tamas). The sixteen ends means the five elements and eleven sense organs (the five receptive and the five active senses together with the manas, the mind, or common sensory organs). The fifty spokes are supposed to produce the motion of the worldly mundane wheel of life. These spokes, or character-

5. We meditate on the river whose water consists of the five streams, which is wild and winding with its five springs, whose waves are the five vital breaths, whose fountain head is the mind, the course of the five kinds of perceptions. It has five whirlpools, its rapids are the five pains; it has fifty kinds of suffering, and five branches.[5]

6. In that vast Brahma-wheel, in which all things live and rest, the bird flutters about, so long as he thinks that the self in him is different from the mover (the god, the lord). When he has been blessed by him, then he gains immortality.[6]

7. But what is praised in the Upanishads is the Highest Brahman, and in it there is the triad.[7] The Highest Brahman is the safe support, it is imperishable. The Brahma-students, when they have known what is within this world, are devoted and merged in the Brahman, free from birth.

8. The Lord (Isa) supports all this together, the perishable and the imperishable, the developed and the undeveloped. The living self, not being a lord, is bound, because he has to enjoy the fruits of works; but when he has known the god (deva), he is freed from all fetters.

9. There are two, one knowing (Isvara), the other not-knowing (giva), both unborn, one strong, the other weak; there is she, the unborn, through whom each man receives the recompense of his works; and there is the infinite Self (appearing) under all forms, but himself inactive. When a man finds out these three, that is Brahma.[8]

[5] Here Isvara is likened to a stream, the minute coincidences are explained by Sankara. The five streams are the five receptive organs, the five springs are the five elements, the five waves are the five active organs. The head is the manas, the mind, or sensory organs, from which the perceptions of the five senses spring. The five whirlpools are the objects of the five senses, the five rapids are the five pains of being in the womb, being born, growing old, growing ill, and dying. The rest is not fully explained by Sankara. The whole river, however, is meant for the Brahman—like the wheel in the preceding verse—in the form of cause and effect, as the phenomenal not the absolutely real world.

[6] If one is blessed by Isvara and has been accepted by the Lord, then he has discovered his own true self in the Lord. Again it must be remembered that both Isvara, the Lord, and the purusha, the individual soul, are phenomenal only, and that the Brahma-wheel is meant for the manifest, but unreal world. This distinction is important in all the Upanishads and Vedanta.

[7] The three are the subject, the object, and the mover.

[8] The three are (1) the lord, the personal god, the creator and ruler; (2) the individual soul or souls; and (3) the power of creation. All three are contained in Brahman.

istics of worldly life, include different kinds of misconceptions, ignorance, doubt, self-love, fear, hatred; twenty-eight types of disabilities or cause of misconceptions, various self-satisfactions and pleasure in a number of perfections.

10. That which is perishable is the Pradhana (the first), the immortal and imperishable is Hara. The one god rules the perishable (the pradhana) and the living self.[9] From meditating on him, from joining him, from becoming one with him there is further cessation of all illusion in the end.

11. When that god is known, all fetters fall off, sufferings are destroyed, and birth and death cease. From meditating on him there arises, on the dissolution of the body, the third state, that of universal lordship.[10] but he only who is alone, is satisfied.[11]

12. This, which rests eternally within the self, should be known; and beyond this not anything has to be known. By knowing the enjoyer,[12] the enjoyed, and the ruler, everything has been declared to be threefold, and this is Brahman.

13. As the form of fire, while it exists in the under-wood is not seen, nor is its seed destroyed, but it has to be seized again and again by means of the stick and the under-wood, so it is in both cases, and the Self has to be seized in the body by means of the pranava (the syllable Om).[13]

14. By making his body the under-wood, and the syllable Om the upper-wood, man, after repeating the drill of meditation, will perceive the bright god, like the spark hidden in the wood.

15. As oil in seeds, as butter in cream, as water in dry riverbeds,[14] as fire in wood, so is the Self seized within the self, if man looks for him by truthfulness and penance.[15]

16. If he looks for the Self that pervades everything, as butter is contained in milk, and the roots whereof are self-knowledge and penance. That is the Brahman taught by the Upanishad.

[9]The self or atman is used here for purusha, the individual soul or souls.
[10]Such a third state is blissful and within the Brahman-world; and while it is not yet perfect freedom it may lead one to it.
[11]This aloneness is produced by the knowledge that the individual self is one with the divine self, and that both the individual and the divine self are only phenomenal forms of the True Self, or Brahman.
[12]The enjoyer here is purusha, the individual soul, the subject. The enjoyed is prakriti, the object, nature. The ruler is Brahman as Isvara.
[13]This is somewhat obscure, but like most of the philosophical metaphors in the Upanishads it becomes quite exact when understood. Max Muller analyzes it in detail: Fire is compared to the Self. It is not seen at first, yet its linga or subtle body cannot have been destroyed because as soon as the stick is drilled in the underwood the fire becomes visible. In the same way the Self, though invisible during a state of ignorance, is there all the time and is perceived when the body has been drilled by the Pranava—that is, after constant repetition of the sacred syllable OM, the body has been subdued and the ecstatic vision of the Self is achieved.
[14]Here again, if the dry river bed is dug into it will yield water. In such a way persistent efforts to dig into one's self will yield results.
[15]The Upanishad implies here that he who is seized is the same as he who looks for the hidden Self.

Third Adhyaya[16]

1. The snarer who rules alone by his powers, who rules all the worlds by his powers, who is one and the same, while things arise and exist—they who know this are immortal.

2. For there is one Rudra only, they do not allow a second, who rules all the worlds by his powers. He stands behind all persons, and after having created all worlds he, the protector, rolls it up at the end of time.[17]

3. That one god, having his eyes, his face, his arms, and his feet in every place, when producing heaven and earth forges them together with his arms and his wings.

4. He, the creator and supporter of the gods, Rudra, the great seer, the lord of all, he who formerly gave birth to Hiranyagarbha, may he endow us with good thoughts.

5. O Rudra, thou dweller in the mountains, look upon us with that most blessed form of thine which is auspicious, not terrible, and reveals no evil!

6. O lord of the mountains, make lucky that arrow which thou, a dweller in the mountains, holdest in thy hand to shoot. Do not hurt man or beast!

7. Those who know beyond this the High Brahman, the vast, hidden in the bodies of all creatures, and alone enveloping everything, as the Lord, they become immortal.[18]

8. I know that great person (purusha) of sunlike lustre beyond the darkness. A man who knows him truly, passes over death; there is no other path to go.

9. This whole universe is filled by this person (purusha), to whom there is nothing superior, from whom there is nothing different, than whom there is nothing smaller or larger, who stands alone, fixed like a tree in the sky.

10. That which is beyond this world is without form and without suffering. They who know it, become immortal, but others suffer pain indeed.

11. That Bhagavat exists in the faces, the heads, the necks

[16]This adhyaya represents the Highest Self as the personified deity, Isa, or Rudra, under the sway of his own creative power or prakriti.

[17]Rudra, after having created all things draws together, and takes back his created into himself at the end of time.

[18]The knowledge implied here consists in knowing either that Brahman is Isa, or that Isa is Brahman. Muller does not seem happy with his translation of this paragraph and writes that he prefers an alternative: "Beyond this is the Higher Brahman, the vast. Those who know Isa, the Lord, hidden in all things and embracing all things to be this (Brahman), become immortal."

of all, he dwells in the cave (of the heart) of all beings, he is all-pervading, therefore he is the omnipresent Siva.

12. That person (purusha) is the great lord; he is the mover of existence, he possesses that purest power of reaching everything, he is light, he is undecaying.

13. The person (purusha), not larger than a thumb, dwelling within, always dwelling in the heart of man, is perceived by the heart, the thought, the mind; they who know it become immortal.

14. The person (purusha) with a thousand heads, a thousand eyes, a thousand feet, having compassed the earth on every side, extends beyond it by ten fingers' breadth.[19]

15. That person alone (purusha) is all this, what has been and what will be; he is also the lord of immortality; he is whatever grows by food.

16. Its hands and feet are everywhere, its eyes and head are everywhere, its ears are everywhere, it stands encompassing all in the world.

17. Separate from all the senses, yet reflecting the qualities of all the senses, it is the lord and ruler of all, it is the great refuge of all.

18. The embodied spirit within the town with nine gates, the bird, flutters outwards, the ruler of the whole world, of all that rests and of all that moves.

19. Grasping without hands, hasting without feet, he sees without eyes, he hears without ears. He knows what can be known, but no one knows him; they call him the first, the great person (purusha).

20. The Self, smaller than small, greater than great, is hidden in the heart of the creature. A man who has left all grief behind, sees the majesty, the Lord, the passionless, by the grace of the creator (the Lord).

21. I know this undecaying, ancient one, the Self of all things, being infinite and omnipresent. They declare that in him all birth is stopped, for the Brahma-students proclaim him to be eternal.

Fourth Adhyaya

1. He, the sun, without any colour, who with set purpose by means of his power (sakti) produces endless colours, in whom

---

[19]This is a famous verse of the Rig Veda (X.90), and is repeated in several Upanishads. Sankara explains the reference to ten fingers' breadth as meaning "endless," or another alternative he suggests is that it may refer to the place of the heart, which is ten fingers above the navel.

all this comes together in the beginning, and comes asunder in the end—may he, the god, endow us with good thoughts.

2. That Self indeed is Agni (fire), it is Aditya (sun), it is Vayu (wind), it is Kandramas (moon); the same also is the starry firmament, it is Brahman (Hiranyagarbha), it is water, it is Pragapati.

3. Thou art woman, thou art man; thou art youth, thou art maiden; thou, as an old man, totterest along on thy staff; thou art born with thy face turned everywhere.

4. Thou art the dark-blue bee, thou art the green parrot with red eyes, thou art the thunder-cloud, the seasons, the seas. Thou art without beginning, because thou art infinite, thou from whom all worlds are born.

5. There is one unborn being (female), red, white, and black, uniform, but producing manifold offspring. There is one unborn being (male) who loves her and lies by her; there is another who leaves her, while she is eating what has to be eaten.[20]

6. Two birds, inseparable friends, cling to the same tree. One of them eats the sweet fruit, the other looks on without eating.

7. On the same tree man sits grieving, immersed, bewildered, by his own impotence (an-isa). But when he sees the other lord (isa) contented, and knows his glory, then his grief passes away.

8. He who does not know that indestructible being of the Rig-veda, that highest ether-like (Self) wherein all the gods reside, of what use is the Rig-veda to him? Those only who know it, rest contented.

9. That from which the maker (mayin)[21] sends forth all this—the sacred verses, the offerings, the sacrifices, the panaceas, the past, the future, and all that the Vedas declare—in that the other is bound up through the maya.

[20]This is another famous verse because it formed an important bone of contention between Vedanta and Sankhya philosophers. The Sankhyas admit two principles—the Purusha, or absolute subject, and the Prakriti, which is generally translated as nature but carries a broader meaning as an energy principle. The Vedanta philosophers admit nothing but the one absolute subject, look upon nature as due to the power inherent within that subject, and are unwaveringly monist. Both schools of philosophy were anxious to find authoritative passages in the Vedas to confirm their opinions, and so both appealed to this and other passages to show that their view of Prakriti was supported by the Veda.

[21]Max Muller notes that there are no equivalents to terms such as maya and mayin. Maya means making, creating, or art. But as all art, making, or creating is phenomenal only (or simply illusion) as far as the Supreme Self is concerned, maya conveys the sense of illusion at the same time as creativity. In the same way mayin is the maker, the artist, but also the juggler, magician, or illusionist. What seems intended here is that all proceeds from Brahman (the nonattributable, the undifferentiated), but that the actual creator or maker of all emanations is Isa (Brahman with attributes), who, as creator, is acting through maya.

10. Know then Prakriti (nature) is Maya (art), and the great Lord of Mayin (maker); the whole world is filled with what are his members.

11. If a man has discerned him, who being one only, rules over every germ (cause), in whom all this comes together and comes asunder again, who is the lord, the bestower of blessing, the adorable god, then he passes for ever into that peace.

12. He, the creator and supporter of the gods, Rudra, the great seer, the lord of all, who saw Hiranyagarbha being born, may he endow us with good thoughts.

13. He who is the sovereign of the gods, he in whom all the worlds rest, he who rules over all two-footed and four-footed beings, to that god let us sacrifice an oblation.

14. He who has known him who is more subtile than subtile, in the midst of chaos, creating all things, having many forms, alone enveloping everything the happy one (Siva), passes into peace for ever.

15. He also was in time the guardian of this world, the lord of all, hidden in all beings. In him the Brahmarshis and the deities are united,[22] and he who knows him cuts the fetters of death asunder.

16. He who knows Siva (the blessed) hidden in all beings, like the subtile film that rises from out the clarified butter,[23] alone enveloping everything,—he who knows the god, is freed from all fetters.

17. That god, the maker of all things, the great Self[24] always dwelling in the heart of man, is perceived by the heart, the soul, the mind—they who know it become immortal.

18. When the light has risen,[25] there is no day, no night, neither existence nor non-existence; Siva (the blessed) alone is there. That is the eternal, the adorable light of Savitri—and the ancient wisdom proceeded thence.

19. No one has grasped him above, or across, or in the middle. There is no image of him whose name is Great Glory.

20. His form cannot be seen, no one perceives him with the eye. Those who through heart and mind know him thus abiding in the heart, become immortal.

---

[22]This is because both the Brahamarshis, the holy seers, and the deities find their true essence in Brahman.
[23]Muller notes that this could be translated "like cream from milk."
[24]In this case the Self carries the clear designation of "high-minded."
[25]Atamas meaning "no darkness," that is, the light of knowledge.

Sixth Adhyaya

1. Some wise men, deluded, speak of Nature, and others of Time as the cause of everything; but it is the greatness of God by which this Brahma-wheel is made to turn.

2. It is at the command of him who always covers this world, the knower, the time of time, who assumes qualities and all knowledge, it is at his command that this work (creation) unfolds itself, which is called earth, water, fire, air, and ether;

3. He who, after he has done that work and rested again, and after he has brought together one essence (the self) with the other (matter), with one, two, three, or eight, with time also and with the subtile qualities of the mind,

4. Who, after starting the works endowed with the three qualities, can order all things, yet when, in the absence of all these, he has caused the destruction of the work, goes on, being in truth different from all he has produced;[26]

5. He is the beginning, producing the causes which unite the soul with the body, and, being above the three kinds of time (past, present, future), he is seen as without parts, after we have first worshipped that adorable god, who has many forms, and who is the true source of all things, as dwelling in our own mind.

6. He is beyond all the forms of the tree (of the world) and of time, he is the other, from whom this world moves round, when one has known him[27] who brings good and removes evil, the lord of bliss, as dwelling within the self, the immortal, the support of all.

7. Let us know that highest great lord of lords, the highest deity of deities, the master of masters, the highest above, as god, the lord of the world, the adorable.

8. There is no effect and no cause known of him, no one is seen like unto him or better; his high power is revealed as manifold, as inherent, acting as force and knowledge.

9. There is no master of his in the world, no ruler of his, not even a sign of him.[28] He is the cause, the lord of the lords of the

[26]These two verses (4 and 5) are extremely obscure, and explanations by Sankara and other commentators are not really very enlightening. After a long, detailed analysis Muller decides that he thinks the subject of the two verses is really the same: that is, the Lord, as manifesting and passing through different states, and at last knowing himself to be above all around him.

[27]As in much of Eastern mysticism, the emphasis here is on experimenting. The poet seems to be saying that when one has worshipped him, or when one has *known him within oneself*, then he is seen as That, as the Lord of Lords, as That Which Is.

[28]The argument here is that if he could be inferred from a sign, there would be no necessity for the Veda to reveal him.

organs,[29] and there is of him neither parent nor lord.

10. That only god who spontaneously covered himself, like a spider, with threads drawn from the first cause (pradhana), grant us entrance into Brahman.

11. He is the one God, hidden in all beings, all-pervading, the self within all beings, watching over all works, dwelling in all beings, the witness, the perceiver, the only one, free from qualities.

12. He is the one ruler of many who seem to act, but really do not act;[30] he makes the one seed manifold. The wise who perceive him within their self, to them belongs eternal happiness, not to others.

13. He is the eternal among eternals, the thinker among thinkers, who, though one, fulfils the desires of many. He who has known that cause which is to be apprehended by Sankhya (philosophy) and Yoga (religious discipline), he is freed from all fetters.[31]

14. The sun does not shine there, nor the moon and the stars, nor these lightnings, and much less this fire. When he shines, everything shines after him. by his light all this is lightened.

15. He is the one bird in the midst of the world; he is also like the fire of the sun that has set in the ocean. A man who knows him truly, passes over death; there is no other path to go.

16. He makes all, he knows all, the self-caused, the knower, the time of time (destroyer of time), who assumes qualities and knows everything, the master of nature and of man, the lord of the three qualities (guna), the cause of the bondage, the existence, and the liberation of the world.[32]

17. He who has become that, he is the immortal, remaining

---

[29]The instrument of perception (karana) here is the organ of sense. The lords of such organs would be all living beings, and their lord the True Lord.

[30]Sankara explains that the acts of living beings are due to their organs, but do not affect the Highest Self, which always remains passive.

[31]Sankara interprets this verse differently than Muller in his translation. Sankara writes: "He is the eternal of eternals; that is, as he possesses eternity among living souls, these living souls also may claim eternity. Or the eternal may be meant for earth, water, etc. And in the same way he is the thinker among thinkers." Sankarananda says: "He is eternal, imperishable, among eternal, imperishable things. He is thinking among thinkers." Vignanatman says of this verse, "The Highest Lord is the cause of eternity in eternal things on earth, and the cause of thought in the thinkers on earth." Yet in the end, common to all these interpretations, is the idea that there is only one eternal, and only one thinker, from whom all that is (or seems to be), eternal and all that is thought on earth is derived.

[32]He binds, sustains, and dissolves worldly existence.

the lord, the knower, the ever-present guardian of this world, who rules this world for ever, for no one else is able to rule it.

18. Seeking for freedom I go for refuge to that God who is the light of his own thoughts, he who first creates Brahman and delivers the Vedas to him;

19. Who is without parts, without actions, tranquil, without fault, without taint, the highest bridge to immortality—like a fire that has consumed its fuel.

20. Only when men shall roll up the sky like a hide, will there be an end of misery, unless God has first been known.

21. Through the power of his penance and through the grace of God has the wise Svetasvatara truly proclaimed Brahman, the highest and holiest, to the best of ascetics, as approved by the company of Rishis.

22. This highest mystery in the Vedanta, delivered in a former age, should not be given to one whose passions have not been subdued, nor to one who is not a son, or who is not a pupil.

23. If these truths have been told to a high-minded man, who feels the highest devotion for God, and for his Guru as for God, then they will shine forth,—then they will shine forth indeed.

Maitri Upanishad[1]

THIRD PRAPATHAKA

1. The Valakhilyas said to Pragapati Kratu: "O Saint, if thou thus showest the greatness of that Self, then who is that other different one, also called self, who really overcome by bright and dark fruits of action, enters on a good or bad birth? Downward or upward is his course, and overcome by the pairs (distinction between hot and cold, pleasure and pain &c.) he roams about."

2. Pragapati Kratu replied: "There is indeed that other different one, called the elemental self (Bhutatma),[2] who, overcome by bright and dark fruits of action, enters on a good or bad birth: downward or upward is his course, and overcome by the pairs he roams about. And this is his explanation: The five

[1] I have followed E.B. Cowell's translation of this Upanishad as "Maitri"; Max Muller translates this Upanishad as Maitrayana-Brahmana. Both titles, however, convey the name of the writer adequately.

[2] The pure Self, called atma, brahma, etc., after entering what he had himself created, and no longer distinguishing himself from the created things (bhuta), was then called Bhutatma.

Tanmatras of sound, touch, form, taste, smell are called Bhuta;
also the five Mahabhutas (gross elements) are called Bhuta.
Then the aggregate of all these is called sar ira, body. And lastly
he of whom it was said that he dwelt in the body, he is called
Bhutatma, the elemental Self. Thus his immortal Self, is like a
drop of water on a lotus leaf, and he himself is overcome by the
qualities of nature. Then, because he is thus overcome, he becomes bewildered, and because he is bewildered, he saw not the
creator, the holy Lord, abiding within himself. Carried along by
the waves of the qualities, darkened in his imaginations, unstable, fickle, crippled, full of desires, vacillating, he enters into
belief, believing 'I am he,' 'this is mine'; he binds his Self by his
Self, as a bird with a net, and overcome afterwards by the fruits
of what he has done, he enters on a good and bad birth; downward or upward is his course, and overcome by the pairs he
roams about."

They asked: "Which is it?" And he answered them:

3. "This also has elsewhere been said: He who acts, is the elemental Self; he who causes to act by means of the organs, is the
inner man (antahpurusha). Now as even a ball of iron, pervaded
(overcome) by fire, and hammered by smiths, becomes manifold
(assumes different forms, such as crooked, round, large, small),
thus the elemental Self, pervaded (overcome) by the inner man,
and hammered by the qualities, becomes manifold. And those
multiplied things are impelled by man (purusha) as the wheel
by the potter. And as when the ball of iron is hammered, the
fire is not overcome, so the inner man is not overcome, but the
elemental Self is overcome, because it has united itself with the
elements."

FOURTH PRAPATHAKA.

1. The Valakhilyas, whose passions were subdued, approached
him full of amazement and said: "O Saint, we bow before thee;
teach thou, for thou art the way, and there is no other for us.
What process is there for the elemental Self, by which, after
leaving this identity with the elemental body, he obtains union
with the true Self?" Pragapati Kratu said to them:

2. "It has been said elsewhere: Like the waves in large rivers,
that which has been done before, cannot be turned back, and,
like the tide of the sea, the approach of death is hard to stem.
Bound by the fetters of the fruits of good and evil, like a
cripple; without freedom, like a man in prison; beset by many
fears, like one standing before Yama (the judge of the dead);
intoxicated by the wine of illusion, like one intoxicated by wine;
rushing about, like one possessed by an evil spirit; bitten by the

world, like one bitten by a great serpent; darkened by passion,
like the night; illusory, like magic; false, like a dream; pithless,
like the inside of the Kadali; changing its dress in a moment,
like an actor; fair in appearance, like a painted wall, thus they
call him; and therefore it is said:

"Sound, touch, and other things are like nothings; if the elemental Self is attached to them, it will not remember the
Highest Place.

3. "This is indeed the remedy for the elemental Self: Acquirement of the knowledge of the Veda, performance of one's
own duty, threfore conformity on the part of each man to the
order to which he happens to belong. This is indeed the rule for
one's own duty, other performances are like the mere branches
of a stem.[3] Through it one obtains the Highest above, otherwise
one falls downward. Thus is one's own duty declared, which is
to be found in the Vedas. No one belongs truly to an order (as-
rama), who transgresses his own law.[4] And if people say, that a
man does not belong to any of the orders, and that he is an ascetic, this is wrong, though, on the other hand, no one who is
not an ascetic brings his sacrificial works to perfection or obtains
knowledge of the Highest Self. For thus it is said:

"By ascetic penance goodness is obtained, from goodness understanding is reached, from understanding the Self is obtained,
and he who has obtained that, does not return.

4. "'Brahman is,' thus said one who knew the science of
Brahman; and this penance is the door to Brahman, thus said
one who by penance had cast off all sin. The syllable Om is the
manifest greatness of Brahman, thus said one who well grounded
in Brahman always meditates on it. Therefore by knowledge, by
penance, and by meditation is Brahman gained. Thus one goes
beyond Brahman (Hiranyagarbha), and to a divinity higher
than the gods; nay, he who knows this, and worships Brahman
by these three (by knowledge, penance, and meditation), obtains
bliss imperishable, infinite, and unchangeable. Then freed from
those things (the senses of the body, etc.) by which he was
filled and overcome, a mere charioteer,[5] he obtains union with
the Self."

5. The Valakhilyas said: "O Saint, thou art the teacher, thou
art the teacher. What thou hast said, has been properly laid up

---

[3]Other sacrificial performances are considered by some commentators as
harmful and to be avoided.

[4]This means the rules of the order to which he belongs.

[5]Muller points out that charioteer, or rathitah, is a very strange word with
several possibilities. A preferred alternative translation Muller feels might
have been: "But then, freed from all those things by which he was filled and
likewise was overcome by them, he obtains union with the Self."

in our mind. Now answer us a further question: Agni, Vayu, Aditya, Time (kala) which is Breath (prana), Food (anna), Brahma,[6] Rudra, Vishnu, thus do some meditate on one, some on another. Say which of these is the best for us." He said to them:

6. "These are but the chief manifestations of the highest, the immortal, the incorporeal Brahman. He who is devoted to one, rejoices here in his world (presence), thus he said. Brahman indeed is all this, and a man may meditate on, worship, or discard also those which are its chief manifestations. With these deities he proceeds to higher and higher worlds, and when all things perish, he becomes one with the Purusha, yes, with the Purusha."

SIXTH PRAPATHAKA

15. There are two forms of Brahman, time and non-time. That which was before the existence of the sun is non-time and has no parts. That which had its beginning from the sun is time and has parts. Of that which has parts, the year is the form, and from the year are born all creatures; when produced by the year they grow, and go again to rest in the year. Therefore the year is Pragapati, is time, is food, is the nest of Brahman, is Self. Thus it is said:

"Time ripens and dissolves all beings in the great Self, but he who knows into what time itself is dissolved, he is the knower of the Veda."

16. This manifest time is the great ocean of creatures. He who is called Savitri (the sun, as begetter) dwells in it, from whence the moon, stars, planets, the year, and the rest are begotten. From them again comes all this, and thus, whatever of good or evil is seen in this world, comes from them. Therefore Brahman is the Self of the sun, and a man should worship the sun under the name of time. Some say the sun is Brahman, and thus it is said:

"The sacrificer, the deity that enjoys the sacrifice, the oblation, the hymn, the sacrifice, Vishnu, Pragapati, all this is the Lord, the witness, that shines in yonder orb."

17. In the beginning Brahman was all this. He was one, and infinite; infinite in the East, infinite in the South, infinite in the West, infinite in the North, above and below and everywhere infinite. East and the other regions do not exist for him, nor across, nor below, nor above. The Highest Self is not to be fixed, he is unlimited, unborn, not to be reasoned about, not to be con-

---

[6]This means, of course, the personal Brahman of the Hindu triad, not the Brahman of Absolute Reality who possesses no attributes.

ceived. He is like the ether (everywhere), and at the destruction
of the universe, he alone is awake. Thus from that ether he
wakes all this world; which consists of thought only, and by him
alone is all this meditated on, and in him it is dissolved. His is
that luminous form which shines in the sun, and the manifold
light in the smokeless fire, and the heat which in the stomach
digests the food. Thus it is said:

"He who is in the fire, and he who is in the heart, and he who
is in the sun, they are one and the same."

He who knows this becomes one with the one.

18. This is the rule for achieving it (viz. concentration of
the mind on the object of meditation): restraint of the breath,
restraint of the senses, meditation, fixed attention, investigation,
absorption, these are called the sixfold Yoga.[7] When beholding
by this Yoga, he beholds the gold-coloured maker, the lord, the
person, Brahman, the cause, then the sage, leaving behind good
and evil, makes everything (breath, organs of sense, body, etc.)
to be one in the Highest Indestructible (in the pratyagatman or
Brahman). And thus it is said:

"As birds and deer do not approach a burning mountain, so
sins never approach those who know Brahman."

19. And thus it is said elsewhere: When he who knows has,
while he is still Prana (breath), restrained his mind, and placed
all objects of the senses far away from himself, then let him remain without any conceptions. And because the living person,
called Prana (breath), has been produced here on earth from
that which is not Prana (the thinking Self), therefore let this
Prana merge the Prana (himself) in what is called the fourth.[8]
And thus it is said:

"What is without thought, though placed in the centre of
thought, what cannot be thought, the hidden, the highest—let a
man merge his thought there: then will this living being (linga)
be without attachment."[9]

20. And thus is has been said elsewhere: There is the superior fixed attention (dharana) for him, viz. if he presses the

---

[7] After having explained the form of what is to be meditated on and the mode
of meditation, the Upanishad now teaches the Yoga which serves to keep
our thoughts in subjection, and to fix our thoughts on the object of meditation.

[8] The fourth stage is the *thinking* Self; the earlier stages being waking, slumbering, and sleep.

[9] E.B. Cowell offers two alternative translations of this passage, which Muller
himself considers difficult. "This which is called prana, i.e. the individual
soul as characterized by the subtil body, will thus no longer appear in its
separate individuality from the absence of any conscious subject; or, this
subtle body bearing the name of intellect will thus become void of all objects."

tip of the tongue down the palate and restrains voice, mind, and breath, he sees Brahman by discrimination (tarka). And when, after the cessation of mind, he sees his own Self, smaller than small, and shining, as the Highest Self, then having seen his Self as the Self, he becomes Self-less, and because he is Self-less, he is without limit, without cause, absorbed in thought. This is the highest mystery, and final liberation. And thus it is said:

"Through the serenity of the thought he kills all actions, good or bad; his Self serene, abiding in the Self, obtains imperishable bliss."

"The gold-coloured bird abides in the heart, and in the sun—a diver bird, a swan, strong in splendour; him we worship in the fire."

Having recited the verse, he discovers its meaning, viz. the adorable splendour of Savitri (sun) is to be meditated on by him who, abiding within his mind, meditates thereon. Here he attains the place of rest for the mind, he holds it within his own Self. On this there are the following verses:

(1) As a fire without fuel becomes quiet in its place, thus do the thoughts, when all activity ceases, become quiet in their place.

(2) Even in a mind which loves the truth and has gone to rest in itself there arise, when it is deluded by the objects of sense, wrongs resulting from former acts.

(3) For thoughts alone cause the round of births; let a man strive to purify his thoughts. What a man thinks, that he is: this is the old secret.

(4) By the serenity of his thoughts a man blots out all actions, whether good or bad. Dwelling within his Self with serene thoughts, he obtains imperishable happiness.

(5) If the thoughts of a man were so fixed on Brahman as they are on the things of this world, who would not then be freed from bondage?

(6) The mind, it is said, is of two kinds, pure or impure; impure from the contact with lust, pure when free from lust.

(7) When a man having freed his mind from sloth, distraction, and vacillation, becomes as it were delivered from his mind, that is the highest point.

(8) The mind must be restrained in the heart till it comes to an end—that is knowledge, that is liberty: all the rest are extensions of the ties which bind us to this life.

(9) That happiness which belongs to a mind which by deep meditation has been washed clean from all impurity and has entered within the Self, cannot be described here by words; it can be felt by the inward power only.

(10) Water in water, fire in fire, ether in ether, no one can

distinguish them; likewise a man whose mind has entered till it cannot be distinguished from the Self attains liberty.

(11) Mind alone is the cause of bondage and liberty for men; if attached to the world, it becomes bound; if free from the world, that is liberty.

Sanatsugatiya Upanishad

Chapter VI

That pure great light which is radiant; that great glory; that, verily, which the gods worship; that by means of which the sun shines forth—that eternal divine being is perceived by devotees. From that pure principle the Brahman is produced, by that pure principle the Brahman is developed; that pure principle, not illumined among all radiant bodies, is itself luminous and illuminates them. That eternal divine being is perceived by devotees. The perfect is raised out of the perfect. It being raised out of the perfect is called the perfect. The perfect is withdrawn from the perfect, and the perfect only remains. That eternal divine being is perceived by devotees. From the Brahman the waters are produced; and then from the waters, the gross body. In the space within that, dwelt the two divine principles. Both enveloping the quarters and sub-quarters, support earth and heaven.[1] That eternal divine being is perceived by devotees. The horse-like senses[2] lead towards heaven him who is possessed of knowledge and divine, who is free from old age, and who stands on the wheel of the chariot-like body, which is transient, but the operations of which are imperishable.[3] That eternal divine being is perceived by devotees. His form has no parallel; no one sees him with the eye. Those who apprehend him by means of the understanding, and also the mind and heart, become immortal.[4] That eternal divine being is perceived by

[1] The two principles between them pervade the universe, the individual self being connected with the material world, the other with heaven.

[2] Sankara adds a comment to this verse: though the senses generally lead one to sensuous objects, they do not do so when under the guidance of true knowledge.

[3] The body is perishable, but action done by the self while in the body leaves its effect.

[4] Sankara comments here that the heart is the place within, where the self is said to be, and it may be taken as indicating the self; the meaning would then be that direct consciousness in the self involves its unity with the Supreme.

devotees. The currents of twelve collections[5] supported by
the Deity, regulate the honey[6] and those who follow after it
move about in this dangerous world. That eternal divine being
is perceived by devotees. The bee[7] drinks that accumulated
honey for half a month.[8] The Lord created the oblation for all
beings.[9] That eternal divine being is perceived by devotees.
Those who are devoid of wings,[10] coming to the Asvattha of
golden leaves,[11] there become possessed of wings, and fly away
happily. That eternal divine being is perceived by devotees. The
upward life-wind swallows up the downward life-wind; the moon
swallows up the upward life-wind; the sun swallows up the
moon;[12] and another swallows up the sun.[13] Moving about above
the waters, the supreme self[14] does not raise one leg. Should he
raise that, which is always performing sacrifices, there will be no
death, no immortality.[15] That eternal divine being is perceived
by devotees. The being which is the inner self, and which is of
the size of a thumb, is always migrating in consequence of the
connexion with the subtle body.[16] The deluded ones do not perceive that praiseworthy lord, primeval and radiant, and
possessed of creative power. That eternal divine being is perceived by devotees. Leading mortals to destruction by their own
action they conceal themselves like serpents in secret recesses.

[5]The five organs of action, the five senses of perception, and the mind and
understanding make up the twelve.

[6]Sankara translates "honey" to mean "fruit of action." A literal translation
is honey-material enjoyment. The regulation means that each current has its
own honey regularly distributed to it under the supervision of the Supreme
Deity.

[7]Some commentators interpret this to mean "one who is given to flying
about—the individual self."

[8]That is, in one life in respect of actions done in a previous life.

[9]The meaning of the whole passage, which is obscure, seems to be that the
Lord has arranged things so that each being receives some of this honey, this
food, which is the fruit of his own action. Then the question arises, Do these
beings continue taking the honey and migrating into other lives perpetually,
or are they ever released? That is answered in the next sentence.

[10]"The wings of knowledge," says Sankara, "those, verily, who have knowledge are possessed of wings, those who are not possessed of knowledge are
devoid of wings."

[11]Sankara explains golden to mean "beneficial and pleasant."

[12]"The moon," says Sankara, "means the mind, and the sun the understanding, as they are the respective deities of those organs." The sun, however, is
said to relate to the eye.

[13]That is, one remains in the state of being identified with Brahman.

[14]Sankara says this is the individual self; the bond being between the
Supreme and the world.

[15]As the whole of the material world is dissolved, when the self is separated
from the delusion which is the cause of it.

[16]The life-winds, the ten organs of sense, mind and understanding.

The deluded men then become more deluded. The enjoyments
afforded by them cause delusion, and lead to worldly life. That
eternal divine being is perceived by devotees. This seems to be
common to all mankind[17]—whether possessed of resources[18] or
not possessed of resources—it is common to immortality and the
other.[19] Those who are possessed of them attain there to the
source of the honey.[20] That eternal divine being is perceived by
devotees. They go, pervading both worlds by knowledge. Then
the Agnihotra though not performed is as good as performed.
Your knowledge of the Brahman, therefore, will not lead you to
littleness. Knowledge is his name. To that the talented ones attain. That eternal divine being is perceived by devotees. The self
of this description absorbing the material cause becomes great.[21]
And the self of him who understands that being is not degraded
here. That eternal divine being is perceived by devotees. One
should ever and always be doing good. There is no death,
whence can there be immortality?[22] The real and the unreal have
both the same real entity as their basis. The source of the existent and the non-existent is but one.[23] That eternal divine being
is perceived by devotees. The being who is the inner self, and
who is of the size of a thumb, is not seen, being placed in the
heart. He is unborn, is moving about day and night, without
sloth. Meditating on him, a wise man remains placid. That eternal divine being is perceived by devotees. From him comes the
wind; in him, likewise, is everything dissolved. From him come
the fire and the moon; and from him comes life. That is the
support of the universe; that is immortal; that is all things perceptible; that is the Brahman, that glory. From that all entities
were produced; and in that they are dissolved. That eternal
divine being is perceived by devotees. The brilliant (Brahman)
supports the two divine principles[24] and the universe, earth and
heaven, and the quarters. He from whom the rivers flow in various directions, from him were created the great oceans. That
eternal divine being is perceived by devotees. Should one fly,

[17]The quality of being one with the Brahman in essence.

[18]Self-restraint, tranquillity, etc.

[19]Whether in the midst of worldly life or in the state of perfect freedom.

[20]The Supreme Brahman. "There" Sankara interprets as "in the supreme
abode of Vishnu."

[21]Sankara says "the cause in which all is absorbed." "Becomes great" means
"becomes the Brahman" according to Sankara.

[22]There is no worldly life with birth and death for one who does good, and
thinks his self to be the Brahman. Hence no rebirths or emancipation.

[23]The Brahman is the real, and on that the unreal material world is imagined.

[24]"The individual soul and God," say some of the commentators on this
verse. The latter, in this case, being distinct from the Supreme Self.

even after furnishing oneself with thousands upon thousands of wings, and even though one should have the velocity of thought, one would never reach the end of the great cause.[25] That eternal divine being is perceived by devotees. His form dwells in the unperceived,[26] and those whose understanding are very well refined perceive him. The talented man who has got rid of affection and aversion perceives him by the mind. Those who understand him become immortal. When one sees this self in all beings stationed in various places, what should one grieve for after that? The Brahmana has as much interest in all beings, as in a big reservoir of water, to which water flows from all sides.[27] I alone am your mother, father; and I too am the son. And I am the self of all this—that which exists and that which does not exist. I am the aged grandfather of this, the father, and the son, O descendant of Bharata! You dwell in my self only. You are not mine, nor I yours. The self only is my seat; the self too is the source of my birth.[28] I am woven through and through (everything). And my seat is free from the attacks of old age. I am unborn, moving about day and night, without sloth. Knowing me, verily, a wise man remains placid. Minuter than an atom, possessed of a good mind,[29] I am stationed within all beings. The wise know the father of all beings to be placed in the lotus-like heart of every one.

[25]"It is therefore endless," says Sankara.

[26]"In a sphere beyond the reach of perception," writes Sankara.

[27]One of Sankara's commentaries differs from this translation: "As a person who has done all he need do, has no interest in a big reservoir of water, so to a Brahmana who sees the self in all beings, there is no interest in all the actions laid down in the Vedas, etc.; as he has obtained everything by mere perception of the self."

[28]Sankara says that "everything has its birth from the self."

[29]Sankara comments that this is a mind free from affection and aversion, hatred, love, or any attachments.

4. Patanjali, Yoga Sutra

Chapter I
Concentration (Samadhi), Its Spiritual Uses

1. Now concentration is explained.

2. Yoga is restraining the mind-stuff (chitta) from taking various forms (vrittis).

3. At that time (the time of concentration) the seer (Purusha) rests in his own unmodified state.

4. At other times (other than that of concentration) the seer is identified with the modifications.

5. There are five classes of modifications, some painful and others not painful.

6. These are right knowledge, indiscrimination, verbal delusion, sleep and memory.

7. Direct perception, inference, and competent evidence, are proofs.

8. Indiscrimination is false knowledge not established in real nature.

9. Verbal delusion follows from words having no (corresponding) reality.

10. Sleep is a vritti which embraces the feeling of voidness.

11. Memory is when vrittis of perceived subjects do not slip away and through impressions come back to consciousness.

12. Their control is by practice and non-attachment.

13. Continuous struggle to keep the vrittis perfectly restrained in practice.

14. It becomes firmly grounded by long constant efforts with great love for the end to be attained.

15. That effect which comes to those who have given up their thirst after objects either seen or heard, and which wills to control the objects, is non-attachment.

16. That is extreme non-attachment which gives up even the qualities, and comes from the knowledge of (the real nature of) the Purusha.

145

17. The concentration called right knowledge is that which is followed by reasoning, discrimination, bliss, unqualified egoism.

18. There is another samadhi which is attained by the constant practice of cessation of all mental activity, in which the chitta retains only the unmanifested impressions.

19. This samadhi when not followed by extreme non-attachment becomes the cause of the re-manifestation of the gods and of those that become merged in nature.

20. To others this samadhi comes through faith, energy, memory, concentration, and discrimination of the real.

21. Success is speedy for the extremely energetic.

22. The success of yogis differs according as the means they adopt are mild, medium or intense.

23. Or by devotion to Isvara.

24. Isvara (the Supreme Ruler) is a special purusha, untouched by misery, actions, their results and desires.

25. In Him becomes infinite that all-knowingness which in others is (only) a germ.

26. He is the Teacher of even the ancient teachers, being not limited by time.

27. His manifesting word is Om.

28. The repetition of this (Om) and meditating on its meaning (is the way).

29. From that is gained (the knowledge of) introspection, and the destruction of obstacles.

30. Disease, mental laziness, doubt, lack of enthusiasm, lethargy, clinging to sense-enjoyments, false perception, non-attaining concentration, and falling away from the state when obtained, are the obstructing distractions.

31. Grief, mental distress, tremor of the body, irregular breathing, accompany non-retention of concentration.

32. To remedy this, the practice of one subject (should be made).

33. Friendship, mercy, gladness and indifference, being thought of in regard to subjects, happy, unhappy, good and evil respectively, pacify the chitta.

34. By throwing out and restraining the breath.

35. Those forms of concentration that bring extraordinary sense perceptions cause perseverance of the mind.

36. Or by the meditation on the Effulgent Light, which is beyond all sorrow.

37. Or by meditation on the heart that has given up all attachment to sense-objects.

38. Or by meditating on the knowledge that comes in sleep.

39. Or by the meditation on anything that appeals to one as good.

40. The yogi's mind thus meditating, becomes unobstructed from the atomic to the infinite.

41. The yogi whose vrittis have thus become powerless (controlled) obtains in the receiver, the instrument of receiving, and the received (the Self, the mind, and eternal objects), concentratedness and sameness, like the crystal before different coloured objects.

42. Sound, meaning, and resulting knowledge, being mixed up, is (called) samadhi with-question.

43. Samadhi called "without-question" comes when the memory is purified, or devoid of qualities, expressing only the meaning (of the meditated object).

44. By this process the concentrations with discrimination and without discrimination, whose objects are finer, are also explained.

45. The finer objects end with the pradhana.[1]

46. These concentrations are with seed.

47. The concentration "without discrimination" being purified, the chitta becomes firmly fixed.

48. The knowledge in that is called "filled with Truth."

49. The knowledge that is gained from testimony and inference is about common objects. That from the samadhi just mentioned is of a much higher order, being able to penetrate where inference and testimony cannot go.

50. The resulting impression from this samadhi obstructs all other impressions.

51. By the restraint of even this impression, which obstructs all other impressions, all being restrained, comes the "seedless" samadhi.

Chapter II
Concentration, Its Practice and Methods (Sadhana)

1. Mortification, study, and surrendering fruits of work to God are called kriya-yoga.[2]

2. (It is for) the practice of samadhi and minimizing the pain-bearing obstructions.

3. The pain-bearing obstructions are—ignorance, egoism, attachment, aversion, and clinging to life.

---

[1] Pradhana is the noumenal, as opposed to the phenomenal: an object of purely rational perception.

[2] Kriya yoga is the yoga of action.

4. Ignorance is the productive field of all these that follow, whether they are dormant, attenuated, overpowered, or expanded.

5. Ignorance is taking the non-eternal, the impure, the painful, and the non-Self, as the eternal, the pure, the happy, and the Atman or Self (respectively).

6. Egoism is the identification of the seer with the instrument of seeing.

7. Attachment is that which dwells on pleasure.

8. Aversion is that which dwells on pain.

9. Flowing through its own nature, and established even in the learned, is the clinging to life.

10. The five samskaras are to be conquered by resolving them into their causal state.

11. By meditation, their gross modifications are to be rejected.

12. The "receptacle of works" has its root in these pain-bearing obstructions, and their experience is in this visible life, or in the unseen life.

13. The root being there, the fruition comes in the form of species, life, and experience of pleasure and pain.

14. They bear fruit as pleasure or pain, caused by virtue or vice.

15. To the discriminating, all is, as it were, painful on account of everything bringing pain, either as consequence, or as anticipation of loss of happiness or as fresh craving arising from impressions of happiness, and also as counter-action of qualities.

16. The misery which is not yet come is to be avoided.

17. The cause of that which is to be avoided is the junction of the seer and the seen.

18. The experienced is composed of elements and organs, is of the nature of illumination, action, and inertia, and is for the purpose of experience and release of the experiencer.

19. The states of the qualities are the defined, the undefined, the indicated only, and the signless.

20. The seer is intelligence only, and though pure, sees through the colouring of the intellect.

21. The nature of the experienced is for him.

22. Though destroyed for him whose goal has been gained, yet it is not destroyed, being common to others.

23. Junction is the cause of the realization of the nature of both the powers, the experienced and its Lord.

24. Ignorance is its cause.

25. There being absence of that ignorance there is absence of junction, which is the thing-to-be-avoided; that is the independence of the seer.

26. The means of destruction of ignorance is unbroken practice of discrimination.

27. His knowledge is of the sevenfold highest ground.

28. By the practice of the different parts of yoga the impurities being destroyed, knowledge becomes effulgent up to discrimination.

29. Yama, Niyama, Asana, Pranayama, Pratyahara, Dharana, Dhyana, and Samadhi, are the eight limbs of yoga.[3]

30. Non-killing, truthfulness, non-stealing, continence, and non-receiving, are called yama.[4]

31. These, unbroken by time, place, purpose and caste-rules, are (universal) great vows.

32. Internal and external purification, contentment, mortification, study, and worship of God, are the niyamas.

33. To obstruct thoughts which are inimical to yoga, contrary thoughts should be brought.

34. The obstructions to yoga are killing, falsehood, etc., whether committed, caused, or approved; either through avarice, or anger or ignorance; whether slight, middling, or great; and result in infinite ignorance and misery. This is the method of thinking the contrary.

35. Non-killing being established, in his presence all enmities cease in others.

36. By the establishment of truthfulness the yogi gets the power of attaining for himself and others the fruits of work without the works.

37. By the establishment of non-stealing all wealth comes to the yogi.

38. By the establishment of continence energy is gained.

39. When he is fixed in non-receiving he gets the memory of past life.

40. Internal and external cleanliness being established, arises disgust for one's own body, and non-intercourse with others.

41. There also arises purification of the sattva, cheerfulness of the mind, concentration, conquest of the organs, and fitness for the realization of the Self.

42. From contentment comes superlative happiness.

45. By sacrificing all to Isvara comes samadhi.
gans and the body, by destroying the impurity.

44. By repetition of the mantra comes the realization of the intended deity.[5]

[3]That is, abstinence, observances, postures, breath control, detachment and withdrawal of senses, concentration, meditation, and identification or trance.

[4]Of these the most important is the first, non-killing, or ahimsa, which is one of the basic tenets of the Jain religion as well.

[5]Mantra has been explained earlier, but in this context it is the repetition of the sacred sound, or, in Western terms, a prayer.

45. By sacrificing all to Isvara comes Samadhi.

46. Posture is that which is firm and pleasant.

47. By lessening the natural tendency (for restlessness) and meditating on the unlimited (posture becomes firm and pleasant).

48. Seat being conquered, the dualities do not obstruct.

49. Controlling the motion of the exhalation and the inhalation follows after this.

50. Its modifications are either external or internal, or motionless, regulated by place, time, and number, either long or short.[6]

51. The fourth is restraining the prana by reflecting on external or internal objects.

52. From that, the covering to the light of the chitta is attenuated.

53. The mind becomes fit for dharana.[7]

54. The drawing in of the organs is by their giving up their own objects and taking the form of the mind-stuff, as it were.

55. Thence arises supreme control of the organs.

Chapter III
Powers (Vibhuti)

We have now come to the chapter in which the yoga powers are described.

1. Dharana is holding the mind on to some particular object.

2. An unbroken flow of knowledge in that object is dhyana.[8]

3. When that, giving up all forms, reflects only the meaning, it is samadhi.

4. (These) three (when practised) in regard to one object is samyama.[9]

5. By the conquest of that comes light of knowledge.

6. That should be employed in stages.

7. These three are more internal than those that precede.

8. But even they are external to the seedless (samadhi).

9. By the suppression of the disturbed impressions of the mind, and by the rise of impressions of control, the mind, which persists in that moment of control, is said to attain the controlling modifications.

[6]Breath control has three stages: puraka or in-breathing, rechaka or out-breathing, and kumbhaka or breath-holding.

[7]Dharana is concentration on anything, subtle or gross.

[8]Dhyana is meditation.

[9]Radhakrishnan defines samyama as "inner discipline."

10. Its flow becomes steady by habit.

11. Taking in all sorts of objects, and concentrating upon one object, these two powers being destroyed and manifested respectively, the chitta gets the modification called samadhi.

12. The one-pointedness of the chitta is when the impression that is past and that which is present are similar.

13. By this is explained the threefold transformation of form, time and state, in fine or gross matter, and in the organs.

14. That which is acted upon by transformations, either past, present or yet to be manifested, is the qualified.

15. The succession of changes is the cause of manifold evolution.

16. By making samyama on the three sorts of changes comes the knowledge of past and future.

17. By making samyama on word, meaning, and knowledge, which are ordinarily confused, comes the knowledge of all animal sounds.

18. By perceiving the impressions, (comes) the knowledge of past life.

19. By making samyama on the signs in another's body, knowledge of his mind comes.

20. But not its contents, that not being the object of the samyama.

21. By making samyama on the form of the body, the perceptibility of the form being obstructed, and the power of manifestation in the eye being separated, the yogi's body becomes unseen.

22. By this the disappearance or concealment of words which are being spoken and such other things, are also explained.

23. Karma is of two kinds, soon to be fructified, and late to be fructified. By making samyama on these, or by the signs called arishta, portents, the yogis know the exact time of separation from their bodies.

24. By making samyama on friendship, mercy, etc. (I. 33), the yogi excels in respective qualities.

25. By making samyama on the strength of the elephant, and others, their respective strength comes to the yogi.

26. By making samyama on the effulgent light (I. 36) comes the knowledge of the fine, the obstructed and the remote.

27. By making samyama on the sun, comes the knowledge of the world.

28. On the moon, comes the knowledge of the cluster of stars.

29. On the pole-star, comes the knowledge of the motion of the stars.

30. On the navel circle, comes the knowledge of the constitution of the body.

31. On the hollow of the throat, comes cessation of hunger.

32. On the nerve called kurma comes fixity of the body.

33. On the light emanating from the top of the head, sight of the siddhas.[10]

34. Or by the power of pratibha all knowledge.[11]

35. In the heart, knowledge of minds.

36. Enjoyment comes by the non-discrimination of the soul and sattva which are totally different. The latter whose actions are for another is separate from the self-centred one. Samyama on the self-centered one gives knowledge of the Purusha.

37. From that arises the knowledge belonging to pratibha and supernatural hearing, touching, seeing, tasting, and smelling.

38. These are obstacles to samadhi: but they are powers in the worldly state.

39. When the cause of bondage of the chitta has become loosened, the yogi, by his knowledge of its channels of activity (the nerves), enters another's body.

40. By conquering the current called udana the yogi does not sink in water, or in swamps, he can walk on thorns, etc., and can die at will.[12]

41. By the conquest of the current samana he is surrounded by a blaze of light.

42. By making samyama on the relation between the ear and the akasa comes divine hearing.

43. By making samyama on the relation between the akasa[13] and the body and becoming light as cotton wool, etc., through meditation on them, the yogi goes through the skies.

44. By making samyama on the "real modifications" of the mind, outside of the body, called great disembodiedness, comes disappearance of the covering to light.

45. By making samyama on the gross and fine forms of the elements, their essential traits, the inherence of the gunas in them and on their contributing to the experience of the soul, comes mastery of the elements.

[10]Siddhas, says Vivekananda, are "perfected ones."

[11]Pratibha is prescience. Vivekananda describes its condition as spontaneous enlightenment that results from purity.

[12]As the prana or vital breath moves through the body it is described according to "zones" within which it manifests; for example, prana that manifests all the way to the toes of the feet is called apana. If it manifests all the way to the head it is udana. It is vyana when the vital breath pervades the complete body. But prana itself is the chief manifestation as it moves through the mouth, nose and into the chest.

[13]Akasa is the ether.

46. From that comes minuteness, and the rest of the powers, "glorification of the body," and indestructibleness of the bodily qualities.

47. The "glorification of the body" is beauty, complexion, strength, adamantine hardness.

48. By making samyama on the objectivity and power of illumination of the organs, on egoism, the inherence of the gunas in them and on their contributing to the experience of the soul, comes the conquest of the organs.

49. From that comes to the body the power of rapid movement like the mind, power of the organs independently of the body, and conquest of nature.

50. By making samyama on the discrimination between sattva and the purusha come omnipotence and omniscience.

51. By giving up even these powers comes the destruction of the very seed of evil, which leads to kaivalya.[14]

52. The yogi should not feel allured or flattered by the overtures of celestial beings, for fear of evil again.

53. By making samyama on a particle of time and its precession and succession comes discrimination.

54. Those things which cannot be differentiated by species, sign and place, even they will be discriminated by the above samyama.

55. The saving knowledge is that knowledge of discrimination which simultaneously covers all objects, in all their variations.

56. By the similarity of purity between the sattva and the purusha comes kaivalya.

Chapter IV
Independence (Kaivalya)

1. The siddhis (powers) are attained by birth, chemical means, power of words, mortification or concentration.

2. The change into another species is by the filling in of nature.

3. Good and bad deeds are not the direct causes in the transformations of nature, but they act as breakers of obstacles to the evolutions of nature: as a farmer breaks the obstacles to the course of water, which then runs down by its own nature.

4. From egoism alone proceed the created minds.

5. Though the activities of the different created minds are various, the original mind is the controller of them all.

[14]Kaivalya as used in the fourth chapter means not only independence, but implies complete isolation or separation.

6. Among the various chittas that which is attained by sa-madhi is desireless.

7. Works are neither black nor white for the yogis; for others they are threefold—black, white, and mixed.

8. From these threefold works are manifested in each state only those desires (which are) fitting to that state alone. (The others are held in abeyance for the time being.)

9. There is consecutiveness in desires, even though separated by species, space and time, there being identification of memory and impressions.

10. Thirst for happiness being eternal desires are without beginning.

11. Being held together by cause, effect, support, and objects, in the absence of these is its absence.

12. The past and future exist in their own nature, qualities having different ways.

13. They are manifested or fine, being of the nature of the gunas.

14. The unity in things is from the unity in changes.

15. Since perception and desire vary with regard to the same object, mind and object are of different nature.

16. Things are known or unknown to the mind, being dependent on the colouring which they give to the mind.

17. The states of the mind are always known because the lord of the mind, the purusha is unchangeable.

18. The mind is not self-luminous, being an object.

19. From its being unable to cognize both at the same time.

20. Another cognizing mind being assumed there will be no end to such assumptions and confusion of memory will be the result.

21. The essence of knowledge (the purusha) being unchangeable, when the mind takes its form, it becomes conscious.

22. Coloured by the seer and the seen the mind is able to understand everything.

23. The mind though variegated by innumerable desires acts for another (the purusha), because it acts in combination.

24. For the discriminating the perception of the mind as At-man ceases.

25. Then bent on discriminating, the mind attains the previous state of kaivalya (isolation).

26. The thoughts that arise as obstructions to that are from impressions.

27. Their destruction is in the same manner as of ignorance, egoism, etc., as said before (II.10).

28. Even when arriving at the right discriminating knowledge of the essences, he who gives up the fruits, unto him comes as the

result of perfect discrimination, the samadhi called the cloud of virtue.

29. From that comes cessation of pains and works.

30. Then knowledge, bereft of covering and impurities, becoming infinite, the knowable becomes small.

31. Then are finished the successive transformations of the qualities, they having attained the end.

32. The changes that exist in relation to moments, and which are perceived at the other end (at the end of a series) are succession.

33. The resolution in the inverse order of the qualities, bereft of any motive of action for the purusha, is kaivalya, or it is the establishment of the power of knowledge in its own nature.

5. The Aphorisms of Sandilya

21. *If you say "faith is to be avoided as being an affection,"—no, because it has the highest aim, like union.*

This aphorism is introduced incidentally from the mention of the Yoga sastra. It may be said that faith also should be altogether avoided by one who wishes for liberation, because it does not differ from the affection characterized and condemned in the Yoga Aphorisms of Patanjali (II. 3), "affection, aversion, and tenacity of mundane existence are the 'afflictions.'" But this is not a true view, because faith has the highest aim, as its object is Iswara. A certain feeling is not to be avoided from the mere fact of its being an affection, but from its being an affection connected with mundane existence; just in the same way as it is not mere 'union' that is to be avoided but union with what is evil, for to be in a state of union with God is a state devoutly to be desired. And so in this alleged inference, "faith in Iswara is to be avoided, because it is an affection," we must supply the limiting condition (or upadhi) which is required to narrow its too great comprehensiveness, viz. its being connected with mundane existence or its not being conducive to liberation. And this faith is not devoid of the quality of "goodness," for this is expressly declared to be its characteristic in that line of the Gita (xvii.4) "those with the quality of goodness worship the gods."

*22. This faith indeed is the highest from the express decla-
ration of its superiority to the performers of sacrificial acts, to
those who follow knowledge and to those who practise concentration.*

This form of worship is indeed the highest,—this faith has the
highest character. This is every way ascertained, since the Gita
declares (VI. 46, 47),

"The yogi is higher than the ascetics, he is counted higher than
even those who follow knowledge,

"The yogi is higher than those who perform sacrificial acts;
therefore, O Arjuna, be thou a yogi.

"And of all yogis, whosoever with his soul intent on me

"In full belief worships me, he is accounted by me the most
devoted."

Here there is to be understood a gradual climax of the different subjects, caused by the successive superiority of their
respective characteristics, asceticism, etc.; but of course no subsidiary can be reckoned superior to its end; therefore faith is
the principal.

*24. But faith is not the same as belief, because it has a wider
range.*

Faith must not be universally supposed to be identical with
belief (sraddha), because belief is merely subsidiary to ceremo-
nial works; but not so is faith in Iswara.

*35. The power of the Supreme is not disputed and it is not thus
in the case of the souls other than He, because they have his
nature.*

The power of the Supreme is not denied in any Veda, that
such a generally received belief should be held untenable. Rather
we learn that power in natural to him from such passages as that
in the Chandogya Upanishad, "he whose will is truth." Nor is
there in his case any reason for his abandoning attributes once
known to belong to him, as we hold that there is to individual
souls, since he is always the Lord and always liberated. But affliction, etc., are not thus natural to the individual souls other than
God,—why? because they have his nature. For we read in the
Chandogya Upanishad (VIII.3), "he attains to the supreme
light and appears in his own nature," and this would be impossible, if affliction were natural to the individual souls. It would
indeed be possible if affliction were natural to the Supreme also,
but this is not so. Therefore we conclude, because liberation, as
defined as becoming identified with Brahman, would otherwise

be impossible, that mundane existence with its inevitable afflictions is only accidental to embodied souls. Although Maya is a non-natural power of the Supreme, still it does not follow that this his disguise will ever be absolutely abolished; but the internal organs, which are the disguisers of the individual souls, will be absolutely abolished wherever faith is produced towards the Supreme. The Maya power of God never ceases, because, as the number of individual souls is infinite, its exercise by him is ever necessary, for their mundane existence and manifold service. And therefore such passages as those in the Sruti (Brihadaranyaka Upan. IV.3,7), "he as it were thinks, he as it were moves," and again (Ib. II.3,6), "hence there is this definition, 'he is not this,' 'he is not this,' etc., refer to the individual soul," not to Brahman.

37. *Brahman is not subject to change since matter is interposed as a screem,[1] following Him as He exists as thought.*

Matter is the material cause of inanimate effects, and is subject to change; but not so Brahman; the creative power of the Supreme is really through the development of himself and his being obeyed by matter. Nor can it be said that matter alone is existence, because this supposition would lead to individual souls being non-existent, as they are other than matter. Therefore we hold that creative power etc., belong naturally to the Supreme, and that he throws a veil before himself in the form of his maya power or matter, on which he works; and therefore he himself is not subject to change, just as a magician who seems to create by illusion is not himself the subject of illusion. Although as the Sankhyas say, the very fact of being an effect means being changed, since the cause and the effect are in their substrate identical, yet when God creates it is not such a change as involves a change of form, as in the case of milk becoming curds. Or again, we may say that God is not subject to change any more than the potter's stick is in reference to the jar, since the stick does not effect any change in itself besides that produced in the jar.[2] Therefore it is said in the Aphorism "since matter is interposed as a screen."

---

[1] Matter, or prakriti, acts as a screen and stops the influence of change on Brahman.
[2] God in this view is the instrumental cause, and the potter's stick is not itself changed.

6. Selections from the Writings of Sankaracharya

The Awakening to the Self

This awakening to the Self is recorded for those whose inner darkness has been worn away by strong effort, who has reached restfulness, from whom passion has departed, who seek perfect Freedom.

Among all causes, wisdom is the only cause of perfect Freedom; as cookery without fire, so perfect Freedom cannot be accomplished without wisdom.

Works cannot destroy unwisdom, as these two are not contraries; but wisdom destroys unwisdom, as light the host of darkness.

At first wrapped in unwisdom, when unwisdom is destroyed the pure Self shines forth of itself, like the radiant sun when the clouds have passed.

When life that was darkened by unwisdom is made clear by the coming of wisdom, unwisdom sinks away of itself, as when water is cleared by astringent juice.

This world is like a dream, crowded with loves and hates; in its own time it shines like a reality; but on awakening it becomes unreal.

This passing world shines as real, like the silver imagined in a pearl-shell, as long as the Eternal is not known, the secondless substance of all.

In the real conscious Self, the all-penetrating everlasting pervader, all manifested things exist, as all bracelets exist in gold.

Just like the ether, the Lord of the senses, the Radiant, clothed in many vestures, seems divided because these are divided, but is beheld as one when the vestures are destroyed.

Through this difference of vesture, race, name, and home are attributed to the Self, as difference of taste and color to pure water.

Built up of fivefold-mingled elements through accumulated works is the physical vesture, the place where pleasure and pain are tasted.

Holding the five life-breaths, mind, reason, and the ten perceiving and acting powers, formed of unmingled elements, is the subtle vesture, the instrument of enjoyment.

Formed through the beginningless, ineffable error of separateness, is the causal vesture. One should hold the Self to be different from these three vestures.

In the presence of the five veils, the pure Self seems to share their nature; like a crystal in the presence of blue tissues.

The pure Self within should be wisely discerned from the veils that surround it, as rice by winnowing, from husk and chaff.

Though ever all-present, the Self is not everywhere clearly beheld; let it shine forth in pure reason like a reflection in a pure mirror.

The thought of difference arises through the vestures, the powers, mind, reason, and nature; but one must find the Self, the witness of all this being, the perpetual king.

Through the busy activity of the powers, the Self seems busy; as the moon seems to course through the coursing clouds.

The vestures, powers, mind, and reason move in their paths under the pure consciousness of the Self, as people move in the sunshine.

The qualities of vestures, powers, and works are attributed to the spotless Self through undiscernment, as blue to the pure sky.

Through unwisdom, the mental vestures actorship is attributed to the Self, as the ripple of the waves to the moon reflected in a lake.

Passion, desire, pleasure, pain move the mind; but when the mind rests in deep sleep they cease; they belong to the mind, not to the Self.

Shining is the sun's nature; coldness, the water's; heat, the fire's; so the Self's nature is Being, Consciousness, Bliss, perpetual spotlessness.

The Self lends Being and Consciousness, and mind lends activity. When these two factors are joined together by undiscernment, there arises the feeling that "I perceive."

The Self never changes; and mind of itself cannot perceive; but the Self through error believes itself to be the habitual doer and perceiver.

The Self is believed to be the habitual life, as a rope is believed to be a snake; and thus fear arises. But when it is known that "I am not the habitual life but the Self" then there can be no more fear.

The Self alone lights up the mind and powers, as a flame

lights up a jar. The Self can never be lit by these dull powers.

In the knowledge of the Self, there is no need that it should be known by anything else. A light does not need another light; it shines of itself.

Putting all veils aside, saying "it is not this! it is not this!" one must find the real unity of the habitual Self and the Supreme Self, according to the words of wisdom.

All outward things, the vestures and the rest, spring from unwisdom; they are fugitive as bubbles. One must find the changeless, spotless "I am the Eternal."

As I am other than these vestures, not mine are their birth, weariness, suffering, dissolution. I am not bound by sensuous objects, for Self is separate from the powers of sense.

As I am other than mind, not mine are pain, rage, hate, and fear. The Self is above the outward life and mind, according to the words of wisdom.

From this Self come forth the outward life and mind, and all the powers; from the Self come ether, air, fire, the waters, and earth upholder of all.

Without quality or activity, everlasting, free from doubt, stainless, changeless, formless, ever free am I the spotless Self.

Like ether, outside and inside all, I am unmoved; always all-equal, pure, unstained, spotless, unchanged.

The ever-pure lonely one, the partless bliss, the secondless, truth, wisdom, endless, the Supreme Eternal; this am I.

Thus the steadily-held remembrance that "I am the Eternal" takes away all unwisdom, as the healing essence stills all pain.

In solitude, passionless, with powers well-ruled, let him be intent on the one, the Self, with no thought but that endless one.

The wise through meditation immersing all outward things in the Self, should be intent on that only Self, spotless as shining ether.

Setting aside name, color, form, the insubstantial causes of separateness, the knower of the supreme rests in perfect Consciousness and Bliss.

The difference between knower, knowing, and known exists not in the Self; for through its own Consciousness and Bliss it shines self-luminous.

Thus setting the fire-stick of thought in the socket of the Self, let the kindled flame of knowledge burn away the fuel of unwisdom.

By knowledge, as by dawn, the former darkness is driven away; then is manifest the Self, self-shining like the radiant sun.

Yet the Self, though eternally possessed, is as though not possessed, through unwisdom. When unwisdom disappears, the Self shines forth like a jewel on one's own throat.

Separate life is conceived in the Eternal by error, as a man is imagined in a post. But the pain of separation ceases when the truth about it is perceived.

By entering into real nature, wisdom swiftly arises. Then the unwisdom of "I" and "mine" disappears, as when a mistake about the position of north and south is set right.

The seeker after union, possessed of all knowledge, sees with the eye of wisdom that all things rest in the Self; and this Self is the One, the All.

Self is all this moving world; other than Self is naught. As all jars are earth, so he beholds all as the Self.

Perfect Freedom even in life is this, that a man should shake himself free from all the limits of his disguises, through the essence of Reality, Consciousness, Bliss, just as the grub becomes the bee.

Crossing the ocean of glamor, and slaying the monsters, passion and hate, the seeker for union, perfect in peace, grows luminous in the garden of the Self.

Free from bondage to outward, unlasting pleasures, and returning to the joy of the Self, he shines pure within like the flame in a lamp.

Even when hidden under disguises, let the Sage stand free from them, like pure ether. Though knowing all, let him be as though he knew nothing; moving untrammelled like the air.

Let the Sage, shaking off his disguises, merge himself utterly in the all-pervading One; as water in water, ether in ether, flame in flame.

The gain above all gains, the joy above all joys, the wisdom above all wisdoms; let him affirm that it is the Eternal.

When this is seen, there is no more to see; when this is attained, there is no more to attain; when this is known, there is no more to know;—let him affirm that this is the Eternal.

Upward, downward, on all sides perfect; Being, Consciousness, Bliss; the secondless, endless, everlasting One;—let him affirm that this is the Eternal.

Through the knowledge that nothing is but the Eternal, the unchanging One is beheld by the wise; the aboriginal, partless joy; let him affirm that this is the Eternal.

As partakers in the bliss of that partless, blissful One, the Evolver and all the powers enjoy their bliss as dependents.

Every being is bound to the Eternal; every movement follows the Eternal; the all-embracing Eternal is in all, as curd is in all milk.

Nor small nor great nor short nor long, nor born nor departing, without form, attribute, color, name;—let him affirm that this is the Eternal.

Through whose shining shine the sun and all lights; but who shines not by any's light; through whom all this shines;—let him affirm that this is the Eternal.

All present within and without, making luminous all this moving, the Eternal shines forth glowing of red-hot iron.

The Eternal is different from the moving world—yet other than the Eternal is naught! What is other than the Eternal shines insubstantial, like the mirage in the desert.

Things seen and heard are not other than the Eternal. Knowledge of reality teaches that all this is the Eternal, the Being, Consciousness, Bliss, the secondless.

The eye of wisdom beholds the ever-present Consciousness, Bliss, the Self, the eye of unwisdom beholds not, as the blind beholds not the shining sun.

The personal life, refined through and through by the fire of wisdom, which right learning and knowledge kindle, shines pure as gold, freed from every stain.

The Self, rising in the firmament of the heart—sun of wisdom, darkness-dispersing, all-present, all-supporting—shines forth and illumines all.

He who, drawing away from space and time, faithfully worships in the holy place of the divine Self—the ever-present, the destroyer of heat and cold and every limit, the stainless, eternally happy—he all-knowing, entering the All, becomes immortal.

(Thus the Awakening to the Self is completed.)

The Awakening to Reality

To the Master, the World-Soul, the Master of seekers for union, obeisance; to the teacher, the giver of wisdom. To fulfill love for those who would be free, this Awakening to Reality is addressed to them.

The Four Perfections

We shall tell of the way of discerning reality, the perfection of freedom, for those who are fitted by possessing the Four Perfections.

What are the Four Perfections?

—The Discerning between lasting and unlasting things; No Rage for enjoying the fruit of works, either here or there; the Six Graces that follow Peace; and then the Longing to be free.

What is the Discerning between lasting and unlasting things?

—The one lasting thing is the Eternal; all, apart from it, is unlasting.

What is No Rage?

—A lack of longing for enjoyments here and in the heaven-world.

What is possession of the Perfections that follow Peace?

—Peace; Self-Control; Steadiness; Sturdiness; Confidence; Intentness.

What is Peace?

—A firm hold on emotion.

What is Self-Control?

—A firm hold on the lust of the eyes and the outward powers.

What is Steadiness?

—A following out of one's own genius.

What is Sturdiness?

—A readiness to bear opposing forces, like cold and heat, pleasure and pain.

What is Confidence?

—Confidence is a reliance on the Voice of the Teacher and Final Wisdom.

What is Intentness?

—One-pointedness of the imagination.

What is the Longing to be free?

—It is the longing: "That Freedom may be mine."

The Discerning of Reality

These are the Four Perfections. Through these, men are fitted to discern Reality.

What is the Discerning of Reality?

—It is this: the Self is real; other than it, all is fancy.

The Crest Jewel of Wisdom
(Vivekachudamani)

First Steps on the Path

THE PUPIL ASKS

"Hear with selfless kindness, Master. I ask this question: receiving the answer from thy lips I shall gain my end.

"What is, then, a bond? And how has this bond come? What cause has it? And how can one be free?

"What is not-Self and what the Higher Self? And how can one discern between them?"

THE MASTER ANSWERS

"Happy art thou. Thou shalt attain thy end. Thy kin is blest in thee. For thou seekest to become the Eternal by freeing thyself from the bond of unwisdom.

"Sons and kin can pay a father's debts, but none but a man's self can set him free.

"If a heavy burden presses on the head others can remove it, but none but a man's self can quench his hunger and thirst.

"Health is gained by the sick who follow the path of healing: health does not come through the acts of others.

"The knowledge of the real by the eye of clear insight is to be gained by one's own sight and not by the teacher's.

"The moon's form must be seen by one's own eyes; it can never be known through the eyes of another.

"None but a man's self is able to untie the knots of unwisdom, desire, and former acts, even in a myriad of ages.

"Freedom is won by a perception of the Self's oneness with the Eternal, and not by the doctrines of Union or of Numbers, nor by rites and sciences.

"The form and beauty of the lyre and excellent skill upon its strings may give delight to the people, but will never found an empire.

"An eloquent voice, a stream of words, skill in explaining the teaching, and the learning of the learned; these bring enjoyment but not freedom.

"When the Great Reality is not known the study of the scriptures is fruitless; when the Great Reality is known the study of the scriptures is also fruitless.

"A net of words is a great forest where the fancy wanders; therefore the reality of the Self is to be strenuously learned from the knower of that reality.

"How can the hymns (Vedas) and the scriptures profit him who is bitten by the serpent of unwisdom? How can charms or medicine help him without the medicine of the knowledge of the Eternal?

"Sickness is not cured by saying 'Medicine,' but by drinking it. So a man is not set free by the name of the Eternal without discerning the Eternal.

"Without piercing through the visible, without knowing the reality of the Self, how can men gain Freedom by mere outward words that end with utterances?

"Can a man be king by saying, 'I am king,' without destroying his enemies, without gaining power over the whole land?

"Through information, digging, and casting aside the stones, a treasure may be found, but not by calling it to come forth.

"So by steady effort is gained the knowledge of those who know the Eternal, the lonely, stainless reality above all illusion; but not by desultory study.

"Hence with all earnest effort to be free from the bondage of the world, the wise must strive themselves, as they would to be free from sickness.

"And this question put by thee to-day must be solved by those who seek Freedom; this question that breathes the spirit of the teaching, that is like a clue with hidden meaning.

"Hear, then, earnestly, thou wise one, the answer given by me; for understanding it thou shalt be free from the bondage of the world."

Self, Potencies, Vestures

The first cause of Freedom is declared to be an utter turning back from lust after unenduring things. Thereafter Restfulness, Control, Endurance; a perfect Renouncing of all acts that cling and stain.

Thereafter, the divine Word, a turning of the mind to it, a constant thinking on it by the pure one, long and uninterrupted.

Then ridding himself altogether of doubt, and reaching wisdom, even here he enjoys the bliss of Nirvana.

Then the discerning between Self and not-Self that you must now awaken to, that I now declare, hearing it, lay hold on it within yourself.

The Vestures
(Verses 72–107)

Formed of the substances they call marrow, bone, fat, flesh, blood, skin and over-skin; fitted with greater and lesser limbs, feet, breast, trunk, arms, back, head; this is called the physical vesture by the wise—the vesture whose authority, as "I" and "my" is declared to be a delusion.

The body, powers, life-breaths, mind, self-assertion, all changes, sensuous things, happiness, unhappiness, the ether and all the elements, the whole world up to the unmanifest—this is not Self.

Glamor and every work of glamor from the world-soul to the body, know this as unreal, as not the Self, built up of the mirage of the desert.

But I shall declare to you the own being of the Self supreme, knowing which a man, freed from his bonds, reaches the lonely purity.

There is a certain selfhood wherein the sense of "I" forever rests; who witnesses the three modes of being, who is other than the five veils; who is the only knower in waking, dreaming, dreamlessness; of all the activities of the knowing soul, whether good or bad—this is the "I";

Who of himself beholds all; whom none beholds; who kindles to consciousness the knowing soul and all the powers; whom none kindles to consciousness; by whom all this is filled; whom no other fills; who is the shining light within this all; after whose shining all else shines;

By whose nearness only body and powers and mind and soul do their work each in his own field, as though sent by the Self;

Because the own nature of this is eternal wakefulness, self-assertion, the body and all the powers, and happiness and unhappiness are beheld by it, just as an earthen pot is beheld. This inner Self, the ancient Spirit, is everlasting, partless, immediately experienced happiness; ever of one nature, pure waking knowledge, sent forth by whom Voice and the life-breaths move.

Here, verily, in the substantial Self, in the hidden place of the soul, this steady shining begins to shine like the dawn; then the shining shines forth as the noonday sun, making all this world to shine by its inherent light; knower of all the changing moods of mind and inward powers; of all the acts done by body, powers, life-breaths; present in them as fire in iron, strives not nor changes at all.

This is not born nor dies nor grows, nor does it fade or change forever; even when this form has melted away, it no more melts than the air in a jar.

Alike stranger to forming and deforming; of its own being, pure wakefulness; both being and non-being is this, besides it there is nothing else; this shines unchanging, this Supreme Self gleams in waking, dream and dreamlessness as "I," present as the witness of the knowing soul.

Bondage and Freedom

(Verses 136–153)

Then, holding firmly mind, with knowing soul at rest, know your self within yourself face to face saying, "This am I." The life-ocean, whose waves are birth and dying, is shoreless; cross over it, fulfilling the end of being, resting firm in the Eternal.

Thinking things not self are "I"—this is bondage for a man; this, arising from unwisdom, is the cause of falling into the weariness of birth and dying; this is the cause that he feeds and anoints and guards this form, thinking it the Self; the unreal, real; wrapping himself in sensuous things as a silk-worm in his own threads.

The thought that what is not That is That grows up in the fool through darkness; because no discernment is there, it wells up, as the thought that a rope is a snake; thereupon a mighty multitude of fatuities fall on him who accepts this error, for he who grasps the unreal is bound; mark this, my companion.

By the power of wakefulness, partless, external, secondless, the Self wells up with its endless lordship; but this enveloping power wraps it round, born of Darkness, as the dragon of eclipse envelops the rayed sun.

When the real Self with its stainless light recedes, a man thinking "this body is I," calls it the Self; then by lust and hate and all the potencies of bondage, the great power of Force that they call extension greatly afflicts him.

Torn by the gnawing of the toothed beast of great delusion; wandered from the Self, accepting every changing mood of mind as himself, through this potency, in the shoreless ocean of birth and death, full of the poison of sensuous things, sinking and rising, he wanders, mean-minded, despicable-minded.

As a line of clouds, born of the sun's strong shining, expands before the sun and hides it from sight, so self-assertion, that has come into being through the Self, expands before the Self and hides it from sight. As when on an evil day the lord of day is swallowed up in thick, dark clouds, an ice-cold hurricane of wind, very terrible, afflicts the clouds in turns; so when the Self is enveloped in impenetrable Darkness, the keen power of extension drives with many afflictions the man whose soul is deluded.

From those two powers a man's bondage comes; deluded by them he errs, thinking the body is the Self.

Of the plant of birth and death, the seed is Darkness, the sprout is the thought that body is Self, the shoot is rage, the sap is deeds, the body is the stem, the life-breaths are the branches, the tops are the bodily powers, sensuous things are the flowers, sorrow is the fruit, born of varied deeds and manifold; and the Life is the bird that eats the fruit.

This bondage to what is not Self, rooted in unwisdom, innate, made manifest without beginning or end, gives life to the falling torrent of sorrow, of birth and death, of sickness and old age.

Not by weapons nor arms, not by storm nor fire nor by a myriad deeds can this be cut off, without the sword of discernment and knowledge, very sharp and bright, through the grace of the guiding power.

He who is single-minded, fixed on the word divine, his steadfast fulfilment of duty will make the knowing soul within him pure; to him whose knowing soul is pure, a knowing of the Self supreme shall come; and through this knowledge of the Self supreme he shall destroy this circle of birth and death and its root together.

The Freeing of the Self
(Verses 148–154)

The Self, wrapped up in the five vestures beginning with the vesture formed of food, which are brought into being by its own power, does not shine forth, as the water in the pond, covered by a veil of green scum.

When the green scum is taken away, immediately the water shines forth pure, taking away thirst and heat, straightway becoming a source of great joy to man.

When the five vestures have been stripped off, the Self shines forth pure, the one essence of eternal bliss, beheld within, supreme, self-luminous.

Discernment is to be made between the Self and what is not Self by the wise man seeking freedom from bondage; through this he enters into joy, knowing the Self which is being, consciousness, bliss.

As the reed from the tiger grass, so separating from the congeries of things visible the hidden Self within, which is detached, not involved in actions, and dissolving all in the Self, he who stands thus, has attained liberation.

The Vesture Formed of Mind

(Verses 167–183)

The mind-formed vesture is formed of the powers of perception and the mind; it is the cause of the distinction between the notions of "mine" and "I"; it is active in making a distinction of names and numbers; as more potent, it pervades and dominates the former vesture.

The fire of the mind-formed vesture, fed by the five powers of perception, as though by five sacrificial priests, with objects of sense like streams of melted butter, blazing with the fuel of manifold sense-impressions, sets the personality aflame.

For there is no unwisdom, except in the mind, for the mind is unwisdom, the cause of the bondage to life; when this is destroyed, all is destroyed; when this dominates, the world dominates.

In dream, devoid of substance, it emanates a world of experiencer and things experienced, which is all mind; so in waking consciousness, there is no difference; it is all the domination of the mind.

During the time of dreamlessness, when mind has become latent, nothing at all of manifestation remains; therefore man's circle of birth and death is built by mind, and has no permanent reality.

By the wind a cloud is collected, by the wind it is driven away again; by mind bondage is built up, by mind is built also liberation.

Building up desire for the body and all objects, it binds the man thereby as an ox by a cord; afterwards leading him to turn from them like poison, that same mind, verily, sets him free from bondage.

Therefore mind is the cause of man's bondage, and in turn of his liberation; when darkened by the powers of passion it is the cause of bondage, and when pure of passion and darkness it is the cause of liberation.

Where discernment and dispassion are dominant, gaining purity, the mind makes for liberation; therefore let the wise man who seeks liberation strengthen these two in himself as the first step.

Mind is the name of the mighty tiger that hunts in the forest glades of sensuous things; let not the wise go thither, who seek liberation.

Mind moulds all sensuous things through the earthly body and the subtle body of him who experiences; mind ceaselessly shapes the differences of body, of color, of condition, of race, as fruits caused by the acts of the potencies.

Mind, beclouding the detached, pure consciousness, binding it with the cords of the body, the powers, the life-breaths, as "I" and "my," ceaselessly strays among the fruits of experience caused by its own activities.

Man's circle of birth anl death comes through the fault of attributing reality to the unreal, but this false attribution is built up by mind; this is the effective cause of birth and death and sorrow for him who has the faults of passion and darkness and is without discernment.

Therefore the wise who know the truth have declared that mind is unwisdom, through which the whole world, verily, is swept about, as cloud belts by the wind.

Therefore purification of the mind should be undertaken with strong effort by him who seeks liberation; when the mind has been purified, liberation comes like fruit into his hand.

Through the sole power of liberation uprooting desire for sensuous things, and ridding himself of all bondage to works, he who through faith in the Real stands firm in the teaching, shakes off the very essence of passion from the understanding.

The mind-formed vesture cannot be the higher Self, since it has beginning and end, waxing and waning; by causing sensuous things, it is the very essence of pain; that which is itself seen cannot be the Seer.

The Vesture Formed of Intelligence

(Verses 184–197)

The intelligence, together with the powers of intelligence, makes the intelligence-formed vesture, whose distinguishing character is actorship; it is the cause of man's circle of birth and death.

The power which is a reflected beam of pure Consciousness, called the understanding, is a mode of abstract Nature; it possesses wisdom and creative power; it thereby focuses the idea of "I" in the body and its powers.

This "I," beginningless in time, is the separate self, it is the initiator of all undertakings; this, impelled by previous imprints, works all works both holy and unholy, and forms their fruits.

Passing through varying births it gains experience, now descending, now ascending; of this intelligence-formed vesture, waking, dream and dreamlessness are the fields where it experiences pleasure and pain.

By constantly attributing to itself the body, state, condition, duties and works, thinking, "These are mine," this intelligence-formed vesture, brightly shining because it stands closest to the higher Self, becomes the vesture of the Self, and, thinking itself to be the Self; wanders in the circle of birth and death.

This, formed of intelligence, is the light that shines in the vital breaths, in the heart; the Self who stands forever wears this vesture as actor and experiencer.

The Self, assuming the limitation of the intelligence, self-deluded by the error of the intelligence, though it is the universal Self, yet views itself as separate from the Self; as the potter views the jars as separate from the clay.

Through the force of its union with the vesture, the higher Self takes on the character of the vesture and assumes its nature, as fire, which is without form, takes on the varying forms of the iron, even though the Self is for ever by nature uniform and supreme.

THE DISCIPLE SPEAKS

Whether by delusion or otherwise, the higher Self appears as the separate self; but, since the vesture is beginningless, there is no conceivable end of the beginningless.

Therefore existence as the separate self must be eternal, nor can the circle of birth and death have an end; how then can there be liberation? Master, tell me this.

THE MASTER ANSWERS

Well hast thou asked, O wise one! Therefore rightly hear! A false imagination created by error is not conclusive proof.

Only through delusion can there be an association with objects, of that which is without attachment, without action, without form; it is like the association of blueness with the sky.

The appearance as the separate self, of the Self, the Seer, who is without qualities, without form; essential wisdom and bliss, arises through the delusion of the understanding; it is not real; when the delusion passes, it exists no longer, having no substantial reality.

Its existence, which is brought into being through false perception, because of delusion, lasts only so long as the error lasts; as the serpent in the rope endures only as long as the delusion; when the delusion ceases, there is no serpent.

The Witness

That Thou Art

(Verses 241–251)

The Eternal and the Self, indicated by the two words "that" and "thou," when clearly understood, according to the Scripture "THAT THOU ART," are one; their oneness is again ascertained.

This identity of theirs is in their essential, not their verbal meanings, for they are *apparently* of contradictory character; like the firefly and the sun, the sovereign and the serf, the well and the great waters, the atom and Mount Meru.

The contradiction between them is built up by their disguises, but this disguise is no real thing at all; the disguise of the Master Self is the world-glamor, the cause of the Celestial and other worlds; the disguise of the *individual* life is the group of five veils—hear this now:

These are the two disguises, of the Supreme and the *individual* life; when they are set aside together, there is no longer the Supreme nor the *individual* life. The king has his kingdom, the warrior his weapons; when these are put away, there is neither warrior nor king.

According to the Scripture saying, "this is the instruction, *the Self is not that, not that*," the twofoldness that was built up sinks away of itself in the Eternal; let the truth of this scripture be grasped through awakening; the putting away of the two disguises must verily be accomplished.

It is not this, it is not this: because this is built up, it is not the real—like the serpent seen in the rope, or like a dream; thus putting away every visible thing by wise meditation, the oneness of the two—*Self and Eternal*—is then to be known.

Therefore the two are to be well observed in their essential unity. Neither their contradictory character nor their non-contradictory character is all; but the real and essential Being is to be reached, in order to gain the essence in which they are one and undivided.

When one says: "This man is Devadatta," the oneness is here stated by rejecting contradictory qualities. With the great word "THAT THOU ART," it is the same; what is contradictory between the two is set aside.

As being essentially pure consciousness, the oneness between the Real and the Self is known by the awakened; and by hundreds of great texts the oneness, the absence of separateness, between the Eternal and the Self is declared.

That is not the physical; it is the perfect, after the unreal is put aside; like the ether, not to be handled by thought. Hence this matter that is perceived is illusive, therefore set it aside; but what is grasped by its own selfhood—"that I am the Eternal"—know that with intelligence purified; know the Self as partless awakening.

Every pot and vessel has always clay as its cause, and its material is clay; just like this, this world is engendered by the Real, and has the Real as its Self, the Real is its material altogether. That Real than which there is none higher, THAT THOU ART, the restful, the stainless, secondless Eternal, the supreme.

The Manifest and the Hidden Self

(Verses 252–268.)

As dream-built lands and times, objects and knowers of them, are all unreal, just so here in waking is this world; its cause is ignorance of the Self; in as much as all this world, body and organs, vital breath and personality are all unreal, in so much THOU ART THAT, the restful, the stainless, secondless Eternal, the supreme.

Far away from birth and conduct, family and tribe, quite free from name and form and quality and fault; beyond space and time and objects—this is the Eternal, THAT THOU ART; become it in the Self.

The supreme, that no word can reach, but that is reached by the eye of awakening, pure of stain, the pure reality of consciousness and mind together—this is the Eternal, THAT THOU ART; become it in the Self.

Untouched by the six infirmities, reached in the heart of those that seek for union, reached not by the organs, whose being neither intellect nor reason knows—this is the Eternal, THAT THOU ART; become it in the Self.

Built of error is the world; in That it rests; That rests in itself, different from the existent and the non-existent; partless, nor bound by causality, is the Eternal, THAT THOU ART; become it in the Self.

Birth and growth, decline and loss, sickness and death it is free from, and unfading; the cause of emanation, preservation, destruction, is the Eternal, THAT THOU ART; become it in the Self.

Where all difference is cast aside, all distinction is cast away, a waveless ocean, motionless; ever free, with undivided form—this is the Eternal, THAT THOU ART; become it in the Self.

Being one, though cause of many, the cause of others, with no cause itself; where cause and caused are merged in one, self-being, the Eternal, THAT THOU ART; become it in the Self.

Free from doubt and change, great, unchanging; where changing and unchanging are merged in one Supreme; eternal, unfading joy, unstained—this is the Eternal, THAT THOU ART; become it in the Self.

This shines forth manifold through error, through being the Self under name and form and quality and change; like gold itself unchanging ever—this is the Eternal, THAT THOU ART; become it in the Self.

This shines out unchanging, higher than the highest, the hidden one essence, whose character is selfhood, reality, consciousness, joy, endless unfading—this is the Eternal, THAT THOU ART; become it in the Self.

Let a man make it his own in the Self—like a word that is spoken, by reasoning from the known, by thought; this is as devoid of doubt as water in the hand, so certain will its reality become.

Recognizing this perfectly illumined one, whose reality is altogether pure, as *one recognizes* the leader of men in the assembled army, and resting on that always, standing firm in one's own Self, sink all this world that is born, into the Eternal.

In the soul, in the hidden place, marked neither as what is nor what is not, is the Eternal, true, supreme, secondless. He who through the Self dwells here in the secret place, for him there is no coming forth again to the world of form.

When the thing is well known even, this beginningless mode of thought, "I am the doer and the enjoyer," is very powerful; this mode of mind lasting strongly, is the cause of birth and rebirth. A looking backward toward the Self, a dwelling on it, is to be effortfully gained; freedom here on earth, say the saints, is the thinning away of that mode of thought.

That thought of "I" and "mine" in the flesh, the eye and the rest, that are not the Self—this transference *from the real to the unreal* is to be cast away by the wise man by steadfastness in his own Self.

Finding the Real Self

Selfhood Transferred to Things not Self

(Verses 277–298)

By resting ever in the Self, the restless mind of him who
seeks union is stilled, and all imaginings fade away; therefore
make an end of transferring Selfhood to things not Self.

Darkness is put away through force and substantial being;
force, through substantial being; in the pure, substantial being is
not put away; therefore, relying on substantial being, make an
end of transferring Selfhood to things not Self.

The body of desire is nourished by all new works begun;
steadily thinking on this, and effortfully holding desire firm,
make an end of transferring selfhood to things not Self.

Thinking: "I am not this separate life but the supreme Eternal," beginning by rejecting all but this, make an end of transferring selfhood to things not Self; it comes from the swift
impetus of imaginings.

Understanding the all-selfhood of the Self, by learning, seeking union, entering the Self; it comes from the Self's reflected
light in other things.

Neither in taking nor giving does the sage act at all; therefore
by ever resting on the One, make an end of transferring selfhood
to things not Self.

Through sentences like "That thou art" awaking to the
oneness of the Eternal and the Self, to confirm the Self in the
Eternal, make an end of transferring selfhood to things not Self.

While there yet lingers a residue undissolved of the thought
that this body is the Self, carefully seeking union with the Self,
make an end of transferring selfhood to things not Self.

As long as the thought of separate life and the world shines,
dreamlike even, so long incessantly, O wise one, make an end of
transferring selfhood to things not Self.

The body of desire, born of father and mother of impure elements, made up of fleshly things impure, is to be abandoned as
one abandons an impure man afar; gain thy end by becoming
the Eternal.

The Real in Things Unreal

As the space in a jar in universal space, so the Self is to be merged without division in the Self supreme; rest thou ever thus, O sage.

Through the separate self gaining the Self, self-shining as a resting-place, let all outward things from a world-system to a lump of clay be abandoned, like a vessel of impure water.

Raising the thought of "I" from the body to the Self that is Consciousness, Being, Bliss, and lodging it there, leave form, and become pure for ever.

Knowing that "I am that Eternal" wherein this world is reflected, like a city in a mirror, thou shalt perfectly gain thy end.

What is of real nature, self-formed, original consciousness, secondless bliss, formless, actless—entering that, let a man put off this false body of desires, worn by the Self as a player puts on a costume.

For the Self, all that is seen is but mirage; it lasts but for a moment, we see, and know it is not "I"; how could "I know all" be said of the personal self that changes every moment?

The real "I" is witness of the personal self and its powers; as its being is perceived always, even in dreamless sleep. The scripture says the Self is unborn, everlasting; this is the hidden Self, distinguished neither as what exists nor what has no existence.

The beholder of every change in things that change, can be the unchanging alone; in the mind's desires, in dreams, in dreamless sleep the insubstantial nature of things that change is clearly perceived again and again.

Therefore put away the false selfhood of this fleshly body, for the false selfhood of the body is built up by thought: knowing the Self as thine own, unhurt by the three times, undivided illumination, enter into peace.

The Power of Mind-Images

Consciousness, eternal, non-dual, partless, uniform, witness of intellect and the rest, different from existent and non-existent; its real meaning is the idea of "I"; a union of being and bliss—this is the higher Self.

He who thus understands, discerning the real from the unreal, ascertaining reality by his own awakened vision, knowing his own Self as partless awakening, freed from these things reaches peace in the Self.

Then melts the heart's knot of unwisdom without residue,

when, through the ecstasy in which there is no doubt, arises the vision of the non-dual Self.

Through the mind's fault are built the thoughts of thou and I and this, in the supreme Self which is non-dual, and beyond which there is nothing; but when ecstasy is reached, all his doubts melt away through apprehension of the real.

Peaceful, controlled, possessing the supreme cessation, perfection in endurance, entering into lasting ecstasy, the ascetic makes the being of the All-self his own; thereby burning up perfectly the doubts that are born of the darkness of unwisdom, he dwells in bliss in the form of the Eternal, without deed or doubt.

They who rest on the Self that is consciousness, who have put away the outward, the imaginations of the ear and senses, and selfish personality, they, verily, are free from the bonds and snares of the world, but not they who only meditate on what others have seen.

The Self is divided by the division of its disguises; when the disguises are removed, the Self is lonely and pure; hence let the wise man work for the removal of the disguises by resting in the ecstasy that is free from doubt.

Attracted by the Self the man goes to the being of the Self by resting on it alone; the grub, thinking on the bee, builds up the nature of the bee.

The grub, throwing off attachment to other forms, and thinking intently on the bee, takes on the nature of the bee; even thus he who seeks for union, thinking intently on the reality of the supreme Self, perfectly enters that Self, resting on it alone.

Very subtle, as it were, is the reality of the supreme Self, nor can it be reached by gross vision; by the exceedingly subtle state of ecstasy it is to be known by those who are worthy, whose minds are altogether pure.

As gold purified in the furnace, rids itself of dross and reaches the quality of its own self, so the mind ridding itself of the dross of substance, force and darkness, through meditation, enters into reality.

When purified by the power of uninterrupted intentness, the mind is thus melted in the Eternal, then ecstasy is purified of all doubt, and of itself enjoys the essence of secondless bliss.

Through this ecstasy comes destruction of the knot of accumulated mind-images, destruction of all works; within and without, for ever and altogether, the form of the Self becomes manifest, without any effort at all.

Let him know that thinking is a hundred times better than scripture; that concentration, thinking the matter out, is a

hundred thousand times better than thinking; that ecstasy free
from doubt is endlessly better than concentration.

Through unwavering ecstasy is clearly understood the reality
of the Eternal, fixed and sure. This cannot be when other
thoughts are confused with it, by the motions of the mind.

Therefore with powers of sense controlled enter in ecstasy
into the hidden Self, with mind at peace perpetually; destroy
the darkness made by beginningless unwisdom, through the clear
view of the oneness of the real.

The first door of union is the checking of voice, the cessation
of grasping, freedom from expectation and longing, the character
bent ever on the one end.

A centering of the mind on the one end, is the cause of the
cessation of sensuality; control is the cause that puts an end to
imaginings; by peace, the mind-image of the personality is
melted away; from this arises unshaken enjoyment of the
essence of bliss in the Eternal for ever, for him who seeks
union; therefore the checking of the imagination is ever to be
practiced effortfully, O ascetic!

Hold voice in the self, hold the self in intellect, hold intellect
in the witness of intellect, and, merging the witness in the perfect Self, enjoy supreme peace.

The seeker for union shares the nature of each disguise—body,
vital breath, sense, mind, intellect—when his thoughts are fixed
on that disguise.

When he ceases from this sharing, the ascetic reaches perfect
cessation and happiness, and is plunged in the essence of Being
and Bliss.

Renouncing inwardly, renouncing outwardly—this is possible
only for him who is free from passion; and he who is free from
passion renounces all attachment within and without, through
the longing for freedom.

Outward attachment arises through sensual objects; inward
attachment, through personality. Only he who, resting in the
Eternal, is free from passion, is able to give them up. Freedom
from passion and awakening are the wings of the spirit. O wise
man, understand these two wings! For without them you cannot
rise to the crown of the tree of life.

Soul-vision belongs to him who is free from passion; steady
inspiration belongs to the soul-seer. Freedom from bondage belongs to the reality of inspiration; enjoyment of perpetual bliss
belongs to the Self that is free.

I see no engenderer of happiness greater than freedom from
passion for him who is self-controlled; if very pure inspiration
of the Self be joined to it, he enters into the sovereignty of
self-dominion. This is the door of young freedom everlasting.

There do thou ever fix they consciousness on the real self, in all ways free from attachment to what is other than this, for the sake of the better way.

Cut off all hope in sensual objects which are like poison, the cause of death; abandon all fancies of birth and family and social state; put all ritual actions far away; renounce the illusion of self-dwelling in the body, center the consciousness on the Self. Thou art the seer, thou art the stainless, thou art in truth the supreme, secondless Eternal.

Firmly fixing the mind on the goal, the Eternal, keeping the outward senses in their own place, with form unmoved, heedless of the body's state, entering into the oneness of Self and Eternal by assimilating the Self and rising above all differences, for ever drink the essence of the bliss of the Eternal in the Self. What profit is there in other things that give no joy?

7. Selections from the Sacred Hymns of the Saivites

Sundarar (Ninth Century)

Hymn 84

"They are learned masters of all that speak of His feet and they experience this truth." "They contemplate your greatness and their hearts melt in love. They become one with you and there arises a voice within—the creative impulse trying to give expression to their mystic union." "They sing. They are not different from you; they are but yourself. Realizing this, when am I to become one with them, big with love to worship you lovingly with grand flowers in my hand so that my miseries (or, the sufferings of my eye in which case he could not have been cured completely of his eye defect) may disappear?"

"He is the great Supreme—Patron, giving me all that is good, even as a thing and a wealth possessed wholly by me. He is Siva, the great significance, vivifying the words pronounced by those who realize Him as the Highest sphere and the Best ideal.

He is the sweet nectar—inside the honey, nay, its clear quintessence. He is the full moon in the skies; the blotless light and also the storm, the water and this earth (sphere); when am I to reach Him as the Great Dancer?"

"The important characteristic features of His are the image form (bhavakam) contemplated by His devotees and servants those who as devoid of all their defects, their path (neri) and their unique musical compositions they recite (icaipparicu). When am I to worship with my heart and praise His holy marks with the help of all that I had studied for fame?" "The devotees stand around Him, playing on the musical drum 'kallavatam' in accompaniment to His dance with which everything in Him and around Him keep time."

"The songs full of the best effects of music and tune—their continuous outpour—the love of the damsels beautiful and bright like the Goddess of Lotus, the great longing of those who wake up exclaiming that He is the first and the greatest Lord who thinks of His devotees only after conferring salvation and freedom on them—these are important marks of His identity. I stand by the side of these, mixed up with them, pining for a way of reaching Him and becoming one with my father and sovereign. He counts even me as of worth and showers His blessing on me so as to save me. When am I to see this Lord of the eye on the forehead (He is indeed the Lord of the eye; for has He not seen the poet) the sweetest fruit?"

"He does not come near the heart of those of deceitful minds. He is the primaeval, first mould and seed of all. He is the nectar unto those who are attached to truth, without any pretensions and who embrace Him with their whole body (and soul), He is the Great Beyond relishing their five (pancagavya) beginning with milk, ghee and curd. When am I to sing of Him as the sovereign protecting me?"

"He is the flame and light, so easy of approach to His servants. He is the rule or order or dharma, the meaning and significance of the holy pure Vedas. He is the eternal One escaping even the poison of the seas. He is the Universe. He is its Beginning and its Chief giving out to the Lords of the Universe the Agamas or the Scriptures. He is the greatest mystic wisdom of great fame. When am I to go and reach Him with all love?"

"He is the Lord. He is the great sound evolved out of Nada. He is the life in this body of flesh, in the form of the brightness of the lamp or jnana or wisdom. He is the green corns, which

feed the lives. He is Beauty. He never leaves even for a while
His attachment to the minds of those great beloved devotees of
His. His ideal followers are blotless. He is the envoy and messenger. He is the bosom companion saving me. He is my Lord
(who listens with His ears, all my requests). When am I His
dog of a slave, to reach Him? He is the sugar candy, the
sweet nectar, the youth of Kanapper."

Hymn 48

"I had no other attachment. I contemplated on your Sacred
feet alone. It was when I attained this escape from the Hiding
Power (Na), I was really born,—till then I was a dead thing,
identified with dead matter (Ma). I reached further the stage of
not dying any more—no sliding back into the malas. Even if I
forget, my tongue will utter this truth 'Namasivaya'."[1]

"I am your lover. I never consider those days when I slight
those who worship your feet (or when I am slighted by them)
except, as days of oblivion and days of destruction. Even if I
forget, my tongue will give expression to the mantra Namasivaya."

"I never consider those days of separation—the days when I
cease thinking of you—except as days of failing consciousness, as
days of departing life and as days of balancing on the funeral
pyre. Even if I forget, my tongue will give expression to the
mantra Namasivaya."

"I, your slave, also was in great fright—overpowered by the
delusion and misery of the world—I cried to you in the hope that
the Beginning of everything is the Fortress for the Frightened.
You have blessed me with your Grace, consonng and encouraging me with the words, 'Fear Not.' Is there now anything of
yours that will be wasted because of this mercy shown? (Why

[1]The sacred mantra of the Saivites is the Pancaksara; the five letters "na,
ma, si, va, ya." The general meaning of these letters when they form a word
is "worship unto Siva," and carries the implication of self-surrender—"I am
not mine but Siva's." Na here stands for the power of the Lord which hides
truth from us till the soul reaches a point of perfection enabling it to perceive Truth. Ma represents Mala or ignorance taking the form of matter,
evil. Si stands for the Absolute, Va for God's Grace, and Ya for the human
soul. The soul escapes Mala or evil by taking refuge in the Grace of the Lord
(Grace being symbolized by the Lord's feet). At one point the soul loses
itself in communion with God, and the distinction between Grace and the
Absolute it expresses disappears. The experience of the Absolute alone remains. This is the experience of Pancaksara described in this hymn. For
further details see M.A.D. Rangaswamy, *The Religion and Philosophy of
Tevaram* (Madras: University of Madras Press, 1959), vol. 3, pp. 661ff.

then do you not continue encouraging me)? Even if I forget, my
tongue will give expression to the mantra Namasivaya."

Hymn 14

"I do not experience the firmly established truth of the Lord
except when I embrace Him.[2] Therefore, I thought, it was
enough if my mind was always contemplating on Him in mental
embrace. He is the Lord who destroys the obstructions and the
three malas as the three castles of the air, swallowing poison to
save His followers. In spite of whatever we may say in extenua-
tion or otherwise, if He is happy when He gains us and is sulky
when He is not so profited. Is there no other Lord but He?"

"The Lord does not speak out, his tongue does not utter
words like these—"these are our men: those are others; this is
good: that is bad', for He makes no such distinction. There is
no external show of his love. He accepts many a people as their
Lord for saving them all but there is not a word of sympathy.
He gives not a single thing. Is there no Lord but He?"

"O, my mind! you melt in love, run in joy and embrace Him
to perform daily the services however menial they be. He blesses
those who do not waste away all their appointed days and who
before that day comes, invoke Him as 'My Lord' even though
they may be devoid of Love. The great Man of mine. If inspite
of all that we may say, He does not put up with our faults and
give us nothing, is there no Lord but He?"

Hymn 59

"He is the One that gives gold and the true reality (of His
own Absolute). What more, it is He who brings about their enjoyment and experience—the enjoyment of the world and His
Grace or the wealth of salvation. He does not stop with that.
He puts up with my excesses. He orders the removal of all
faults. He is my father impossible to be known specifically. He
is the munificent patron so easy to reach. Is it proper or possible
to forget this Lord of Arur?"

"He is the One who weeds out our sufferings and fetters of
disease. He weeds out the cruel diseases and filthy desires (or
desires left off by great minds). It is impossible to leave such a
one if you had once been in communion with Him. He orders
the prevention of the affliction of the past and future scandals."

[2] Some translate this line to mean "when the miseries batter on me."

"He showers as rain on the cloud-clad mountains. He is the significance of all arts and yet becomes one with the soul enjoying the arts, at the same time feeling sympathy for it. He stands as day and night—(as the time frame of art). He is the organs of senses—(the instruments of enjoyment). He is the ear that listens through, the sound to its significance and joy; He is the tongue experiencing the taste. He is the eye that sees. (He is the objects creating the impressions in artists' minds which gives expression to them as art). He is the roaring sea and the mountain."

"He is the greatest. He weeds out our pains. He is the *Vedas.* He is the light for all the living beings of this world, though He is impossible to approach to those who do not think of Him with loving contemplation. He is so easy of reach to me, His slave."

"God's followers worship Him losing themselves in Him and doing nothing of their own but standing in His presence. (Such is their self-surrender.) These get the rulership of the Heavens. To the ears of the people of this world this news reaches. And yet they do not worship Him every day with flowers. Nor do they realize the truth of his saving us. Having heard this, I labour hard to the point of prostration. Thinking that He will be the help and prop to all our relations I call upon many of them to become His servants."

"I nourish and increase my flesh alone. I cannot cross the miseries—inflicting me as a result of the hankerings of many days. Nor, do I see a way out. Alas! I cannot (out of pity) throw anything into the hands of those who beg with sunken eyes."

"He is the flower of my crown; He, after accepting me as His servant under a promise to save, has gone away and hidden Himself. He is the day-light and darkness. He is the honey, springing up in the minds of those contemplating on Him; He is the sugar candy, the strained juice of sugar cane."

"He is the basis of all, fit to be described as the one great city for all the people of the world. He is the real category, the Absolute in communion with everything."

Lal Ded (Lalla) (Fourteenth Century)

An ascetic wandereth from holy place to holy place,
To seek the union brought about by (visiting a god, and yet he
  is but) visiting himself.
O my soul! study thou (the mystery that God is thy Self) and
  be not unbelieving.
The farther thou wilt look (from thy Self), the more green will
  seem the heap of grass.[1]

Holy books will disappear, and then only the mystic formula
  will remain.
When the mystic formula departed, naught but mind was left.
When the mind disappeared naught was left anywhere,
And a void became merged with the Void.[2]

If thou take and rule a kingdom, even then is there no respite.
And if thou give it to another, still in thy heart is no content.
But the soul that is free from desire will never die.
If, while it is yet alive, it die, then that alone is the true knowl-
  edge.[3]

Quietism and self-command are not required for (the knowledge
  of) the Self,
Nor by the mere wish wilt thou reach the door of final release.
E'en though a man become absorbed (in his contemplations) as
  salt is absorbed in water,
Still rarely doth he attain to the discernment of the nature of
  his Self.[4]

[1]Lal Ded means here that the uselessness of seeking God by long pilgrimages
is foolish because He is really the Self of the seeker. The further a man's
thoughts wander from the consideration of the Supreme and the Self, the
more tempting will these worldly pursuits appear.

[2]This is a typical Lal Ded verse, highly symbolic and ardent for the vastness
of her vision. The void is the apparent material world, which is really empty
nothingness, and when final release is attained its apparent existence disappears in the Great Transcendental Void.

[3]This hymn is in praise of freedom from desire, another popular Lal Ded
theme. Freedom from desire alone brings content. A man cannot grasp the
true knowledge till he understands that he should be as one dead, even while
still alive—that is, dead by being free from all desire.

[4]Extraordinary desire, or even ardent asceticism, are common, but without the
knowledge of the true nature of the Self, they are of no avail for achieving
ultimate release.

Slay thou desire; meditate thou on the nature of the Self.

Abandon thou thy vain imaginings; for know thou that that knowledge is rare and of great price.

Yet is it near by thee; search for it not afar.

(It is naught but a void); and a void has become merged within the Void.

God of the dark blue throat! As Thou hast the six, so the same six have I.

And yet, estranged from Thee, into misery have I fallen.

Only this discord was there, that, though betwixt Thee and me there was no difference,

Thou wast the Lord of six, while I by six was led astray.[5]

He who rightly inhaleth his vital airs, and bringeth them under the bridle,

Him, verily, nor hunger nor thirst will touch.

He who is skilled in doing this unto the end,

Fortunate in this universe will he be born.[6]

Give the heart to the bellows, like as the blacksmith gives breath to the bellows,

And your iron will become gold. Now it is early morning, seek out your friend (i.e. God).

(A man) will not find a shore to the sea, neither is there a bridge over it, nor any other means of crossing.

Make to yourself wings and fly. Now it is early morning, seek out your friend.

O negligent man, speedily step out, take care, and leave off wickedness.

If you will not, then you are a fool. Now while it is early morning, seek out your friend.

Don but such apparel as will cause the cold to flee.

Eat but so much food as will cause hunger to cease.

[5]Siva was believed to have a dark-blue throat. In Hindu legend the gods extracted immortality-giving nectar from the ocean. The first potion to rise from the churning ocean was the deadly Kalakuta poison, which Siva immediately swallowed to prevent its doing any harm. The poison dyed his neck dark blue. In Hindu philosophy there are numerous groupings of six. The Supreme Deity has six attributes: omniscience, contentment, knowledge of the past from eternity, absolute self-sufficiency, irreducible potency, and omnipotence. Lalla here exclaims that since she became as one with Him, she also had these six, although she was not in control of them as was the Supreme, and she was misled by another six. The "other six" could mean a variety of byways. They may be the six enemies, such as sexual desire, wrath, desire, arrogance, delusion, and jealousy; or they may be the six human infirmities, or the six periods of the human life, etc.

[6]Puruka, or inhalation of the breath, is one of the methods used to restrain the vital airs and encompass the pranayama, or vital energy. It is a necessary process for obtaining the complete yoga, or union with the Supreme.

O Mind! devote thyself to discernment of the Self and of the Supreme,
And recognize thy body as but food for forest crows.

A royal chowry, sunshade, chariot, throne,
Happy revels, the pleasures of the theatre, a bed of cotton down,—
Bethink thee which of these is lasting in this world,
And how can it take from thee the fear of death.
In thy illusion why didst thou sink in the stream of the ocean of existence?
When thou hadst destroyed the high-banked road, there came before thee the slough of spiritual darkness.
At the appointed time will Yama's apparitors drag thee off in woeful plight.
Who can take from thee the fear of death?
Works two are there, and causes three. On them practise thou the kumbhaka-yoga.
Then, in another world, wilt thou gain the mark of honour.
Arise, mount, pierce through the sun's disk.
Then will flee from thee the fear of death.
Clothe thou thy body in the garb of knowledge.
Brand thou on thy heart the verses that Lalla spake.
With the help of the pranava Lalla absorbed herself
In union with the Soul-light, and so expelled the fear of death.[7]
I came into this universe of birth and rebirth, and through asceticism gained I the self-illuminating light of knowledge.
If any man die, it is naught to me; and if I die it is naught to him.
Good is it if I die, and good is it if I live long.[8]

[7]This verse needs some clarification. The chowry, which is a fly whisk, and the sunshade are both emblems of royalty. The "highbanked road" is the way of truth, by which the Self is able to approach the Supreme Self. "Yama" is the god who rules the land of the dead. His minions carry off the soul after death for judgment by him, and are generally treated very cruelly along the way. "Works" are of two kinds, good and bad. The three causes of the apparent material world (which are technically known as malas or impurities) are: (1) anava-mala, the impurity of the soul deeming itself to be finite; (2) mayiya-mala, the impurity due to thinking or perceiving that one thing is different from another; (3) karma-mala, the producer of pleasure and pain, which results in action. It is the devotee's purpose to destroy the fruits of all works, and thereby destroy these malas. This is done by practicing yoga. And one important form of yoga is the kumbhaka-yoga mentioned, in which the breath is entirely suspended; literally "bottling up the breath." And finally, the pranava is one of the names of the mystic syllable Om.

[8]This last verse is in praise of pefect contentment, for the full realization of life and death, and its place in the scheme of things has been attained. One of the commentators translates this verse as: "As I stand in thy imperishable body, which is composed of the cosmos, and is of the nectar of pure spirit,

1. Put thou thy thoughts upon the path of immortality.
   If thou leave them without guidance, into evil state will
   they fall.
   There, be thou not fearful, but be thou very courageous.
   For they are like unto a suckling child, that tosseth restless
   on its mother's bosom.

2. He who hath deemed another and himself as the same,
   He who hath deemed the day (of joy) and the night (of
   sorrow) to be alike,
   He whose mind hath become free from duality,
   He, and he alone, hath seen the Lord of the chiefest of gods.

3. For a moment saw I a river flowing.
   For a moment saw I no bridge or means of crossing.
   For a moment saw I a bush all flowers.
   For a moment saw I nor rose nor thorn.
   For a moment saw I a cooking hearth ablaze.
   For a moment saw I nor hearth nor smoke.
   For a moment saw I the mother of all the Pandavas.
   For a moment saw I an aunt of a potter's wife.

4. Some, though they be sound asleep, are yet awake;
   On others, though they be awake, hath slumber fallen.
   Some, though they bathe in sacred pools, are yet unclean;
   Others, though they be full of household cares, are yet free
   from action.

5. By a way I came, but I went not by the way.
   While I was yet on the midst of the embankment, with its
   crazy bridges, the day failed for me.
   I looked within my poke and not a cowry was there.
   What shall I give for the ferry fee?

6. O heedless one! speedily lift up thy foot:
   Now it is dawn: seek thou for the Friend.
   Make to thyself wings: lift thou up the winged (feet);
   Now it is dawn: seek thou for the Friend.

7. With a rope of untwisted thread am I towing a boat upon
   the ocean.
   Where will my God hear? Will He carry even me over?
   Like water in goblets of unbaked clay do I slowly waste
   away.
   My soul is in a dizzy whirl. Fain would I reach my home.

---

and as I everlastingly worship the Lord, let me have life or let me have
death for it matters not."

8. Ah, restless mind! have no fear within thy heart.
The Beginningless One Himself taketh thought for thee.
(And considereth) how thy hunger may fall from thee.
Utter, therefore, to Him alone the cry of salvation.

9. I, Lalla, wearied myself seeking for him and searching.
I laboured and strove even beyond my strength.
I began to look for him, and lo, I saw that bolts were on his
   door;
And even in me, as I was, did longing for him become fixed;
And there, where I was, I gazed upon Him.

Sambandar (Seventh Century)

7. He is the pith of holy writ;
   And in the tangle of His hair
The spotless crescent's ray is lit;
   He is both Lord and Lady fair.
He our great sovereign doth abide
   In Kachchi Ehambam's fair town.
My mind can think of naught beside,
   Naught beside Him, and Him alone.

8. All goodness hath He and no shadow of ill.
   Grey-white is His bull, fair Uma shares His form.
His wealth is past searching. Chirapalli's hill
   Is His, whom to praise keeps my heart ever warm.

9. Thou art right and Thou art wrong,
   Lord of holy Alavay;
Kinsman, I to Thee belong;
   Never fades Thy light away.
Thou the sense of books divine,
   Thou my wealth, my bliss art Thou,
Thou my all, and in Thy shrine
   With what praises can I bow?

10. Thou Light whom Brahma, being's fount, and Vishnu could
       not see,
No righteousness have I, I only speak in praise of Thee.
Come, Valivalam's Lord, let no dark fruit of deeds, I pray,
Torment Thy slave who with his song extols Thee day by
   day.

13. Those who repeat it while love's tears outpour,

It gives them life, and guides them in the way.
'Tis the true substance of the Vedas four,
 The Lord's great name, wherefore "Hail Siva," say.

14. For the Father in Arur
 Sprinkle ye the blooms of love;
In your heart will dawn true light,
 Every bondage will remove.

15. Him the holy in Arur
 Ne'er forget to laud and praise;
Bonds of birth will severed be,
 Left behind all worldly ways.

16. In Arur, our loved one's gem,
 Scatter golden blossoms fair.
Sorrow ye shall wipe away,
 Yours be bliss beyond compare.

Tirunavukkarasu Swami (Apparswami)
(Seventh Century)

The Soul's Bitter Cry

29. In right I have no power to live,
 Day after day I'm stained with sin;
I read, but do not understand;
 I hold Thee not my heart within.
O light, O flame, O first of all,
 I wandered far that I might see,
Athihai Virattanam's Lord,
 Thy flower-like feet of purity.

30. Daily I'm sunk in worldly sin;
 Naught know I as I ought to know;
Absorbed in vice as 'twere my kin,
 I see no path in which to go.
O Thou with throat one darkling gem,
 Gracious, such grace to me accord,
That I may see Thy beauteous feet,
 Athihai Virattanam's Lord.

31. My fickle heart one love forsakes,
    And forthwith to some other clings;
Swiftly to some one thing it sways,
    And e'en swiftly backward swings.
O Thou with crescent in Thy hair,
    Athihai Virattanam's Lord,
Fixed at Thy feet henceforth I lie,
    For Thou hast broken my soul's cord.

32. The bond of lust I cannot break;
    Desire's fierce torture will not die;
My soul I cannot stab awake
    To scan my flesh with seeing eye.
I bear upon me load of deeds,
    Load such as I can ne'er lay down.
Athihai Virattanam's Lord,
    Weary of joyless life I've grown.

33. While violence is in my heart,
    Care of my body cage is vain.
My spoon no handle hath when I
    Thy honey's grace to drink am fain.
As in the serpent's mouth the frog,
    Caught in life's terrors, wild I rave.
Thou, King of holy Ottiyur,
    Wilt Thou not care for me and save?

34. When on life's angry waves I launch,
    My heart's the raft I take to me,
My mind's the pole I lean upon,
    Vexation's freight I bear to sea.
I strike upon the rock of lust!
    O then, though witless quite I be,
Grant, King of holy Ottiyur,
    Such wisdom that I think of Thee.

35. Evil, all evil, my race, evil my qualities all,
    Great am I only in sin, evil is even my good.
Evil my innermost self, foolish, avoiding the pure,
    Beast am I not, yet the ways of the beast I can never for-
        sake.
I can exhort with strong words, telling men what they should
        hate,
Yet can I never give gifts, only to beg them I know.
Ah! wretched man that I am, whereunto came I to birth?

36. The moving water He made stand unmoving in His hair;

And He my thoughtless heart hath fixed in thought of Him
    alone;
He taught me that which none can learn, what none can see
    laid bare;
What tongue tells not He told; me He pursued and made
    His own.
    The spotless pure, the holy One, my fell disease He
      healed,
    And in Punturutti to me, e'en me, Himself revealed.

37. O wealth, my treasure, sweetness, lustre fair of heavenly
    hosts,
    Of lustre glory that excels, embodied One, my kin,
My flesh, yea heart within my flesh, image within my heart,
    My all-bestowing tree, my eye, pupil my eye within,
Picture seen in that pupil, lord of Aduturai cool,
    Immortals' king, keep far from me strong pain of fruits
      of sin.

38. Thou to me art parents, Lord,
    Thou all kinsmen that I need,
Thou to me art loved ones fair,
    Thou art treasure rich indeed.
Family, friends, home art Thou,
    Life and joy I draw from Thee,
False world's good by Thee I leave,
    Gold, pearl, wealth art Thou to me.

39. As the vina's pure sound, as the moonlight at even,
    As the south wind's soft breath, as the spring's growing
      heat,
As the pool hovered over by whispering bees,
    So sweet is the shade at our Father-Lord's feet.

45. Ears of mine, hear His praise,
    Siva, our flaming king.
Flaming as coral red His form:
    Ears, hear men praises sing.

46. What kinsmen in that hour
    When life departs, have we?
Who but Kuttalam's dancing lord
    Can then our kinsman be?

47. How proud shall I be there,
    One of His heavenly host,

At His fair feet who holds the deer,
How proud will be my boast!

48. I sought Him and I found.
Brahm sought in vain on high.
Vishnu delved vainly underground.
Him in my soul found I.

Manikka Vasahar (Ninth–Tenth Century)

Selections from the Tiru Vasaham

86. Amid the fruits of deeds I lay. Thou didst thyself reveal
With words of comfort saying "Come, I will destruction
deal
To evil fruit of deeds," and thus thou mad'st me all Thy
slave.
And yet I stand as if a statue made of steel, nor rave,
Nor sing, nor cry, nor wail—woe's me—nor in my spirit
faint
With deep desire, so dull am I. O being ancient,
Thou art beginning, Thou art end: tell me, how can I be
So dead at heart? The end of this I do not dare to see.

87. Him though men seek, none fully know; in Him no evil is.
None are His kindred; knowledge perfect, effortless is His.
A cur am I, yet He hath giv'n to me in sight of men
A place on earth, and shewed me things far beyond mortal
ken.
He told me what no ears can hear; from future births He
sav'd.
Such magic wrought my Lord who me hath lovingly en-
slaved.

88. Our God of gods, whom e'en the devas' king knows but in
part,
Ruleth the three who in the fair world-gardens life impart,
And life maintain, and life destroy; our First, Reality,
Father of old, whose consort Uma is, our sovereign, He
Came down in grace and made e'en me to be His very own.
Henceforth before no man I bow; I fear but Him alone.
Now of His servants' servants I have joined the sacred
throng,

And ever more and more I'll bathe in bliss, with dance and
    song.

89. The meanest cur am I; I know not how to do the right;
    'Twere but what I deserve, should'st Thou my wickedness
        requite
    With the dread fate of those who never saw Thy flowery
        feet;
    For though mine eyes have seen, my ears have heard saints
        guileless, meet,
    Who reached Thy fragrant presence, yet I stay, for false am
        I,
    Fit for naught save to eat and dress, Lion of victory.

90. None but myself has sunk myself. Thy name be ever praised!
    No blame lay I on Thee, lauds to my Master be upraised!
    Yet to forgive is aye a mark of greatness. Praise to Thee!
    Lord of the land celestial, Praise! O end this life for me.

I CLING TO THEE

132. King of the heavenly ones! All-filling Excellence!
    E'en to vile me Thou Thy wonders hast shown;
    Balm of true bliss, ending false earthly bliss of sense,
    Thou my whole household did'st take for Thine own.
    Meaning of holy writ! Wondrous Thy glory!
    True wealth, our Siva, to Thee, Lord, I cling.
    Never to loose my hold, firmly I cling to Thee;
    Where canst Thou go, leaving me sorrowing?

133. King of celestial ones, ever with bull for steed,
    Evil am I, yet my riches art Thou;
    Lest I should rot in my foul flesh, and die indeed,
    Thou hast preserved me, and Thine am I now.
    Thou art our God; Thou of grace art a boundless sea,
    Saved from my flesh, now to Thee, Lord, I cling.
    Never to let Thee loose, firmly I cling to Thee;
    Where can'st Thou go, leaving me sorrowing?

134. Thou did'st come into my vile fleshly body,
    E'en as 'twere into some great golden shrine
    Soft'ning and melting it all, Thou hast saved me,
    Lord condescending, Thou gem all divine!
    Sorrow and birth, death, all ties that deceived me,
    Thou did'st remove, all my bonds severing;
    True bliss, our kindly Light, firmly I cling to Thee;
    Where canst Thou go leaving me sorrowing?

NAUGHT BUT THY LOVE

135. I ask not kin, nor name, nor place,
    Nor learned men's society.
Men's lore for me no value has;
    Kuttalam's lord, I come to Thee.
Wilt thou one boon on me bestow,
    A heart to melt in longing sweet,
As yearns o'er new-born calf the cow,
    In yearning for Thy sacred feet?

LONGING FOR UNION

136. I had no virtue, penance, knowledge, self-control.
    A doll to turn
At others' will, I danced, whirled, fell. But me
    He filled in every limb
With love's mad longing, and that I might climb there
    whence is no return,
    He shewed His beauty, made me His. Ah me, when shall
    I go to Him?

THE WONDER OF GRACE

137. Fool's friend was I, none such may know
    The way of freedom; yet to me
He shew'd the path of love, that so
    Fruit of past deeds might ended be.
    Cleansing my mind so foul, He made me like a god.
    Ah who could win that which the Father hath be-
    stowed?

138. Thinking it right, sin's path I trod.
    But, so that I such paths might leave,
And find His grace, the dancing God,
    Who far beyond our thought doth live,
    O wonder passing great!—to me His dancing shewed.
    Ah who could win that which the Father hath be-
    stowed?

Part Two

BUDDHISM

Introduction

As with most great men, legend intermingles bewilderingly with fact in Buddha's life. His history is shrouded with pious memory, imagination, and devout mystery. Accounts closest to his actual lifetime (c. 560-480 B.C.) were written five or six hundred years later. One clear, modern description can be found in Sir Edwin Arnold's *Light of Asia*.[1] Buddha was born in or near the city of Kapilavastu, the capital territory that now contains part of southern Nepal and northern India. His actual surname was Siddhartha Gautama. His father, Suddhodana, was a petty prince or chieftain of the Sakya clan. While Buddha was born in nobility and luxury, he was not a Brahman and therefore was not one of the traditional holders of Indian sacred knowledge.

As with other spiritual geniuses, wonders were alleged to have accompanied his birth. His mother is said to have dreamed of the future Buddha entering her womb shaped as a white elephant; flowers bloomed out of season; miracles were seen in the sky; spontaneous healings occurred. He was said to have been born from his mother's side, his body bearing the thirty-two marks of his future greatness. A sage warned his father that the boy would become a homeless wanderer or a great king. The king had also been warned that Siddhartha would be a wanderer if he witnessed the "four signs"—an old man, a diseased man, a dead man, and a monk. As much as the king attempted to seclude his son in a golden cage of luxury, the young Siddhartha eventually did come upon the four men of the prophecy. Each of the sights profoundly impressed the overly protected young man. This first acquaintance with the painful facts of infirmity, disease, and death puzzled him deeply. When he met the monk, who seemed so serene and full of spiritual determination, he vowed to learn the meaning and purpose of life. Siddhartha immediately renounced the world, including his wife, newly born son, and all his wealth and privilege and became a wandering ascetic.

[1] Another "life" of Buddha is Asvaghosa's *Buddhacarita*, translated by Samuel Beal; and also a condensed version by Dr. E. Conze in his *Buddhist Scriptures*, 1959.

While there are numerous Buddhist sects throughout the world, all have preserved the central doctrines of nirvana and the Four Noble Truths (Satyani) derived from the young Siddhartha's dramatic meeting with the four men and his eventual enlightenment. This "Great Renunciation," as it is called, occurred when he was twenty-nine and initiated his search to discover the causes of human suffering and its spiritual cure.

Siddhartha finally achieved enlightenment after six years of wandering, during which he underwent extreme austerities of the body. His conclusion that such asceticism was damaging and not at all helpful toward spiritual insight would be the motivation for his later teachings of moderation, or "the middle way." Buddha was apparently torn between either simply going his own way or attempting to teach what he had learned during his enlightenment. He realized his difficulty was communicating his experience in the imperfect medium of human speech. But once it became clear that he should try, he preached his first sermon at Sarnath and won his first converts. For more than forty years thereafter he walked the Indian countryside, expanding, clarifying, refining his ideas.

The Buddha lived in a society where the poor suffered indescribable miseries of poverty, disease, and early death. He questioned the very structure of a world dominated by rigid caste ideas, which was kept in strong repair by the Brahmans for their own advantage. Of the caste system he said, "A man does not become a Brahmana by his family or by birth. In whom there is truth and righteousness, he is blessed, he is a Brahmana."

Some of the lower castes were even considered unworthy of salvation. To this dogma Buddha replied: "My doctrine makes no distinctions between high and low, rich and poor; it is like the sky, it has room for all; like water, it washes all alike." In short, Buddha was a rebel by virtue of his independent seeking of a just and righteous truth applicable to all. In this sense Buddha was like Jesus, for both in their need to purify the religion of their day brought about religious and social revolutions.

As the American philosopher E. A. Burtt has described his philosophical powers, the Buddha "was one of the giant intellects of human history, exhibiting a keenness of analytical understanding that has rarely been equalled."[2] He never appealed to authority or tradition, and in fact discarded any claim to special revelation. He relied rather upon reason and rational analysis. He emphasized the need to strive earnestly after truth and to avoid being deceived by the manifest games of both one's ego and the pressures of peers or society. In his famous

[2]*Teachings of the Compassionate Buddha* (New York: Mentor, 1955), p. 22.

"believe nothing" statement he establishes the best general rule of thumb for independent inquiry ever uttered.

> Believe nothing because a wise man said it,
> Believe nothing because it is generally held,
> Believe nothing because it is written,
> Believe nothing because it is said to be divine,
> Believe nothing because someone else believes it,
> But believe only what you yourself judge to be true.

This emphasis on self-inquiry, on seeking the truth regardless of where it leads, is one of Buddhism's most attractive characteristics—one that all too many religions and philosophers ignore, including some Buddhist sects! When Buddha finally died at the age of eighty he exhibited the same fierce independence that marked his religious thought throughout his life. As he passed away in the arms of Ananda, his most beloved disciple, he is reputed to have whispered, "Decay is inherent in all compound things. Work out your own salvation with diligence."

Buddha's system is highly complex and demands hard and honest work. Unlike many other religions, nothing can be accomplished for you by beneficent external forces, by grace from a compassionate god, by instantaneous insights or spontaneous revelations such as those brought on by drug states. And if one was too consumed by his own ego-ridden delusions, by arrogance, by worldly attachments, by rationalizations, to seek truth or enlightenment, then his ignorance would still blind him and his immersion in delusion and suffering would continue. Perhaps Buddha's persistent emphasis on rational inquiry partially explains the religion's attraction for so many Western intellectuals.

BASIC TENETS OF BUDDHISM

Buddhism was originally an Indian religion, just as Christ's original teachings were the direct result of his Jewish heritage. Yet, strangely, Buddhism attracted its greatest number of adherents outside of India early in its development, even though Buddha's teachings were initially similar in some ways to Hinduism, and a branch of the Aryan way of life.[3] Some still consider

---

[3] The American philosopher W. T. Stace, however, argues that Buddha's peculiar conception of nirvana and his acceptance of reincarnation are the sole examples of similarities between the two teachings. In all other ways, Stace contends, Buddha's ideas were revolutionary regarding Indian tradition. See W. T. Stace, *Teachings of the Mystics* (New York: Mentor, 1960), pp. 70ff. Another exceptional scholar, P. T. Raju, argues that Buddhism was an Indian

Buddhism a protestation from the mother religion of Hinduism. Max Muller, for example, thinks it the doctrine of the Upanishads carried out to its last consequences. Buddha himself called his teachings "Aryan Truths," a term of respect meaning "noble." (This word carried no racial connotation at all.)

Buddha built his dharma (doctrine) from the human anguish he witnessed as a young man. It began with his Four Noble Truths: (1) Life is permeated by dissatisfaction (dukkha) and suffering; (2) the origin of suffering is in craving or grasping (tanha); (3) the cessation of suffering is possible by eliminating craving and attachment; and (4) the way or method one eliminates these cravings is encompassed by the Noble Eightfold Path.

Buddha's realization that extreme physical mortification was only a form of self-indulgence that ended in delusion gave rise to his doctrine of the "middle way," which became a central theme recurring throughout his teachings. It is contained in his Noble Eightfold Way, or eight stages toward enlightenment, which directs the aspirant to attain: (1) right views (beliefs or understanding); (2) right aspiration (intention or resolve); (3) right speech; (4) right conduct; (5) right livelihood; (6) right effort; (7) right mindfulness; (8) right concentration. These basic Buddhist practices involve both the mental and the physical life of the individual. Buddha himself is traditionally said to have described them in the Maha-sati-patthana Sutta.[4]

The steps of spiritual growth also required an initial proper "state of mind," so that the "right views" and "right aspirations" could be arrived at before going on to the more difficult stages. The next three stages are ethical insights that created their new reality within the aspirant and determined conduct; this also conditioned one for further growth. The final three stages involve the contemplative discipline necessary for the aspirant to achieve control of the mind and to reach the stage of enlightenment where a profound serenity, an unsurpassing peace and insight called nirvana, is experienced.[5] This state is a Buddhist's highest aspiration, for it frees one not only from delusion

[4]*Dialogues of the Buddha,* trans. by T. W. and C. A. F. Rhys Davids, Part II (London: Pali Text Society, and Luzac & Co. Ltd., 1910), pp. 343-45.
[5]The complexities of Buddhist nirvana will be discussed later.

religion and has many similarities, especially with Upanishadic teachings. See "Religions of India," Part One, in *The Great Asian Religions,* trans. and edited by Wing-tsit Chan, et al. (London, New York: Collier-Macmillan, 1969). See also Max Muller, *Theosophy or Psychological Religion* (London: Longmans Green, 1893), p. 308; and vol. 15, *Sacred Books of the East,* p. lii, where Muller contends many Buddhist ideas had their origin in the Vedic world.

of craving and worldly attachments, but from the cycles of rebirth.

Three main doctrinal elements compose Buddhism. One is, of
course, the historical facts of Buddha's life. The second is the
Vinaya Pitaka, or "Discipline Basket," concerned with the
monastic order (Sangha) Buddha founded after his enlightenment. Early on, Buddhism separated its monks and the laity:
Monks lived according to the Five Precepts (pancasila), forbid-
ding the taking of any animal life, stealing, improper sexual relations, the use of drugs or alcohol, and the wrong use of speech
(including boasting or malicious gossip). Members of the
Sangha wore yellow robes, were tonsured, and were enjoined to
live lives of utmost simplicity. At first women were excluded
from the Sangha, but they were soon admitted, including Buddha's wife, as were other respected matrons and even prostitutes.
A special characteristic of Buddhist discipline was mindfulness
(sati), in which the monk would always attempt to understand
his own motives. Drugs and alcohol were forbidden not from
prudishness, but because they confused the mind and self-
awareness.

The third basic element of Buddhist doctrine was the dharma
(dhamma in Pali), mentioned earlier. One of the monk's primary tasks was to teach the dharma (the Four Truths and the
Eightfold Path) to others and to continue to improve himself
by self-control and meditation. These three categories are considered the "Three Gems" of Buddhism; the Buddhist creed has
often been reduced to a popular, simple formula: "I take refuge
in Buddha, the Doctrine, and the Order."

THE INEVITABLE SCHISM:
HINAYANA AND MAHAYANA SCHOOLS

As with other religions, the inevitable schism developed in
Buddhism. It evolved into two main schools (there were traditionally eighteen basic teachings): the Theravada (Doctrine of
the Elders), the present form of the Hinayana or "Lesser Vehicle"; and the Mahayana or "Great Vehicle." Ironically, Buddhism did not long survive in its homeland. The Theravadin
teachings found a permanent home in Southeast Asia, and Mahayana was most successful in China, Japan, and Korea.

Hinayana and Mahayana developed during the early centuries—from about 200 B.C. to A.D. 200. The term "Hinayana"
was popularized during the great schism by Mahayanists (hence,
the "Lesser Vehicle" title), and to emphasize the superiority of

their own, broader way. Naturally the Hinayanists resented this
role of a "lesser way" forced upon them and preferred to call
their way Theravada,[6] or "Way of the Elders," emphasizing
their faithfulness to what they considered the original teachings
of Buddha.

The Theravadin doctrines probably did represent Buddha's
original thought the most faithfully, but the differences between
the two schools were not merely the result of a struggle for supremacy within one country. As the two schools traveled from
their homeland the reforms and modifications multiplied. The
Hinayana doctrine of southern Asia (Ceylon, Burma, Thailand,
etc.) differs substantially from the Mahayana teachings of the
Far Eastern Buddhist countries (China, Korea, and Japan), and
the Vajrayana, or Diamond Vehicle, of Tibet.

Buddha's life and teachings were obviously influenced by Hinduism, yet while he sometimes seemed to accept the ancient
pantheism, key doctrines were clearly altered to suit his own
views. The numerous Hindu gods were minimized in Buddhism,
as the emphasis was placed on karma and a man being responsible completely for his own fate, for reaping what he had sown.
Transmigration of souls became more important after Buddha
emphasized that rebirth was a series of stages on humanity's long
trek to nirvana and freedom from the burdens of earthly life.
Eventually, Mahayana probably had the greatest mass appeal
because it offered the hope of salvation and eternal bliss of nirvana in the present life. Hinayana, or Theravada, was more
literal in its interpretations of Buddha's ideas and taught that a
succession of virtuous lives was necessary for final freedom from
misery and the attainment of nirvana.

Our knowledge of early Buddhism comes primarily from the
Theravadin scriptures, even though modern scholarship considers
many Mahayana texts as old.[7] The Theravadin texts (called the
Pali Canon) are divided into three pitakas ("baskets" or sections), and contain the early doctrines and monastic rules set
down by Buddha. While they may not be Buddha's actual
words, for they were written by Buddhists in Ceylon and
southern India about 240 years after Buddha's death, they are
generally believed to represent the Buddha's basic ideas. Some
historians believe their composition was around the first century
B.C. The three baskets of Pali scriptures are together known as

[6]The Theravadins were themselves originally only a sect of the larger so-
called Hinayana school.

[7]The problem of scriptural accuracy is compounded by the fact that the
Buddhist canon was not fixed until the reign of King Asoka, more than two
hundred years after Buddha's death.

the Tipitaka (Tripitaka in Sanskrit), and include the Vinaya, the Dhama (or Sutta), and the Abhidhamma.

The Vinaya Pitaka concerns the monastic rules of the Sangha and is therefore known as the "Discipline Basket." The Dhamma Pitaka consists of collections of Buddha's principal sermons or discourses, and is considered the primary authority for Buddhist doctrine ("Sermon" or "Discourse Basket"). The Dhamma Pitaka is the most important and contains some of the most ancient and beautiful Buddhist poems, including the Dhammapada or Way of Virtue, which is included in this volume. Abhidhamma Pitaka, the "Exposition Basket, is an analysis and exposition of Theravadin doctrine. It is in these writings that the basic distinctions between the Mahayana and Theravadin teachings begin.

The Mahayana canons are mostly written in Sanskrit and overlap considerably with the Pali scriptures of the southern school. Together with later scriptures, such as the famous collection of metaphysical writings known as the Prajnaparamita Sutras, the Mahayana documents were translated into Chinese, Japanese, and Tibetan, where additions and commentaries were made. The Tibetan canon is written in Tibetan and Sanskrit and is known as the Kanjur, and contains the Prajnaparamita Sutras, among other Mahayana writings, as well as Tantric texts.

As can be seen, Buddhist writings are vast, complicated, and overlap into different schools. Mahayanists generally accept Pali scriptures but argue that they must be supplemented by further analysis, which is embodied in their own sutras. In scriptural terms some striking differences between the Theravada and Mahayana can be found. The early Theravadins, for example, tended to accept the scriptures simply as historical and analytical accounts of Buddha's life and teachings. They generally denied that Buddha had any esoteric doctrines and believed that his teachings are contained in their entirety in the Pali Canon. Some Mahayanists, however, identified so intensely with the scriptures that they considered them as being the "Truth Body" of Buddha (meaning identical with the Absolute or Ultimate Reality). While the Theravadins viewed Buddha's thoughts on the written page only as propositional knowledge, some Mahayana schools considered the writings *themselves* as sacred and co-equal to the ideas they contained. In effect, this identification transferred the object of worship from Buddha himself to the texts. All of these revisions were wrong from Buddha's point of view, for he argued intensely against worshipping gods, teachers, or sages, and against raising the written word to sacred dimensions. The text become so revered in some Mahayana sects, however, that salvation was considered obtainable simply by uttering with faith a single sentence of the Lotus Sutra.[8]

The doctrinal differences between the Mahayana and Theravada Buddhists were substantial. Theravadins tended to believe Buddha was not a god, but a teacher whose memory was to be revered. Yet, many Mahayana sects exalted Buddha to god status early in their development. The Theravadins also emphasized the doctrine of "process" in order to undermine the ideas of individuality, reality of self, or soul-substance, rather than to offer any scheme of cosmic unity (which many later Mahayana sects did).[9] Theravadins considered the universe an eternal continuum in which individuals rise and pass on in endless succession. This same infinite process applies to the psychophysical reality of individual consciousness. Thus, the self is not an entity or complete unit unto itself, but rather a stream of energy whose elements change at every moment. The physical self that dies (this includes Buddha's death and going into nirvana, which is called parinirvana) is no more permanent than the impermanent "self" that composes the individual at any given moment. In death a transfer of energy occurs, like a flame moving from candle to candle. Is it the same flame? The Buddhist will answer that such a "death" is the same "dying" one experiences during life, and the changing conditions of moment-to-moment existence. In short, all life is so in flux that both forms of death are merely modification of a continuing stream of energy. This interpretation follows Buddha's conception, which the Theravadins were more faithful to than the early Mahayanists, of an entirely impersonal universe where there is no God, no First Cause, no Supreme Creator, or even Ultimate Purposiveness. The universe is thus conceived as an impersonal process whose ultimate nature can only be discussed as patterned

[8] An outstanding example of this phenomenon is Nichirin (1222-1282) and his followers. Nichirin, a Japanese Buddhist who created a school known as Hokkes, taught a militant form of Buddhism that was intolerant of all other forms of worship—including other Buddhist sects. In contrast to Nichirin's reliance on the chanted text, the Ch'an and Zen Buddhists of China and Japan taught that the words of the scriptures themselves must be transcended, which is illustrated by the famous Zen painting of a holy man tearing up the scriptures. For further discussion of this interesting aspect of Buddhism, see Ninian Smart, "Buddhism," in *The Encyclopedia of Philosophy*, vol. 1 (New York, London: Collier-Macmillan, 1967).

[9] The Buddhist conception of the world as a process rather than a static or substantive reality has much in common with A. N. Whitehead's philosophy of "pan-psychism," and especially in his de-emphasis of self-consciousness. For discussion of this comparison see W. L. King, *In the Hope of Nibbana* (LaSalle, Ill.: Open Court, 1964), pp. 37ff. Other modern pan-psychists whose philosophical views compare interestingly with Buddhist theory are Fechner, Schiller, Paulsen, and Teilhard de Chardin.

and in constant flux.[10] Theravadins therefore do not question the reality of the world, but emphasize its transience instead. In contrast, some Mahayanists challenged the very reality of the physical universe, and proclaimed the universe a void, neither real nor unreal.[11] In short, the Theravadin doctrine of the "no-self" (anatta) became the "void" (sunyata) of the Mahayanists.

The enlightened Theravadin is called an Arhat, and is the highest saint in Hinayana Buddhism, just as the Bodhisattva is in Mahayana.[12] But the Arhat basically works out his own salvation. The Mahayanists argued that this was too selfish and did not harmonize with Buddha's own compassionate concern for his fellow humans. Thus, the Mahayana Bodhisattva delays his entry into nirvana in order to be reborn and labor for his fellow beings. This belief lies behind one Bodhisattva's statement that he would only enter nirvana after the last living being had preceded him. Scriptural justification was found in Buddha's temptation by Mara (the Buddhist Satan), who suggested that he could enter into nirvana immediately upon experiencing enlightenment. Buddha, however, chose to remain and preach salvation, which as the Mahayanists point out is the role of the Bodhisattva. Naturally, an "ideal" Bodhisattva arose, one who through many births accrued merit which he then transferred to others less worthy. Such selfless actions allowed a Bodhisattva's followers to gain a paradise where the conditions for obtaining nirvana are particularly favorable. The *Pure Land Sutras* in the second volume of this anthology represent this Mahayana school. These types of Bodhisattvas were eventually raised to a divine status.

The early Theravadins also resolutely refused to change their belief that an utter cessation of individual existence occurs in nirvana. They ardently rejected the Mahayana idea (which had absorbed some Hindu Vedantist elements by now) that the anatta doctrine of non-self referred only to the destruction of a lower self, while the higher or larger self persisted in a kind of exalted cosmic Self once in nirvana. Nirvana for the Theravadins was just what their detractors called it, a "graveyard of the mind," the absolute termination of individualized existence.[13]

[10]For a complete discussion of Theravadin beliefs see W. L. King, *In the Hope of Nibbana.*

[11]Many important Mahayana concepts, such as sunyata, the Mind-Only, etc., are not discussed here because they rightly belong with the Mahayana texts in vol. 2 of *Eastern Mysticism.*

[12]For a thorough discussion of the ideals of the Mahayana Bodhisattva and the Hinayana Arhat, see Har Dayal, *The Bodhisattva Doctrine in Buddhist Sanskrit Literature* (London, 1932); and I. B. Horner, *Early Buddhist Theory of Man Perfected* (London, 1936).

[13]See W. L. King, *In the Hope of Nibbana*, pp. 82ff.

The Theravadins believed that Buddha had entered that "state of cessation from which there is no return" (nirvana). For them he no longer existed except as an example of the perfect being we should imitate. But the Mahayanists insisted that Buddha continued to exist; that he refused nirvana out of compassion for the world. Such supreme renunciation can only be accomplished by a being so perfected that he becomes the "Compassionate Absolute." The difference between the two schools then was finally symbolized by their individual versions of "saints"—by the distinction in motivation and spiritual purpose of the Arhat and the Bodhisattva.

These philosophical arguments were further refined by formulating the Three-body (triyaka) Doctrine, or conceiving Buddha as three different levels of being. At one level the Buddha is Nirmanakaya, or "Transformation Body," whose essence is made manifest on the earth and exists in the flesh. (The historical personage of Buddha, called the Sakyamuni in many writings, is for the Mahayanists the eternal Buddha manifesting himself to the world, much as Christ is conceived in his man-form as God come to earth.) At another level Buddha appears as a celestial being whose essence is made manifest in various Buddhist heavens. This is the "Body of Bliss," the Sambhogakaya, a Buddha who is omniscient and omnipotent but not yet Supreme. The third and most important level is the Dharmakaya, the "Essence" or "Truth Body," [14] where Buddhahood is considered identical with the Absolute; a body in which he became an infinite and eternal reality for the Mahayanists. In the Dharmakaya body Buddha is divine knowledge (prajna) and Wisdom (bodhi) and Suchness (tattva).

This equation of Buddha with the Absolute focused attention on attaining nirvana, the ultimate goal of Buddhism. Buddha as the "Truth Body" thereby became the final goal of all aspirants. This in turn complemented the idea, eventually held by both schools, that all people had the Buddha nature potentially within.

THE BUDDHIST CONCEPTION OF SELF

Self-control and discipline were vitally important to Buddha, for without them the desired progression toward enlightenment

[14] You may recall that some sects (like Nichirin's) thought of the sacred writings as Buddha's "Truth Body" mentioned earlier. For a more complete description of the Trikaya doctrine see Heinrich Zimmer, *Philosophies of India* (New York: Pantheon, 1951). See also vol. 2 of *Eastern Mysticism*, "The Platform Sutra of the Sixth Patriarch," where the Trikaya doctrine is presented by Hui-neng according to the teachings of the Ch'an (Zen) Buddhist school.

nirvana would be impossible. His thoughts on the individual
"self," however, are exceedingly complex. In broad terms individuals possess three characteristics: suffering (dukkha), absence
of an eternal self (anatta), and impermanence of being (anicca).
Anatta, or absence of an eternal self, in effect repudiates the
idea of a real underlying self or soul. There is no "I," soul, self,
or personal identity that persists within human beings. An individual was in fact considered "temporary" even within a single
lifetime, for one changes or alters one's self from moment to
moment—that is, one "dies" and is "born" many times during
one's lifetime. Such infinitesimal changes and their rapidity
make them indiscernible to ordinary perception or understanding. Psychologically this means that the present moment is the
key to moral progress and change. The psychological "now" contains all the potential for ethical action and ultimate liberation
at one's command. There is only the using of it.

To clarify the apparent contradiction of working to improve a
"self" he taught did not exist, Buddha contended that there does
exist a kind of awareness, a stream of consciousness within individuals. The mind therefore possesses a continuing identity only
in the sense, say, of a wave passing over the surface of water
having a distinctive unity. To continue the analogy: In Western
religious beliefs the soul or true self is an eternal spiritual actuality and retains some singular aspect of itself even after death.
If, for example, a boat were to travel over the surface of the
water rather than a wave, the boat would be a tangible fixed
symbol of the self, and would retain its characteristics even
after passing beyond our metaphorical picture. Buddha argued
that the self is not tangible like the boat, but is in effect an integral part of the total life process. Everything is an energetic
flux of particles, including human consciousness.[15] Thus the famous Theravadin doctrine of non-self (anatta) considers there is
no underlying real self in individuals. Belief in an eternal, inner
self is one of the first "fetters" a Theravadin aspirant must rid
himself of.

The confusion over the conception of self exists because Buddha can be quoted in support of both arguments. Buddha, for
example, admonishes aspirants to be rid of the self in one place,
yet in another he says, "I am the doer" (Anguttara Nikaya, III.
337). What or who is the "I" Buddha refers to here? In yet another place he resists answering the direct question "Is there a

[15]This view of life process based upon energetic particles is familiar to modern physicists. Buddha's conception of the individual self is also surprisingly
similar to Taoist attitudes, arrived at by Lao Tzu almost a hundred years
before Buddha. The Buddhist view of self and ego is discussed further, along
with other major Eastern religious concepts, in the general introduction.

self?" (Samyutta IV.400) by replying that if he says there is a self it would be assumed he was an eternalist, a believer in an eternal, unchanging self; and if he responded that there is no self, he would be considered an annihilationist.

In one part of the Dhammapada, a scripture accepted by both Hinayanists and Mahayanists, Buddha says: "Self is the Lord of Self: Self is the goal of self." And then in another place he says: "Neither self nor aught belonging to self can really and truly be accepted." In the Samyutta Sutta (IV.83), for example, Buddha says that what is impermanent is not the self. Buddha's stating that something "is *not* the self," of course, implies a self beyond what he rejects—exactly the deduction he tried to avoid in the Samyutta Sutta quoted above (IV.400). A plausible explanation for such scriptural and doctrinal confusion is that Buddha was talking about several different aspects of "self"—one, the personal craving, deluded, transitory, worldly "self" that must be destroyed; and the other, a greater, eternal "Higher Self" that one aspires to uncover within oneself. The answer may be in scriptures like the Anguttara Sutta (III.359) where it is stated, "He who has reached enlightenment has utterly destroyed the fetters of becoming. To him who is, by perfect wisdom, emancipated there does not occur the thought that 'anyone is better than I or equal to me or less than I.' Even so, the Buddha replied, men of the true stamp tell what they have gained, but do not speak of 'I'. " This sutta states fairly clearly that "self-naughting," or diminishing of selfhood, is the only practical way to achieve enlightenment. Further, diminishing the sense of the "I" reduces craving, the single most important cause of suffering and rebirth according to Buddha.

Based upon this analysis Mahayanists claim that the anatta doctrine of non-self relates only to personal identity, and that ultimately there is a Universal Self to which enlightenment brings blissful union. And Buddha's arguments taken overall seem to accept a selfhood that exists in the transitory manifestation of worldly personality, but which in terms of any eternal principles is an illusion and cannot therefore be considered "real" in any ultimate sense.

How then do Buddhists explain individual personality? And how do they justify demanding ethical conduct from an individual who they say is not real? To early Buddhists, the ego was a compound of five groups of aggregates called the five skandhas. Together they are believed to constitute the "I" personality of this world. The skandhas are aggregates of (1) matter, (2) feelings, (3) ideas, (4) that of the samskaras which involve instincts, habits, potentials, and (5) the vijnana, or bits, series, of consciousness. The individual is therefore considered a conglomerate or aggregate of stages and energies all interacting with the universe. In Buddhism the key to individual consciousness is activity (the samskaras), the individual's germinative forces made manifest in the world. These forces exist prior to the nescient individual himself and produce the separate being; but the forces are modified, increased or decreased by the activity of the individual. (It is not as in ancient China where each person born is believed to have only a given amount of energy that can be husbanded or squandered.)

Samskaras are called "habit-energies"; forces active in creating both the individual's physical and spiritual being in each incarnation. These energies underlying each life are in fact trans-individualistic or cosmic, and every individual is therefore constituted both by psychological forces formed by past and present action, and by cosmic roots. This intimate interrelationship between individual and universal energy determines a person's specific being in each life. Such an intimate relationship between one's actions and one's "state of being" justifies the acceptance of another major Buddhist concept, that of karma (kamma in Pali). The law of karma is an active principle that determines that for every action there is a corresponding influence on the psychophysical being of the individual. This influence effects the entire "process" of the individual's present life and future incarnations.

To the Buddhist, karma is the moral law of the universe acting within individual lives. This primary "moral law" is an important part of Buddhist salvation, for its action in every sphere (whether mind or body) becomes one of the keys by which a Buddhist can either perpetuate the inexorable cycle of rebirth or stop it and achieve nirvana. If asked by what standards of "morality" such an impersonal principle as karma functions, the Buddhist reply is simply that action always produces a response. A destructive act such as killing, or even anger becomes an integral part of the person who created it; so eventually one must come face to face with whatever one has created. The moral impact is simple but devastating: You act according to that which you know will become a real, visceral part of you. This is a concept exceedingly close, of course, to both the Confucian and Christian Golden Rule, as well as the common ethical belief that "as you sow, so shall you reap."

NIRVANA AND BUDDHIST MYSTICISM

Corruption is a constant companion to the more subtle thoughts of philosophers and great religious reformers. Given enough time and enough followers, the most clear and admirable thinking is muddled and turned sour. Nirvana is such a concept. Etymologically the word means "blown out" or "extinction" in Sanskrit, and has had a confusing reception in the Western world. Since its discovery by Western scholars it has been defined as either annihilation of one's soul or alternatively, as the soul's eternal existence in a state of bliss. Both statements misrepresent Buddha's original view. As we saw from the previous discussion he personally refused to express any opinion at all on either metaphysical absolutes (such as the "self" existing or not) or survival after death.[16] He concentrated instead on teaching a practical way to achieve salvation. This perhaps wise policy, however, left a metaphysical vacuum which philosophers have ever since rushed to fill.

Buddhism has been popularly termed an atheistic philosophy rather than a religion. But this is incorrect. Buddhism (like Islamism, Zoroastrianism, Sikhism, and Jainism) is a mystical religion because it originated from its founder's personal enlightenment; and because the mystical experience of enlightenment is the very core of its teachings and the goal to which all Buddhists' aspire. It can more legitimately be considered a "mystical" religion than Christianity, for example, which did not depend upon Jesus' experiencing a mystical interlude or period of enlightenment. For this reason perhaps, mysticism is more of a minor element in Christianity.[17] Some have argued that Buddha's enlightenment experience was not actually a mystical one. However, although he did not describe it in detail, enough hints exist to indicate that it was that type of unitary consciousness experience where multiplicity was dissolved. In other words, it was a typical experience of undifferentiated unity, which, as the American philosopher Walter Stace has argued convincingly, is the essence of all introvertive mysticism.[18] In fact, because of Buddha's enlightenment experience, the inner illumination that it implied was sought after intensely by Buddhists. In the Theragatha (clxvi), verses composed by Buddhist monks and nuns, there is something of the intensity and quality of the early Buddhist's quest for enlightenment. The poems are clearly mystical, even in their sensual and metaphorical use of nature.

> The peacock's shriek. Ah, the lovely crests and tails,
> And the sweet sound of the blue-throated peacocks.
> The great grassy plain with water now

---

[16]See the selections on the Lankavatara Sutra for an example of this.
[17]See E. A. Burtt, The Teachings of the Compassionate Buddha.
[18]W. T. Stace, The Teachings of the Mystics, pp. 67ff.

Beneath the thunder-clouded sky. Your body is fresh;
   you are vigorous now and fit
To test the teaching. Reach now for that saintly rapture,
So bright, so pure, so hard, to fathom, ·
The highest, the eternal place.

To truly understand the mystical elements in Buddhism one
must turn to its origins in the mystical philosophy of the Upanishads and especially to the idea of nirvana.[19] The most important single concept to both Hinduism and Buddhism, and the
key mystical element in both religions, is nirvana. It is the
direct result of enlightenment, and is the end product of an individual's spiritual discipline and growth—in short, it is salvation!

The problem in describing nirvana accurately, or even adequately, however, is the same as with all religious ultimates.
This is especially true of mystical religions, for their constant
emphasis is on the necessity for the individual to "experience"
the Absolute, which is the only way that clear understanding is
produced. The Buddhist nirvana follows this tradition insis-
tently—in both Hinayana and Mahayana—for nirvana is continually described as essentially ineffable. One can only describe
"qualities" of the experience, but never the substance of it.[20]
To some Buddhists nirvana is the utter peace resulting from
complete freedom from attachment and passion; it is a state of
permanent emancipation, bliss, and purity. Some describe it as
the progressive realization of emptiness of all selfhood; hence, it
is often communicated in negative terms like "non-being." Other
descriptions of nirvana by various Buddhist schools include
sunyata ("void"), a condition where everything is relative which
results in no object-subject polarity; dharma-kaya, or the
"essence of Buddha"; dharma-dhata, or "ultimate reality"; ta-
thata, or "ultimate actuality," and so on.

Theravadins did indeed consider the anatta (non-self) doctrine as the prelude to nirvana, the "graveyard of the mind," a
complete extinction of the self. Progress toward nirvana to the
Theravadins meant not only the destruction of craving, but the
progressive realization of the emptiness of all selfhood. Consciousness in all its forms, which clings to the distinctions of
this world, was to be completely annihilated. But annihilation
means different things to Western ears. The image that comes to
mind is one of utter darkness, a condition where all our senses

[19]The mystical elements of Hinduism and a discussion of key concepts are
more fully presented in Part One, "Hinduism."

[20]The difficulty in talking about the ineffable is discussed more thoroughly in
the general introduction.

and perceptions are diminished to zero. But annihilation, as used by Eastern mystical religions generally, can be taken to mean augmentation, or expansion to the point of becoming, in the words of Tennyson, a "boundless being." It is a point where egoistic personality fades out of existence. Nirvana in this sense can be considered as a candle placed against the face—and full power—of the sun. The candle would, from the viewpoint of any-one observing it, be completely extinguished by the brilliance and power of the sunlight, but would continue to exist as part of the light, as part of the entire universe of energy that brought it into being in the first place.

There are other arguments against the exclusive interpretation of nirvana as annihilation of the complete self. While this *via negativa* interpretation has been given the most publicity, Buddha himself has described it in the Pali Canon as "Whatever is the extinction of passion, of aversion, of confusion, this is called nirvana."[21]

That nirvana is capable of being experienced implies some form of experiencer. In some Theravadin texts, for example, nirvana is considered knowable even after death; what is called kilesa-parinibbana, or the "full extinction of defilements." This qualita-tively described nirvana introduces the idea of it as the extinction of greed, lust, avarice, anger, and other defilements of the world. So, even though the Theravadin nirvana is indeed a "graveyard of the mind" it is also utterly desirable, the *summum bonum*, the single legitimate object for which men can passionately strive. While it is considered an Absolute Nullity, it is also an Absolute Good. The positive elements of nirvana are then un-surprisingly numerous. Rhys Davids compiled an impressive list of positive qualities culled from the Theravadin literature. Nirvana is "the harbour of refuge, the cool cave, the island amidst the floods, the place of bliss, liberation, the tranquil, the calm, the end of suffering, the unshaken, the immaterial, the im-perishable, the abiding, the supreme joy, the ineffable, the de-tachment, the holy city."[22]

Finally, then, even though as explained here nirvana is only a characterization, a description of qualities, the Theravadins do interpret nirvana not only as extinction, but as changeless, time-less, suprapersonal, as Ultimate Good and indescribably blissful. And while there is no union with the divine in Theravadin nir-vana, contrary to most mystical experiences in this book, the immediate, direct, and personal apprehension of Supreme Real-ity, of an absolute state of being, does transcend all the distinc-

---

[21]Samyutta Nikaya (IV. 251).
[22]Quoted in W. L. King, *In the Hope of Nibbana*, p. 87.

tions of worldly consciousness.[23] Nirvana is not then merely a subjective awareness, but a different form of cognitive experience so powerful that it carries the weight of an objective reality beyond all description to those who experience it, beyond all finite things.

EDITOR'S NOTES

To summarize in this introduction the teachings of the numerous schools and their doctrinal differences is impossible as well as misleading, for Buddhism contains a sophisticated system of psychology, a subtle, analytical philosophy, and mystical insights regarding human beings and nature that challenge the most complete and profound philosophies of the West. After seriously studying Buddhism there develops in one a strange sense of awe when confronted by its scope and grandeur of conception. Its subtlety and complexity is such that one feels in the presence of an idea that spirals upward in an infinite helix. In material Western terms, Buddhism creates the metaphorical picture in one's mind of a great translucent gothic cathedral.

Most of the Buddhist material in this volume is Hinayana, and the majority of texts in the second volume are Mahayana. This arrangement corresponds to the characteristics of the influence of each school geographically: the first volume includes the Hinayana scriptures in the Near East and the Southeast (India, Ceylon, Burma, Thailand, etc.); and the second volume, the Mahayana scriptures of the Far East. As with all anthologies an enormous amount of material has been left out only because of space and the economics of publishing. This is especially true with Buddhism where numerous volumes of excellent translations in English exist.

Buddha has many names which the reader will come upon in these writings. Buddha itself means "Enlightened One" and is a title of respect the man known as Buddha could claim only after his own enlightenment. Prior to that he is referred to as a Bodhisattva. The Bodhisattva is also frequently thought of as a "future Buddha." H. C. Warren translates the word literally as "He Whose Essence is Wisdom."

The Buddha's given name in Sanskrit is Siddhartha Gautama (in Pali, a southern dialect, Siddhattha Gotama), and means "successful in his aims," or in another rendering, "He who has

---

[23]For an example of the Mahayana doctrines of Absolute Mind, see Volume Two of *Eastern Mysticism*, but especially the selections from the *Surangama Sutra* where it is argued (much in the tradition of western idealistic philosophy) that ultimate reality is Absolute Mind.

accomplished his goals." His surname, Gautama, is also the name of his clan, the Sakya. Sakya means "powerful," and Buddha is therefore sometimes called Sakyamuni, or "the sage of the Sakyas." One of his most frequent and mysterious titles is Tathagata, which means "He who has arrived at the truth." It is a title of reverence. Some render it as one who has achieved spiritual perfection, "the Perfect One," or "He who has fully come through." In the latter sense Tathagata is considered "Thus-gone," as "Suchness," or one whose life can only be implied but never described.

In the second volume of *Eastern Mysticism* the reader will find even more titles for Buddha. In Chinese Buddhist texts Tathagata is Ju Lai, meaning "He who has fully arrived." The many scriptures of the Pure Land School of Chinese and Japanese Buddhism often refer to Tathagata as Amitabha (or in Japanese Amida). One should be familiar with these terms, for they will frequently appear.

1. The Foundation of the Kingdom of Righteousness (Buddha's First Sermon)

Reverence to the Blessed One, the Holy One, the Fully-Enlightened One.

1. Thus have I heard. The Blessed One was once staying at Benares, at the hermitage called Migadaya. And there the Blessed One addressed the company of the five Bhikkhus,[1] and said:

2. "There are two extremes, O Bhikkhus, which the man who has given up the world ought not to follow—the habitual practice, on the one hand, of those things whose attraction depends upon the passions; and especially of sensuality—a low and pagan way of seeking satisfaction, unworthy, unprofitable, and fit only for the worldly-minded—and the habitual practice, on the other hand, of asceticism or self-mortification, which is painful, unworthy, and unprofitable.

3. "There is a middle path, O Bhikkhus, avoiding these two extremes, discovered by the Tathagata[2]—a path which opens the eyes, and bestows understanding, which leads to peace of mind, to the higher wisdom, to full enlightenment, to Nirvana.[3]

4. "What is that middle path, O Bhikkhus, avoiding these two extremes, discovered by the Tathagata—that path which opens the eyes, and bestows understanding, which leads to peace of mind, to the higher wisdom, to full enlightenment, to Nirvana? Verily! it is this noble eightfold path; that is to say:

[1] Bhikkhus means literally "beggars," but is a term in Buddhism that conveys the idea of a monk, or spiritual mendicant. These five monks are those who had waited on Buddha during his austerities. They eventually became his first disciples.

[2] The Tathagata is an epithet of Buddha, and means one who has already gone through the path to complete Enlightenment.

[3] Nirvana, which means literally "blown out," like a candle, is the ultimate goal of all Buddhist effort. It involves the extinction of all attachment and desire. It also stands for a state of bliss or blessedness.

"Right views;
Right aspirations;
Right speech;
Right conduct;
Right livelihood;
Right effort;
Right mindfulness; and
Right contemplation.

"This, O Bhikkhus, is that middle path, avoiding these two extremes, discovered by the Tathagata—that path which opens the eyes, and bestows understanding, which leads to peace of mind, to the higher wisdom, to full enlightenment, to Nirvana!

5. "Now this, O Bhikkhus, is the noble truth concerning suffering. "Birth is attended with pain, decay is painful, disease is painful, death is painful. Union with the unpleasant is painful, painful is separation from the pleasant; and any craving that is unsatisfied, that too is painful. In brief, the five aggregates [4] which spring from attachment (the conditions of individuality and their cause) are painful.

"This then, O Bhikkhus, is the noble truth concerning suffering.

6. "Now this, O Bhikkhus, is the noble truth concerning the origin of suffering.

"Verily, it is that thirst or craving, causing the renewal of existence, accompanied by sensual delight, seeking satisfaction now here, now there—that is to say, the craving for the gratification of the passions, or the craving for a future life, or the craving for success in this present life.

"This then, O Bhikkhus, is the noble truth concerning the origin of suffering.

7. "Now this, O Bhikkhus, is the noble truth concerning the destruction of suffering.

"Verily; it is the destruction, in which no passion remains, of this very thirst; the laying aside of, the getting rid of, the being free from, the harbouring no longer of this thirst.

"This then, O Bhikkhus, is the noble truth concerning the destruction of suffering.

8. "Now this, O Bhikkhus, is the noble truth concerning the way which leads to the destruction of sorrow. Verily! it is this noble eightfold path; that is to say:

---

[4] The five aggregates, or skandhas, create the temporal integration of the individual; that is, the body, feelings, ideas, volitions, and conscious perception.

"Right views;
Right aspirations;
Right speech;
Right conduct;
Right livelihood;
Right effort;
Right mindfulness; and
Right contemplation.

"This then, O Bhikkhus, is the noble truth concerning the destruction of sorrow.

9. "That this was the noble truth concerning sorrow, was not, O Bhikkhus, among the doctrines handed down, but there arose within me the eye to perceive it, there arose the knowledge of its nature, there arose the understanding of its cause, there arose the wisdom to guide in the path of tranquillity, there arose the light to dispel darkness from it.

10. "And again, O Bhikkhus, that I should comprehend that this was the noble truth concerning sorrow, though it was not among the doctrines handed down, there arose within me the eye, there arose the knowledge, there arose the understanding, there arose the wisdom, there arose the light.

11. "And again, O Bhikkhus, that I had comprehended that this was the noble truth concerning sorrow, though it was not among the doctrines handed down, there arose within me the eye, there arose the knowledge, there arose the understanding, there arose the wisdom, there arose the light.

12. "That this was the noble truth concerning the origin of sorrow, though it was not among the doctrines handed down, there arose within me the eye; but there arose within me the knowledge, there arose the understanding, there arose the wisdom, there arose the light.

13. "And again, O Bhikkhus, that I should put away the origin of sorrow, though the noble truth concerning it was not among the doctrines handed down, there arose within me the eye, there arose the knowledge, there arose the understanding, there arose the wisdom, there arose the light.

14. "And again, O Bhikkhus, that I had fully put away the origin of sorrow, though the noble truth concerning it was not among the doctrines handed down, there arose within me the eye, there arose the knowledge, there arose the understanding, there arose the wisdom, there arose the light.

15. "That this, O Bhikkhus, was the noble truth concerning the destruction of sorrow, though it was not among the doctrines handed down; but there arose within me the eye, there

arose the knowledge, there arose the understanding, there arose
the wisdom, there arose the light.

16. "And again, O Bhikkhus, that I should fully realize the
destruction of sorrow though the noble truth concerning it was
not among the doctrines handed down, there arose within me
the eye, there arose the knowledge, there arose the understanding, there arose the wisdom, there arose the light.

17. "And again, O Bhikkhus, that I had fully realized the
destruction of sorrow, though the noble truth concerning it was
not among the doctrines handed down, there arose within me
the eye, there arose the knowledge, there arose the understanding, there arose the wisdom, there arose the light.

18. "That this was the noble truth concerning the way
which leads to the destruction of sorrow, was not, O Bhikkhus,
among the doctrines handed down; but there arose within me
the eye, there arose the knowledge, there arose the understanding, there arose the wisdom, there arose the light.

19. "And again, O Bhikkhus, that I should become versed in
the way which leads to the destruction of sorrow, though the
noble truth concerning it was not among the doctrines handed
down, there arose within me the eye, there arose the knowledge,
there arose within me the eye, there arose the knowledge, there
arose the light.

20. "And again, O Bhikkhus, that I had become versed in the
way which leads to the destruction of sorrow, though the noble
truth concerning it was not among the doctrines handed down,
there arose within me the eye, there arose the knowledge, there
arose the understanding, there arose the wisdom, there arose the
light.

21. "So long, O Bhikkhus, as my knowledge and insight were
not quite clear, regarding each of these four noble truths in this
triple order, in this twelvefold manner—so long was I uncertain
whether I had attained to the full insight of that wisdom which
is unsurpassed in the heavens or on earth, among the whole race
of Samanas and Brahmans, or of gods or men.

22. "But as soon, O Bhikkhus, as my knowledge and insight
were quite clear regarding each of these four noble truths, in
this triple order, in this twelvefold manner—then did I become
certain that I had attained to the full insight of that wisdom
which is unsurpassed in the heavens or on earth, among the
whole race of Samanas and Brahmans, or of gods or men.

23. "And now this knowledge and this insight has arisen
within me. Immovable is the emancipation of my heart. This is
my last existence. There will now be no rebirth for me!"

24. Thus spake the Blessed One. The company of the five
Bhikkhus, glad at heart, exalted the words of the Blessed One.

And when the discourse had been uttered, there arose within the
venerable Kondanna the eye of truth, spotless, and without a
stain, and he saw that whatsoever has an origin, in that is also
inherent the necessity of coming to an end.

25. And when the royal chariot wheel of the truth had thus
been set rolling onwards by the Blessed One, the gods of the
earth gave forth a shout, saying:

"In Benares, at the hermitage of the Migadaya, the supreme
wheel of the empire of Truth has been set rolling by the Blessed
One—that wheel which not by any Samana or Brahman, not by
any god, not by any Brahma or Mara,[5] not by any one in the
universe, can ever be turned back!"

26. And when they heard the shout of the gods of the earth,
the attendant gods of the four great kings (the guardian angels
of the four quarters of the globe) gave forth a shout, saying:

"In Benares, at the hermitage of the Migadaya, the supreme
wheel of the empire of Truth has been set rolling by the Blessed
One—that wheel which not by any Samana or Brahman, not by
any god, not by any Brahma or Mara, not by any one in the
universe, can ever be turned back!"

27. And thus as the gods in each of the heavens heard the
shout of the inhabitants of the heaven beneath, they took up
the cry until the gods in the highest heaven of heavens gave
forth the shout, saying:

"In Benares, at the hermitage of the Migadaya, the supreme
wheel of the empire of Truth has been set rolling by the Blessed
One—that wheel which not by any Samana or Brahman, not by
any god, not by any Brahma or Mara, not by any one in the
universe, can ever be turned back!"

28. And thus, in an instant, a second, a moment, the sound
went up even to the world of Brahma: and this great ten-
thousand-world-system quaked and trembled and was shaken vio-
lently, and an immeasurable bright light appeared in the universe,
beyond even the power of the gods!

29. Then did the Blessed One give utterance to this exclama-
tion of joy: "Kondanna hath realized it. Kondanna hath realized
it!" And so the venerable Kondanna acquired the name of
Annata-Kondanna ("the Kondanna who realized").[6]

[5]Mara is the Evil One.
[6]Kondanna was one of the five monks who became Buddha's first disciples.
The ordination of the other four, Vappa, Bhaddiya, Mahanama, and Assagi,
took place on the following days. The Maha Vagga completes the verse as
follows: "And then the venerable Annata-Kondanna having seen the truth,
having arrived at the truth, having known the truth, having penetrated the
truth, having past beyond doubt, having laid aside uncertainty, having
attained to confidence and being dependent on no one beside himself for

2. Lamp Unto Yourself
(Buddha's Last Sermon)

Now when the Blessed One had remained as long as he wished at Ambapali's grove, he addressed Ananda, and said: "Come, Ananda,[1] let us go on to Beluva."[2]

"So be it, Lord," said Ananda, in assent, to the Blessed One.

Then the Blessed One proceeded, with a great company of the brethren, to Beluva, and there the Blessed One stayed in the village itself.

Now the Blessed One there addressed the brethren, and said: "O mendicants, do you take up your abode round about Vesali, each according to the place where his friends, intimates, and close companions may live, for the rainy season of vassa. I shall enter upon the rainy season here at Beluva."

"So be it, Lord!" said those brethren, in assent, to the Blessed One. And they entered upon the rainy season round about Vesali, each according to the place where his friends or intimates or close companions lived: whilst the Blessed One stayed even there at Beluva.

Now when the Blessed One had thus entered upon the rainy season, there fell upon him a dire sickness, and sharp pains came upon him, even unto death. But the Blessed One, mindful and self-possessed, bore them without complaint.

Then this thought occurred to the Blessed One, "It would not be right for me to pass away from existence without addressing the disciples, without taking leave of the order. Let me now, by

[1]Ananda means literally "joy" or "bliss"; he was the cousin and foremost disciple of the Buddha.

[2]Beluva is a village at the foot of a hill near Vesali.

knowledge of the religion of the teacher, spake thus to the Blessed One:

" 'May I become, O my Lord, a novice under the Blessed One, may I receive full ordination!'

" 'Welcome, O brother!' said the Blessed One, 'the truth has been well laid down. Practice holiness to the complete suppression of sorrow!'

"And that was the ordination of the Venerable One."

a strong effort of the will, bend this sickness down again, and keep my hold on life till the allotted time be come."

And the Blessed One, by a strong effort of the will, bent that sickness down again, and kept his hold on life till the time he fixed upon should come. And the sickness abated upon him.

Now very soon after, the Blessed One began to recover; when he had quite got rid of the sickness, he went out from the monastery, and sat down behind the monastery on a seat spread out there. And the venerable Ananda went to the place where the Blessed One was, and saluted him, and took a seat and respectfully on one side, and addressed the Blessed One, and said: "I have beheld, Lord, how the Blessed One was in health, and I have beheld how the Blessed One had to suffer. And though at the sight of the sickness of the Blessed One my body became weak as a creeper, and the horizon became dim to me, and my faculties were no longer clear, yet notwithstanding I took some little comfort from the thought that the Blessed One would not pass away from existence until at least he had left instructions as touching the order."

"What, then, Ananda? Does the order expect that of me? I have preached the truth without making any distinction between exoteric and esoteric doctrine: for in respect of the truths, Ananda, the Tathagata has no such thing as the closed fist of a teacher, who keeps some things back. Surely, Ananda, should there be any one who harbours the thought, 'It is I who will lead the brotherhood,' or, 'The order is dependent upon me,' it is he who should lay down instructions in any matter concerning the order. Now the Tathagata, Ananda, thinks not that it is he who should lead the brotherhood, or that the order is dependent upon him. Why then should he leave instructions in any matter concerning the order! I too, O Ananda, am now grown old, and full of years, my journey is drawing to its close, I have reached my sum of days, I am turning eighty years of age; and just as a worn-out cart, Ananda, can only with much additional care be made to move along, so, methinks, the body of the Tathagata can only be kept going with much additional care. It is only, Ananda, when the Tathagata, ceasing to attend to any outward thing, or to experience any sensation, becomes plunged in that devout meditation of heart which is concerned with no material object—it is only then that the body of the Tathagata is at ease.

"Therefore, O Ananda, be ye lamps unto yourselves. Be ye a refuge to yourselves. Betake yourselves to no external refuge. Hold fast to the truth as a lamp. Hold fast as a refuge to the truth. Look not for refuge to any one besides yourselves. And how, Ananda, is a brother to be a lamp unto himself, a refuge to himself, betaking himself to no external refuge, holding fast to the truth as a lamp, holding fast as a refuge to the truth, look-ing not for refuge to any one besides himself?

"Herein, O Ananda, let a brother, as he dwells in the body, so regard the body that he, being strenuous, thoughtful, and mind-ful, may, whilst in the world, overcome the grief which arises from bodily craving—while subject to sensations let him continue so to regard the sensations that he, being strenuous, thoughtful, and mindful, may, whilst in the world, overcome the grief which arises from the sensations—and so, also, as he thinks, or reasons, or feels, let him overcome the grief which arises from the crav-ing due to ideas, or to reasoning, or to feeling.

"And whosoever, Ananda, either now or after I am dead, shall be a lamp unto themselves, and a refuge unto themselves, shall betake themselves to no external refuge, but holding fast to the truth as their lamp, and holding fast as their refuge to the truth, shall look not for refuge to any one besides themselves—it is they, Ananda, among my Bhikkhus, who shall reach the very topmost Height!—but they must be anxious to learn."

3. The Questions of
King Milinda

Book II

Chapter 1
The Doctrine of Not-Self[1]

Now Milinda the king went up to where the venerable Nagasena was, and addressed him with the greetings and compliments of

[1]The literal title of this book is "The Distinguishing Characteristics of Ethi-cal Qualities," but it has gained attention for its exposition of the doctrine of the Theravadin "not-self." The Questions of King Milinda states most clearly obscure Buddhist teachings for the half-European, Greco-Bactrian King Menandros. It is shallower than other writings because of this, but the questions and answers for "King Milinda" offer a painless, even pleas-ant introduction to the complicated principles and beliefs of the Hina-yana (Theravadin) or southern Buddhist teachings. The Questions of King Milinda represent the Theravadin aspect of the Buddhist "wisdom" or prajna texts.

friendship and courtesy, and took his seat respectfully apart. And Nagasena reciprocated his courtesy, so that the heart of the king was propitiated.

And Milinda began by asking, "How is your Reverence known, and what, Sir, is your name?"

"I am known as Nagasena, O king, and it is by that name that my brethren in the faith address me. But although parents, O king, give such a name as Nagasena, or Surasena, or Virasena, or Sihasena, yet this, Sire,—Nagasena and so on—is only a generally understood term, a designation in common use. For there is no permanent individuality (no soul) involved in the matter." [2]

Then Milinda called upon the Yonakas and the brethren to witness: "This Nagasena says there is no permanent individuality (no soul) implied in his name. Is it now even possible to approve him in that?" And turning to Nagasena, he said: "If, most reverend Nagasena, there be no permanent individuality (no soul) involved in the matter, who is it, pray, who gives to you members of the Order your robes and food and lodging and necessaries for the sick? Who is it who enjoys such things when given? Who is it who lives a life of righteousness? Who is it who devotes himself to meditation? Who is it who attains to the goal of the Excellent Way, to the Nirvana of Arahatship? And who is it who destroys living creatures? who is it who takes what is not his own? who is it who lives an evil life of worldly lusts, who speaks lies, who drinks strong drink, who (in a word) commits any one of the five sins which work out their bitter fruit even in this life? If that be so there is neither merit nor demerit; there is neither doer nor causer of good or evil deeds; there is neither fruit nor result of good or evil Karma. If, most reverent Nagasena, we are to think that were a man to kill you there would be no murder, then it follows that there are no real masters or teachers in your Order, and that your ordinations are void.—You tell me that your brethren in the Order are in the habit of addressing you as Nagasena. Now what is that Nagasena? Do you mean to say that the hair is Nagasena?"

"I don't say that, great king."

"Or the hairs on the body, perhaps?"

"Certainly not."

"Or is it the nails, the teeth, the skin, the flesh, the nerves, the bones, the marrow, the kidneys, the heart, the liver, the abdomen, the spleen, the lungs, the larger intestines, the lower intestines, the stomach, the fæces, the bile, the phlegm, the pus, the blood, the sweat, the fat, the tears, the serum, the saliva,

[2] This means that there is no permanent subject underlying the temporary phenomena visible in a man's individuality.

the mucus, the oil that lubricates the joints, the urine, or the brain, or any or all of these, that is Nagasena?"

And to each of these he answered no.

"Is it the outward form then (Rupa) that is Nagasena, or the sensations (Vedana), or the ideas (Sanna), or the confections (the constituent elements of character, Samkhara), or the consciousness (Vinnana), that is Nigasena?"

And to each of these also he answered no.

"Then is it all these skandhas combined that are Nagasena?"

"No! great king."

"But is there anything outside the five skandhas that is Nagasena?"

And still he answered no.

"Then thus, ask as I may, I can discover no Nagasena. Nagasena is a mere empty sound. Who then is the Nagasena that we see before us? It is a falsehood that your reverence has spoken, an untruth!"

And the venerable Nagasena said to Milinda the king: "You, Sire, have been brought up in great luxury, as beseems your noble birth. If you were to walk this dry weather on the hot and sandy ground, trampling under foot the gritty, gravelly grains of the hard sand, your feet would hurt you. And as your body would be in pain, your mind would be disturbed, and you would experience a sense of bodily suffering. How then did you come, on foot, or in a chariot?"

"I did not come, Sir, on foot. I came in a carriage."

"Then if you came, Sire, in a carriage, explain to me what that is. Is it the pole that is the chariot?"

"I did not say that."

"Is it the axle that is the chariot?"

"Certainly not."

"Is it the wheels, or the framework, or the ropes, or the yoke, or the spokes of the wheels, or the goad, that are the chariot?"

And to all these he still answered no.

"Then is it all these parts of it that are the chariot?"

"No, Sir."

"But is there anything outside them that is the chariot?"

And still he answered no.

"Then thus, ask as I may, I can discover no chariot. Chariot is a mere empty sound. What then is the chariot you say you came in? It is a falsehood that your Majesty has spoken, an untruth! There is no such thing as a chariot! You are king over all India, a mighty monarch. Of whom then are you afraid that you speak untruth?" And he called upon the Yonakas and the brethren to witness, saying: "Milinda the king here has said that he came by carriage. But when asked in that case to explain what the carriage was, he is unable to establish what he averred. Is it, forsooth, possible to approve him in that?"

When he had thus spoken the five hundred Yonakas shouted their applause, and said to the king: "Now let your Majesty get out of that if you can?"

And Milinda the king replied to Nagasena, and said: "I have spoken no untruth, reverend Sir. It is on account of its having all these things—the pole, and the axle, the wheels, and the framework, the ropes, the yoke, the spokes, and the goad—that it comes under the generally understood term, the designation in common use, of 'chariot.' "

"Very good! Your Majesty has rightly grasped the meaning of 'chariot.' And just even so it is on account of all those things you questioned me about the thirty-two kinds of organic matter in a human body, and the five constituent elements of being— that I come under the generally understood term, the designation in common use, of 'Nagasena.' For it was said, Sire, by our Sister Vagira in the presence of the Blessed One:

" 'Just as it is by the condition precedent of the co-existence of its various parts that the word "chariot" is used, just so is it that when the Skandhas are there we talk of a "being." ' "

"Most wonderful, Nagasena, and most strange. Well has the puzzle put to you, most difficult though it was, been solved. Were the Buddha himself here he would approve your answer. Well done, well done, Nagasena!"

FAITH

The king said, "Venerable Nagasena, what is the characteristic mark of faith?"

"Tranquillisation, O king, and aspiration."

"And how is tranquillisation the mark of faith?"

"As faith, O king, springs up in the heart it breaks through the five hindrances—lust, malice, mental sloth, spiritual pride, and doubt—and the heart, free from these hindrances, becomes clear, serene, untroubled."

"Give me an illustration."

"Just, O king, as a suzerain king, when on the march with his fourfold army, might cross over a small stream, and the water, disturbed by the elephants and cavalry, the chariots and the bowmen, might become fouled, turbid, and muddy. And when he was on the other side the monarch might give command to his attendants, saying: 'Bring some water, my good men. I would fain drink.' Now suppose the monarch had a water-clearing

gem,[3] and those men, in obedience to the order, were to throw
the jewel into the water; then at once all the mud would precip-
itate itself, and the sandy atoms of shell and bits of water-
plants would disappear, and the water would become clear,
transparent, and serene, and they would then bring some of it to
the monarch to drink. The water is the heart; the royal servants
are the recluse; the mud, the sandy atoms, and the bits of
water-plants are evil dispositions; and the water-cleansing gem is
faith."

"And how is aspiration the mark of faith?"

"In as much as the recluse, on perceiving how the hearts of
others have been set free, aspires to enter as it were by a leap
upon the fruit of the first stage, or of the second, or of the third
in the Excellent Way, or to gain Arahatship itself, and thus applies himself to the attainment of what he has not reached, to
the experience of what he has not yet felt, to the realisation of
what he has not yet realised,—therefore is it that aspiration is
the mark of faith."

"Give me an illustration."

"Just, O king, as if a mighty storm were to break upon a
mountain top and pour out rain, the water would flow down according to the levels, and after filling up the crevices and chasms
and gullies of the hill, would empty itself into the brook below,
so that the stream would rush along, overflowing both its banks.
Now suppose a crowd of people, one after the other, were to
come up, and being ignorant of the real breadth or depth of the
water, were to stand fearful and hesitating on the brink. And
suppose a certain man should arrive, who knowing exactly his
own strength and power should gird himself firmly and, with a
spring, land himself on the other side. Then the rest of the
people, seeing him safe on the other side, would likewise cross.
That is the kind of way in which the recluse, by faith,[4] aspires
to leap, as it were by a bound, into higher things. For this has
been said, O king, by the Blessed One in the Samyutta Nikaya:

"By faith he crosses over the stream,
By earnestness the sea of life;
By steadfastness all grief he stills,
By wisdom is he purified."

[3] A magic gem is probably meant here, particularly the allusion to the Wondrous Gem of the mythical King of Glory.
[4] Faith, that is, in Buddha and the sufficiency of the Excellent Way. There
must also be faith in the capacity of man to walk along the Way. The Buddhist and Christian views of faith are similar, as Rhys Davids puts it, in that
"the two conditions of heart are strikingly similar in both origin and in
consequence."

"Well put, Nagasena!"

The king said: "What, Nagasena, is the characteristic mark of perseverance?"

"The rendering of support, O king, is the mark of perseverance. All those good qualities which it supports do not fall away."

"Give me an illustration."

"Just as a man, if a house were falling, would make a prop for it of another post, and the house so supported would not fall; just so, O king, is the rendering of support the mark of perseverance, and all those good qualities which it supports do not fall away."

"Give me a further illustration."

"Just as when a large army has broken up a small one, then the king of the latter would call to mind every possible ally and reinforce his small army, and by that means the small army might in its turn break up the large one; just so, O king, is the rendering of support the mark of perseverance, and all those good qualities which it supports do not fall away. For it has been said by the Blessed One: 'The persevering hearer of the noble truth, O Bhikkhus, puts away evil and cultivates goodness, puts away that which is wrong and develops in himself that which is right, and thus does he keep himself pure.'"

"Well put, Nagasena!"

MINDFULNESS (SATI)

The king said: "What, Nagasena, is the characteristic mark of mindfulness?"[5]

"Repetition, O king, and keeping up."

"And how is repetition the mark of mindfulness?"

"As mindfulness, O king, springs up in his heart he repeats over the good and evil, right and wrong, slight and important, dark and light qualities, and those that resemble them, saying to himself: 'These are the four modes of keeping oneself ready and mindful, these the four modes of spiritual effort, these the four bases of extraordinary powers, these the five organs of the moral sense, these the five mental powers, these the seven bases of Arahatship, these the eight divisions of the Excellent Way, this

[5]T. W. Rhys Davids notes that the word sati, which he translates as mindfulness here, is one of the most difficult words in the whole Buddhist system of ethical psychology to translate. Others have rendered sati as conscience, meditation (both of which Rhys Davids thinks is wrong), or self-possession. Its etymological meaning is "memory," but it means considerably more than that in Buddhist terminology. It carries within it the idea of activity of mind, of constant presence of mind, wakefulness of heart. The word is very important because it is a constant theme of the Buddhist moralist.

is serenity and this insight, this is wisdom and this emancipation.' Thus does the recluse follow after those qualities that are desirable, and not after those that are not; thus does he cultivate those which ought to be practised, and not those which ought not. That is how repetition is the mark of mindfulness."

"Give me an illustration."

"It is like the treasurer of the imperial sovran, who reminds his royal master early and late of his glory, saying: 'So many are thy war elephants, O king, and so many thy cavalry, thy war chariots and thy bowmen, so much the quantity of thy money, and gold, and wealth, may your Majesty keep yourself in mind thereof.'"

"And how, Sir, is keeping up a mark of mindfulness?"

"As mindfulness springs up in his heart, O king, he searches out the categories of good qualities and their opposites, saying to himself: 'Such and such qualities are good, and such bad; such and such qualities helpful, and such the reverse.' Thus does the recluse make what is evil in himself to disappear, and keeps up what is good. That is how keeping up is the mark of mindfulness."

"Give me an illustration."

"It is like the confidential adviser of that imperial sovran who instructs him in good and evil, saying: 'These things are bad for the king and these good, these helpful and these the reverse.' And thus the king makes the evil in himself die out, and keeps up the good."

"Well put, Nagasena!"

MEDITATION

The king said: "What, Nagasena, is the characteristic mark of meditation?"

"Being the leader, O king. All good qualities have meditation as their chief, they incline to it, lead up towards it, are as so many slopes up the side of the mountain of meditation."

"Give me an illustration."

"As all the rafters of the roof of a house, O king, go up to the apex, slope towards it, are joined on together at it, and the apex is acknowledged to be the top of all; so is the habit of meditation in its relation to other good qualities."

"Give me a further illustration."

"It is like a king, your Majesty, when he goes down to battle with his army in its fourfold array. The whole army—elephants, cavalry, war chariots, and bowmen—would have him as their chief, their lines would incline towards him, lead up to him, they would be so many mountain slopes, one above another, with him as their summit, round him they would all be ranged. And it has been said, O king, by the Blessed One: "Cultivate in yourself, O Bhikkhus, the habit of meditation. He who is established therein knows things as they really are.'"

"Well put, Nagasena!"

WISDOM

The king said: "What, Nagasena, is the characteristic mark of wisdom?"

"I have already told you, O king, how cutting off, severance, is its mark, but enlightenment is also its mark."

"And how is enlightenment its mark?"

"When wisdom springs up in the heart, O king, it dispels the darkness of ignorance, it causes the radiance of knowledge to arise, it makes the light of intelligence to shine forth, and it makes the Noble Truths plain. Thus does the recluse who is devoted to effort perceive with the clearest wisdom the impermanency of all beings and things, the suffering that is inherent in individuality, and the absence of any soul."

"Give me an illustration."

"It is like a lamp, O king, which a man might introduce into a house in darkness. When the lamp had been brought in it would dispel the darkness, cause radiance to arise, and light to shine forth, and make the objects there plainly visible. Just so would wisdom in a man have such effects as were just now set forth."

"Well put, Nagasena!"

The king said: "These qualities which are so different, Nagasena, do they bring about one and the same result?"

"They do. The putting an end to evil dispositions."

"How is that? Give me an illustration."

"They are like the various parts of an army—elephants, cavalry, war chariots, and archers—who all work to one end, to wit: the conquest in battle of the opposing army."

"Well put, Nagasena!"

THE POWER OF LOVE

"Venerable Nagasena, it has been said by the Blessed One: 'Eleven advantages, O brethren, may be anticipated from practising, making a habit of, enlarging within one, using as a means of advancement, and as a basis of conduct, pursuing after, accumulating, and rising well up to the very heights of the emancipation of heart, arising from a feeling of love towards all beings. And what are these eleven? He who does so sleeps in peace, and in peace does he awake. He dreams no sinful dreams. He becomes dear to men, and to the beings who are not men.[6] The gods watch over him. Neither fire, nor poison, nor sword works any harm to him. Quickly and easily does he become tranquillised. The aspect of his countenance is calm. Undismayed does he meet death, and should he not press through to the Supreme Condition of Arahatship, then is he sure of rebirth in the Brahma world.' But on the other hand you members of the Order say that Sama the Prince, while dwelling in the cultivation of a loving disposition toward all beings, and when he was in consequence thereof wandering in the forest followed by a herd of deer, was hit by a poisoned arrow shot by Piliyakkha the king, and there, on the spot, fainted and fell.' Now, venerable Nagasena, if the passage I have quoted from the words of the Blessed One be right, then this statement of yours must be wrong. But if the story of Prince Sama be right, then it cannot be true that neither fire, nor poison, nor sword can work harm to him who cultivates the habit of love to all beings. This too is a double-edged problem. so subtle, so abstruse, so delicate, and so profound, that the thought of having to solve it might well bring out sweat over the body even of the most subtle-minded of mortals. This problem is now put to you. Unravel this mighty knot. Throw light upon this matter to the accomplishment of the desire of those sons of the Conqueror who shall arise hereafter."

"The Blessed One spake, O king, as you have quoted. And Prince Sama dwelling in the cultivation of love, and thus followed by a herd of deer when he was wandering in the forest, was hit by the poisoned arrow shot by king Piliyakkha, and then and there fainted and fell. But there is a reason for that. And what is the reason? Simply that those virtues (said in the passage you quoted to be in the habit of love) are virtues not attached to the personality of the one who loves, but to the actual presence of the love that he has called up in his heart.[7] And when Prince Sama was upsetting the water-pot, that moment he lapsed from the actual feeling of love. At the moment, O king, in which an individual has realised the sense of love, that moment neither fire, nor poison, nor sword can do him harm. If any men bent on doing him an injury come up, they will not see him, neither will they have a chance of hurting him. But these

[6]This doesn't mean gods, but various spirits on the earth, such as fairies, dryads, and nayads.

[7]The Pali word used here, bhanana, means more than simply "cultivation" of the heart or love. It is the actual presence, the felt sense of a particular state being cultivated—as in this case, of love. Rhys Davids has translated it also as "meditation."

virtues, O king, are not inherent in the individual, they are in the actual felt presence of the love that he is calling up in his heart.

"Suppose, O king, a man were to take into his hand a Vanishing Root of supernatural power; and that, so long as it was actually in his hand, no other ordinary person would be able to see him. The virtue, then, would not be in the man. It would be in the root that such virtue would reside that an object in the very line of sight of ordinary mortals could, nevertheless, not be seen. Just so, O king, is it with the virtue inherent in the felt presence of love that a man has called up in his heart.

"Or it is like the case of a man who has entered into a well-formed mighty cave. No storm of rain, however mightily it might pour down, would be able to wet him. But that would be by no virtue inherent in the man. It would be a virtue inherent in the cave that so mighty a downpour of rain could not wet the man. And just so, O king, is it with the virtue inherent in the felt presence of love that a man has called up in his heart."[8]

"Most wonderful is it, Nagasena, and most strange how the felt presence of love has the power of warding off all evil states of mind."

"Yes! The practice of love is productive of all virtuous conditions of mind both in good (beings) and in evil ones. To all beings whatsoever, who are in the bonds of conscious existence, is this practice of love of great advantage, and therefore ought it to be sedulously cultivated."

[8] The early Buddhists did believe in the power of a subjective love over external circumstances. It is true that the best examples of this power of love were over their hearts, and hence indirectly over their actions. There is the story that Devadatta had let loose against the Buddha the fierce, manslaying elephant Nalagiri, but the Buddha is said to have permeated the beast with his love and the elephant moved up to him to be stroked. And another tale relates how the five disciples intended to show Buddha no respect when he went to Benares, but the Buddha is said to have "concentrated that feeling of his love, which was able to pervade generally all beings in earth and heaven," and to have this "sense of his love diffused through their hearts." As he came nearer they rose from their seats and bowed down before him and welcomed him, no longer capable of resisting his love.

4. If He Should Desire
(Akankheyya)

Thus have I heard. The Blessed One was once staying at Savatthi in Anatha Pindika's park.

There the Blessed One addressed the Brethren, and said, "Bhikkhus." "Yea, Lord!" said the Brethren, in assent, to the Blessed One.

Then spake the Blessed One:

"Continue, Brethren, in the practice of Right Conduct, adhering to the Rules of the Order; continue enclosed by the restraint of the Rules of the Order, devoted to uprightness in life; train yourselves according to the Precepts, taking them upon you in the sense of the danger in the least offence.

"If a Bhikkhu should desire, Brethren, to become beloved, popular, respected among his fellow-disciples, let him then fulfil all righteousness, let him be devoted to that quietude of heart which springs from within, let him not drive back the ecstasy of contemplation, let him look through things,[1] let him be much alone!

"If a Bhikkhu should desire, Brethren, to receive the requisites—clothing, food, lodging, and medicine, and other necessaries for the sick—let him then fulfil all righteousness, let him be devoted to that quietude of heart which springs from within, let him not drive back the ecstasy of contemplation, let him look through things, let him be much alone!

"If a Bikkhu should desire, Brethren, that to those people among whom he receives the requisites—clothing, food, lodging, and medicine, and other necessaries for the sick—that charity of theirs should redound to great fruit and great advantage, let him then fulfil all righteousness, let him be devoted to that quietude of heart which springs from within, let him not drive back the ecstasy of contemplation, let him look through things, let him be much alone!

[1] This involves insight into objective phenomena, and is one of the three major qualities constantly referred to as a prerequisite of Arhatship. The Arhat is the highest saint of Buddhists, and exempt from further rebirth.

"If a Bhikkhu should desire, Brethren, that those relatives of his, of one blood with him, dead and gone, who think of him with believing heart should find therein great fruit and great advantage,[2] let him then fulfil all righteousness, let him be devoted to that quietude of heart which springs from within, let him not drive back the ecstasy of contemplation, let him look through things, let him be much alone!

"If a Bhikkhu should desire, Brethren, that he should be victorious over discontent and lust, that discontent should never overpower him, that he should master and subdue any discontent that had sprung up within him, let him then fulfil all righteousness, let him be devoted to that quietude of heart which springs from within, let him not drive back the ecstasy of contemplation, let him look through things, let him be much alone!

"If a Bhikkhu should desire, Brethren, that he should be victorious over spiritual danger and dismay, that neither danger nor dismay should ever overcome him, that he should master and subdue every danger and dismay, let him then fulfil all righteousness, let him be devoted to that quietude of heart which springs from within, let him not drive back the ecstasy of contemplation, let him look through things, let him be much alone!

"If a Bhikkhu should desire, Brethren, to realise the hopes of those spiritual men who live in the bliss which comes, even in this present world, from the four Ghanas, should he desire not to fall into the pains and difficulties which they avoid, let him then fulfil all righteousness, let him be devoted to that quietude of heart which springs from within, let him not drive back the ecstasy of contemplation, let him look through things, let him be much alone![3]

"If a Bhikkhu should desire, Brethren, to reach with his body and remain in those stages of deliverance which are incorporeal, and pass beyond phenomena, let him then fulfil all righteousness, let him be devoted to that quietude of heart which springs from within, let him not drive back the ecstasy of contemplation, let him look through things, let him be much alone!

"If a Bhikkhu should desire, Brethren, by the complete destruction of the three Bonds to become converted, to be no longer liable to be reborn in a state of suffering, and to be assured of final salvation, let him then fulfil all righteousness, let him be devoted to that quietude of heart which springs from within, let him not drive back the ecstasy of contemplation, let him look through things, let him be much alone!

"If a Bhikkhu should desire, Brethren, by the complete

[2] Even after death those who remember the Buddha, the Truth, or the Order with believing heart can reap spiritual advantage.

[3] The bliss here described is the "ecstasy of contemplation."

destruction of the three Bonds, and by the reduction to a mini-
mum of lust, hatred, and delusion, to become a Sakadagamin,
and thus on his first return to this world to make an end of sorrow, let him then fulfil all righteousness, let him be devoted to
that quietude of heart which springs from within, let him not
drive back the ecstasy of contemplation, let him look through
things, let him be much alone!

"If a Bhikkhu should desire, Brethren, by the complete
destruction of the five Bonds which bind people to this earth, to
become an inheritor[4] of the highest heavens, there to pass entirely away, thence never to return, let him then fulfil all righteousness, let him be devoted to that quietude of heart which
springs from within, let him not drive back the ecstasy of contemplation, let him look through things, let him be much alone!

"If a Bhikkhu should desire, Brethren, to comprehend by his
own heart the hearts of other beings and of other men; to discern the passionate mind to be passionate, and the calm mind
calm; the angry mind to be angry, and the peaceable peaceable;
the deluded mind to be deluded, and the wise mind wise; the
concentrated thoughts to be concentrated, and the scattered to
be scattered; the lofty mind to be lofty, and the narrow mind
narrow; the sublime thoughts to be sublime, and the mean to be
mean; the steadfast mind to be steadfast, and the wavering to
be wavering; the free mind to be free, and the enslaved mind to
be enslaved; let him then fulfil all righteousness, let him be devoted to that quietude of heart which springs from within, let
him not drive back the ecstasy of contemplation, let him look
through things, let him be much alone!

"If a Bhikkhu should desire, Brethren, to be able to call to
mind his various temporary states in days gone by; such as one
birth, two births, three, four, five, ten, twenty, thirty, forty,
fifty, a hundred or a thousand, or a hundred thousand births;
his births in many an æon of destruction, in many an æon of
renovation, in many an æon of both destruction and renova-

[4] T. W. Rhys Davids comments that this is another of those words that simply cannot be translated adequately to convey the Buddhist idea behind it.
It means a being who springs into existence without the intervention of
parents, and is therefore uncaused, and who seemingly appears by chance.
All the higher devas (gods or angels) are created this way (opapatika), there
being no sex or birth in the highest heavens. From the Buddhist point of
view, which admits nothing without a cause, the sufficient cause for the
appearance of the opapatika was the passing away of a being somewhere
else and that person's karma. But Buddhist theory could not accept the
heretical idea of a soul flying away after the death of its body from one
world to another, so it necessitated an expression (opapatika) that could
utilize the composite characteristics of that individual's being as the basis
for the creation of another totally different one.

tion,[5] so as to be able to say: In that place such was my
name, such my family, such my caste, such my subsistence, such
my experience of comfort or of pain, and such the limit of my
life; and when I passed from thence, I took form again in that
other place where my name was so and so, such my family, such
my caste, such my subsistence, such my experience of comfort
or of joy, and such my term of life; and when I fell from
thence, I took form in such and such a place;—should he desire
thus to call to mind his temporary states in days gone by in all
their modes and all their details let him then fulfil all righteousness, let him be devoted to that quietude of heart which springs
from within, let him not drive back the ecstasy of contemplation, let him look through things, let him be much alone!

"If a Bhikkhu should desire, Brethren, to see with pure and
heavenly vision, surpassing that of men, beings as they pass
from one state of existence and take form in others; beings base
or noble, good-looking or ill-favoured, happy or miserable, according to the karma they inherit—if he should desire to be able
to say: These beings, reverend sirs, by their bad conduct in action, by their bad conduct in word, by their bad conduct in
thought, by their speaking evil of the Noble Ones,[6] by their
adhesion to false doctrine, or by their acquiring the karma of
false doctrine, have been reborn, on the dissolution of the body
after death, in some unhappy state of suffering or woe. These
beings, reverend sirs, by their good conduct in action, by their
good conduct in word, by their good conduct in thought, by
their not speaking evil of the Noble Ones, by their adhesion to
right doctrine, by their acquiring the karma of right doctrine,
have been reborn, on the dissolution of the body after death,
into some happy state in heaven;—should he desire thus to see
with pure and heavenly vision, surpassing that of men, beings as
they thus pass from one state of existence and take form in others; beings base or noble, good-looking or ill-favoured, happy or
miserable, according to the karma they inherit; let him then fulfil all righteousness, let him be devoted to that quietude of heart
which springs from within, let him not drive back the ecstasy of
contemplation, let him look through things, let him be much
alone!

"If a Bhikkhu should desire, Brethren, by the destruction of
the great evils (Asavas),[7] by himself, and even in this very

[5]This is based on the Buddhist theory of the periodical destruction and creation of the universe, each of which takes countless years to come about.

[6]This is a collective term meaning several different types of Buddhas (Pak-
keka Buddhas, Arahats, Anagamins, Sakadagamins, and Sotapannas), who
are walking the Noble Eightfold Path.

[7]That is, sensuality, individuality, delusion, and ignorance.

world, to know and realise and attain to Arahatship, to emancipation of heart, and emancipation of mind, let him then fulfil all righteousness, let him be devoted to that quietude of heart which springs from within, let him not drive back the ecstasy of contemplation, let him look through things, let him be much alone!"

Thus spake the Blessed One. And those Brethren, delighted in heart, exalted the word of the Blessed One.

5. The Way of Purity
(Visuddhi-Magga)

THE NINETEENTH CHAPTER, CALLED PURITY FROM THE REMOVAL OF DOUBT

The knowledge of the dependence of name and form and the consequent removal of doubt in the three divisions of time is called the Purity Ensuing on the Removal of Doubt.

The priest who is desirous of this knowledge enters on a search for the causes and dependence of name and form, just as a skilful physician seeing a disease will search to find how it arose, or just as a compassionate man seeing a small, weakly, helpless boy-baby lying on its back in the middle of the road will try to discover its parents.

And at first he reflects as follows: "Name and form can not be without a cause, as they are not the same everywhere, at all times, and for all people; nor yet are they caused by any personal power or the like, for there is no such power behind name and form; nor, again, are they right who say that name and form themselves constitute such a power, as the name and form thus called a personal power or the like are not a cause. Therefore it must needs be that name and form have causes and a dependence. And what are they?

"Having made these reflections, he begins to investigate the causes and dependence of form, as follows: When this body comes into existence, it does not arise in the midst of nymphaeas, nelumbiums, lotuses, and water-lilies, etc., nor of jewels, pearl-necklaces, etc.; but ill-smelling, disgusting, and repulsive, it arises between the stomach and the lower intestines, with the belly-wall behind and the backbone in front, in the midst of the entrails and mesentery, in an exceedingly contracted, ill-smelling, disgusting, and repulsive place, like a worm in rotten fish, carrion, or rancid gruel, or in a stagnant or dirty pool or the like. As it thus comes into being, these four—ignorance, desire, attachment, and karma—are the cause of it, inasmuch as they produce it; food is its dependence, inasmuch as it supports it. These five are its causes and dependence. Three of these—ignorance, etc.—are the basis for this body, as is the mother for the child; karma is the begetter, as is the father of the son; food is the sustainer, like the nurse."

Having thus grasped the dependence of form, he then grasps the dependence of name, as follows: "In dependence on the eye and in respect to form, eye-consciousness arises," etc.

When he has thus perceived the dependent manner of existence of name and form, he reaches the insight: "As name and form have at the present time a dependent manner of existence, so also had they in the past time, and so will they have in the future." In reaching this insight, that which is called the fivefold questioning concerning the past, namely:

"Did I exist in past time?

"Did I not exist in past time?

"What was I in past time?

"How was I in past time?

"Did I in past time change from one existence to another?" and that called the fivefold questioning concerning the future, namely:

"Shall I exist in future time?

"Shall I not exist in future time?

"What shall I be in future time?

"How shall I be in future time?

"Shall I in the future change from one existence to another?" and that called the sixfold questioning concerning the present, throwing doubt on his present existence, namely:

"Am I?

"Am I not?

"What am I?

"How am I?

"Whence came this existing being?

"Whither is it to go?"—
are all abandoned.

Another observes the twofold dependence of name as general and specific, and the fourfold one of form, as karma, etc.

For the dependence of name is twofold—general and specific. The six sense-apertures: eye, etc., and the six objects of sense: form etc., are the general dependence of name in respect of giv-

ing rise to any kind of name whether meritorious or not; but attention, etc., are special. For philosophic attention, listening to
the Good Doctrine, etc., are the dependence of only meritorious
name. Their opposites are the dependence of that which is demeritorious; karma, etc., of fruition; existence-substratum, etc.,
of action.

Of form, however, karma, etc., *i.e.*, karma, thoughts, the seasons, and nutriment, constitutes the fourfold dependence.

Of these four, it is past karma which is the dependence of
form springing from karma; present thoughts of that springing
from thoughts; the seasons and nutriment are the dependence
for the continuance of that springing from the seasons and from
nutriment.

Thus does one priest grasp the dependence of name and form.
And when he has perceived their dependent manner of existence
he reaches the insight: "As name and form have at the present
time a dependent manner of existence, so also had they in past
time, and so will they have in the future." And when he reaches
this insight, the questioning concerning the three divisions of
time is abandoned as aforesaid.

Another observes in respect of these constituents of being,
called name and form, their growing old and their subsequent
dissolution, as follows: "The old age and death of the constituents of being exist when birth exists, birth when existence exists,
existence when attachment exists, attachment when desire exists,
desire when sensation exists, sensation when contact exists, contact when the six organs of sense exist, the six organs of sense
when name and form exist, name and form when consciousness
exists, consciousness when karma exists, karma when ignorance
exists." Thus does he grasp the dependence of name and form by
considering Dependent Origination in the reverse direction. And
his questioning is abandoned as aforesaid.

Another grasps the dependence of name and form by first considering the formula of Dependent Origination in the forward
direction, in full, "Behold! On ignorance depends karma," etc.
And his questioning is abandoned as aforesaid.

Another grasps the dependence of name and form by considering the round of karma and the round of its fruit as follows:

"Behold! in a former karma-existence, infatuation-ignorance,
initiatory karma, longing desire, approximating attachment, and
thought-existence—these five factors were the dependence for
conception into this existence; rebirth-consciousness, the descent
of name and form, the sensitiveness of the organs of sense, the
contact experienced, the sensation felt, these five factors belonging to the originating-existence of the present life depend on the
karma of a previous existence; when the senses have matured,

then infatuation-ignorance, . . . thought-existence—these five factors of a present karma-existence are the dependence of rebirth
in the future."

Now karma is fourfold:

That which bears fruit in the present existence;

That which bears fruit in rebirth;

That which bears fruit at no fixed time; and

Bygone karma.

The karma which bears fruit in the present existence is the
meritorious or demeritorious thoughts constituting the first
swiftness in the seven thoughts of a stream of swiftnesses. That
brings forth fruit in this existence. But if it fail to do so, then it
is bygone karma, and it is to be said of it in respect to the three
divisions of time, as follows: "That karma has gone by: there
was no fruit from it, nor will there be, nor is there."

The karma which bears fruit in rebirth is the efficacious
thought which constitutes the seventh swiftness. That bears fruit
in the next existence. But if it fail to do so, it is bygone karma,
as described above.

The karma which bears fruit at no fixed time is the thoughts
constituting the five intermediate swiftnesses. That bears fruit in
the future whenever it may find opportunity, and as long as the
round of rebirth continues there is no bygone karma.

There is another fourfold division of karma:

The weighty;

The abundant;

The close at hand; and

The habitual.

Weighty karma—whether meritorious or demeritorious, such as
matricide and other serious crimes of the sort, or lofty deeds—
bears fruit before that which is not weighty.

That which is abundant, whether good conduct or bad conduct, bears fruit before that which is not abundant.

That which is close at hand is karma remembered at the moment of death. For the karma which a man remembers at the
point of death springs up with him in rebirth.

But distinct from all these three is karma that has become
habitual through much repetition. This brings on rebirth when
the other three are absent.

There is another fourfold division of karma:

Productive;

Supportive;

Counteractive; and

Destructive.

Productive karma may be either meritorious or demeritorious.

It produces both form and the other fruition-groups, not only at the time of conception, but as long as they continue.

Supportive karma can not produce fruit, but when rebirth has been given by other karma, and fruit has been produced, it supports the ensuing happiness or misery, and brings about its continuance.

Counteractive karma, when rebirth has been given by other karma, and fruit has been produced, counteracts the ensuing happiness or misery, suppresses it, and does not suffer it to continue.

Destructive karma, whether meritorious or demeritorious, destroys other weak karma, and, preventing it from bearing fruit, makes room for its own fruition. The fruit which thus arises is called apparitional.

The distinction between these twelve different karmas and their fruits have their inner nature plainly revealed to the insight into karma and its fruit possessed by the Buddhas, but this insight is not shared in by their disciples. The man of insight, however, should know the general distinction between karma and the fruit of karma. Therefore it is that these distinctions of karma are only explained in rough outline.

Thus does this one, in merging these twelve karmas together in the round of karma, grasp the dependence of name and form by considering the round of karma and the round of its fruit.

He who, by thus considering the round of karma and the round of fruit, grasps the dependent manner of existence of name and form, reaches the insight: "As name and form have in the present time a dependent manner of existence by means of a round of karma and a round of fruit, so also had they in past time, and so will they have in the future."

Thus does he have karma and fruit, a round of karma and a round of fruit, karma's manner of existing and the fruit's manner of existing, the karma-series and the fruit-series, action and the effect of action. And he attains to the insight:

> "A round of karma and of fruit;
> The fruit from karma doth arise,
> From karma then rebirth doth spring;
> And thus the world rolls on and on."

When he has attained this insight, the sixteen above-mentioned doubts concerning the past, present, and future, "Did I exist?" etc., are all abandoned. And it becomes evident to him that it is merely name and form which passes through the various modes, classes, stages, grades, and forms of existence by means of a connection of cause and effect. He sees that behind

the action there is no actor, and that, although actions bear
their fruit, there is no one that experiences that fruit. He then
sees clearly, in the light of the highest knowledge, that when a
cause is acting, or the fruit of an action ripens, it is merely by a
conventional form of speech that the wise speak of an actor or
of any one as experiencing the fruit of an action. Therefore have
the ancients said,

"No doer is there does the deed,
Nor is there one who feels the fruit;
Constituent parts alone roll on;
This view alone is orthodox.

"And thus the deed, and thus the fruit
Roll on and on, each from its cause;
As of the round of tree and seed,
No one can tell when they began.

"Nor is the time to be perceived
In future births when they shall cease.
The heretics perceive not this,
And fail of mastery o'er themselves.

" 'An Ego'," say they, 'doth exist,
Eternal, or that soon will cease';
Thus two-and-sixty heresies
They 'mongst themselves discordant hold.

"Bound in the bonds of heresy,
By passion's flood they're borne along;
And borne along by passion's flood,
From misery find they no release.

"If once these facts he but perceive,
A priest whose faith on Buddha rests,
The subtile, deep, and self-devoid
Dependence then will penetrate.

"Not in its fruit is found the deed,
Nor in the deed finds one the fruit;
Of each the other is devoid,
Yet there's no fruit without the deed.

"Just as no store of fire is found
In jewel, cow-dung, or the sun,

Nor separate from these exists,
Yet short of fuel no fire is known;

"Even so we ne'er within the deed
Can retribution's fruit descry,
Nor yet in any place without;
Nor can in fruit the deed be found.

"Deeds separate from their fruits exist,
And fruits are separate from the deeds:
But consequent upon the deed
The fruit doth into being come.

"No god of heaven or Brahma-world
Doth cause the endless round of birth;
Constituent parts alone roll on,
From cause and from material sprung."

When he has thus grasped the dependence of name and form
by considering the round of karma and the round of fruit, and
has abandoned all questioning in the three divisions of time, he
then understands the past, future, and present elements of being
at death and at conception. This is exact determination. And he
knows as follows:

Those groups which came into existence in the past existence
in dependence on karma perished then and there. But in dependence on the karma of that existence other groups have come
into being in this existence. Not a single element of being has
come into this existence from a previous one. The groups which
have come into being in this existence in dependence on karma
will perish, and others will come into being in the next existence,
but not a single element of being will go from this existence into
the next. Moreover, just as the words of the teacher do not pass
over into the mouth of the pupil who nevertheless repeats them;
and just as holy water drunk by the messenger sent for the purpose does not pass into the belly of the sick man and nevertheless in dependence on this water is the sickness allayed; and just
as the features of the face do not pass to the reflection in mirrors and the like and nevertheless in dependence on them does
the image appear; and just as the flame does not pass over from
the wick of one lamp to that of another and nevertheless the
flame of the second lamp exists in dependence on that of the
former: in exactly the same way not a single element of being
passes over from a previous existence into the present existence,
nor hence into the next existence; and yet in dependence on the
groups, organs of sense, objects of sense, and sense-conscious-

nesses of the last existence were born those of this one, and
from the present groups, organs of sense, objects of sense, and
sense-consciousnesses will be born the groups, organs of sense,
objects of sense, and sense-consciousnesses of the next existence.

> Just as, indeed, eye-consciousness
> Doth follow on mentality,
> Yet cometh not from out the same,
> Nor yet doth fail to come to be;
>
> So, when conception comes to pass,
> The thoughts a constant series form;
> The last thought of the old birth dies,
> The first thought of the new springs up.
>
> No interval is 'twixt them found,
> No stop or break to them is known;
> There's naught that passes on from hence,
> And yet conception comes to pass.

When he thus understands the elements at death and at
conception, and the knowledge gained by grasping the dependence of name and form has become thoroughly established, then
the sixteen doubts are still more completely abandoned. And
not merely they, but also the eight doubts concerning The
Teacher, etc., are abandoned, and the sixty-two heresies are es-
topped.

The knowledge thus gained by this manifold grasping of the
dependence of name and form, and by the ensuing removal of
doubt in the three divisions of time, is what should be understood by the phrase, "the purity ensuing on the removal of
doubt." The knowledge of the continuance of the factors of
being, the knowledge of the truth and correct insight, are
synonyms of it.

For it has been said as follows:

"The knowledge of the continuance of the factors of being
consists of the wisdom gained by grasping their dependence, as,
for example, 'On ignorance depends karma, in dependence has it
originated. Both of these factors of being have originated by dependence.'"

In considering the factors of being in the light of their transitoriness, what is the knowledge of truth thus achieved? wherein
consists correct insight? how does it become plain that all the
constituents of being are transitory? where is doubt abandoned?

In considering the factors of being in the light of their

misery, . . . in considering the factors of being in the light of their lack of an Ego, . . . where is doubt abandoned?

In considering the factors of being in the light of their transitoriness is achieved the knowledge of the truth of causes; in this knowledge lies what is called correct insight; as the result of this knowledge it becomes plain that all the constituents of being are transitory; here is where doubt is abandoned.

In considering the factors of being in the light of their misery is achieved the knowledge of the truth of what exists; in this knowledge lies what is called correct insight; as the result of this knowledge it becomes plain that all the constituents of being are misery; here is where doubt is abandoned.

In considering the factors of being in the light of their lack of an Ego is achieved the knowledge of the truth both of the causes of existence and of existence; in this knowledge lies what is called correct insight; as the result of this knowledge it becomes plain that all the constituents of being are wanting in an Ego; here is where doubt is abandoned.

Now do the various expressions, "knowledge of the truth," "correct insight," and "removal of doubt," designate various truths, or are they various expressions for one truth? Knowledge of the truth, correct insight, and removal of doubt are various expressions for one truth.

Now the man of insight, having by this knowledge obtained confidence in the dispensation of the Buddha, and a footing in it, and having his destiny established, is called newly converted.

> Therefore should a mindful priest,
> Who may desire his doubts removed,
> Search everywhere that he may grasp
> On what his name and form depend.

Thus says the "Way of Purity," composed for the delectation of good people, and in the section on the development of wisdom.

6. Existence and Nirvana in Hinayana Buddhism

EXISTENCE AND ATTACHMENT

The Fire-Sermon[1]

Then the Blessed One, having dwelt in Uruvela as long as he wished, proceeded on his wanderings in the direction of Gaya Head, accompanied by a great congregation of priests, a thousand in number, who had all of them aforetime been monks with matted hair. And there in Gaya, on Gaya Head, the Blessed One dwelt, together with the thousand priests.

And there the Blessed One addressed the priests:

"All things, O priests, are on fire. And what, O priests, are all these things which are on fire?

"The eye, O priests, is on fire; forms are on fire; e~ ~ sciousness is on fire; impressions received by the eye are and whatever sensation, pleasant, unpleasant, or in originates in dependence on impressions received by the ~ that also is on fire.

"And with what are these on fire?

"With the fire of passion, say I, with the fire of hatred, with the fire of infatuation: with birth, old age, death, sorrow, lamentation, misery, grief, and despair are they on fire.

"The ear is on fire; sounds are on fire; the nose is on fire; odors are on fire; the tongue is on fire; tastes are on fire; the body is on fire; things tangible are on fire; the mind is on fire; ideas are on fire; mind-consciousness is on fire; impressions received by the mind are on fire; and whatever sensation, pleasant, unpleasant, or indifferent, originates in dependence on impressions received by the mind, that also is on fire.

"And with what are these on fire?

[1]Translated from the Maha-Vagga (I.21), the Fire Sermon describes in vivid form the Theravadin emphasis on averting everything that is "on fire with craving," so that one may achieve the deliverance of nirvana.

"With the fire of passion, say I, with the fire of hatred, with the fire of infatuation; with birth, old age, death, sorrow, lamentation, misery, grief, and despair are they on fire.

"Perceiving this, O priests, the learned and noble disciple conceives an aversion for the eye, conceives an aversion for forms, conceives an aversion for eye-consciousness, conceives an aversion for the impressions received by the eye; and whatever sensation, pleasant, unpleasant, or indifferent, originates in dependence on impressions received by the eye, for that also he conceives an aversion. Conceives an aversion for the ear, conceives an aversion for sounds, conceives an aversion for the nose, conceives an aversion for odors, conceives an aversion for the tongue, conceives an aversion for tastes, conceives an aversion for the body, conceives an aversion for things tangible, conceives an aversion for the mind, conceives an aversion for ideas, conceives an aversion for mind-consciousness, conceives an aversion for the impressions received by the mind; and whatever sensation, pleasant, unpleasant, or indifferent, originates in dependence on impressions received by the mind, for this also he conceives an aversion. And in conceiving this aversion, he becomes divested of passion, and by the absence of passion he becomes free, and when he is free he becomes aware that he is free; and he knows that rebirth is exhausted, that he has lived the holy life, that he has done what it behooved him to do, and that he is no more for this world."

Attachment[2]

In looking upon Form and the other Groups as having a nature resembling bubbles of foam and the like, the meditative priest ceases to look upon the unsubstantial as substantiality. To particularize:

In looking upon subjective Form as impure, he comes thoroughly to understand material food, abandons the perverse mistaking of the impure for the pure, crosses the torrent of sensual pleasure, breaks loose from the yoke of sensual pleasure, is freed from the depravity of sensual pleasure, severs the myriad bonds of covetousness, and does not attach himself by the Attachment of Sensual Pleasure;

In looking upon Sensation as misery, he comes thoroughly to

[2] Translated from the Visuddhi-Magga (chap. XIV).

understand the nutriment called contact, abandons the perverse
mistaking of misery for happiness, crosses the torrent of existence, breaks loose from the yoke of existence, is freed from the
depravity of passion for existence, severs the myriad bonds of
malevolence, and does not attach himself by the Attachment of
Fanatical Conduct;

In looking upon Perception and the Predispositions as not an
Ego, he comes thoroughly to understand the nutriment called
karma, abandons the perverse mistaking of what is no Ego for
an Ego, crosses the torrent of heresy, breaks loose from the yoke
of heresy, is freed from the depravity of heresy, severs the
myriad bonds of dogmatism, and does not attach himself by the
Attachment of the Assertion of an Ego;

In looking upon Consciousness as transitory, he comes thoroughly to understand the nutriment called consciousness, abandons the perverse mistaking of the transitory for the permanent,
crosses the torrent of ignorance, breaks loose from the yoke of
ignorance, is freed from the depravity of ignorance, severs the
myriad bonds of an affectation of fanatical conduct, and does
not attach himself by the Attachment of Heresy.

Existence[3]

In the proposition, *On attachment depends existence,*

> The sense, the different elements,
> The use, divisions, summings up,
> And which the dependence makes of which,
> Must now be understood in full.

"Existence" is so called because it is an existing. It is
twofold; karma-existence, and originating-existence. As it has
been said: "Existence is twofold: there is a karma-existence, and
there is an originating-existence." Here *karma-existence* is
equivalent to karma; and in like manner *originating-existence* is
equivalent to originating. Originating is called existence because
it is an existing; but karma is called existence because it causes
existence, just as the birth of a Buddha is called happy because
it results in happiness.

This, then, is the full understanding of the sense.

The different elements: Karma-existence is in brief thought

[3]Translated from the Visuddhi-Magga (chap. XVII).

and the elements covetousness etc., which go under the name of karma and exist conjoined with thought. As it has been said,

"What is karma-existence? Meritorious karma, demeritorious karma, and karma leading to immovability, all these are called karma-existence, whether they be of little or great extent. Moreover all karma conducive to existence is karma-existence."

In the above, the term meritorious karma includes thirteen thoughts, demeritorious karma includes twelve, and the term, karma leading to immovability, includes four thoughts. Also, by the phrase, "Whether of little or great extent," is meant the slight or large amount of fruition of these same thoughts, and, by the phrase, "And all karma conducive to existence," are meant covetousness and so on conjoined with thought.

Originating-existence, however, is in brief the groups which have come into existence through karma, and it has a ninefold division. As it is said,

"What is originating-existence? Existence in the realm of sensual pleasure, existence in the realm of form, existence in the realm of formlessness, existence in the realm of perception, existence in the realm of non-perception, existence in the realm of neither perception nor yet non-perception, existence once infected, existence four times infected, existence five times infected, all these are originating-existence."

In the above, existence in the realm of sensual pleasure is the existence called sensual pleasure, and similarly in respect of existence in the realm of form, and of existence in the realm of formlessness. Existence in the realm of perception is so called either because perception constitutes that existence, or because there is perception in that existence. The converse is the case with existence in the realm of nonperception. Existence in the realm of neither perception nor yet non-perception is so called because, as there is no gross perception there, but only a subtile one, there is neither perception nor yet non-perception in that existence. Existence once infected is existence infected with the form-group alone, or it is called existence once infected because there is but one infection to that existence, and similarly in regard to existences four times and five times infected.

Existence in the realm of sensual pleasure is the five attachment-groups, and existence in the realm of form is the same. Existence in the realm of formlessness is four attachment-groups. Existence in the realm of perception is five attachment-groups, and existence in the realm of non-perception is one attachment-group. Existence in the realm of neither perception nor yet non-perception is four attachment-groups, and existence once infected etc., is one, four, or five attachment-groups.

This, then, is the full understanding of *the different elements*.

The use: It is true that the meritorious and the other karmas have been already spoken of in the exposition of karma. However, this karma was the karma of a previous existence and hence given as constituting the dependence for conception into this one,—while in the present case they are present karma and given as constituting the dependence for conception into a future existence. Thus the repetition is of use. Or again, when it was said, "What is meritorious karma? It is meritorious thoughts in the realm of sensual pleasure," and so on, only thoughts were included in the term karma, while in the present instance where it is said, "And all karma conducive to existence," there are also included the elements of being which are conjoined with thoughts. Or again, only that karma which is the dependence of consciousness was in the first instance intended by the term karma, but now that also which gives rise to an existence in the realm of non-perception. But why make a long story of it? By the meritorious karma etc. intended in the proposition, "On ignorance depends karma," meritorious and demeritorious factors of being only are meant; but in the present case, in the proposition, "On attachment depends existence," inasmuch as originating-existence is included, all elements of being, whether meritorious or demeritorious or indeterminate are intended. Accordingly the repetition is useful from every point of view.

This, then, is the full understanding of *the use.*

In regard to their summings up, however, by putting karma-existence and originating-existence together we have existence in the realm of sensual pleasure and the therewith included existences, existence in the realm of form, and existence in the realm of formlessness, making three existences which depend on the attachment of sensual pleasure; and similarly in regard to the remaining attachments. Thus there sum up twelve existences besides the therewith included existences, all of which depend on attachment. Moreover, to speak absolutely, karma-existence is karma which leads to existence in the realm of sensual pleasure and is dependent on attachment, and the groups which spring from it are originating-existence.

We may have one who, because of what he hears reported or by inference from what he sees, reflects as follows: "Sensual pleasures obtain in the world of men in wealthy families of the warrior caste and so forth and so on, and also in the six heavens of sensual pleasures." Then he becomes deceived by listening to false doctrine and takes a wrong way to attain them, and thinking, "By this kind of karma I shall obtain sensual pleasures," he adopts the attachment of sensual pleasure and does evil with his body, evil with his voice, and evil with his mind, and when he has fulfilled his wickedness he is reborn in a lower state of exis-

tence. Or again, he adopts the attachment of sensual pleasure
through being desirous of sensual pleasure and of protecting that
which he has already obtained, and does evil with his body, evil
with his voice, and evil with his mind, and when he has fulfilled
his wickedness he is reborn in a lower state of existence. Here
the karma that was the cause of his rebirth is karma-existence.
The groups which sprang from that karma were originating-existence. Existence in the realm of perception and existence five
times infected are therewith included.

Another, however, strengthens his knowledge by listening to
the Good Doctrine, and thinking, "By this kind of karma I shall
obtain sensual pleasures," adopts the attachment of sensual pleasure and does good with his body, good with his voice, and good
with his mind; and when he fulfilled his righteousness he is reborn either among the gods or among men. Here the karma that
was the cause of his rebirth is karma-existence. The groups which
sprang from that karma were originating-existence. Existence in
the realm of form and existence five times infected are therewith
included. Accordingly the attachment of sensual pleasure is the
dependence of existence in the realm of sensual pleasure together with its divisions and whatever existences are therewith
included.

The Middle Doctrine[4]

The world, for the most part, O Kaccana, holds either to a
belief in being or to a belief in non-being. But for one who in
the light of the highest knowledge, O Kaccana, considers how
the world arises, belief in the non-being of the world passes
away. And for one who in the light of the highest knowledge, O
Kaccana, considers how the world ceases, belief in the being of
the world passes away. The world, O Kaccana, is for the most
part bound up in a seeking, attachment, and proclivity [for the
groups], but a priest does not sympathize with this seeking and
attachment, nor with the mental affirmation, proclivity, and prej-
udice which affirms an Ego. He does not doubt or question that
it is only evil that springs into existence, and only evil that
ceases from existence, and his conviction of this fact is dependent on no one besides himself. This, O Kaccana, is what constitutes Right Belief.

That things have being, O Kaccana, constitutes one extreme

of doctrine; that things have no being is the other extreme. These extremes, O Kaccana, have been avoided by the Tathagata, and it is a middle doctrine he teaches:

On ignorance depends karma;
On karma depends consciousness;
On consciousness depend name and form;
On name and form depend the six organs of sense;
On the six organs of sense depends contact;
On contact depends sensation;
On sensation depends desire;
On desire depends attachment;
On attachment depends existence;
On existence depends birth;
On birth depend old age and death, sorrow, lamentation, misery, grief, and despair. Thus does this entire aggregation of misery arise.

But on the complete fading out and cessation of ignorance ceases karma;
On the cessation of karma ceases consciousness;
On the cessation of consciousness cease name and form;
On the cessation of name and form cease the six organs of sense;
On the cessation of the six organs of sense ceases contact;
On the cessation of contact ceases sensation;
On the cessation of sensation ceases desire.
On the cessation of desire ceases attachment;
On the cessation of attachment ceases existence;
On the cessation of existence ceases birth;
On the cessation of birth cease old age and death, sorrow, lamentation, misery, grief, and despair. Thus does this entire aggregation of misery cease.

Questions Which Tend Not to Edification[5]

Thus have I heard.

On a certain occasion the Blessed One was dwelling at Savatthi in Jetavana monastery in Anathapindika's Park. Now it happened to the venerable Malunkyaputta, being in seclusion and plunged in meditation, that a consideration presented itself to his mind, as follows:

[5]Translated from the Majjhima-Nikaya, and constituting Sutta 63. Also called the Lesser Malunkyaputta Sermon.

"These theories which The Blessed One has left unelucidated, has set aside and rejected—that the world is eternal, that the world is not eternal, that the world is finite, that the world is infinite, that the soul and the body are identical, that the soul is one thing and the body another, that the saint exists after death, that the saint[6] does not exist after death, that the saint both exists and does not exist after death, that the saint neither exists nor does not exist after death—these the Blessed One does not elucidate to me. And the fact that the Blessed One does not elucidate to me. And the fact that the Blessed One does not elucidate them to me does not please me nor suit me. Therefore I will draw near to the Blessed One and inquire of him concerning this matter. If the Blessed One will elucidate to me, in that case will I lead the religious life under the Blessed One. If the Blessed One will not elucidate to me, either that the world is eternal, or that the world is not eternal, or that the saint neither exists nor does not exist after death, in that case will I abandon religious training and return to the lower life of a layman."

Then the venerable Malunkyaputta arose at eventide from his seclusion, and drew near to where the Blessed One was; and having drawn near and greeted the Blessed One, he sat down respectfully at one side. And seated respectfully at one side, the venerable Malunkyaputta spoke to the Blessed One as follows:

"Reverend Sir, it happened to me, as I was just now in seclusion and plunged in meditation, that a consideration presented itself to my mind, as follows: 'These theories which the Blessed One has left unelucidated, has set aside and rejected—that the world is eternal, that the world is not eternal . . . that the saint neither exists nor does not exist after death—these the Blessed one does not elucidate to me.'

"Pray, Malunkyaputta, did I ever say to you, 'Come, Malunkyaputta, lead the religious life under me, and I will elucidate to you either that the world is eternal, or that the world is not eternal, or that the saint neither exists nor does not exist after death'?"

"Nay, verily, Reverend Sir."

"Or did you ever say to me, 'Reverend Sir, I will lead the religious life under the Blessed One, on condition that the Blessed One elucidate to me either that the world is eternal, or that the world is not eternal, or that the saint neither exists nor does not exist after death'?"

"Nay, verily, Reverend Sir."

"Malunkyaputta, any one who should say, 'I will not lead the

---

[6]The Hinayana arahat (Arhat) is one who has achieved liberation, and is perhaps equivalent in language to "saint."

religious life under the Blessed One until the Blessed One shall elucidate to me either that the world is eternal, or that the world is not eternal, or that the saint neither exists nor does not exist after death';—that person would die, Malunkyaputta, before the Tathagata had ever elucidated this to him.

"It is as if, Malunkyaputta, a man had been wounded by an arrow thickly smeared with poison, and his friends and companions, his relatives and kinsfolk, were to procure for him a physician or surgeon; and the sick man were to say, 'I will not have this arrow taken out until I have learnt whether the man who wounded me belonged to the warrior caste, or to the Brahman caste, or to the agricultural caste, or to the menial caste.'

"Or again he were to say, 'I will not have this arrow taken out until I have learnt the name of the man who wounded me, and to what clan he belongs.'

"Or again he were to say, 'I will not have this arrow taken out until I have learnt whether the man who wounded me was tall, or short, or of the middle height.'

"Or again he were to say, 'I will not have this arrow taken out until I have learnt whether the shaft which wounded me was wound round with the sinews of an ox, or of a buffalo, or of a ruru deer, or of a monkey.'

"That man would die, Malunkyaputta, without ever having learned this.

"In exactly the same way, Malunkyaputta, any one who should say, 'I will not lead the religious life under the Blessed One until the Blessed One shall elucidate to me either that the world is eternal, or that the world is not eternal, or that the saint neither exists nor does not exist after death';—that person would die, Malunkyaputta, before the Tathagata had ever elucidated this to him.

"The religious life, Malunkyaputta, does not depend on the dogma that the world is eternal; nor does the religious life, Malunkyaputta, depend on the dogma that the world is not eternal. Whether the dogma obtain, Malunkyaputta, that the world is eternal, or that the world is not eternal, there still remain birth, old age, death, sorrow, lamentation, misery, grief, and despair, for the extinction of which in the present life I am prescribing.

"Accordingly, Malunkyaputta, bear always in mind what it is that I have not elucidated, and what it is that I have elucidated. And what, Malunkyaputta, have I not elucidated? I have not elucidated, Malunkyaputta, that the world is eternal; I have not elucidated that the world is not eternal; I have not elucidated that the world is finite; I have not elucidated that the world is infinite; I have not elucidated that the soul and the body are

identical; I have not elucidated that the soul is one thing and
the body another; I have not elucidated that the saint exists after death; I have not elucidated that the saint does not exist
after death; I have not elucidated that the saint both exists
and does not exist after death; I have not elucidated that the
saint neither exists nor does not exist after death. And why,
Malunkyaputta, have I not elucidated this? Because,
Malunkyaputta, this profits not, nor has to do with the fundamentals of religion, nor tends to aversion, absence of passion,
cessation, quiescence, the supernatural faculties, supreme wisdom, and Nirvana; therefore have I not elucidated it.

"And what, Malunkyaputta, have I elucidated? Misery,
Malunkyaputta, have I elucidated; the origin of misery have I
elucidated; the cessation of misery have I elucidated; and the
path leading to the cessation of misery have I elucidated. And
why, Malunkyaputta, have I elucidated this? Because,
Malunkyaputta, this does profit, has to do with the fundamentals of religion, and tends to aversion, absence of passion, cessation, quiescence, knowledge, supreme wisdom, and Nirvana;
therefore have I elucidated it. Accordingly, Malunkyaputta, bear
always in mind what it is that I have not elucidated, and what
it is that I have elucidated."

MEDITATION AND NIRVANA

The Attainment of the Paths[1]

"Behold how empty is the world,
Mogharaja! In thoughtfulness
Let one remove belief in self
And pass beyond the realm of death.
The king of death can never find
The man who thus the world beholds."

When in the course of his application of the Three Characteristics the ascetic has thus considered the constituents of being in
the light of their emptiness, he abandons all fear and joy in regard to them, and becomes indifferent and neutral, and does not
deem them as "I" or "mine," like a man who has given up his
wife.

Just as a man might have a wife beloved, delightful, and

[1] Translated from the Visuddhi-Magga (chap. XXI).

charming, from whom he could not bear to be separated for a moment, and on whom he excessively doted. If he then were to see that woman standing or sitting in company with another man, and talking and joking with him, he would be angry and displeased, and experience bitter grief. But if subsequently he were to discover that she had been guilty of a fault, he would lose all desire for her and let her go, and no longer look on her as "mine." From that time on, whenever he might see her engaged with any one else, he would not be angry or grieved, but simply indifferent and neutral. In exactly the same way the ascetic by grasping the constituents of being with the reflective insight becomes desirous of being released from them, and perceiving none of them worthy of being deemed "I" or "mine," he abandons all fear and joy in regard to them, and becomes indifferent and neutral. When he has learnt and perceived this, his mind draws in, contracts, and shrinks away from the three modes of existence, the four species of being, the five destinies in rebirth, the seven stages of consciousness, the nine grades of being, and does not spread out, and only indifference or disgust abides.

Just as drops of water on a gently inclined lotus-leaf draw in, contract, and shrink away, and do not spread out; in exactly the same way his mind draws in, contracts, and shrinks away from the three modes of existence, the four species of being, the five destinies in rebirth, the seven stages of consciousness, the nine grades of being, and does not spread out, and only indifference or disgust abides. Just as a cock's feather, . . . if thrown into the fire, draws in, contracts, and shrinks away, and does not spread out; in exactly the same way his mind draws in, contracts, and shrinks away from the three modes of existence, the four species of being, the five destinies in rebirth, the seven stages of consciousness, the nine grades of being, and does not spread out, but only indifference or disgust abides. Thus has he attained to the knowledge consisting in indifference to the constituents of being.

If this knowledge be such that it sees Nirvana, the abode of peace, to be the good, then it gives up everything made of the constituents of being, and leaps towards it; but if it be not such that it sees Nirvana to be the good, it will again and again take the constituents of being as its object, resembling in this the crow of the sailors.

They say that sea-faring traders take what is called a land-sighting crow when they go aboard ship. And when the ship is tossed about by the winds, and out of its course, and land no longer to be seen, then they let go that landsighting crow. Such a bird springs into the air from the mast-head, and going to all

the quarters and intermediate quarters flies to the shore if he
sees it; but if he does not see it, he returns again and again and
alights on the mast. In exactly the same way, if the knowledge
consisting in indifference to the constituents of being be such
that it sees Nirvana, the abode of peace, to be the good, then it
gives up everything made of the constituents of being, and leaps
towards it; but if it be not such that it sees Nirvana to be the
good, it will again and again take the constituents of being as its
object. It grasps the constituents of being in many different
ways, as if they were so much meal being sorted in the kitchen,
or so much cotton unrolled and being shredded, and having
abandoned all fear and joy in regard to them and become neutral by its sifting of the constituents of being, it abides as the
threefold insight. And abiding thus, it becomes the threefold
starting-point of deliverance, and the dependence for the distinction of the seven noble individuals.

Now this knowledge, existing as the threefold insight, becomes
by the predominance of three qualities the threefold starting-
point of deliverance. For the three insights are called the three
starting-points of deliverance. As it is said:

"Moreover, deliverance has three starting-points for escape
from the world: the consideration of the beginnings and endings
of the constituents of being for the thoughts to spring to the
unconditioned; the agitating of the mind concerning the constituents of being for the thoughts to spring to the desireless;
the consideration of all the elements of being as not an Ego for
the thoughts to spring to the empty. These are the three starting-points of deliverance for escape from the world."

Here *the beginnings and endings*—the beginnings and endings
in the springing up and disappearance of things. For the insight
into transitoriness, by coming to the conclusion, "The constituents of being did not exist before they sprang up," determines
beginnings; and by observing their destiny, and coming to the
conclusion, they continue no more after they have disappeared,
but vanish right then," determines endings.

The *agitating of the mind*—the agitating of the thoughts. For
by insight into the misery of the constituents of being the
thoughts are agitated.

The *consideration of all elements of being as not an Ego*—
considering them as not an "I" or "mind."

Accordingly these three propositions are to be understood as
spoken concerning the insight into transitoriness etc. Therefore
was it thereafter said in answer to a question,

"To one who considers them in the light of their transitoriness the constituents of being seem perishable. To one who considers them in the light of their misery they seem frightful. To

one who considers them in the light of their want of an Ego
they seem empty.

But how many are the deliverances of which these insights are
the starting-points? There are three: the unconditioned, the desireless, and the empty. For it has been said as follows:

"He who considers them [the constituents of being] in the
light of their transitoriness abounds in faith and obtains the
unconditioned deliverance; he who considers them in the light
of their misery abounds in tranquillity and obtains the desireless
deliverance; he who considers them in the light of their want of
an Ego abounds in knowledge and obtains the empty deliverance."

Here *the unconditioned deliverance* is the Noble Path realized
by meditation on Nirvana in its unconditioned aspect. For the
Noble Path is unconditioned from having sprung out of the
unconditioned, and it is a deliverance from being free from the
corruptions. In the same way the Noble Path when realized by
meditation on Nirvana in its desireless aspect is to be understood as *desireless;* when realized by meditation on Nirvana in
its empty aspect as *empty.*

The Summum Bonum[2]

"And craving, O priests, the summum bonum, the incomparable peaceful state, I came in the course of my journeyings
among the Magadhans to Uruvela, the General's Town. There I
perceived a delightful spot with an enchanting grove of trees,
and a silvery flowing river, easy of approach and delightful, and
a village near by in which to beg. And it occurred to me, O
priests, as follows:

" 'Truly, delightful is this spot, enchanting this grove of trees,
and this silvery river flows by, easy of approach and delightful,
and there is a village near by in which to beg. Truly, there is
here everything necessary for a youth of good family who is desirous of struggling.'

"And there I settled down, O priests, as everything was
suitable for struggling.

"And being, O priests, myself subject to birth, I perceived the
wretchedness of what is subject to birth, and craving the incomparable security of a Nirvana free from birth, I attained
the incomparable security of a Nirvana free from birth; myself

[2]Translated from the Majjhima-Nikaya, and constituting Sutta 26.

subject to old age, ... disease, ... death, ... sorrow, ... corruption, I perceived the wretchedness of what is subject to corruption, and craving the incomparable security of a Nirvana free from corruption, I attained the incomparable security of a Nirvana free from corruption. And the knowledge and the insight sprang up within me, 'My deliverance is unshakable; this is my last existence; no more shall I be born again.' And it occurred to me, O priests, as follows:

" 'This doctrine to which I have attained is profound, recondite, and difficult of comprehension, good, excellent, and not to be reached by mere reasoning, subtile, and intelligible only to the wise. Mankind, on the other hand, is captivated, entranced, held spell-bound by its lusts; and forasmuch as mankind is captivated, entranced, and held spell-bound by its lusts, it is hard for them to understand the law of dependence on assignable reasons, the doctrine of Dependent Origination, and it is also hard for them to understand how all the constituents of being may be made to subside, all the substrata of being be relinquished, and desire be made to vanish, and absence of passion, cessation, and Nirvana be attained. If I were to teach the Doctrine, others would fail to understand me, and my vexation and trouble would be great.'

"Then, O priests, the following stanzas occurred to me, not heard of before from any one else:

" 'This Doctrine out of toil begot
I see 't is useless to proclaim:
Mankind's by lusts and hates enthralled,
'T is hopeless they should master it.

" 'Repugnant, abstruse would it prove,
Deep, subtile, and beyond their ken;
Th' infatuates live in clouds of lusts,
And cannot for the darkness see.'

"Thus, O priests, did I ponder, and my mind was disinclined to action, and to any proclaiming of the Doctrine.

"Then, O priests, Brahma Sahampati perceived what was in my mind, and it occurred to him as follows:

" 'Lo, the world is lost, is ruined! For the mind of The Tathagata, The Saint, The Supreme Buddha, is disinclined to action, and to any proclaiming of the Doctrine.' "

"Then, O priests, Brahma Sahampati, as quickly as a strong man might stretch out his bent arm, or might draw in his outstretched arm, even so, having vanished from the Brahma-world, appeared in my presence.

"Then, O priests, Brahma Sahampati threw his upper garment over his shoulder and, stretching out to me his joined palms, spoke as follows:

" 'Reverend Sir, let the Blessed One teach the Doctrine. let The Happy One teach the Doctrine. There are some beings having but little moral defilement, and through not hearing the Doctrine they perish. Some will be found to understand the Doctrine.'

"Thus, O priests, spoke Brahma Sahampati, and having thus spoken, he continued as follows:

" 'The Magadhans hold hitherto a doctrine
Impure, thought out by men themselves not spotless.
Ope thou the door that to the deathless leadeth:
Him let them hear who is himself unspotted.

" 'As one who standeth on a rocky pinnacle,
Might thence with wide-extended view behold mankind,
Climb thou, Wise One, the top of Doctrine's palace,
And thence gaze down serene on all the peoples,
Behold how all mankind is plunged in sorrow,
And how old age and death have overwhelmed them.

" 'Rise thou, O Hero, Victor in the Battle!
O Leader, Guiltless One, go 'mongst the nations!
The Doctrine let The Buddha teach,
Some will be found to master it.'

"Then I, O priests, perceiving the desire of Brahma, and having compassion on living beings, gazed over the world with the eye of a Buddha. And as I gazed over the world with the eye of a Buddha, I saw people of every variety: some having but little moral defilement, and some having great moral defilement; some of keen faculties, and some of dull faculties; some of good disposition, and some of bad disposition; some that were docile, and some that were not docile; and also some who saw the terrors of the hereafter and of blameworthy actions. Just as in a pond of blue lotuses, of water-roses, or of white lotuses, some of the blossoms which have sprung up and grown in the water, do not reach the surface of the water but grow under water; some of the blossoms which have sprung up and grown in the water, are even with the surface of the water; and some of the blossoms which have sprung up and grown in the water, shoot up above the water and are not touched by the water; in exactly the same way, O priests, as I gazed over the world with the eye of a Buddha, I saw people of every variety: some having but little moral defilement, and some having great moral defilement; some of keen faculties, and some of dull faculties; some of good disposition, and some of bad disposition; some that were docile, and some that were not docile; and also some who saw the terrors of the hereafter and of blameworthy actions. And when I had seen this, O priests, I addressed Brahma Sahampati in the following stanza:

" 'Let those with ears to hear come give me credence,
For lo! the door stands open to the deathless.
O Brahma, 't was because I feared annoyance
That I was loath to tell mankind the Doctrine.'

"Then, O priests, thought Brahma Sahampati, 'The Blessed One has granted my request that he should teach the Doctrine,' and saluting me, he turned his right side towards me, and straightway disappeared.

The Trance of Cessation[8]

What is the trance of cessation?

It is the stoppage of all mentality by a gradual cessation. . . . A priest who is desirous of entering on cessation will take his breakfast, wash carefully his hands and his feet, and seat him cross-legged on a well-strewn seat in some retired spot, with body erect, and contemplative faculty active. He then enters the first trance, and rising from it obtains insight into the transitoriness, misery, and lack of an Ego of the constituents of being.

This insight, however, is threefold: the insight into the constituents of being, the insight belonging to the attainment of the Fruits, and the insight belonging to the trance of cessation.

Whether the insight into the constituents of being be dull or keen, it is in either case a preparation for the Paths.

The insight belonging to the attainment of the Fruits can only be keen, like the realization of the Paths.

The insight, however, belonging to the trance of cessation should not be too dull nor yet too keen. Therefore he will contemplate the constituents of being with an insight that is neither very dull nor very keen.

Thereupon he enters the second trance, and rising from it obtains insight into the constituents of being in the same manner

---

[8]Translated from the Visuddhi-Magga (chap. XXIII).

as before. Thereupon he enters the third trance, the fourth trance, the realm of the infinity of space, the realm of the infinity of consciousness, and rising from it obtains insight into the constituents of being in the same manner as before. Then he enters the realm of nothingness, and rising from it performs the four preliminary duties; the protection of less intimate belongings, respect for the Order, a summons from The Teacher, limitation of time.

Limitation of time—limitation of the time of life. For this priest should be skilful respecting the limitation of time. He should not enter this trance without first reflecting whether his span of life is to last seven days longer or not. For if he were to enter this trance without perceiving that his vital powers were to break up within the seven-day limit, his trance of cessation would not be able to ward off death, and as death cannot take place during cessation, he would have to rise from the midst of his trance. Therefore he must enter it only after having made the above reflection. For it has been said that it is permissible to neglect the other reflections, but not this one.

When he has thus entered the realm of nothingness, and risen from it and performed these preliminary duties, he enters the realm of neither perception nor yet non-perception; and having passed beyond one or two thoughts, he stops thinking and reaches cessation. But why do I say that beyond two thoughts the thoughts cease? Because of the priest's progress in cessation. For the priest's progress in gradual cessation consists in an ascent through the eight attainments by the simultaneous use of both the quiescence and insight methods, and does not result from the trance of the realm of neither perception nor yet non-perception alone. Thus it is because of the priest's progress in cessation that beyond two thoughts the thoughts cease.

Now the priest who should rise from the realm of nothingness, and enter the realm of neither perception nor yet non-perception without having performed his preliminary duties would not be able to lose all thought, but would fall back into the realm of nothingness. In this connection I will add a simile of a man traveling on a road over which he has never passed before.

A certain man traveling on a road over which he has never passed before, comes on his way to a deep ravine containing water, or to a slough in which is a stepping-stone that has been over-heated by the sun; and essaying to descend into the ravine, without having first adjusted his tunic and his upper garment, he is obliged to retreat again to the top of the bank, through fear of wetting his requisites; or stepping upon the stone he scorches his feet so badly that he jumps back to the hither

bank. In the above simile, just as the man, through not having
adjusted his tunic and his upper garment, retreated to where he
had started from, as soon as he had descended into the ravine,
or had stepped on the heated stone; in exactly the same way the
ascetic, if he have not performed the preliminary duties, as soon
as he reaches the realm of neither perception nor yet non-perception, retreats again into the realm of nothingness.

As, however, another man who has traveled on that road before, when he reaches that spot, will gird his tunic tightly and
cross the ravine with the other garment in his hand, or will
touch the stone as little as possible in passing to the further
bank; in exactly the same way a priest who has performed his
preliminary duties, and entered the realm of neither perception
nor yet non-perception, will pass beyond and lose all thought,
and dwell in cessation.

How long will he stay in it? He who has entered it in the
above-described manner will remain in it during the limit of
time which he has set for it, provided that the termination of
his life, or respect for the Order, or a summons from The
Teacher does not interfere.

How does he rise from it? In a twofold manner. The priest
who is in the path of never returning, with the attainment of
the fruit of never returning, the saint with the attainment of the
fruit of saintship.

When he has risen from it, to what is his mind inclined? It is
inclined to Nirvana. For it has been said as follows:

"Brother Visakha, the mind of a priest who has risen from the
trance of the cessation of perception and sensation is inclined to
isolation, has a tendency to isolation, is impelled to isolation."

What is the difference between a dead man and one who has
entered this trance? This matter also is treated of in this discourse. As it is said:

"Brother, of the man who has died and become a corpse,
bodily karma has ceased and become quieted, vocal karma has
ceased and become quieted, mental karma has ceased and become quieted, vitality has become exhausted, natural heat has
subsided, and the senses have broken up. Of the priest who has
entered on the cessation of perception and sensation, bodily
karma has ceased and become quieted, vocal karma has ceased
and become quieted, mental karma has ceased and become
quieted, but vitality has not become exhausted, natural heat has
not subsided, and the senses have not broken up."

In regard to the questions "Is the trance of cessation conditioned or unconditioned?" it cannot be said either that it is conditioned or that it is unconditioned, either that it is worldly or
that it is transcendent. And why not? On account of the non-

existence of any positive reality. Inasmuch, however, as it can be entered upon, therefore it is correct to say that it is brought about, not that it is not brought about.

> Whereas the wise who cultivate
> The wisdom which doth make a saint
> Are they who reach this holy trance—
> This trance by saints at all times prized,
> And ever by them held to be
> Nirvana in the present life—
> Therefore the faculty to reach
> This state of trance which is conferred
> By wisdom in the holy paths
> A blessing of those paths is called.

The Attainment of Nirvana[4]

Acquisition of honor: The blessings to be derived from the realization of this transcendent wisdom include not only the ability to enter the trance of cessation, but also the acquisition of honor etc. For the individual who has developed his wisdom by the development of the fourfold wisdom of the paths is worthy of the worship, the veneration, the votive offerings, and the reverence of all the world of gods and men, and is an unsurpassed source of merit for the world.

To particularize:

He who, being of weak faculties, develops the wisdom of the first path with a dull insight is reborn seven times at most; after seven rebirths in states of bliss he will make an end of misery: he who develops it with medium faculties and insight is a roamer; after two or three rebirths he will make an end of misery: he who develops it with keen faculties and insight takes root but once, only one human birth will he pass through and make an end of misery.

He who develops the wisdom of the second path returns once; once more will he return to this world and then make an end of misery.

He who develops the wisdom of the third path never returns. His destiny is fivefold, as follows: In the descending order of the worth of his faculties he passes into Nirvana in the midst, at

[4] Translated from the Visuddhi-Magga (chap. XXIII).

the end, without instigation, with instigation, or passes up current to the Sublime Gods.

Here the one who passes into Nirvana *in the midst* is reborn in some one of the Pure Abodes and passes into Nirvana before attaining half the normal length of life of that heaven; he who passes into Nirvana *at the end* passes into Nirvana after attaining half the normal length of life; he who passes into Nirvana *without instigation* achieves the fourth path without instigation or urging; he who passes into Nirvana *with instigation* achieves the higher path with instigation or urging; and he who *passes up current to the Sublime Gods* starts from the particular heaven into which he may be reborn, and ascends as far as to the Sublime Gods and there passes into Nirvana.

Of those who develop the wisdom of the fourth path, one is freed by faith, another is freed by wisdom, another is doubly freed, another possesses the threefold knowledge, another the Six High Powers, but the greatest of all is he who has mastered the four analytical sciences and has lost all depravity. Concerning this last it has been said:

"At the time he is in the paths he is disentangling the snarl, at the time he is in the fruits he has disentangled the snarl, and there is in all the world of gods and men none more worthy of votive gifts."

> Since, then, such blessings manifold
> From noble wisdom take their rise,
> Therefore the understanding man
> Should place therein his heart's delight.

The above constitutes the explanation of the development of wisdom and of its blessings in the Way of Purity as taught in the stanza,

> "What man his conduct guardeth, and hath wisdom,
> And thoughts and wisdom traineth well,
> The strenuous and the able priest,
> He disentangles all this snarl."

The Questions of King Milinda on Nirvana[5]

The king said: "Is cessation Nirvana?"

"Yes, your Majesty."

"How is that, Nagasena?"

"All foolish individuals, O king, take pleasure in the senses and in the objects of sense, find delight in them, continue to cleave to them. Hence are they carried down by that flood of human passions, they are not set free from birth, old age, and death, from grief, lamentation, pain, sorrow, and despair—they are not set free, I say, from suffering. But the wise, O king, the disciple of the noble ones, neither takes pleasure in those things, nor finds delight in them, nor continues cleaving to them. And inasmuch as he does not, in him craving ceases, and by the cessation of craving grasping ceases, and by the cessation of grasping becoming ceases, and when becoming has ceased birth ceases, and with its cessation birth, old age, and death, grief, lamentation, pain, sorrow, and despair cease to exist. Thus is the cessation brought about the end of all that aggregation of pain. Thus is it that cessation is Nirvana."

"Very good, Nagasena!"

The king said: "Venerable Nagasena, do all men receive Nirvana?"

"Not all, O king. But he who walks righteously, who admits those conditions which ought to be admitted, perceives clearly those conditions which ought to be clearly perceived, abandons those conditions which ought to be abandoned, practises himself in those conditions which ought to be practised, realises those conditions which ought to be realised—he receives Nirvana."

"Very good, Nagasena!"

The king said: "Venerable Nagasena, does he who does not receive Nirvana know how happy a state Nirvana is?"

"Yes, he knows it."

"But how can he know that without his receiving Nirvana?"

"Now what do you think, O king? Do those whose hands and feet have not been cut off know how sad a thing it is to have them cut off?"

"Yes, Sir, that they know."

[5]Translated from the Questions of King Milinda, Book III, chapters 4 and 5.

"But how do they know it?"

"Well, by hearing the sound of the lamentation of those whose hands and feet have been cut off, they know it."

"Just so, great king, it is by hearing the glad words of those who have seen Nirvana, that they who have not received it know how happy a state it is."

"Very good, Nagasena!"

Buddha's Nirvana

The king said: "Have you, Nagasena, seen the Buddha?"

"No, Sire."

"Then have your teachers seen the Buddha?"

"No, Sire."

"Then, venerable Nagasena, there is no Buddha!"

"But, great king, have you seen the river Uha in the Himalaya mountains?"

"No, Sir."

"Or has your father seen it?"

"No, Sir."

"Then, your Majesty, is there therefore no such river?"

"It is there. Though neither I nor my father has seen it, it is nevertheless there."

"Just so, great king, though neither I nor my teachers have seen the Blessed One, nevertheless there was such a person."

"Very good, Nagasena!"

The king said: "Is there such a person as the Buddha, Nagasena?"

"Yes."

"Can he then, Nagasena, be pointed out as being here or there?"

"The Blessed One, O king, has attained Nirvana by that kind of Parinirvana in which nothing remains which could tend to the formation of another individual. It is not possible to point out the Blessed One as being here or there."

"Give me an illustration."

"Now what do you think, O king? When there is a great body of fire blazing, is it possible to point out any one flame that has gone out, that it is here or there?"

"No, Sir. That flame has ceased, it has vanished."

"Just so, great king, has the Blessed One passed away by that kind of passing away in which no root remains for the formation of another individual. The Blessed One has come to an end, and it cannot be pointed out of him, that he is here or there. But in the body of his doctrine he can, O king, be pointed out. For the doctrine was preached by the Blessed One."

"Very good, Nagasena!"

7. The Way of Virtue (Dhammapada)

Chapter I The Twin-verses

1. All that we are is the result of what we have thought: it is founded on our thoughts, it is made up of our thoughts. If a man speaks or acts with an evil thought, pain follows him, as the wheel follows the foot of the ox that draws the carriage.

2. All that we are is the result of what we have thought: it is founded on our thoughts, it is made up of our thoughts. If a man speaks or acts with a pure thought, happiness follows him, like a shadow that never leaves him.

3. "He abused me, he beat me, he defeated me, he robbed me"—in those who harbour such thoughts hatred will never cease.

4. "He abused me, he beat me, he defeated me, he robbed me"—in those who do not harbour such thoughts hatred will cease.

5. For hatred does not cease by hatred at any time: hatred ceases by love—this is an old rule.

6. The world does not know that we must all come to an end here; but those who know it, their quarrels cease at once.

7. He who lives looking for pleasures only, his senses uncontrolled, immoderate in his food, idle and weak, Mara the tempter will certainly overthrow him, as the wind throws down a weak tree.

8. He who lives without looking for pleasures, his senses well controlled, moderate in his food, faithful and strong, him Mara will certainly not overthrow, any more than the wind throws down a rocky mountain.

9. He who wishes to put on the yellow dress without having cleansed himself from sin, who disregards also temperance and truth, is unworthy of the yellow dress.

10. But he who has cleansed himself from sin, is well grounded in all virtues, and endowed also with temperance and truth: he is indeed worthy of the yellow dress.

11. They who imagine truth in untruth, and see untruth in truth, never arrive at truth, but follow vain desires.

12. They who know truth in truth, and untruth in untruth, arrive at truth, and follow true desires.

13. As rain breaks through an ill-thatched house, passion will break through an unreflecting mind.

14. As rain does not break through a well-thatched house, passion will not break through a well-reflected mind.

15. The evil-doer mourns in this world, and he mourns in the next; he mourns in both. He mourns and suffers when he sees the evil result of his own work.

16. The virtuous man delights in this world, and he delights in the next; he delights in both. He delights and rejoices, when he sees the purity of his own work.

17. The evil-doer suffers in this world, and he suffers in the next; he suffers in both. He suffers when he thinks of the evil he has done; he suffers more when going on the evil path.

18. The virtuous man is happy in this world, and he is happy in the next; he is happy in both. He is happy when he thinks of the good he has done; he is still more happy when going on the good path.

19. The thoughtless man, even if he can recite a large portion of the law, but is not a doer of it, has no share in the priesthood, but is like a cowherd counting the cows of others.

20. The follower of the law, even if he can recite only a small portion of the law, but, having forsaken passion and hatred and foolishness, possesses true knowledge and serenity of mind, he, caring for nothing in this world or that to come, has indeed a share in the priesthood.

Chapter II On Earnestness

21. Earnestness is the path of immortality (Nirvana), thoughtlessness the path of death. Those who are in earnest do not die, those who are thoughtless are as if dead already.

22. Having understood this clearly, those who are advanced

in earnestness delight in earnestness, and rejoice in the knowledge of the elect.

23. These wise people, meditative, steady, always possssed of strong powers attain to Nirvana, the highest happiness.

24. If an earnest person has roused himself, if he is not forgetful, if his deeds are pure, if he acts with consideration, if he restrains himself, and lives according to law—then his glory will increase.

25. By rousing himself, by earnestness, by restraint and control, the wise man may make for himself an island which no flood can overwhelm.

26. Fools follow after vanity. The wise man keeps earnestness as his best jewel.

27. Follow not after vanity, nor after the enjoyment of love and lust! He who is earnest and meditative, obtains ample joy.

28. When the learned man drives away vanity by earnestness, he, the wise, climbing the terraced heights of wisdom, looks down upon the fools: free from sorrow he looks upon the sorrowing crowd, as one that stands on a mountain looks down upon them that stand upon the plain.

29. Earnest among the thoughtless, awake among the sleepers, the wise man advances like a racer, leaving behind the hack.

30. By earnestness did Maghavan (Indra) rise to the lordship of the gods. People praise earnestness; thoughtlessness is always blamed.

31. A Bhikshu (mendicant) who delights in earnestness, who looks with fear on thoughtlessness, moves about like fire, burning all his fetters, small or large.

32. A Bhikshu (mendicant) who delights in reflection, who looks with fear on thoughtlessness, cannot fall away from his perfect state—he is close upon Nirvana.

Chapter III Thought

33. As a fletcher makes straight his arrow, a wise man makes straight his trembling and unsteady thought, which is difficult to guard, difficult to hold back.

34. As a fish taken from his watery home and thrown on the dry ground, our thought trembles all over in order to escape the dominion of Mara, the tempter.

35. It is good to tame the mind, which is difficult to hold in

and flighty, rushing wherever it listeth; a tamed mind brings happiness.

36. Let the wise man guard his thoughts, for they are difficult to perceive, very artful, and they rush wherever they list: thoughts well guarded bring happiness.

37. Those who bridle their mind which travels far, moves about alone, is without a body, and hides in the chamber of the heart, will be free from the bonds of Mara, the tempter.

38. If a man's faith is unsteady, if he does not know the true law, if his peace of mind is troubled, his knowledge will never be perfect.

39. If a man's thoughts are not dissipated, if his mind is not perplexed, if he has ceased to think of good or evil, then there is no fear for him while he is watchful.

40. Knowing that this body is fragile like a jar, and making his thought firm like a fortress, one should attack Mara, the tempter, with the weapon of knowledge, one should watch him when conquered, and should never rest.

41. Before long, alas! this body will lie on the earth, despised, without understanding, like a useless log.

42. Whatever a hater may do to a hater, or an enemy to an enemy, a wrongly-directed mind will do him greater mischief.

43. Not a mother, not a father, will do so much, nor any other relatives; a well-directed mind will do us greater service.

Chapter IV Flowers

47. Death carries off a man who is gathering flowers, and whose mind is distracted, as a flood carries off a sleeping village.

48. Death subdues a man who is gathering flowers, and whose mind is distracted, before he is satiated in his pleasures.

49. As the bee collects nectar and departs without injuring the flower, or its colour or scent, so let a sage dwell in his village.

50. Not the perversities of others, not their sins of commission or omission but his own misdeeds and negligences should a sage take notice of.

51. Like a beautiful flower, full of colour, but without scent, are the fine but fruitless words of him who does not act accordingly.

52. But like a beautiful flower, full of colour and full of

scent, are the fine and fruitful words of him who acts accordingly.

Chapter V The Fool

60. Long is the night to him who is awake; long is a mile to him who is tired; long is life to the foolish who do not know the true law.

61. If a traveller does not meet with one who is his better, or his equal, let him firmly keep to his solitary journey; there is no companionship with a fool.

62. "These sons belong to me, and this wealth belongs to me?" with such thoughts a fool is tormented. He himself does not belong to himself; how much less sons and wealth?

63. The fool who knows his foolishness, is wise at least so far. But a fool who thinks himself wise, he is called a fool indeed.

64. If a fool be associated with a wise man even all his life, he will perceive the truth as little as a spoon perceives the taste of soup.

65. If an intelligent man be associated for one minute only with a wise man, he will soon perceive the truth, as the tongue perceives the taste of soup.

66. Fools of poor understanding have themselves for their greatest enemies, for they do evil deeds which bear bitter fruits.

67. That deed is not well done of which a man must repent, and the reward of which he receives crying and with a tearful face.

68. No, that deed is well done of which a man does not repent, and the reward of which he receives gladly and cheerfully.

69. As long as the evil deed done does not bear fruit, the fool thinks it is like honey; but when it ripens, then the fool suffers grief.

Chapter VI The Wise Man

76. If you see a man who shows you what is to be avoided, who administers reproofs, and is intelligent, follow that wise

man as you would one who tells of hidden treasures; it will be better, not worse, for him who follows him.

77. Let him admonish, let him teach, let him forbid what is improper!—he will be beloved of the good, by the bad he will be hated.

78. Do not have evil-doers for friends, do not have low people for friends: have virtuous people for friends, have for friends the best of men.

79. He who drinks in the law lives happily with a serene mind: the sage rejoices always in the law, as preached by the elect.

80. Well-makers lead the water wherever they like; fletchers bend the arrow; carpenters bend a log of wood; wise people fashion themselves.

81. As a solid rock is not shaken by the wind, wise people falter not amidst blame and praise.

82. Wise people, after they have listened to the laws, become serene, like a deep, smooth, and still lake.

Chapter VII The Venerable

92. Men who have no riches, who live on recognized food, who have perceived void and unconditioned freedom (Nirvana), their path is difficult to understand, like that of birds in the air.

93. He whose appetites are stilled, who is not absorbed in enjoyment, who has perceived void and unconditioned freedom (Nirvana), his path is difficult to understand, like that of birds in the air.

Chapter VIII The Thousands

100. Even though a speech be a thousand (of words), but made up of senseless words, one word of sense is better, which if a man hears, he becomes quiet.

101. Even though a Gatha (poem) be a thousand (of words), but made up of senseless words, one word of a Gatha is better, which if a man hears, he becomes quiet.

102. Though a man recite a hundred Gathas made up of

senseless words, one word of the law is better, which if a man hears, he becomes quiet.

103. If one man conquer in battle a thousand times a thousand men, and if another conquer himself, he is the greatest of conquerors.

109. He who always greets and constantly reveres the aged, four things will increase to him: life, beauty, happiness, power.

115. And he who lives a hundred years, not seeing the highest law, a life of one day is better if a man sees the highest law.

Chapter IX Evil

116. A man should hasten towards the good, and should keep his thought away from evil; if a man does what is good slothfully, his mind delights in evil.

117. If a man commits a sin, let him not do it again; let him not delight in sin: the accumulation of evil is painful.

118. If a man does what is good, let him do it again; let him delight in it: the accumulation of good is delightful.

119. Even an evil-doer sees happiness so long as his evil deed does not ripen; but when his evil deed ripens, then does the evil-doer see evil.

120. Even a good man sees evil days so long as his good deed does not ripen; but when his good deed ripens, then does the good man see good things.

121. Let no man think lightly of evil, saying in his heart, It will not come nigh unto me. Even by the falling of water-drops a water-pot is filled; the fool becomes full of evil, even if he gather it little by little.

122. Let no man think lightly of good, saying in his heart, It will not come nigh unto me. Even by the falling of water-drops a waterpot is filled; the wise man becomes full of good, even if he gather it little by little.

123. Let a man avoid evil deeds, as a merchant, if he has few companions and carries much wealth, avoids a dangerous road; as a man who loves life avoids poison.

124. He who has no wound on his hand, may touch poison with his hands; poison does not affect one who has no wound; nor is there evil for one who does not commit evil.

125. If a man offend a harmless, pure, and innocent person, the evils falls back upon that fool, like light dust thrown up against the wind.

Chapter X Punishment

129. All men tremble at punishment, all men fear death; remember that you are like unto them, and do not kill, nor cause slaughter.

130. All men tremble at punishment, all men love life; remember that thou are like unto them, and do not kill, nor cause slaughter.

131. He who, seeking his own happiness, punishes or kills beings who also long for happiness, will not find happiness after death.

132. He who, seeking his own happiness, does not punish or kill beings who also long for happiness, will find happiness after death.

133. Do not speak harshly to anyone; those who are spoken to will answer thee in the same way. Angry speech is painful: blows for blows will touch thee.

134. If, like a shattered metal plate (gong), thou utter nothing, then thou hast reached Nirvana; anger is not known to thee.

135. As a cowherd with his staff drives his cows into the stable, so do Age and Death drive the life of men.

141. Not nakedness, not plaited hair, not dirt, not fasting, or lying on the earth, not rubbing with dust, not sitting motionless, can purify a mortal who has not overcome desires.

142. He who, though dressed in fine apparel, exercises tranquillity, is quiet, subdued, restrained, chaste, and has ceased to find fault with all other beings, he indeed is a Brahmana, an ascetic (sramana), a friar (bhikshu).

143. Is there in this world any man so restrained by shame that he does not provoke reproof, as a noble horse the whip?

Chapter XI Old Age

152. A man who has learnt little, grows old like an ox; his flesh grows, but his knowledge does not grow.

Chapter XII Self

157. If a man hold himself dear, let him watch himself carefully; during one at least out of the three watches a wise man should be watchful.

158. Let each man direct himself first to what is proper, then let him teach others; thus a wise man will not suffer.

159. If a man make himself as he teaches others to be, then, being himself well subdued, he may subdue others; for one's own self is difficult to subdue.

160. Self is the lord of self, who else could be the lord? With self well subdued, a man finds a lord such as few can find.

161. The evil done by one's self, self-forgotten, self-bred, crushes the foolish, as a diamond breaks even a precious stone.

162. He whose wickedness is very great brings himself down to that state where his enemy wishes him to be, as a creeper does with the tree which it surrounds.

163. Bad deeds, and deeds hurtful to ourselves, are easy to do; what is beneficial and good, that is very difficult to do.

164. The foolish man who scorns the rule of the venerable (Arhat), of elect (Ariya), of the virtuous, and follows a false doctrine, he bears fruit to his own destruction, like the fruits of the Katthaka reed.

165. By one's self the evil is done, by one's self one suffers; by one's self evil is left undone, by one's self one is purified. The pure and the impure stand and fall by themselves, no one can purify another.

166. Let no one forget his own duty for the sake of another's, however great; let a man, after he has discerned his own duty, be always attentive to his duty.

Chapter XIV The Buddha—The Awakened

182. Difficult to obtain is the conception of men, difficult is the life of mortals, difficult is the hearing of the True Law, difficult is the birth of the Awakened (the attainment of Buddhahood).

183. Not to commit any sin, to do good, and to purify one's mind, that is the teaching of all the Awakened.

184. The Awakened call patience the highest penance, long-suffering the highest Nirvana; for he is not an anchorite (pravragita) who strikes others, he is not an ascetic (sramana) who insults others.

185. Not to blame, not to strike, to live restrained under the law, to be moderate in eating, to sleep and sit alone, and to dwell on the highest thoughts—this is the teaching of the Awakened.

186. There is no satisfying lusts, even by a shower of gold pieces; he

187. who knows that lusts have a short taste and cause pain, he is wise; even in heavenly pleasures he finds no satisfaction, the disciple who is fully awakened delights only in the destruction of all desires.

188. Men, driven by fear, go to many a refuge, to mountains and forests, to groves and sacred trees.

189. But that is not a safe refuge, that is not the best refuge; a man is not delivered from all pains after having gone to that refuge.

190-2. He who takes refuge with Buddha, the Law, and the Church; he who, with clear understanding, sees the four holy truths: pain, the origin of pain, the destruction of pain, and the eightfold holy way that leads to the quieting of pain;—that is the safe refuge, that is the best refuge; having gone to that refuge, a man is delivered from all pain.

193. A supernatural person (a Buddha) is not easily found: he is not born everywhere. Wherever such a sage is born, that race prospers.

194. Happy is the arising of the Awakened, happy is the teaching of True Law, happy is peace in the church, happy is the devotion of those who are at peace.

195. He who pays homage to those who deserve homage, whether

196. the awakened (Buddha) or their disciples, those who have overcome the host of evils, and crossed the flood of sorrow, he who pays homage to such as have found deliverance and know no fear, his merit can never be measured by anyone.

Chapter XV Happiness

197. We live happily indeed, not hating those who hate us! among men who hate us we dwell free from hatred! We live happily indeed, free from ailments among the ailing! among men who are ailing let us dwell free from ailments!

198. We live happily indeed, free from greed among the greedy! among men who are greedy let us dwell free from greed!

199. We live happily indeed, though we call nothing our own! We shall be like the bright gods, feeding on happiness!

201. Victory breeds hatred, for the conquered is unhappy. He who has given up both victory and defeat, he, the contented, is happy.

202. There is no fire like passion; there is no losing throw like hatred; there is no pain like this body; there is no happiness higher than rest.

203. Hunger is the worst of diseases, the elements of the body the greatest evil; if one knows this truly, that is Nirvana, the highest happiness.

204. Health is the greatest of gifts, contentedness the best riches; trust is the best of relationships, Nirvana the highest happiness.

205. He who has tasted the sweetness of solitude and tranquillity, is free from fear and free from sin, while he tastes the sweetness of drinking in the law.

Chapter XVI Pleasure

215. From lust comes grief, from lust comes fear; he who is free from lust knows neither grief nor fear.

216. From love comes grief, from love comes fear; he who is free from love knows neither grief nor fear.

217. From greed comes grief, from greed comes fear; he who is free from greed knows neither grief nor fear.

Chapter XVII Anger

221. Let a man leave anger, let him forsake pride, let him overcome all bondage! No sufferings befall the man who is not attached to name and form, and who calls nothing his own.

222. He who holds back rising anger like a rolling chariot, him I call a real driver; other people are but holding the reins.

223. Let a man overcome anger by love, let him overcome evil by good; let him overcome the greedy by liberality, the liar by truth!

224. Speak the truth, do not yield to anger; give, if thou art asked for little; by these three steps thou wilt go near the gods.

225. The sages who injure nobody, and who always control their body, they will go to the unchangeable place (Nirvana), where, if they have gone, they will suffer no more.

231. Beware of bodily anger, and control thy body! Leave the sins of the body, and with thy body practise virtue!

232. Beware of the anger of the tongue, and control thy tongue! Leave the sins of the tongue, and practise virtue with thy tongue!

233. Beware of the anger of the mind, and control thy mind! Leave the sins of the mind, and practise virtue with thy mind!

234. The wise who control their body, who control their tongue, the wise who control their mind, are indeed well controlled.

Chapter XVIII Impurity

238. Make thyself an island, work hard, be wise! When thy impurities are blown away, and thou art free from guilt, thou wilt not enter again into birth and decay.

239. Let a wise man blow off the impurities of himself, as a smith blows off the impurities of silver, one by one, little by little, and from time to time.

240. As the impurity which springs from the iron, when it

springs from it, destroys it; thus do a transgressor's own works lead him to the evil path.

251. There is no fire like passion, there is no shark like hatred, there is no snare like folly, there is no torrent like greed.

252. The fault of others is easily perceived, but that of one's self is difficult to perceive; a man winnows his neighbour's faults like chaff, but his own fault he hides, as a cheat hides the bad die from the player.

253. If a man looks after the faults of others, and is always inclined to be offended, his own passions will grow, and he is far from the destruction of passions.

Chapter XIX The Just

260. A man is not an elder because his head is grey; his age may be ripe, but he is called "Old-in-vain."

261. He in whom there is truth, virtue, pity, restraint, mod-. eration, he who is free from impurity and is wise, he is called an elder.

266. A man is not a mendicant (bhikshu) simply because he asks others for alms; he who adopts the whole law is a Bhikshu, not he who only begs.

267. He who is above good and evil, who is chaste, who with care passes through the world, he indeed is called a Bhikshu.

268. A man is not a Muni because he observes silence if he is foolish

269. and ignorant; but the wise who, as with the balance, chooses the good and avoids evil, he is a Muni, and is a Muni thereby; he who in this world weighs both sides is called a Muni.

270. A man is not an elect (Ariya) because he injures living creatures; because he has pity on all living creatures, therefore is a man called Ariya.

Chapter XX The Way

273. The best of ways is the eightfold; the best of truths the four words; the best of virtues passionlessness; the best of men he who has eyes to see.

277. "All created things perish": he who knows and sees this becomes passive in pain; this is the way to purity.

278. "All created things are grief and pain": he who knows and sees this becomes passive in pain; this is the way that leads to purity.

279. "All forms are unreal": he who knows and sees this becomes passive in pain; this is the way that leads to purity.

280. He who does not rouse himself when it is time to rise, who, though young and strong, is full of sloth, whose will and thought are weak, that lazy and idle man never finds the way to knowledge.

282. Through zeal knowledge is gained, through lack of zeal knowledge is lost; let a man who knows this double path of gain and loss thus place himself that knowledge may grow.

283. Cut down the whole forest of desires, not a tree only! Danger comes out of the forest of desires. When you have cut down both the forest of desires and its undergrowth, then, Bhikshus, you will be rid of the forest and of desires!

Chapter XXIV Thirst

334. The thirst of a thoughtless man grows like a creeper; he runs from life to life, like a monkey seeking fruit in the forest.

335. Whomsoever this fierce poisonous thirst overcomes, in this world, his sufferings increase like the abounding Birana grass.

336. But from him who overcomes this fierce thirst, difficult to be conquered in this world, sufferings fall off, like water-drops from a lotus leaf.

337. This salutary word I tell you, "Do ye, as many as are here assembled, dig up the root of thirst, as he who wants the sweet-scented Usira root must dig up the Birana grass, that Mara, the tempter, may not crush you again and again, as the stream crushes the reeds."

338. As a tree, even though it has been cut down, is firm so long as its root is safe, and grows again, thus, unless the feeders of thirst are destroyed, this pain of life will return again and again.

339. He whose thirty-six streams are strongly flowing in the channels of pleasure, the waves—his desires which are set on passion—will carry away that misguided man.

340. The channels run everywhere, the creeper of passion

stands sprouting; if you see the creeper springing up, cut its root by means of knowledge.

341. A creature's pleasures are extravagant and luxurious; given up to pleasure and deriving happiness, men undergo again and again birth and decay.

342. Beset with lust, men run about like a snared hare; held in fetters and bonds, they undergo pain for a long time, again and again.

343. Beset with lust, men run about like a snared hare; let therefore the mendicant drive out thirst, by striving after passionlessness for himself.

344. He who, having got rid of the forest of lust after having reached Nirvâna, gives himself over to forest-life (to lust), and who, when free from the forest (from lust), runs to the forest (to lust), look at that man! though free, he runs into bondage.

345. Wise people do not call that a strong fetter which is made of iron, wood, or hemp; passionately strong is the care for precious stones and rings, for sons and a wife.

346. That fetter wise people call strong which drags down, yields, but is difficult to undo; after having cut this at last, people leave the world, free from cares, and leaving the pleasures of love behind.

347. Those who are slaves to passions, run down the stream of desires, as a spider runs down the web which he has made himself; when they have cut this, at last, wise people go onwards, free from cares, leaving all pain behind.

348. Give up what is before, give up what is behind, give up what is between when thou goest to the other shore of existence; if thy mind is altogether free, thou will not again enter into birth and decay.

349. If a man is tossed about by doubts, full of strong passions, and yearning only for what is delightful, his thirst will grow more and more, and he will indeed make his fetters strong.

350. If a man delights in quieting doubts, and, always reflecting, dwells on what is not delightful, he certainly will remove, nay, he will cut the fetter of Mara.

351. He who has reached the consummation, who does not tremble, who is without thirst and without sin, he has broken all the thorns of life: this will be his last body.

352. He who is without thirst and without affection, who understands the words and their interpretation, who knows the order of letters (those which are before and which are after), he has received his last body, he is called the great sage, the great man.

353. "I have conquered all, I know all, in all conditions of life I am free from taint; I have left all, and through the destruc-

tion of thirst I am free; having learnt myself, whom should I indicate as my teacher?"

354. The gift of the law exceeds all gifts; the sweetness of the law exceeds all sweetness; the delight in the law exceeds all delights; the extinction of thirst overcomes all pain.

355. Riches destroy the foolish, if they look not for the other shore; the foolish by his thirst for riches destroys himself, as if he were destroying others.

356. The fields are damaged by weeds, mankind is damaged by passion; therefore a gift bestowed on the passionless brings great reward.

357. The fields are damaged by weeds, mankind is damaged by hatred: therefore a gift bestowed on those who do not hate brings great reward.

358. The fields are damaged by weeds, mankind is damaged by vanity: therefore a gift bestowed on those who are free from vanity brings great reward.

359. The fields are damaged by weeds, mankind is damaged by lust: therefore a gift bestowed on those who are free from lust brings great reward.

Chapter XXV The Bhikshu

360. Restraint in the eye is good, good is restraint in the ear, in the nose restraint is good, good is restraint in the tongue.

361. In the body restraint is good, good is restraint in speech, in thought restraint is good, good is restraint in all things. A Bhikshu, restrained in all things, is free from all pain.

362. He who controls his hand, he who controls his feet, he who controls his speech, he who is well controlled, he who delights inwardly, who is collected, who is solitary and content, him they call Bhikshu.

363. The Bhikshu who controls his mouth, who speaks wisely and calmly, who teaches the meaning and the law, his word is sweet.

364. He who dwells in the law, delights in the law, meditates on the law, recollects the law: that Bhikshu will never fall away from the true law.

365. Let him not despise what he has received, nor ever envy others: a mendicant who envies others does not obtain peace of mind.

366. A Bhikshu who, though he receives little, does not despise what he has received, even the gods will praise him, if his life is pure, and if he is not slothful.

367. He who never identifies himself with name and form, and does not grieve over what is no more, he indeed is called a Bhikshu.

368. The Bhikshu who behaves with kindness, who is happy in the doctrine of Buddha, will reach the quiet place (Nirvana), happiness arising from the cessation of natural inclinations.

369. O Bhikshu, empty this boat! if emptied, it will go quickly; having cut off passion and hatred, thou wilt go to Nirvana.

370. Cut off the five fetters, leave the five, rise above the five. A Bhikshu, who has escaped from the five fetters, he is called Oghatinna—"saved from the flood."

371. Meditate, O Bhikshu, and be not heedless! Do not direct thy thought to what gives pleasure, that thou mayest not for thy heedlessness have to swallow the iron ball in hell, and that thou mayest not cry out when burning, "This is pain."

372. Without knowledge there is no meditation, without meditation there is no knowledge: he who has knowledge and meditation is near unto Nirvana.

373. A Bhikshu who has entered his empty house, and whose mind is tranquil, feels a more than human delight when he sees the law clearly.

374. As soon as he has considered the origin and destruction of the elements of the body, he finds happiness and joy which belong to those who know the immortal (Nirvana).

375. And this is the beginning here for a wise Bhikshu: watchfulness over the senses, contentedness, restraint under the law; keep noble friends whose life is pure, and who are not slothful.

376. Let him live in charity, let him be perfect in his duties; then in the fullness of delight he will make an end of suffering.

377. As the Vassika plant shed its withered flowers, men should shed passion and hatred, O ye Bhikshus!

378. The Bhikshu whose body and tongue and mind are quieted, who is collected, and has rejected the baits of the world, he is called quiet.

379. Rouse thyself by thyself, examine thyself by thyself, thus self-protected and attentive wilt thou live happily, O Bhikshu!

380. For self is the lord of self, self is the refuge of self; therefore curb thyself as the merchant curbs a noble horse.

381. The Bhikshu, full of delight, who is happy in the doctrine of Buddha will reach the quiet place (Nirvana), happiness consisting in the cessation of natural inclinations.

382. He who, even as a young Bhikshu, applies himself to the

doctrine of Buddha, brightens up this world, like the moon when free from clouds.

Chapter XXVI The Brahmana

383. Stop the stream valiantly, drive away the desires, O Brahmana! When you have understood the destruction of all that was made, you will understand that which was not made.

384. If the Brahmana has reached the other shore in both laws, in restraint and contemplation, all bonds vanish from him who has obtained knowledge.

385. He for whom there is neither the hither nor the further shore, nor both, him, the fearless and unshackled, I call indeed a Brahmana.

386. He who is thoughtful, blameless, settled, dutiful, without passions, and who has attained the highest end, him I call indeed a Brahmana.

387. The sun is bright by day, the moon shines by night, the warrior is bright in his armour, the Brahmana is bright in his meditation; but Buddha, the Awakened, is bright with splendour day and night.

388. Because a man is rid of evil, therefore he is called Brahmana; because he walks quietly, therefore he is called Samana; because he has sent away his own impurities, therefore he is called Pravragita (pabbagita, a pilgrim).

389. No one should attack a Brahmana, but no Brahmana, if attacked, should let himself fly at his aggressor! Woe to him who strikes a Brahmana, more woe to him who flies at his aggressor!

390. It advantages a Brahmana not a little if he holds his mind back from the pleasures of life; the more all wish to injure has vanished the more all pain will cease.

391. Him I call indeed a Brahmana who does not offend by body, word, or thought, and is controlled on these three points.

392. He from whom he may learn the law, as taught by the Well-awakened (Buddha), him let him worship assiduously, as the Brahmana worships the sacrificial fire.

393. A man does not become a Brahmana by his plaited hair, by his family, or by birth; in whom there is truth and righteousness, he is blessed, he is a Brahmana.

394. What is the use of plaited hair, O fool! what of the raiment of goatskins? Within thee there is ravening, but the outside thou makest clean.

395. The man who wears dirty raiments, who is emaciated and covered with veins, who meditates alone in the forest, him I call indeed a Brahmana.

396. I do not call a man a Brahmana because of his origin or of his mother. He is indeed arrogant, and he is wealthy: but the poor, who is free from all attachments, him I call indeed a Brahmana.

397. Him I call indeed a Brahmana who, after cutting all fetters, never trembles, is free from bonds and unshackled.

398. Him I call indeed a Brahmana who, after cutting the strap and the thong, the rope with all that pertains to it, has destroyed all obstacles, and is awakened.

399. Him I call indeed a Brahmana who, though he has committed no offence, endures reproach, stripes, and bonds: who has endurance for his force, and strength for his army.

400. Him I call indeed a Brahmana who is free from anger dutiful, virtuous, without appetites, who is subdued and has received his last body.

401. Him I call indeed a Brahmana who does not cling to sensual pleasures like water on a lotus leaf, like a mustard seed on the point of a needle.

402. Him I call indeed a Brahmana who, even here, knows the end of his own suffering, has put down his burden, and is unshackled.

403. Him I call indeed a Brahmana whose knowledge is deep, who possesses wisdom, who knows the right way and the wrong, and has attained the highest end.

404. Him I call indeed a Brahmana who keeps aloof both from laymen and from mendicants, who frequents no houses, and has but few desires.

405. Him I call indeed a Brahmana who without hurting any creatures, whether feeble or strong, does not kill nor cause slaughter.

406. Him I call indeed a Brahmana who is tolerant with the intolerant, mild with the violent, and free from greed among the greedy.

407. Him I call indeed a Brahmana from whom anger and hatred, pride and hypocrisy have dropped like a mustard seed from the point of a needle.

408. Him I call indeed a Brahmana who utters true speech, instructive and free from harshness, so that he offend no one.

409. Him I call indeed a Brahmana who takes nothing in the world that is not given him, be it long or short, small or large, good or bad.

410. Him I call indeed a Brahmana who fosters no desires

for this world or for the next, has no inclinations, and is unshackled.

411. Him I call indeed a Brahmana who has no interests,
and when he has understood the truth, does not say How, how?
and who has reached the depth of the Immortal.

412. Him I call indeed a Brahmana who in this world has
risen above both ties, good and evil, who is free from grief, from
sin and from impurity.

413. Him I call indeed a Brahmana who is bright like the
moon, pure, serene, undisturbed, and in whom all gaiety is extinct.

414. Him I call indeed a Brahmana who has traversed this
miry road, the impassible world, difficult to pass, and its vanity,
who has gone through, and reached the other shore, is thoughtful, steadfast, free from doubts, free from attachment, and content.

415. Him I call indeed a Brahmana who in this world, having abandoned all desires, travels about without a home, and in
whom all concupiscence is extinct.

416. Him I call indeed a Brahmana who, having abandoned
all longings, travels about without a home, and in whom all
covetousness is extinct.

417. Him I call indeed a Brahmana who, after leaving all
bondage to men, has risen above all bondage to the gods, and is
free from all and every bondage.

418. Him I call indeed a Brahmana who has left what gives
pleasure and what gives pain, who is cold, and free from all
germs of renewed life: the hero who has conquered all the
worlds.

419. Him I call indeed a Brahmana who knows the destruction and the return of beings everywhere, who is free from
bondage, welfaring (Sugata), and awakened (Buddha).

420. Him I call indeed a Brahmana whose path the gods do
not know, nor spirits (Gandharvas), nor men, whose passions
are extinct, and who is an Arhat.

421. Him I call indeed a Brahmana who calls nothing his
own, whether it be before, behind, or between, who is poor, and
free from the love of the world.

422. Him I call indeed a Brahmana, the manly, the noble,
the hero, the great sage, the conqueror, the indifferent, the accomplished, the awakened.

423. Him I call indeed a Brahmana who knows his former
abodes, who sees heaven and hell, has reached the end of births,
is perfect in knowledge, a sage, and whose perfections are all
perfect.

Part Three

ZOROASTRIANISM, JAINISM, AND SIKHISM

There is no fundamental connection between the three religions included in Part Three. In fact, each is closer to other religions in the book than to either of the others: Zoroastrianism has more intimate ties with early Hinduism (the Vedas) and Persian Sufism; the Jains have closer ties to Buddhism; and Sikhism has more important relationships with Buddhism, Sufism, and Hinduism. They are grouped together here merely for editorial and structural convenience; as Eastern mystical religions they were too important to exclude entirely from the book, yet they were not central enough to Eastern mysticism to demand a large number of pages by themselves. There is a separate introduction for each of the religions.

Introduction to Zoroastrianism

Although Zoroastrianism has been traditionally and popularly presented in a simplistic, superficial fashion, it is one of the most ancient religions and, in unique ways, is highly subtle. Zoroaster (Greek for the Persian Zarathustra or Zarathushtra) lived during the sixth century B.C. His exact dates, and even his actual existence, are questionable. The oldest classical writers, such as Xanthus, Plato, Pliny, and Plutarch, place his life anywhere from 6000 to 1000 B.C. The Zoroastrian tradition itself places his life from c. 660-583 B.C. Another acceptable date is c. 570-500 B.C.

There are four main periods in Zoroastrianism: the early inspiration and teachings of Zoroaster himself; the religion of the Achaemenid period (c. 550-330 B.C.); the Sassanian period (c. 226-640 A.D.); and the period after the fall of the Persian empire to the Arab invaders in 635.

The Achaemenid rulers begin with Darius I (521-486 B.C.) and include Cyrus, Xerxes, Artaxerxes, and lesser figures. During this period the ritual and ethical aspects of the religion were emphasized. Following the Achaemenidae, Zoroastrianism was all but demolished by Alexander's invasion and religious factionalism. But when the Sassanian dynasty was founded by Ardashir in 226, Zoroastrianism was reestablished as the state religion. During the Sassanian period (the last native Persian dynasty before the Arab conquest), the theological emphasis was magical and demon-obsessed. But it was also a period of intense speculation about the workings of the universe and in particular the cosmology of Zoroastrianism. Although during the late, or final, period the faithful were dispersed under brutal Muslim oppression, the religion was not entirely extinguished. Zoroastrianism survived in various elements of the Muslim mystical Sufis of Iran, and in small groups that traveled to India rather than accept the religion of Islam. This minority, which successfully settled in India, where they still exist today, came to be known as the Parsis—literally, "Persians."

Zoroaster apparently reformed many of the ancient Persian nature-worship practices. The original sacrificial religion of the Persians focused on the protection of domestic animals, increas-

ing the harvest, and propitiating the basic life forces, such as
fire, earth, and water. Zoroaster incorporated many of the old
Persian pantheon into his religion, but divided this polytheism
into two primal dieties: one beneficent, the other malevolent.
Ahura Mazda, or Ormuzd, was the chief God of light and goodness; while Angra Mainyu, or Ahriman, was the God of malevolence and darkness. This ditheism is a strong part of the whole
Zoroastrian religion, but it should be remembered that it is not
entirely dualistic, for Zoroaster predicted that the ultimate triumph of good (Ormuzd) over evil (Ahriman) would eventually
take place.

Zoroaster himself was clearly a mystic in the prophetic tradition. He was inspired and in frequent communion with his God
Ormuzd. Sometimes he doubted himself, as can be seen throughout the Zoroastrian sacred scripture, the Zendavesta. But he is
convinced he "knows" that God is speaking through his mouth
when he preaches to the people. Ormuzd is not, however, an
awesome Jehovah, as in the Old Testament. He is instead a wise,
benevolent Holy Lord. "Speak to me," Zoroaster says to his
Lord, "as friend to friend. Grant us the support which friend
would give to a friend." For Zoroaster such a friendship between
God and man is possible only because his God is a righteous, benevolent one. The Zoroastrian prayer often implies recognition
of the sublimity of the surrounding universe. Such prayers are
full of reverence and awe (so the "friendship" between man and
God does not make the Lord less powerful and great), and in
this sense they are mystical, for life is transmuted into praise of
the Good Spirit, the Wise Lord of creation:

> Waste, and Solitary places where we taste
> The pleasure of believing what we see,
> Is boundless, as we wish our souls to be.

Previously the gods of ancient Persia had been tyrannical
despots, open to flattery and gifts that were little more than
bribes. With Ormuzd, Zoroaster replaces a deity of caprice with
a God of law and absolute equity. For Zoroaster, righteousness—
that is, good thought, good word, and good deed, the three commandments of Ormuzd—leads to bliss.[1] By living righteously a
man expresses his God-gift of free will, diminishes the power of
evil, and strengthens the power of good. Thus Ormuzd achieves
final victory over evil only with mankind's freely given help.

The Zoroastrian influence spread to many mystically oriented
teachings. In the second century B.C. the Essene Manual of

[1]See *The Hymns of Zarathustra*, by Jacques Duchesne-Guillemin (London:
John Murray, Inc., 1952), p. 7.

Discipline, for example, describes the origin of evil in Zoroastrian terms. The Essenes wrote that God created two active principles in the beginning, Truth and Perversity, which is clearly a Zoroastrian concept. A Gnostic writing entitled The Apocalypse of Zoroaster presents the world as caught in a conflict between the powers of Light and Darkness. There are even Zoroastrian influences in the writings of the mystical sects of Judaism, and the Greek writings of the Magi in Asia Minor in the second century B.C.[2] And, of course, both Zoroastrianism and Gnosticism were melded in Persia by Mani, or Manes (216?-276?), in the Manichaean religion in order to establish a universal religion.

One of the difficulties of outlining the mystical elements in Zoroastrianism is that only ancient sources are available, and the cosmic principles that glimmer tantalizingly before one are sparse and undeveloped. Zoroastrian dualism simply expressed, for example, states that there were two original spirits—good and evil. As an isolated fact this seems an unenlightened, even primitive concept, except that it was conceived by Zoroaster many centuries before other similar dualistic religious ideas were developed. But an important qualifying fact modifies Zoroaster's simple dualism into a provocative idea, for the two original spirits were not called "two persons" as with anthropomorphic dualism, as one might expect, but rather were described as "principles"—a better principle and a worse one.[3] The qualifying terms are also all in the neuter, and contain no personifying characteristics.[4] As these two spirits, or principles, came together by natural affinity, they composed the dynamic polarities and phenomena of all life. If one follows this interpretation, the Zoroastrian dualism which initially seemed like a simple ditheism becomes a far more complex conception of cosmic birth. It sounds surprisingly like the birth of the opposing phenomenal aspects of yin and yang in Taoism, which emanated from the originating cosmic principle of chi. This parallel with Taoism, however, is not complete without noting that the chi principle

[2] See "The Gnostics," in Sidney Spencer, *Mysticism in World Religion* (Baltimore: Penguin, 1963), p. 148. Also see Francis Legge, *Forerunners and Rivals of Christianity* (New York, New Hyde Park: University Books, 1964), 2 vols., pp. 155-56, 181.

[3] See Yasna XXX of the Zendavesta for an example of this. Verse 3 is rendered from the Gathic as: "Thus the two spirits who uttered first in the world each his own principle; that is, who each uttered, one his own good and the other his own sin, these were a pair, in thought, word, and deed, a highest and a degraded one." *Sacred Books of the East*, trans. by L.H. Mills, vol. 31, Part III (Oxford at the Clarendon Press, 1887), pp. 29-30.

[4] L.H. Mills, *Sacred Books of the East*, vol. 31, p. 25.

of Taoism is complemented by the intriguing Zoroastrian deity
Zurvan, or Infinite Time.

According to one version of Zoroastrian cosmology, Ormuzd
created the universe by means of thought, and since He is God,
He foresees the evil one, Ahriman. The "thought" of evil gives
birth to Ahriman and evil thereby comes into being. But this
conception presented particular difficulties for Zoroastrian theologians, for if Ormuzd created evil by His own thought, then evil
must exist within a God specifically conceived of by Zoroaster as
good. It was difficult, to say the least, to defend a God who apparently contained corruption or evil within Himself. Such a deity was less than pure or supreme.

While Zoroastrianism is, in practical terms, a ditheistic religion, its cosmology allows for resolving its dualism in a mystical
monism. This monism is expressed primarily in sacrificial mysticism and in the doctrines of Zurvan, for in these beliefs the
road to salvation is toward "One World" which, of necessity, is
attained through the long journey and struggle in choosing between the "Two."[5] Zurvan, who is thought of very early as either a maker of paths leading to the hereafter or as "Infinite
Time" (and also as "Time of the Long Dominion"), is first
mentioned on Nuzi tablets of the thirteenth and twelfth centuries B.C.

In Zurvanian cosmology Ormuzd is first brought into being after Zurvan had sacrificed for a thousand years. This is admittedly a strange concept, for the idea of a Supreme God offering
sacrifice does seem puzzling. But it is actually one of the subtler
concepts of Zoroastrianism. For a modern analytical Westerner
the obvious question is, what and to whom does a Supreme God
sacrifice? In ancient Persia and India, sacrifice had a very specific meaning and impact. Sacrifice meant creation rather than
propitiation, and in this sense some have called it sacrificial
mysticism.[6] There was not so much an asking as a participation
in action. In the ancient forms of sacrifice, the sacrificer who
lighted his morning fire was not only making an offering, but
participating in making the sun rise. In the Indian Upanishads,

[5]For an elaboration of this analysis of Zoroastrianism, see Jacques Duchesne-
Guillemin, *The Hymns of Zarathustra*, A Translation of the Gathas together
with Commentary. Other sources that analyze Zoroastrianism from this per-
spective are: Jacques Duchesne-Guillemin, *Zoroastrianism, Symbols and
Values* (New York: Harper Torchbooks, 1966); Sir Rustom Masani, *Zoro-
astrianism, The Religion of the Good Life* (New York: Collier Books, 1962);
and the lengthy commentaries by L.H. Mills, "The Zendavesta," in *Sacred
Books of the East*, volume 31; and Franz Cumont, *The Mysteries of Mithra*
(New York: Dover, 1956; a reprint of the original edition published by
Open Court Publishing Co., Chicago, 1903).

[6]See S.N. Dasgupta, *Hindu Mysticism* (New York: Ungar, 1927, 1959).

for example, which are more or less coeval with Zoroaster, fire is present throughout the whole universe, expecially in the stars and lightning. The universe itself was considered a vast sacrificial fire.[7] This idea can be found in the Rig Veda and Upanishad selections included in *Eastern Mysticism*, where Agni, Fire, is all-pervading. Thus, the totality of a supreme and universal Godhead "sacrificing" to bring into being the twin contrasts of good and evil, which in turn manifest the finite world, was not illogical, mysterious, or lacking in meaning or religious value for the ancient Persians.[8] In short, sacrifical mysticism presents man with other means of uniting himself to his God besides virtuous action or grace. As Duchesne-Guillemin phrases it, proper sacrifice was thought able to "create a mystic bond between men and God." So we can begin to sense some of the originality in Zoroaster's religion.

Two important aspects of the ancient Indo-Iranian cultures (Zoroastrianism and Hinduism) involve first *action* or *sacrifice,* and second the *effect of thought.* In the first, sacrifice involves ancient man in universal functions, he becomes a part of natural processes, and in this sense he practices a mystical religion; and by involving oneself in this *totality* of life, the conception of not only the origin of life, but the impact of "human thought" upon the processes of the universe is implied. In this sense the "mind," which was admittedly an incomplete idea to the ancient Persians and Indians, evolves into a clearer concept through the individual's personal involvement with divine processes, and the developing awareness of one's sense of "self" and the possibility of choice. Hence, Zoroastrianism initiated a gnostic view of the universe, and was perhaps the first religion to offer a sophisticated philosophical view of free will: men *can* choose either evil or good, either Ahriman or Ormuzd; and by their choice each individual partakes of the ultimate outcome of the universal plan. For Zoroaster has made clear that Ormuzd will reign supreme at the end only with the help of men making the right choice; that is, on the side of "righteousness" and "good thought."

Zoroastrian gnosticism, however, was not an isolated development. The power of thought is present in the religions of ancient Egypt, India, and Greece, as well as in the opening chapter of Genesis. Here, Divine Creativity is interpreted by many as

---

[7]See Jacques Duchesne-Guillemin, *The Hymns of Zarathustra,* p. 11.

[8]As a Supreme God who sacrifices in order to create, Zurvan has a counterpart in the Indian High God Prajapati. Both Zurvan and Prajapati offered sacrifices in order to create offspring; and in both cases there is the strong yearning for progeny. Hence man is the child of God in both religions and contains the seeds of divinity within him. See also the Vedic Hymns, Part One, note 5, for comments on Vedic sacrifice.

"thought," expressed by a word or Logos, which in turn gives being to the universe and all phenomenal life.[9] To Zoroaster, thought or mind is the origin of all, and it, combined with sacrifice, wedded mankind to the processes of nature as thoroughly as any mystical cosmology could. Zoroaster in fact describes his God as "Good Thought" throughout the Zendavesta, as his "Wise Lord," and details the subtlety and structure of His divinity as "He who, through the mind, filled the blessed spaces with light . . ."

The Zoroastrian concept of heaven and hell is another example of the underlying concept of mind. They are not separate domains, a stockyard, country club, torture chamber, or limbo where deities place various grades of good or bad people to reward or punish. Hell is conceived of as being the "worst life" and heaven is considered "the best mental state"; which is surprisingly close to Milton's vision of "The mind is its own place and in itself can make a heaven of hell, a hell of heaven." The evil principle, or Ahriman, becomes Satan and is considered "Evil Thought," or "the worst mind."[10] As L.H. Mills argues, this is the proper Zoroastrian concept of creation, heaven, and hell. It is undeniably original and highly abstract—especially considering its early date.

Ahriman, the Zoroastrian Satan, came into existence also as a projection of thought. He was born as the result of a moment of doubt occuring to Zurvan during the creation of Ormuzd, when a fleeting negative thought made Him wonder about the efficacy of His sacrificing. Among some Zurvanians it is believed that Zurvan Himself was born from Light, and during the process had a moment of doubt, and from this doubt darkness and Satan was born.[11] Zurvan then can be considered beyond good and evil, or, as Duchesne-Guillemin argues, as an "undetermined" First One who gives birth to the "determined." He is a Supreme Being who dwells in an eternal condition, beyond the contrasts that exist in the finite world. His giving birth to the twins of good and evil, to Ormuzd and Ahriman, makes the contrast be-

[9]This Zoroastrian "Logos" is closer to the Greek Stoic's concept of Logos as the active principle of the universe, rather than to either the Old Testament Apocrypha writers who used the word to personify "wisdom," or the Alexandrian-Jewish philosophers like Philo who considered it "Divine Reason." No mention of Logos is found in the synoptic gospels, and Christian associations with the concept of Logos occur almost entirely through the early Apocrypha, the Christian gnostics, and St. John's gospel.

[10]See L.H. Mills, "The Zendavesta," *Sacred Books of the East*, vol. 31, p. 26.

[11]Thought, the mind, and doubt have an interesting connection with the Vedas and Buddhism. Buddhaghosa, for example, has explained the important Buddhist principle of self-mastery as being accomplished "by the absence of doubt," which brings one's mind under control.

tween good and evil meaningful only in the temporal world
where conflict can exist. Zurvan remains, therefore, associated
with light, power, wisdom, and infinity; but not with the phenomenal expression of good and evil.

Thus Zoroaster was one of the first sages to perceive God in
terms of "pure thought" and to relate humanity to the divine
through the medium of "mind." As described in more detail in
the general introduction, the concept of "mind" plays a central
role in all mystical philosophies; so Zoroaster has a legitimate
claim to being the first to perceive a necessary communion between humanity and the divine with the "mind" acting as the
ultimate arbiter of reality. As Zoroaster himself wrote,

> He who first by the mind filled the blessed
>   spaces with light,
> He created Righteousness by his will,
> By which he upholds Best Mind.
>
> Thou hast, O Wise One, increased it by thy Spirit
> Which is even now one with thee, O Lord!
> Through the mind, O Wise One, have I known thee
> As the Father of Good Mind,
> When I perceived thee with mind-eyes
>   as the true creator of Right
> As the Lord in the deeds of existence.

Selections from Zoroastrian Gathas, Yashts, and Hymns

> Lord Mazada Ahura!, grant unto us
> To realise the difference between
> Our two selves, the physical lower one,
> And th' other, higher, of the better mind.
> Of these two selves that Mazda gave to us,
> The higher self points ever to the Right,
> The lower one misleads towards the Wrong;
> Determined by these two are all our acts.

The Brighter Self unto the Darker says:
Neither our minds, nor well-cognised beliefs,
Nor duties, manners, words, nor our deeds,
Nor our religions, nor our souls agree.

Gatha 28.2; 30.11; 45.2

Lord of benignant Spirit, Mazada!,
Listen to this my prayer, and teach me well
What he should do who would with a pure mind
Seek earnestly to find the Peace of Brahm'!
... May we find Brahma in the House of Songs.

Gatha, 48.1

May Ahura give us the truth of Brahm',
May He unite us with that Absolute,
When we have undergone successfully
The disciplines whereby the Vice in us
Is overthrown by Virtue, which make man
Divinely meritorious, and which bring
Salvation unto men and gods alike.

Gatha, 46.17

Thee only do I know to be Supreme!
All others I dismiss from this my mind!
I know Him to be none except Thy-Self!
He who is known as Ahura Mazada—
With duteous deeds we worship Him alone.
We know Thee as Supreme above all lives.

Gatha, 44.11; 34.7; 45.10; 34.5

All things that may be dear to us are dear
For the sweet sake of our-Self alone.

Gatha, 43.2

Give me the gift that is the best of all,
Give me the Inmost Self of all the Selves.

Gatha, 45.5

These two Primordial Principles in One,
Of Light and Darkness, Good and Ill, that seem
Apart from one another, yet are bound
Inseparably together, each to each—
In Thought, in Word, in Action, everywhere

Are they in operation; and the wise
Walk on the side of Light, while the unwise
Follow the other until they grow wise.
These ancient Two, in mutual wrestle-play
Give birth to Twin-Desires, high and low,
That shape as Hate-Mentality in some,
In others as the Better Mind of Love.
O Mighty Lord of Wisdom, Mazada!,
Supreme, Infinite, Universal mind!,
Ahura!, thou that givest Life to all!,
Grant me the power to control this mind,
This Lower Mind of mine, this egoism,
And put an end to all Duality,
And gain the reign of One—as is desired.

Gatha, 30.3,4; 32.16

Ad Astra

Glory to thee, O Mazdah! Lo, I turn
From dazzling visions of Thy home of light,
And find me weary in the strife again,
To battle with the watchful fiends that line
Man's path to Heaven. Yet in the sacred Fire
I pray Thee let my waking thoughts recall
Sights that can soothe and strengthen.
                                    I beheld,
And lo, from out the eternal House of Song,
One came and answered my unspoken prayer:—
"How came I hither? Thou must tell the tale
Of what I was, a mortal, for the years
Of bliss have swept the memory away.
It may be the fell demons of disease
Vanquished my body, while the Death-fiend nigh
Waited the hour to swoop upon her prey.
What recked I? I was free.
                          Three days I watched
Hard by the spot whence weeping friends had borne
The demon-haunted frame that once was mine.
New light had dawned on all the earthly scenes
Where once I seemed to struggle all alone
Against the Lie; for myriad angel forms

Thronged o'er the foughten field, and silently
Strengthened the weary warrior with their aid.
And joy whose like the world had never known
Bade me forget the tears that death had drawn
And death should dry.
                    Four glorious Dawns had risen,
And with the wakening loveliness of day
Came breezes whispering from the southern sky,
Laden with fragrant sweetness. I beheld,
And floating lightly on the enamoured winds
A Presence sped and hovered over me,
A maiden, roseate as the blush of morn,
Stately and pure as heaven, and on her face
The freshness of a bloom untouched of Time.
Amazed I cried, 'Who art thou, Maiden fair,
Fairer than aught on earth these eyes have seen?'
And she in answer spake, 'I am Thyself,
Thy thoughts, thy words, thy actions, glorified.
By every conquest over base desire,
By every offering of a holy prayer
To the Wise Lord in Heaven, every deed
Of kindly help done to the good and pure.
By these I come thus lovely, come to guide
Thy steps to the dread Bridge where waits for thee
The Prophet, charged with judgement.'
                              On the winds
A little space we flew, yet spanned therein
Ten times the gulf that severs sun and star,
On to the South, where like a buried noon
Glimmered a growing glory—onward still,
Till heavens burning with ethereal light
Revealed the House of Song. High-towered it stood,
With flashing diamonds walled, suspense in air;
And, far beneath, a chasm fathomless
To keenest vision, whence a muffled wail
Strained through the solid darkness and betrayed
Fell Angra Mainyu's realm. Long time I gazed
Dazzled at Heaven, or blinded upon Hell;
Till o'er the abyss I saw a thin bright line
Stretched up to that fair portal, and I knew
The Bridge of Judgement. Lo, an angel dread
Sat there beside, and in his hand the scales
To weigh the good and evil. At his bar
I stood, yet feared not, while good angels pled
And demons fierce accused me, till the scale
Sank with the load of everlasting joy.

So with my Angel forth I sped and passed
The Bridge of Judgement, passed the Heavens Three,
Good Thought, Good Word, Good Action, and beyond
Soared to the place of Everlasting Light,
Ahura Mazdah's boundless House of Song.
A Saint's voice hailed me, "How hast hither come,
From carnal world to spiritual, from the realm
Of death to life, to bliss that cannot die?
And from the Throne came answer, 'Question not
Him that hath trod the dread and unknown path
Which parts the body and the soul for aye.' "

Yasht 22

O Thou Wise Lord, who when Thy world was young
    Didst pierce the grim night of the eastern sky
    With gladsome rays of truth and purity,
Forgive the error of this venturous song
That strives to hymn Thy bounty. May my tongue
    Tell of Thy Seer, and how against the Lie
    Pure thoughts, pure words, pure actions' victory
Rang from his herald trumpet loud and long:—
So from the blaze wherein Thy glories dwell
    Once more athwart the sunless gloom a Star
    Shall flash its guiding message, and from far
The Sage of Iran answer to the spell,
    And speed with trophies of a faith long dim
    To find his Lord and bow the knee to Him.

Anonymous

This I Ask Thee

This I ask Thee—tell it to me truly, Lord!
Who the Sire was, Father first of Holiness?
Who the pathway for the sun and stars ordained?
Who, through whom its moon doth wax and wane again?
This and much else do I long, O God, to know.

This I ask Thee—tell it to me truly, Lord!
Who set firmly earth below, and kept the sky
Sure from falling? Who the streams and trees did make?

Who their swiftness to the winds and clouds hath yoked?
Who, O Mazda, was the Founder of Good Thought?

This I ask Thee—tell it to me truly, Lord!
Who, benignant, made the darkness and the light?
Who, benignant, sleep and waking did create?
Who the morning, noon, and evening did decree
As reminders to the wise, of duty's call?

Persian tenth century B.C.

Introduction to Jainism

Jainism, a word derived from Jina, which means victor or con-queror (implying one who has overcome all human passions), is an ancient Indian religion born about the same time as Bud-dhism. Both religions apparently emerged as a protest against the orthodox ritualism and rigid impersonality of sixth-century-B.C. Brahmanism. The Jains, however, do not accept the later dates for the origin of their religion and consider their faith as prehistoric, perhaps even the original faith of the Brahmans. The Jains are sometimes called a Hindu sect, which they resent with some justification, for their religion is quite distinct from Hinduism. For example, while orthodox Hinduism is polytheis-tic, Jainism is atheistic in the sense that Jains possess no per-sonal god. There is also little Jain theology, for gods, spirits, demons—all supernaturalism, with one exception—are rejected. The only supernatural beings Jains accept are the Tirthankaras ("Perfect Saints"), who are good men made perfect. The pro-gression from good to perfect is long and arduous, and is at-tained only after following strict rules of living.

The Jain patron saint, Mahavira (d. 528 B.C., or 468 B.C.; 599-527 B.C. is generally acceptable), became the prophet of the religion after spending twelve years in meditation and asceticism. This was to become the standard for later yeti, or ascetics. Twelve years of rigorous self-discipline is believed to be adequate time for them to attain nirvana. The yeti must also live according to five important vows: to injure no living creature (ahimsa), to speak only the truth, to abstain from theft, to renounce all worldly goods, and to practice sexual continence. If the yeti lives according to this code of conduct it is believed he will gain self-mastery.

The Jain believes strongly in salvation through right action and self-sacrifice. The soul may return, for example, after achieving release in nirvana in order to help weaker spirits attain freedom from the cycle of rebirths—which is very similar to the Buddhist Bodhisattva tradition of self-sacrifice and service. Reincarnation is one of the foundations of Jain theology, which holds that everything in the universe, including matter, is eternal. How one conducts oneself throughout one's successive incarnations determines one's capacity for good or evil actions. This cumulative effect of one's actions upon later lives is the Jain concept of karma. The possession of and immersion in karmic ties impel the soul to seek body after body successively. After nine incarnations even a lay member (not a yeti) of the Jain sect may attain nirvana, or freedom from reincarnations and the restrictions of matter. But both the lay and yeti Jain must follow basic principles of conduct. These principles, by which every individual who wishes to attain salvation must be guided, are right faith, right cognition, and right conduct.[1]

The Jains differ importantly from the other religions originating in India, for their concept of soul does not include searching for or realizing a "higher self," as in Vedanta and Buddhism. In Jainism the whole self of the individual is a principle that is unchanging[2]—the general Jain term for soul is jiva, which is identical to the self (aya or atman). For this reason Jains use the term "yoga" very differently from the Hindus.[3] While the Hindu term "yoga" is defined generally as "yoke," "union," or "unifying," the Jain use of the word means specifically the joining of the pure atman (self or soul) with karma (action). The Jains do not differentiate at all between the atman meaning self or soul, and jiva, a word also meaning soul. The words are in fact often used synonymously. The jiva is considered the atman in bondage, and conversely the atman is the jiva liberated. As the individual progresses spiritually, then, the atman is augmented and becomes more fully realized in one's life, as the jiva is diminished or given up.[4]

[1] Note the similarity here with the Buddha's steps to enlightenment.

[2] This is similar, however, to some schools of Buddhism and Hinduism, which also conceive of the higher self as an unchanging principle.

[3] The "yoga" of the sage Patanjali is also distinctive from the Jain use of the word. Patanjali developed yoga as a psychological and physical discipline by which one could attain freedom (moksha) of the soul from involvement with the material world.

[4] This is one of the most important distinctions in Kunda Kunda Acharya's writing *Niyamasara* (c. first century B.C.). See *The Great Asian Religions*,

Unlike other systems the soul or highest self is not perceived as sleeping within a hidden chamber at the base of the spine, or as a point of light deep within a mysterious recess, or even in a special gland, but rather it permeates the whole being, the complete physical matter of the earthly body at all times. There is no separateness between the two, except one of degree. And there are numberless lives, or souls (jivas), not only embodied in men but in animals, plants, and even in the four elements of earth, water, fire, and wind.[5] Such a pervasive principle as jiva, or "life monad" as Heinrich Zimmer calls it, seems to transform itself into a mystical vitalism at a given point, even though the philosophical and cosmological systems guiding this vitalism are highly complex and functions according to grades of significance.

Mysticism is solipsistic in certain of its characteristics, and this aspect is brought to its fullest expression in Jainism. The mystical foundations of Jainism are expressed through the individual soul's purification and exaltation. The soul or self is the single "spiritual" factor in their religion. There is no god with which the soul seeks union, and in this sense Jainism does share with Buddhism and later classical yoga a nondeistic and nontheistic form of mysticism. Neither the Jain nor the yogic Ajivika (or classical) school possessed a "god" within which they could become immersed or find grace.

A Jain can annihilate the material aspects of life and free the soul from mundane entanglements through the use of tapas, or extreme austerity. In such a way the soul becomes purified and exalted to a universal condition—the Jain form of nirvana. Even though the individual monad or life force achieves its own salvation, Mahavira claimed attainment of a higher kind of experience quite similar to the Buddhist nirvana. The Jain life monad therefore gains a form of omniscience once it is emancipated from the web of matter. Again, similar to the Buddhist and Hindu conception (as well as some other Eastern religions), the Jain achieves this state of enlightenment or intense sense of universality from knowledge gained from the contemplative experience.

The Jain nirvana, however, differs considerably from the Hindu samadhi or moksha, for there is no absorption in Brahman as in Hinduism. To the Jain, the pure, undifferentiated state which they call nirvana is a "life" that is blissful and uneventful (and in that sense differs from Buddhism). But each

[5]See Hermann Jacobi, "Akaranga Sutra," in *Sacred Books of the East*, vol. 22, Part I, p. 3, note 2.

edited by Wing-tsit Chan, Isma'il Ragi al Farugi, Joseph Kitagawa, and P.T. Raju (London and New York: Collier-Macmillan, 1969), pp. 67-69.

person's individuality is intact, for the individual self is and always has been eternal. Once the soul or self is unfettered from the five material sheaths that clog its release from the karmic cycles of physical life, the individual soul becomes eternal and pure. This strong dependence upon one's own will, upon individual effort to achieve the soul's freedom from material bondage, creates a unique kind of mysticism. The soul is purified through effort and sacrifice, then exalted, and finally made eternally one with all life. But the lack of any deity, the complete dedication to one's own soul development, the reverence and care for all life forms, the absolute prohibitions against injuring any living creature even to eat, all create a religion that is quite complicated with many unique aspects. Parallels can, of course, always be made with other religions; especially with Taoism and Buddhism, which have no concern for an anthropomorphic deity or Godhead, and are also dedicated to freeing one's self from worldly bondage. But Jainism remains nevertheless one of the most remarkable, mysterious, and arduous of Eastern mystical religions.

Selections from Jaina Sutras

The Akaranga Sutra

Fifth Lecture
Called
Essence of the World

FIRST LESSON

Many entertain cruel thoughts against the world with a motive or without one; they entertain cruel thoughts against these six classes of living beings. To him pleasures are dear. Therefore he is near death. Because he is near death, he is far from liberation. But he who is neither near death nor far from liberation, considers the life of a slow and ignorant fool as similar to a dew-drop trembling on the sharp point of the blade of Kusa grass which falls down when shaken by the wind. A fool, doing cruel acts, comes thereby ignorantly to grief. "Through delusion he is born, dies, etc." Being conversant with the deliberation about this delusion, one is conversant with the samsara; being not conversant with that deliberation, one is not conversant with the samsara. He who is clever, should not seek after sexual inter-course. But having done so, it would be a second folly of the weak-minded not to own it. Repenting and excluding from the mind the begotten pleasures, one should instruct others to follow the commandment. Thus I say.

See! many who desire colours,[1] are led around in the samsara, they experience here again and again feelings (i.e. punishment). Many live by injurious deeds against the world, they live by injurious deeds against these living beings. Also the fool, suffering for his passions, delights in bad acts here, mistaking that for sal-vation which is none. Many heretics lead the life of a hermit in order to avoid worldly sorrows and pains.

Such a man has much wrath, much pride, much conceit, much greed; he delights in many works, acts frequently like a stage-player or a rogue, forms many plans, gives way to his impulses, is influenced by his acts though he pretends to be awakened: thinking that nobody will see him. Through the influence of ig-norance and carelessness the fool never knows the law. Men! un-happy creatures, world-wise are those who, not freeing them-selves from ignorance, talk about final liberation: they turn round and round in the whirlpool of births. Thus I say.

SECOND LESSON.

Many do not live by injurious deeds against the world, they do not live by injurious deeds against these living beings. Ceas-ing from them, making an end of them, he perceives: this is a favourable opportunity;[2] he who searches for the right moment for this body should never be careless. This is the road taught by the noble ones.

When he has become zealous for the law, he should never be careless, knowing pain and pleasure in their various forms. Men act here on their own motives; it has been declared that they suffer for their own sins. Neither killing nor lying, he should pa-tiently bear all unpleasant feelings when affected by them. That man is called a true monk.

[1] Color stands for all perceptions of the senses. Specifically, what is meant is the attachment to sensual pleasures.
[2] Favorable, that is, for adopting the right conduct.

Those who are not given to sinful acts are nevertheless attacked by calamities; but then the steadfast will bear them. He has to bear them afterwards as he has done before his conversion. The body is of a fragile, decaying nature, it is unstable, transient, uneternal, increasing and decreasing, of a changeable nature. Perceive this as its true character. For him who well understands this, who delights in the unique refuge,[3] for the liberated and inactive there is no passage from birth to birth. Thus I say.

Many are attached to something in the world—be it little or much, small or great, sentient or nonsentient—they are attached to it here amongst these householders. Thus some incur great danger. For him who contemplates the course of the world and does not acknowledge these attachments there is no such danger. Knowing that that which is well understood is well practised, man! with thy eyes on the highest good, be victorious in control. Among such men only is real Brahmanhood. Thus I say.

I have heard this, and it is in my innermost heart; and the freedom from bonds is in your innermost heart. He who has ceased to have worldly attachments, the houseless, suffers with patience a long time.

The careless stand outside, the careful lead a religious life.

Maintain rightly this state of a sage. Thus I say.

THIRD LESSON

Many are not attached to something in this world, they are not attached to it among these householders. He is a wise man who has heard and understood the word of the learned ones. Without partiality the law has been declared by the noble ones. As I have destroyed here the connection with the world, so is the connection elsewhere difficult to destroy. Therefore I say: One should not abandon firmness. Some who early exert themselves, do not afterwards slide back; some who early exert themselves, afterwards slide back; those who do not early exert themselves, can of course not slide back. That man also is of this description, who knowing the world as worthless nevertheless follows its ways. "Knowing this, it has been declared by the sage." Here the follower of the commandment, the wise, the passionless, he who exerts himself before morning and after evening, always contemplating virtue[4] and hearing the merit of it will become free from love and delusion. "Fight with this your

[3] This refuge means the Ayatana, the triad: right knowledge, right intuition, right conduct.
[4] This virtue consists in vows, restraint of the senses, avoidance of sin, and other corrections of one's behavior and life style.

body! why should you fight with anything else?" Difficult to attain is this human body which is worth the fight. For the clever ones have praised the discernment of wisdom; the fool who falls from it, is liable to birth etc. In this religion of the Jainas the cause of the fool's fall has been declared to depend on colour and killing. But a sage who walks the beaten track to liberation, regards the world in a different way. "Knowing thus the nature of acts in all regards, he does not kill," he controls himself, he is not overbearing.

Comprehending that pleasure and pain are individual, advising kindness, he will not engage in any work in the whole world: keeping before him the one great aim, liberation, and not turning aside, "living humbly, unattached to any creature." The rich in control who with a mind endowed with all penetration recognises that a bad deed should not be done, will not go after it. What you acknowledge as righteousness, that you acknowledge as sagedom (mauna); what you acknowledge as sagedom, that you acknowledge as righteousness. It is inconsistent with weak, sinning, sensual, ill-conducted house-inhabiting men. "A sage, acquiring sagedom, should subdue his body." "The heroes who look at everything with indifference, use mean and rough food, etc." Such a man is said to have crossed the flood of life, to be a sage, to have passed over the samsara, to be liberated, to have ceased from acts. Thus I say.

FOURTH LESSON

For a monk who has not yet reached discrimination, it is bad going and difficult proceeding when he wanders alone from village to village. Some men when going wrong will become angry when exhorted with speech. And a man with wary pride is embarrassed with great delusion. There are many obstacles which are very difficult to overcome for the ignorant and the blinded. Let that not be your case! That is the doctrine of the clever one (Mahavira). Adopting the akarya's views, imitating his indifference for the outer world, making him the guide and adviser of all one's matters, sharing his abode, living carefully, acting according to his mind, examining one's way,[5] not coming too near the akarya, minding living beings, one should go on one's business.

[5]The monk must inspect carefully everything he comes into contact with in order to avoid killing living things; this is also true when walking, sitting, sleeping, eating, drinking, and so forth. This is the most extreme form that ahimsa, or nonviolence, takes.

FIFTH LESSON

Thus I say: a lake is full of water, it is in an even plain, it is free from dust, it harbours many fish.[6] Look! he (the teacher) stands in the stream of knowledge and is guarded in all directions. Look! there are great Seers in the world, wise, awakened, free from acts. Perceive the truth: from a desire of a pious end they chose a religious life. Thus I say.

He whose mind is always wavering, does not reach abstract contemplation.[7] Some, bound by worldly ties, are followers (i.e. understand the truth); some who are not bound, are followers. How should he not despond who amongst followers is a non-follower? "But that is truth beyond doubt, what has been declared by the Jinas."

Whatever a faithful, well-disposed man, on entering the order, thought to be true, that may afterwards appear to him true; what he thought to be true, that may afterwards appear to him untrue; what he thought to be untrue, that may afterwards appear to him true; what he thought to be untrue, that may afterwards appear to him true. What he thinks to be true, that may, on consideration, appear to him true, whether it be true or untrue. What he thinks to be untrue, that may, on consideration, appear to him untrue, whether it be true or untrue. But he who reflects should say unto him who does not reflect: Consider it to be true. Thus the connection (i.e. the continuity of sins) is broken.

Regard this as the course of the zealous one, who stands in obedience to the spiritual guide. In this point do not show yourself a fool!

As it would be unto thee, so it is with him whom thou intendest to kill. As it would be unto thee, so it is with him whom thou intendest to tyrannise over. As it would be unto thee, so it is with him whom thou intendest to torment. In the same way (it is with him) whom thou intendest to punish, and to drive away. The righteous man who lives up to these sentiments, does therefore neither kill nor cause others to kill living beings. He should not intentionally cause the same punishment for himself.[8]

The Self is the knower or experiencer, and the knower is the Self. That through which one knows, is the Self. With regard to

---

[6] The lake here is like a teacher who is full of wisdom, lives in a quiet country, is free from passion, and protects all living beings.

[7] This means samadhi, and is the means of a religious death.

[8] He will suffer in his next life for the same pain he has caused others in this life.

this (to know) it (the Self) is established.[9] Such is he who
maintains the right doctrine of Self. This subject has truly been
explained. Thus I say.

SIXTH LESSON

Some not instructed in the true law make only a show of
good conduct; some, though instructed, have no good conduct.
Let that not be your case! That is the doctrine of the clever
one. Adopting the akarya's views, imitating his indifference for
the outer world, making him the guide and adviser in all one's
matters, sharing his abode, conquering sinfulness, one sees the
truth; unconquered one should be one's own master, having no
reliance on anything in the world. He who is great and with-
draws his mind from the outer world, should learn the teaching
of the Tirthakaras through the teaching of the akarya; by his
own innate knowledge, or through the instruction of the highest,
or having heard it from others. A wise man should not break the
commandment. Examining all wrong doctrines from all sides and
in all respects, one should clearly understand and reject them.
"Knowing the delight of this world,[10] circumspect and restrained, one should lead the life of an ascetic." Desiring liberation, a hero should, through the sacred lore, ever be victorious.
Thus I say.

The current of sin is said to come from above, from below,
and from the sides;[11] these have been declared to be the currents
through which, look, there is sinfulness.

"Examining the whirlpool,[12] a man, versed in the sacred lore,
should keep off from it." Leaving the world to avert the current
of sin, such a great man, free from acts, knows and sees the
truth; examining pleasures he does not desire them. Knowing
whence we come and whither we go, he leaves the road to birth
and death, rejoicing in the glorious liberation. "All sounds recoil
thence, where speculation has no room," nor does the mind penetrate there.[13] The saint[14] knows well that which is without support.[15]

[9]This means that knowledge is a modification (parinama) of the Self, and
therefore one with it, but not as a quality or action of the Self different
from it.
[10]That is, self-control.
[11]The door of asrava, which is the current or three directions mentioned here,
are the three divisions of the universe. Objects of desire in each induce men
to sin.
[12]The whirlpool of worldly desires and their objects is meant here.
[13]It is impossible to express the nature of final liberation in words, since it
cannot be reached even by the mind.
[14]That is, he who is free from love and hate.
[15]This means liberation, or the state of the liberated.

The liberated is not long nor small nor round nor triangular nor quadrangular nor circular; he is not black nor blue nor red nor green nor white; neither of good nor bad smell; not bitter nor pungent nor astringent nor sweet; neither rough nor soft; neither heavy nor light; neither cold nor hot; neither harsh nor smooth; he is without body, without resurrection, without contact of matter, he is not feminine nor masculine nor neuter; he perceives, he knows, but there is no analogy whereby to know the nature of the liberated soul; its essence is without form; there is no condition of the unconditioned. There is no sound, no colour, no smell, no taste, no touch—nothing of that kind. Thus I say.

End of the Fifth Lecture, called Essence of the World.

RANDOM SELECTIONS FROM JAINA TEXTS

> Perhaps It is; or may be It is not;
> Or it may be that It both is and not;
> Or it is only Indescribable;
> Or though unspeakable It perhaps is;
> Or it both is not and unspeakable;
> Or, seventhly, it may be that It is
> And is not and unspeakable also!

From the Syad-Vada

> May He abide always within my heart,
> "The Supreme Self," the One God of all gods,
> Transcending all "this-world's" ephemera,
> By deepest meditation reachable!
> They who have passed beyond all arguments
> And doubts and false attachments of this world,
> They only can behold in purity
> "The Supreme Self," and in It merge themselves.
> Who take their refuge in that "Supreme-Self,"
> Stainless, beyond particularities,
> And fix their minds on It devotedly,
> Unfailingly they gain Its Blessedness.

From the Amita-Gait,
Samayika-patha

> Three-staged the Path of souls inherently;
> Each soul must pass through all successively;
> First is the stage of vicious selfishness;
> To it succeeds the time of virtuousness;
> Last comes the stage free from all loves and hates,

All personal desires. This last, the path
Lighted by Duty only, helps the soul
To break the bonds of sin and merit, too,
Forged by the passions which imprison it;
And takes it safe across life's stormy sea.
Give up the wish to earn merit for heaven;
But do not therefore cease from purity,
Nor dream of ever doing deed of sin.
Observe the rules prescribed for piety,
Till the mind merges in the fount and source
Of Purity. Bear patiently the states,
Now high, now low, which fortune brings to thee;
Guard watchfully 'gainst errings of the mind;
See it falls not from noble to base mood.
Such is the only way to fill with Peace
Of mind and heart the life upon this earth;
Such is the essence of what Jina taught.

From Bhaga Chandra

Introduction to Sikhism

Sikhism is a relatively modern religion. It was founded by Guru Nanak (1469-1539), the first guru, who taught a monotheistic religion but emphasized the fundamental unity of all religions. Nanak opposed many of the basic Hindu practices of his time, including the caste system, the maintenance of a priesthood, and the practice of suttee, in which a wife was required to throw her body on her husband's flaming funeral pyre.

The ascetics (udasis) were separated from the laity by the third guru, Angad (1504-1552), who eliminated most of the remaining features of Hinduism. In place of a priesthood the Sikh religion relied heavily upon the guru system. The guru, or spiritual leader of the Sikhs, became a hereditary system (ironically not unlike the priesthood system it labored to replace) in the mid-seventeenth century. At the same time the Sikhs split into many factions. Govind Singh (1666-1708), who was the tenth and last guru, welded the Sikhs once again into a unitive force. But Govind Singh drastically altered many of the previous practices and beliefs initiated by Nanak. He reestablished, for example, the caste practices of the Hindus that Nanak had opposed, as well as the polytheistic beliefs typical of Hinduism of that period. He also created a new Sikh military, including the establishment of a military caste structure, which moved Sikhism further than ever from the original gentle unitarian spiritualism of Nanak.

Nanak's creed was not a complicated or sophisticated spiritual structure, yet his teachings and tradition best represent the mystical aspects of Sikhism. Nanak's belief can be summed up in the simple formula of the "Unity of God and the Brotherhood of Man." He incorporated the doctrines of reincarnation and karma from Hinduism, along with the concepts of maya (illusion) and nirvana (final freedom), and blissful union with God. Nanak, however, considered God immanent in each soul, and the soul's journey in this world is seen as a necessary struggle to reunite itself with God. This is, of course, a conception basic to most mystics.

The early Hindus worshipped a great number of gods and goddesses; and one of the fundamental differences between Sikhism and Hinduism was the Sikh's strong emphasis on one God who is without equal, who is complete in His uniqueness and unity. The mul mantra (key verse) in the Sikh sacred scriptures expresses this singularity.

There is but one God. If you care to name Him call Him Sati (Satya), one Who was, Who is, and Who shall be. He is the doer, all pervading, without fear, without enmity. His existence is unlimited by time. He is unborn and self-existent, can be realized through the grace of the Guru.

This final emphasis on the grace of the guru introduces another fundamentally important concept in Sikhism. To the Sikh the guru is supreme in his attainment of spiritual experience. He has, by definition, experience of God. It is believed by all Sikhs that those who follow the guru's instructions faithfully must ultimately reach the same stage of spiritual enlightenment, and enjoy the same eternal bliss within which the guru lives. It follows then that a Sikh would completely surrender himself to his guru. The guru is a guide, a teacher who motivates and realizes the truth of God within all his followers. The ideal conclusion for a Sikh who faithfully follows his guru is captured in the Dhanasari, where it is written:

My heart is full of Him, this vision I have realized through the Guru.
I regard everybody as my friend, and am the well-wisher of all men.

The Lord has destroyed the pangs of separation and united me
　unto Himself.
The perverse mentality has been destroyed.
It rains nectar now, and the Word of the Guru tastes sweet.
I have seen Ram, who pervades waters and deserts and fills both
　the earth and the heaven.[1]

And so the guru brings the faithful to a mystical union with
all the universe. The anguish of life, of being separate from the
divine love the faithful yearns for, is resolved by living within
the orb of the guru, and absorbing oneself in the God-centered
life. To achieve this spiritual progress one need not renounce everything in the world and become a forest ascetic, for true
renunciation in Sikhism is found in giving up ungodly things
such as lust, greed, and anger. By living such a life, by working
at some worthy activity, and by following the words of one's
guru, salvation and experience of God can be attained while living
in this world. This is the important condition of Jiwan-mukat,
and is possible because one's spiritual progress is dependent
upon one's own will and activity. Heaven and hell are mental
states of the soul, and soul development or regression occurs
through the repetition of words, deeds, and thoughts. As these
elements of the human character are repeated and become habits
the soul itself is marked; so it becomes vitally important for the
Sikh to live the right way. The Sikh view of the mundane world
is far more realistic psychologically than that of many other religions, for the Sikh teach that asceticism merely for the sake of
denying the physical world is wasted endeavor. Hindrances within
the path of spiritual progress, which do involve the physical
world and all its enticements, are placed there by God as a necessary obstacle, for in conquering such obstacles one develops spiritual strength just as exercising one's body develops bodily strength.
It is by engaging the mundane world that we may attain spiritual
advancement. Life is seen, then, as a sort of spiritual wrestling
bout for which one must be constantly alert and able.[2]

Sikhism is what I call a "core" or basically mystical religion,
for it does not avoid the basic or difficult questions that every
religion faces, such as "How can we be sure of God's existence?"
Some religions avoid answering this question directly by answering it at great length, by indulging in long and often tortuous
theological treatises, which generally end up somewhere in the
vicinity of where they began. The mystic's response, and the response of mystically inclined religions, is simple and direct reli-

[1] Guru V, 4.3.

[2] See C.H. Loehlin, *The Sikhs and their Scriptures* (Lucknow, India: Lucknow
Publishing House, 1964), p. 46.

ance on experience. Guru Nanak gives the mystic's classical answer to this question: Nanak says that "your soul can have communion with God, *so we can be as sure* of His existence as we are of anything else in life our experience tells us exists." Such an empirical challenge is basic to all mystics, but is especially emphasized in most of the Eastern mystical religions.

The Sikh gurus were mystical devotees as well as practical organizers and men of the world. But the gurus themselves, and the guru system generally, was heavily influenced by the Hindu concept of bhakti. "Bhakti" comes from the Sanskrit root "bhaj" and means, in its religious sense, devotion, worship, love, and homage. "Loving devotion" and "adoration" are common translations of the word. Practically all the great Hindu religious leaders were initiators or followers of the bhakti movement: Gautama Buddha, Mahavira, Krishna, and the Sikh gurus themselves. The bhakti movement, which is perhaps the foundation of Hindu and Sikh mysticism, grew out of the monotheism that developed as a reaction to excessive polytheism. Sikhism is uncompromisingly monotheistic, and its adoration of God is equal in intensity to the combined polytheistic devotions of the earlier Hindus. Bhakti also involves a concept called prapatti, or total surrender of self. All one's actions are for God. This utter devotion leads to the realization of God within us, and to the union of the soul with Him. "One should worship in supreme love" writes a Shaivite saint, "Him who does kindness to the world." Such is the power of Grace, which the bhakti Hindu mystic, the Sufi, and the Sikh all perceive in their God, that complete "worship in supreme love" is the only response possible for those who experience it.[3]

THE INFLUENCE OF SUFISM

It is perhaps the natural Sikh tendencies toward monotheism and intense adoration that made the mutual influencing of Sikhism and Sufism inevitable. The orthodox Muslim God of stern justice did not attract the Sikh, but rather the immanent, gentle mysticism of the Sufi; for the Sikh's conception of God was much closer to the Sufis'. The Sikh God is wise and compassionate, a generous friend rather than a taskmaster or judge. He is called a "Friend of Sinners," or "Destroyer of Sorrow."

While it is true that Islam conquered India in the eleventh century and its aggressive proselytizers won many converts to orthodox Muslim faith, it was the Sufis that attracted the more mystically inclined bhakti Hindus and Sikhs. The ascetics

[3]Bhakti is one of the single most important aspects of Near Eastern mysticism, and is discussed in more detail in the Hindu section in this volume.

and gurus of each religion learned the ways of the other. It was a time of mutual mystical attraction in a world of violence and oppression. Ascetic and meditational practices changed hands, and each learned to respect the other's religion. Each was strongly devotional and possessed the identical obsession of returning to one's God, a God who they both believed unified all the world under His single, unitive aspect. What did it matter the name He was called? Their mystically perceived experience of Him was identical and gave them both the same assurance of His reality.

The effect of this exchange is seen today in estimates that two-thirds of India and Pakistan are presently under the influence of the deeply mystical, ascetic dervish Sufi orders. It is highly probable that the Sikh gurus themselves were also profoundly affected by the Sufis. In fact, it is likely that faiths with such strong mystical tendencies as Sufism, bhakti Hinduism, and Sikhism did merge at many points. Indeed, one of the main purposes stated by the first gurus was to form a synthesis between Hinduism and Islam. Further, several Sikh gurus are considered to be Sufis, if not in fact, at least in inclination. For example, Guru Arjan (1563-1606) was considered a Sufi by the Sufis because he emphasized that God was the "Causer" of everything. The names of Guru Nanak and Kabir have become intimately linked, for their religious beliefs and practical desires for synthesizing their religions were so similar that Guru Nanak considered Kabir a Sikh, while the Hindus considered him Hindu. In reality he was neither and both, for he was a passionate unitarian. Both men represented a common bhakti tradition of devotion, and both tried intensely throughout their lives to meld the teachings of Hinduism and Islam. With the exception of the Ten Gurus themselves, Kabir is more represented in the Adi Granth than any other individual or group, with well over a thousand of his verses included in the Sikh holy book. Kabir was also extremely fond of a Koranic verse, which was held in equally high esteem by both the Sufis and the Tenth Guru Gobind Singh.

> Were I to make all the islands my paper, and the seven seas my ink;
> Were I to cut down all trees, and turn them into pens for writing;
> Were I to make Saraswati dictate for millions of ages;
> Were I to write with the hand of Ganesh,
> O Thou who holdest the destroying sword, I could please Thee even a little without offering Thee homage.[4]

[4]Koran, XVIII. 109.

The Sikhs, then, sprang from the fertile religious soil of Hinduism, and yet blended much of the Sufi passion and the Hindu bhakti mystical devotion into a distinctive new religion. The Sikh religion and its scriptures, the Adi Granth, represent something quite special in religious history and for the contemporary world. It is more than a simple syncretism one finds in other parts of the world, such as Confucianism, Buddhism, and Taoism coexisting for ages; as a religion Sikhism is a monument to the creative and synthesizing effort that brought together traditionally differing religions. It represents a spiritual lesson for the dogmatic and traditionally antipathetic relations between other world religions. For Nanak the fundamental truth was that the approach to God lies in self-abnegation, and this is the Sikh's humbling message to the more aggressive, proselytizing religions of the world that insist on conquering the hearts and spirits of men by force, coercion, or disdain rather than as Nanak did—by gentle example and guidance.

Selections from Sikh Scriptures

Guru Nanak's Mool Mantra

There is One God
His Name is Truth.
He is the Creator,
He is without fear and without hate.
He is beyond time Immortal,
His Spirit pervades the universe.
He is not born,
Nor does He die to be born again,
He is self-existent.
By the guru's grace shalt thou worship Him.[1]

---

[1] The mool mantra (mool=root), or mul mantra, is Guru Nanak's root or basic mantra, and it represents the foundation of the Sikh creed. The sacred book of the Sikhs, the Adi Granth, begins with this statement, and it is repeated prior to every prayer. The following selection, the Japji, is the Sikh

The Japji

THERE is but one God whose name is true, the Creator,[2] devoid of fear and enmity, immortal, unborn, self-existent; by the favour of the Guru.

Repeat His Name

The True One was in the beginning; the True One was in the primal age.

The true One is now also, O Nanak; the True One also shall be.[3]

I

By thinking I cannot obtain a conception of Him, even though I think hundreds of thousands of times.

Even though I be silent and keep my attention firmly fixed on Him, I cannot preserve silence.

The hunger of the hungry for God subsideth not though they obtain the load of the worlds.

If man should have thousands and hundreds of thousands of devices, even one would not assist him in obtaining God.

How shall man become true before God? How shall the veil of falsehood be rent?

By walking, O Nanak, according to the will of the Commander as preordained.

[2]The Creator here is Karta purukh, and means male or creative agency. The all-pervading spirit in union with a female element uttered a word from which sprang creation.

[3]This has also been translated as: "God was true in the beginning, He was true in primal age; He is true now also, Nanak, and He also will be true."

morning prayer and considered by most scholars as the essence of all that Nanak, the founder and primary sage of Sikhism, had taught. The Japji is so important that all Sikhs are admonished to have it by heart, otherwise they are not considered orthodox Sikhs. The Japji was probably composed by Guru Nanak at an advanced age. See M.A. Macauliffe, *The Sikh Religion*, (Oxford, 1909, vol. V), p. 195.

II

By His order bodies are produced; His order cannot be described.

By His order souls are infused into them; by His order greatness is obtained.

By His order men are high or low; by His order they obtain preordained pain or pleasure.

By His order some obtain their reward;[4] by His order others must ever wander in transmigration.

All are subject to His order; none is exempt from it.

He who understandeth God's order, O Nanak, is never guilty of egoism.[5]

III

Who can sing His power? Who hath power to sing it?

Who can sing His gifts or know His signs?

Who can sing His attributes, His greatness, and His deeds?

Who can sing His knowledge whose study is arduous?

Who can sing Him, who fashioneth the body and again destroyeth it?

Who can sing Him, who taketh away life and again restoreth it?

Who can sing Him, who appeareth to be far, but is known to be near.

Who can sing Him, who is all-seeing and omnipresent?[6]

In describing Him there would never be an end.

Millions of men give millions upon millions of descriptions of Him, but they fail to describe Him.

The Giver giveth; the receiver groweth weary of receiving.

In every age man subsisteth by His bounty.

The Commander by His order hath laid out the way of the world.

Nanak, God the unconcerned is happy.

---

[4] That is, they are blended with God.

[5] The literal translation here is that one should not be guilty of saying that he exists by himself independently of God. This is the sin of spiritual pride.

[6] This and the preceding lines are also translated: "Some sing His power according to their abilities; Some sing His gifts according to their knowledge of His signs; Some sing His attributes, His greatness, and His deeds; Some sing his knowledge whose study is arduous; Some sing that He fashioneth the body and again destroyeth it; Some that He taketh away the soul and again restoreth it; Some that He appeareth far from mortal gaze; Some that He is all-seeing and omnipresent."

IV

True is the Lord, true is His name; it is uttered with endless love.[7]

People pray and beg, "Give us, give us"; the Giver giveth His gifts;
Then what can we offer Him whereby His court may be seen?
What words shall we utter with our lips, on hearing which He may love us?
At the ambrosial hour of morning meditate on the true Name and God's greatness.
The Kind One will give us a robe of honour, and by His favour we shall reach the gate of salvation.[8]

Nanak, we shall thus know that God is altogether true.[9]

V

He is not established, nor is He created.
The pure one existeth by Himself.
They who worshipped Him have obtained honour.
Nanak, sing His praises who is the Treasury of excellences.
Sing and hear and put His love into your hearts.
Thus shall your sorrows be removed, and you shall be absorbed in Him who is the abode of happiness.
Under the Guru's instruction God's word is heard; under the Guru's instruction its knowledge is acquired; under the Guru's instruction man learns that God is everywhere contained.[10]

The Guru is Shiv; the Guru is Vishnu and Brahma; the Guru is Parbati, Lakhshmi,[11] and Saraswati.[12]

[7]This is also translated: "His attributes are described in endless languages."
[8]This is also translated: "By our former acts we acquire this human vesture, and by God's favor reach the gate of salvation." This is done as the body is first formed, and then the soul from another body enters it. The actions of previous birth are adjusted when the soul attains a human body; for it is the acts done in a human body which accompany the soul to future states of existence. This is the action of karma.
[9]Another common rendering of this verse is "we shall then *know* that God is all in all Himself."
[10]Several additional instructions or verses are sometimes added to this: "The voice of God is found as well in other compositions as in the Veds; the voice of God is all-pervading." "The pious know the Guru's instructions, *that* God is everywhere contained." "The voice of the Guru is as the Veds for the holy; they are absorbed in it."
[11]This is the Hindu goddess of wealth and riches, consort of Vishnu, and the mother of Kam the god of love.
[12]The goddess of eloquence and learning, and patroness of arts and sciences.

If I knew Him, should I not describe Him? He cannot be described by words.

My Guru hath explained one thing to me—

That there is but one Bestower on all living beings; may I not forget Him!

VI

If I please Him, that is my place of pilgrimage to bathe in; if I please Him not, what ablutions shall I make?

What can all the created beings I behold obtain without previous good acts?

Precious stones, jewels, and gems shall be treasured up in thy heart if thou hearken to even one word of the Guru.

The Guru hath explained one thing to me—

That there is but one Bestower on all living beings; may I not forget Him!

VII

Were man to live through the four ages, yea ten times longer;

Were he to be known on the nine continents, and were everybody to follow in his train.[13]

Were he to obtain a great name and praise and renown in the world;

If God's look of favour fell not on him, no one would notice him.

He would be accounted a worm among worms, and even sinners would impute sin to him.

May we have the protection of All-steel!

May we have the protection of All-death!

May we have the protection of All-steel!

Hymns of Guru Nanak

What can deep water do to a fish? What can the sky do to a bird?

What can cold do to a stone? What can married life do to a eunuch?

Even though thou apply sandal to a dog, he will still preserve his canine nature:

[13]That is, to show him respect.

Even though thou instruct a deaf man, and read for him the Simritis;

Even though thou place a light before a blind man, and burn fifty lamps for him, all would be of no avail.

Even though thou put gold before a herd of cattle, they would still pick out the grass to eat.

If a flux be put into iron it will melt, but not become cotton.[14]

*   *   *

They who in the early morning praise God and meditate on Him with single heart,

Are perfect kings, and die fighting when occasion ariseth.[15]

In the second watch there are many ways in which the attention of the mind is distracted.

Many persons fall into the fathomless water, and cannot emerge however much they struggle.

In the third watch when hunger and thirst are both barking, food is put into the mouth.

What is eaten becometh filth, yet man again desireth food.

In the fourth watch drowsiness cometh, man closeth his eyes and goeth into dreamland.[16]

Again rising in the morning he engageth in turmoil, and yet maketh preparations to live a hundred years.

If man feel love for God every moment during the eight watches of the day,

O Nanak, God will dwell in his heart and true shall be his ablution.

One obtains the pure fear from singing the praises of God;
    God, Himself, lives in all hearts;
God is in the spirit of man, and God fills everything;
    Within and without, there is one God; the worshippers Of
    God assemble and laud His name.

At the second circumambulation, Nanak (says), "Innumerable musical instruments began to be sounded."

The third circumambulation (is made) in the name of God; the minds of the Bhairagis are filled with joy; I sacrifice myself to thee, O God!

The holy have union with God, and he, who obtains God, great is his fortune; I sacrifice myself to Thee, O God!

---

[14]Its nature will not be altered in any way.
[15]This is meant to imply that they will fight to the death with their deadly sins.
[16]The word for dreamland here is "pawar," which properly means a trance, or suspended animation.

He, who obtains the Pure God, and sings God's praises, his
  mouth always utters His words;
The holy are very fortunate, for they, who obtain God, tell
  forth the untellable tale of God;
In the hearts of all, the thought of God arises; that soul
  only can take his name, in whose fate it is so written.

Emperors pass away, but God ever flourisheth.
There is only Thou, there is only Thou, O God!

Neither demigods, nor demons, nor men,
Nor Sidhs, nor Strivers, nor this earth shall abide.
There is One; is there any other?
There is only Thou, there is only Thou, O God!

Neither the just nor the generous,
Nor the seven regions beneath the earth shall remain.
There is One: is there any other?
There is only Thou, there is only Thou, O God!

Not the regions of the sun and the moon,
Nor the seven continents, nor the seven seas,
Nor corn, nor wind shall abide.
There is only Thou, there is only Thou, O God!

Our maintenance is in nobody's power but God's:
To all of us but one hope abideth—
There is one: is there any other?
There is only Thou, there is only Thou, O God!

Birds have no money in their possession:
They only depend on trees and water.
God is their Giver.
There is only Thou, there is only Thou, O God!

Nanak, no one can erase
What is written on the forehead.
God it is who giveth man power and again taketh it away.
There is only Thou, there is only Thou, O God!

When Thou art near, what more do I desire? I speak verily.
He who is deceived by false worldly occupations reacheth not
God's palace:
His heart is hard and he loseth his service.
The house which containeth not the True One, should be
destroyed and rebuilt.

When its owner is weighed, how shall he be found of full weight?

If he lose his pride, no one will say he is of short weight.

The genuine shall be assayed, and selected at the gate of the All-seeing.

The true goods are only in one shop; they are obtained from the perfect Guru.

Without the True One all are false and practise falsehood.

Without the True One the false shall be bound and led away;

Man shall not be emancipated without the Guru's instruction; see and ponder upon this.

Even though man performed hundreds of thousands of ceremonies, all would still be darkness without the Guru.

What shall we say to those who are blind and devoid of wisdom?

Without the Guru the way cannot be seen; how shall we reach the goal?

Man calleth the counterfeit genuine; but he knoweth not what the genuine is.

A blind man he calleth an assayer; wonderful is this age.

Man saith, the sleeper is awake, and he who is awake sleepeth;

He saith, they who are alive are dead, and he weepeth not for those who are really dead;

He saith that he who is coming hath gone, and that he who hath gone is coming;

He calleth another's property his own, and with his own he is not satisfied;

He calleth what is sweet bitter, and what is bitter sweet;

He slandereth those who love God—such is what I have seen in this age.

Man serveth a handmaiden,[17] but the Master he seeth not.

He churneth tank water, and no butter is produced.

He who can explain this is the Guru for me.

Nanak, he who knoweth himself is unequalled and unrivalled.

Painful is the night for the young bride; without her Beloved she sleepeth not.[18]

[17]The handmaiden meant here is "Mammon."

[18]The tradition of the longing for God being compared to the longing of the young bride for her lover is worldwide. It is true of Western mysticism, as seen in the Song of Songs, St. Teresa, Eckhart, and Ruysbroeck among others; throughout the Eastern mystical tradition, especially in the Hindu Govinda Gita, and in the fervent Sufi pursuit of God. These verses of Guru Nanak's are perfect examples of the same metaphor in the Sikh mystic.

She pineth away through grief at His absence:

The woman pineth away through grief at His absence, saying "How shall I look upon Him?"

Ornaments, dainty food, sensuous enjoyments are all vain and of no account for her.

Intoxicated with the wine of youth and melting with pride milk cometh not to her breasts.

Nanak, she meeteth her Spouse when He causeth her to meet Him; without Him no sleep cometh to her.

The bride is unhonoured without her beloved Lord.

How shall she be happy without embracing Him?

Without a spouse there is no domestic happiness; ask thy friends and companions.

Without the Name there is no love or affection; but, with the True One, woman abideth in happiness.

They in whose hearts there is truth and contentment, meet the Friend; under the Guru's instruction the Bridegroom is recognized.

Nanak, the woman who abandoneth not the Name shall be easily absorbed in God through it.

Come, friends and companions, let us enjoy our Beloved.

I will ask my Guru and write His words of love.

The Guru hath communicated to me the true Word; the perverse shall regret they have not received it.

When I recognized the True One, my roaming mind became fixed.

The wisdom of the True One is ever new, so is the love of His Word.

Nanak, true peace of mind is obtained from His look of favour; meet Him, my friends and companions.

My desires have been fulfilled; the Friend hath come home to me.

A song of rejoicing was sung at the union of Husband and wife.

His praises and a song of joy were sung; the bride is happy in His love and her heart is in raptures.

Her friends are also happy, her enemies unhappy; true profit is obtained by repeating the name of the True One.

With clasped hands the woman prayeth that she may night and day be steeped in God's love.

Nanak, the Beloved and His spouse unite in dalliance; my desires have been fulfilled.

When bronze, gold, and iron break,
The blacksmith weldeth them by means of fire.

When a husband falleth out with his spouse,
A reconciliation is effected in this world through children.
When the king asketh and his subjects give, a bond is established between them.
When a hungry man eateth, he establisheth an alliance with the world.
Drought formeth an alliance with rivers when they are flooded with rain.
There is an affinity between love and sweet words.
If any one speak the truth, he formeth a bond with knowledge.
By goodness and truth the dead establish a bond with the living.
Such are the affinities that are established in the world.
The only way to establish friendship with a fool is to smite him on the mouth.[19]
By praising God man establisheth an alliance with God's court.
Nanak saith this deliberately.

My state in longing for Thee, O God is that of the taker of
  intoxicating drugs, when he cannot get those intoxicating
  drugs, and as that of fishes when they cannot get water;
And, he, who is absorbed with his Lord, he is satisfied with
  everything (and says,)
I will go and sacrifice myself, and cut myself into pieces, for
  the sake of my Lord's Name.
The Lord is that most fruitful Tree, the name of which is Immortality;
And he, who drinks thereof, becomes satisfied, and to Him
  will I sacrifice myself;
He cannot be seen by me, although He lives with all;
How will one's thirst be allayed, if one only put one's head on
  a high wall (in the middle of the tank, out of reach of the
  water).
Nanak is Thy salesman (banian); Thou art my capitalist and
  all my stock;
All doubts will be removed from my mind, when I shall continually remember thy praise.[20]

[19]This is also translated "to remain silent," which seems a better rendering
here.
[20]This verse from the Wadahans Rag is typical of Nanak, for he often admonishes us to remember God. It is a continuing theme in Nanak and is
comparable in Western mysticism to the Eastern Orthodox Church's invocations in the Philokalia or Prayer of the Heart. In a discourse with Gupal, a
teacher, when he was only seven Nanak was reputed to have sung the Siri

"Listen, my respected mother and parent! the Name of God only pleases me;[21]

I wander about sad, when the Lord God does not come into my thoughts.

If he come not into my thoughts, I wander about sad; God only satisfies my soul;

Listen my maid and companion[22] is filled with love (for God), and my young heart is full of (His) youth;

And I cannot live without my Beloved (God), for one instant or second, and sleep comes not to my eyes (without Him).

Nanak says truly, 'Listen, my mother! the Name of God only pleases me.'

Listen! my mother and parent! the saints possess nothing but the Name of God;

My soul was dark; the holy men adorned it in such a way, that it always returns to the holy.

It returns ever to the holy; the holy have no wealth but the Name of God;

And the Name of God is such, that it will never diminish in worth.

Although it may rain, it becomes no greener, and, if the sunshine wax a hundredfold, it never dries up;

When one departs, one's excessive youth and great loveliness will not go with one.

Nanak says truly; 'Listen, my mother and dearest parent, the saints possess nothing but the Name of God.'

Listen, my respected mother and parent! this my heart will tell these a tale;

My Lord God often came not into my mind, and was continually forgotten through negligence;

I have forgotten Him through negligence, O mother! because my mind was absorbed in worldliness;

Every living head will there have to give an account, whether he have done evil or good;

[21]Like most other sages and founders of religions, Guru Nanak left family and home to wander the countryside seeking God. In the Siri and Suhi Rags Nanak sings verses that are a response to his mother's pleading for him to return home to his family. One can almost envision Jesus speaking quietly in such a way to his own mother as he turned away entirely from his family to encounter God.

[22]These are Nanak's passions and desires.

Rag in which he admonishes the teacher to stop being concerned with his facts and remember the True God, for beyond that no accounting will be made of him. "The remembering of God is a token of the true threshold," the seven-year-old Nanak said, and it is by such remembrance that God is obtained.

My wedding day is fixed, and a few days only remain (to it),
but my heart is still telling its tale of God!
Nanak says truly, 'Listen my respected mother and parent.
He is forgotten by me through negligence'!
O my respected mother and parent! the wedding party (i.e.
death) has arrived;
I am the bride; the angel of death is the wedding party; and
death is the bridegroom,
Death is such a bridegroom, O mother! that when one departs,
one can say nothing;
The five attendants[23] go to another home, and the house remains
quite empty;
And he, who is to marry me, he is taking me away, and I cannot
stop him:
Nanak says truly! 'Listen, my mother! death is my bride-
groom!' "

Love the Lord as the lotus loves the waters,
Even though with its waves the lotus is lashed, yet it does not
abandon its love, instead blooms all the more.
It knoweth in water is its life. So whether it loves or hates it,
without its love it cannot survive.
O mind! I can never give up His love.
The Teacher dwells in the disciple and confers on him the boon
of devotion.
O, my mind! Love the Lord as the fish loves the water.
As the water increases it grows happy and its body develops and
enjoys.
The Lord alone knoweth the fish's agony for want of water, not
I nor you.
O, mind! love the Lord as the Chatak bird loves the clouds.
Although the water on the earth may be full in ponds and rivers
but it looks not to them, but waits only for the drops of rain
from the overhanging cloud.
On whomsoever He confers His Grace, he achieves the goal, not
the egoist who depends on his effort.
O, mind! love the Lord as the water loves the milk.
When heated it burns itself so that its friend the milk may not
suffer or dry up.
Parting with its life, it raises the value of milk.
O, mind! Love the Lord as the bird Chakvi loves the moon,
It does not sleep a minute seeing its Beloved far away from it,
The egoist does not know the secret of love, only he knows it
full well who is a surrender to the Lord.

[23]That is, lust, anger, pride, covetousness, and worldly love.

The egoist is wasting time in counting odds. He does not know
  that the Lord is the final Dispenser (not his effort).
He knoweth not the mind of the Lord who rests his faith solely
  on fate.
Only he who has his mind turned to the Lord can know the
  secret and attain bliss and not the egoist.
So is your mind rivetted on Him and do you contemplate on
  His beatitude?
True love never suffers if the Satguru guides. The lover gains
  wisdom from Him which discloses the world's secret to him.
He who is a genuine seeker, gets initiation into the Name of the
  Lord, which never forsakes him till eternity.
Those birds who dwelt in beautiful ponds and ate pearls have
  passed away.
When death cometh ye cannot get a moment's leave, there is no
  knowing when the game of life may be over.
He meets the Lord on Whom He conferreth His grace and that
  one reaches His Abode.
Love does not appear without the grace of the Guru nor is ego
  killed without his grace.
His grace reveals the Word and gains power for the seeker.
Love is recognised by purity of heart.
Who is one with the Lord he needs no instructions for guidance.
He is one with the Word and revels ever in Him.
The egoist cannot meet the Lord. He always suffers separation
  and pain.
The abode Divine is one, there is no home besides.
So says Nanak.

The Songs of Kabir

Between the poles of the conscious and the unconscious, there
  has the mind made a swing:
Thereon hang all beings and all worlds, and that swing never
  ceases its sway.
Millions of beings are there: the sun and the moon in their
  courses are there:
Millions of ages pass, and the swing goes on.
All swing! the sky and the earth and the air and the water; and
  the Lord Himself taking form:
And the sight of this has made Kabir a servant.

When people say I am Thy bride, I am ashamed; for I have not
    touched Thy heart with my heart.
Then what is this love of mine? I have no taste for food, I have
    no sleep; my heart is ever restless within doors and without.
As water is to the thirsty, so is the lover to the bride. Who is
    there that will carry my news to my beloved?
Kabir is restless: he is dying for sight of Him.

I have stilled my restless mind, and my heart is radiant: for in
    Thatness I have seen beyond Thatness, in company I have
    seen the Comrade Himself.
Living in bondage, I have set myself free: I have broken away
    from the clutch of all narrowness.
Kabir says: "I have attained the unattainable, and my heart is
    coloured with the colour of love."

I am intoxicated with love: why should I be conscious of forms?
I crave freedom from this world, what attachment have I to the
    world?
They who are separated from their Beloved wander aimlessly
    from door to door.
My friend dwells within me, there is no waiting for me any
    more!
The entire creation doth crackle much of its head for Fame.
For me, the Name of my Lord is True: what attachment have I
    to the world?
Not for a moment the Beloved forsakes me: nor I can leave the
    Dear one.
I am in love with Him: There is no restlessness for me.
Intoxicated with love, dispel thou the duality from thy heart.
Delicate is the path thou hast to tread; why carry a heavy bur-
    den on the head?
So says Kabir.

O how may I ever express that secret word?
O how can I say He is not like this, and He is like that?
If I say that He is within me, the universe is ashamed:
If I say that He is without me, it is falsehood.
He makes the inner and the outer worlds to be indivisibly one;
The conscious and the unconscious, both are His footstools.
He is neither manifest nor hidden, He is neither revealed nor
    unrevealed:
There are no words to tell that which He is.

I am neither pious nor ungodly,
I live neither by law nor by sense,

I am neither a speaker nor hearer,
I am neither a servant nor master,
I am neither bond nor free,
I am neither detached nor attached.
I am far from none: I am near to none.
I shall go neither to hell nor to heaven.
I do all works; yet I am apart from all works.
Few comprehend my meaning: he who can comprehend it, he sits
    unmoved.
Kabir seeks neither to establish nor to destroy.

The true Name is like none other name!
The distinction of the Conditioned from the Unconditioned is
    but a word.
The Unconditioned is the seed, the Conditioned is the flower and
    the fruit.
Knowledge is the branch, and the Name is the root.
Look, and see where the root is: happiness shall be yours when
    you come to the root.
The root will lead you to the branch, the leaf, the flower, and
    the fruit:
It is the encounter with the Lord, it is the attainment of bliss,
    it is the reconciliation of the Conditioned and the Uncondi-
    tioned.

O servant, where dost thou seek me?
Lo! I am beside thee.
I am neither in temple nor in mosque: I am neither in Kaaba
    nor in Kailash[24]
Neither am I in rites and ceremonies, nor in Yoga and renuncia-
    tion.
If thou art a true seeker, thou shalt at once see me: thou shalt
    meet Me in a moment of time.
Kabir says, "O Sadhu! God is the breath of all breath."

The river and its waves are one surf: where is the difference be-
    tween the river and its waves?
When the wave rises, it is the water; and when it falls, it is the
    same water again. Tell me, Sir, where is the distinction?
Because it has been named as wave, shall it no longer be con-
    sidered as water?
Within the Supreme Brahma, the worlds are being told like
    beads:
Look upon that rosary with the eyes of wisdom.

[24]These two are places sacred to the worshippers of Mohammed and Shiva;
and this verse is a good example of Kabir's lifelong refusal to accept or
exclude any particular religion or belief.

O Sadhu! the simple union is the best.

Since the day when I met with my Lord, there has been no end
    to the sport of our love.

I shut not my eyes, I close not my ears, I do not mortify my
    body;

I see with eyes open and smile, and behold His beauty every-
    where:

I utter His Name, and whatever I see, it reminds me of Him;
    whatever I do, it becomes His worship.

The rising and the setting are one to me; all contradictions are
    solved.

Wherever I go, I move round Him,

All I achieve is His service:

When I lie down, I lie prostrate at His feet.

He is the only adorable one to me: I have none other.

My tongue has left off impure words, it sings His glory day and
    night:

Whether I rise or sit down, I can never forget Him; for the
    rhythm of His music beats in my ears.

Kabir says: "My heart is frenzied, and I disclose in my soul
    what is hidden. I am immersed in that one great bliss which
    transcends all pleasure and pain."

Hymns of Guru Arjan

O God, mercifully unite with Thee those who by their past
acts are separated from Thee!

Weary of wandering in the four corners of the world and in
every direction, we have come to Thy protection.

A cow without milk is of no avail:

Without water the tree withereth and beareth no fruit.

If we meet not the Lord God, the Friend, how shall we find
rest?

The city or village or house where God is not seen is as a furnace.

All decorations, betel, and tasteful viands are unstable together with the body.

Without the Lord God all friends are as the god of death.

Nanak's supplication is, "Mercifully grant me Thy name;

"O Lord God, whose abode is immovable, unite me with
Thee."

In Chet[25] worship God and you shall greatly rejoice.

You shall obtain Him by meeting saints and repeating His name.

It is only those who have found their God, whose advent into the world is of account:

Vain is his birth who liveth even for a moment without Him.

God is equally contained in sea and land, the nether regions, the firmament, and the forests.

With how much pain shall man reckon if God enter not his heart?

They who repeat God's name are very fortunate.

Nanak, my mind desireth, my mind thirsteth for a sight of God.

I shall touch his feet who causeth me to meet God in the month of Chet.

In Baisakh how can they find consolation who are separated from God, in whose hearts there is no love,

Who forget Him the Friend, and attach themselves to deceitful mammon?

Son, wife, wealth remain not; God alone perisheth not.

The whole world is strangled in its love of false occupations.

All but the name of the one God shall be lost on man's last journey.

He who forgetteth God is ruined; there is none but Him.

Pure is the fame of those who are attached to the feet of the Beloved.

Nanak's prayer, O God, is—"Unite me with Thee that I may obtain Thee."

Baisakh is then delightful when the saints cause man to meet God.

In Jeth man should unite with God before whom all bow.

He who clingeth to the skirt of God, the Friend, shall never be bound by any one.

God's name is like gems and pearls which none may steal.

In God are all the loves which delight the mind.

What God desireth He doeth, and creatures act according to His will.

They whom God hath made His own are blest.

Could men on their own account meet God,[26] why should they weep in separation?

---

[25] These hymns of Guru Arjan's are from his The Twelve Months, and each of the terms starting these hymns, such as "Chet," "Baisakh," and "Jeth," refers to these periods.

[26] That is, without the interposition of the Guru.

Hymns of Guru Ram Das

O refractory soul who comest from afar, how shalt thou meet God?[27]

When I found the Guru by perfect good fortune, the Beloved came and embraced me.

O refractory soul,[28] meditate upon the True Guru;

O refractory and wretched soul, meditate on God's name,

And when thy account is called for, God Himself will release thee.

O refractory soul, once very pure, the filth of pride hath now attached to thee.

The Beloved Spouse was present in thy house; when thou didst separate from Him, thou wert punished.

O refractory soul, my dear, search for God within thee.

He is not found by contrivance; the Guru showeth Him in thy heart.

O refractory soul, my dear, day and night fix thine attention on God.

When thou findest God through the Guru thou shalt go home and obtain the painted palace.

O refractory soul, my friend, abandon hypocrisy and greed:

The hypocritical and the greedy shall be smitten; Death will punish them with his mace.

O refractory soul, who art dear to me as my life, rid thyself of the filth of hypocrisy and superstition.

The perfect Guru is a tank of divine nectar; when the company of saints is obtained filth departeth.

O refractory soul, my dear, listen only to the instruction of one guide the Guru—

Worldly love may be widely diffused, yet at last nothing shall go with one—

---

[27] In this hymn, which is entitled Gauri Karhale, Guru Ram Das is admonishing men to keep watch over their refractory minds. "Karhale" is a camel, but in a secondary sense means a camel that does not obey its bridle and is exceedingly stubborn. An alternative translation for the word also means to "make effort."

[28] The word here translated as "soul" can also mean sometimes "man." But Macauliffe, the translator of this verse, writes that it appears to mean here the soul which has migrated from a distant body.

O refractory soul, my friend, take God's name for thy travelling expenses, and thou shalt obtain honour.

Thou shalt have a dress of honour in God's court, and God Himself will embrace thee—

O refractory soul, he who obeyeth the Guru shall under the Guru's instruction accomplish his work.

Make obeisance before the Guru, O slave Nanak, and he will blend thee with God.

O refractory soul, gifted with the power of reflection, meditate and carefully look.

They who dwell in forests are tired of wandering in them; while they may under the Guru's instruction behold the Beloved in their own hearts.

O refractory soul, remember God;

O refractory and wretched soul, the perverse are caught in a great net,

While the pious are delivered by remembering God's name.

O refractory soul, my beloved, search for the True Guru in the society of the saints.

Attached to the society of the saints meditate on God and He will go with thee.

O refractory soul, greatly fortunate are they on whom the one God looketh with favour.

If God deliver thee, thou shalt be delivered; worship the true Guru's feet.

O refractory soul, my beloved, think of the Light within thy body.

O my Gobind,[29] Thou art in my heart, thou art in my heart: because Thou art in my heart, I am dyed with Thy love.

O my Gobind, the sportive Hari is with me, yet cannot be seen; but the perfect Guru hath shown me the Unseen.

O my Gobind, all poverty and misery depart from him to whom the name of God hath been made manifest.

The highly fortunate have obtained God, the highest dignity, O Gobind, and are absorbed in His name.

O my Gobind, my beloved, hath any one seen the Lord God with his eyes?

My mind and body are very sad, O my Gobind, without God I a woman waste away.

On meeting the saints, O my Gobind, I have found my God, Friend, and Companion.

[29]In this hymn Guru Ram Das expresses his happiness upon meeting God. Both Gobind and Hari are names of God.

God, the life of the world, hath come to me, O my Gobind; I pass the night in happiness.

Ye saints, cause me to meet my God, the Friend; my soul and body hunger for Him.

I cannot live without seeing my Beloved; separation from Him weigheth upon my heart.

God is my Friend and Beloved; the Guru introduced me to Him and my heart revived.

The desires of my soul and body have been fulfilled, O my Gobind; on meeting God my heart expanded.

I am a sacrifice, O my Gobind, my Beloved; I am a hundred times a sacrifice unto Thee.

In my soul and body is the love of the Beloved, O my Gobind, O God preserve my capital.[30]

O my Gobind, let me meet the true Guru, the mediator who will show me the way, and cause me to meet God!

I suffer from separation from God's name and from God.[31]

May I meet my Lord, my Friend, and obtain happiness!

On beholding the Lord God I survive, O my mother,

His name is my companion and brother.

Ye dear saints, sing the praises of my Lord God.

Ye greatly fortunate ones, repeat the Name under the Guru's instruction.

God and God's name are my life and soul.

Hymns of Guru Gobind Singh

Have no doubt whatever of this.

I am the slave of the Supreme Being,

And have come to behold the wonders of the world.

I tell the world what God told me,

And will not remain silent through fear of mortals.

I bow to the one primal God.

Who extended sea and land, the nether regions, and the firmament.

He is the primal Being, unseen, and immortal;

His light is manifest in the fourteen worlds.

[30]This is meant to make his human life profitable in God's way.

[31]In this moving short hymn the Sikh's longing for God, his intense seeking, is very representative of the whole Sikh approach to God. Like most mystics it is a highly personal and passionate search.

He is contained in the ant as in the elephant;
He deemeth the rich and the poor alike;
He is unequalled, unseen, and eternal;
He is the Searcher of all hearts;
He is invisible, indestructible, and without distinguishing
dress;[32]
He is without passion, colour, form, or outline;
He is devoid of caste marks of every kind;
He is the primal Being, peerless and changeless;
He hath no enemy, no friend, no father, no mother;
He is far from all and near all;
His dwelling is in sea and land, the nether and upper
regions.
Boundless is His form, and boundless His voice;
In the shelter of His feet dwelleth Bhawani;[33]
Brahma and Vishnu have not found His limits;
The four-faced Brahma pointeth out that God is indes-
cribable.
He made millions of Indars and Bawans;[34]
He created and destroyed Brahmas and Shivs.
The fourteen worlds He made as a play.
And again blended them with Himself.
He made endless demons, deities, serpents,
Celestial singers, Yakshas, excellent and beautiful.
He is spoken of in the past, the future, and the present,
And He knoweth the secrets of every heart.
He is not attached to any one love;
He is contained in the light of all souls;
He recognizeth all people and all places;
He is free from death and immortal;
He is the invisible, imperceptible Being, distinct from all the
world.
He is immortal, undecaying, imperishable, and of changeless
purpose.
He is the Destroyer and Creator of all;
He is the Remover of sickness, sorrow, and sin.
He who with single heart meditateth on Him even for a mo-
ment
Shall not fall into Death's noose.

As God spoke to me I speak,
I pay no regard to any one besides.

[32]This phrase is from the word "anbhekh," which also means "without form."
[33]Bhawani is the consort of Siv (Shiva), and is also called Durga.
[34]Bawan was the dwarf incarnation of Vishnu.

I am satisfied with no religious garb;
I sow the seed of the Invisible.
I am not a worshipper of stones,
Nor am I satisfied with any religious garb.
I will sing the Name of the Infinite,
And obtain the Supreme Being.
I will not wear matted hair on my head,
Nor will I put on earrings;
I will pay no regard to any one but God.
What God told me I will do.
I will repeat the one Name
Which will be everywhere profitable.
I will not repeat any other name,
Nor establish any other God in my heart.
I will meditate on the name of the Endless One,
And obtain the supreme light.
I am imbued with Thy name, O God;
I am not intoxicated with any other honour.
I will meditate on the Supreme,
And thus remove endless sins.
I am enamoured of Thy form;
No other gift hath charms for me.
I will repeat Thy name,
And avoid endless sorrow.
Sorrow and sin have not approached those
Who have meditated on Thy name.
They who meditate on any one else
Shall die of arguments and contentions.
The divine Guru sent me for religion's sake:
On this account I have come into the world—
"Extend the faith everywhere;
Seize and destroy the evil and the sinful."
Understand this, ye holy men, in your souls.
I assumed birth for the purpose
Of spreading the faith, saving the saints,
And extirpating all tyrants.
All the first incarnations.
Caused men to repeat their names.
They killed no one who had offended against God,
And they struck out no path of real religion.
The Ghauses[35] and Prophets who existed
Left the world talking of themselves.
None of them recognized the Great Being
Or knew anything of real religion.
Nothing is to be obtained by putting hopes in others;

[35]These are Mohammedan saints who practice excessive devotion.

Put the hopes of your hearts in the One God alone.
Nothing is obtained by hoping in others;
Put the hopes of your hearts in Him.

As from one fire millions of sparks arise; though rising separately, they unite again in the fire;
As from one heap of dust several particles of dust fill the air, and on filling it again blend with the dust;
As in one stream millions of waves are produced; the waves being made of water all become water;
So from God's form non-sentient and sentient things[36] are
[36]This can also mean corporeal and incorporeal beings.
manifested, and, springing from Him, shall all be united in Him again.

Part Four

ISLAM: SUFI AND PERSIAN MYSTICISM

Introduction

Islam is the proper term for the religion variously referred to as Muslim, Moslem, Mohammedan. It emerged from the Arabian desert in the seventh century when its prophet, Mohammed (570-632), the unlettered son of a merchant, revealed that he had received divine visions and instructions. Islam is the name that Mohammed himself gave to his faith. It is an Arabic verb meaning "to submit," and the followers of Mohammed referred to themselves as Muslims or Moslems, the past participle of the same verb, which means "those who have submitted themselves."

The tribes before Mohammed's birth worshipped spirits in stones, trees, rivers, winds, the sun, the moon, and the stars; they served the numerous deities that they believed pervaded the world surrounding them. But by the seventh century Allah began to dominate the others. Allah, however, was an ancient deity known to the Arabs long before Mohammed's time.

The name "Allah" conveys to the Muslim more than simply "God," which is another term in Arabic, "ilah." Allah is composed of the article "al" (the), and "ilah" (a god), and is an ancient Semitic word connected with the Hebrew el and elohim. Allah is considered "ta' hala," Allah the most high, the Supreme God of all gods in the ancient faith. To the Muslim Allah is eternal, not limited to any form, not circumscribed by any measure, is one and indivisible, has no plurality, comprehends all things and is comprehended by nothing. In the Koran, Allah is described by ninety-nine attributes, by which He is invoked by the faithful.

At the time of Mohammed's birth many gods were still worshipped, but Allah was supreme. Mohammed's appearance on the scene, and his vision of a single, unitive God manifesting in all things, brought the developing Arabic monotheism to its culmination. In fact, Mohammed's great contribution to Arabic culture, and his greatest achievement as a prophet, was in successfully communicating his doctrine of one God to widely scattered tribes steeped in animism and polytheism. The prophet's constant emphasis throughout his ecstatic utterances, as written in the Koran, and as repeated throughout the Hadith (commentaries on Mohammed's teachings and life), were directed toward eradicating the prevailing primitive polytheism. His teachings were also directed toward the destruction of two other important religious doctrines of his age: He preached against Persian ditheism (Zoroastrianism), and the degenerate Near Eastern Christianity of the period. His monotheism and devotion to the idea of one God was fanatic, and he succeeded in communicating this vision to his people.

In the beginning Mohammed was without honor in his own country, and his fits and hysteria were considered either the result of madness or possession by evil spirits. Some called him a fake and impostor. With few exceptions his early followers were not of the educated or wealthy, but of the lowest and meanest sort—the dregs of a small Arabian town. It was an inauspicious beginning indeed for a seer who would change the face of Arabia, who would meld warring factions, each with a different idol or spirit-deity, into a spiritual and temporal whole.

SUFISM: THE MYSTIC HEART OF ISLAM

In Mecca the muezzin chants:

"We are nearer to a man than his jugular vein . . .
When I love him, I am the hearing he hears with,
And the sight he sees with, and the hand he
Strikes with and the foot he walks with . . ."

Early Islamic teachings were dominated by the prophetic and visionary dynamism of Mohammed's personal experiences. The climate during the early period (after Mohammed's death) was not particularly favorable for mystics, although a long tradition of desert wanderers seeking God through prayers, isolation, and asceticism already existed. These spiritual mendicants were called hanifs, and represented the contemplative heritage upon which Mohammed himself had based his periods of meditation and isolation. Without question Mohammed was an ecstatic who experienced many visions and revelations. His early "Mecca" revelations are full of ecstatic descriptions. Chapter 53 was selected for the Islamic section because it is one of Mohammed's earlier Mecca visions, and incorporates his famous Revelation of the Night Journey, but most important, because it was the single chapter most revered by the later Sufi mystics. Each Sufi would memorize and repeat to himself the first eighteen verses of this surah (chapter) in the hope that he also would be transported into the divine realms.[1] In effect, Sufism represents the inner aspect of Islamic religion, and in this sense its doctrines are an esoteric commentary on Mohammed's teachings and the Koran.[2]

Like all mystical sects, Sufism strives for the involvement in and worship of the Creator—never the worship of creatures or even the works of the Lord's creation. Although pantheistic influence in Sufism was very strong during some periods of Sufi history, it did not involve a simple worship of nature, as was true in other pantheistic religions. In fact, some Sufis became so intensely committed to excluding all but the thought of unifying themselves with God that schisms with orthodox Muslim teachings became inevitable. A good example is Rabi'a al-'Adawiya (717-801), a former slave girl who lived during the formative period of Sufism, and who became known as the "Muslim Saint Teresa" in the West. When someone asked Rabi'a, "How very dear is the Prophet Muhammed to Thee?" she answered, "The love of the Creator leaves no place in my heart and mind for the love of the creature." This type of response would obviously not please the Muslim orthodoxy, which revered Mohammed, lived strictly by his Koranic teachings, and were concerned with piety, morality, social order, salvation through good works, and unconditional obedience to Allah.

Another anecdote describes this Sufi saint's utter devotion to her own experience of the "Creator." One evening a servant asked her to come view the beautiful spring sunset. "Come out and behold the works of God," asked the man. Rabi'a responded negatively. "Come you inside," she said, "that you may behold their maker. Contemplation of the Maker has turned me aside from contemplating what He has made." For Rabi'a, as for many of the Sufis in that early period, her devotion to God involved renunciation not only of her body and egoic self, but all earthly things—even that which was accepted by the Sufis as something created by God. Later Sufis showed greater appreciation of divine influence in worldly beauty, and even came to regard beauty and nature as part of the divine power, as a mirror in which the splendor of God could be seen and adored. These later Sufis believed that Allah created the world and that it is an image of Himself created out of love.

In contrast to the otherworldliness of early Sufis like Rabi'a,

---

[1] See "Mysticism," R.A. Nicholson, in *The Legacy of Islam*, edited by Sir Thomas Arnold and Alfred Guillaume (Oxford: Oxford University Press, 1931), p. 212.

[2] See Titus Burckhardt, *An Introduction to Sufi Doctrine*, trans. by D.M. Matheson (Kashmiri Bazar, Lahore, Pakistan: Sh. Muhammad Ashraf, 1959, 1971), p. 40.

one of the Sufis' unique characteristics as a mystical sect in
later times was that the material world was not denied. A Sufi
could at once be a successful merchant, a man of the world, and
a mystic. One day he could be found arguing over the price of
cloth in the marketplace and on another in deep trance and in
ecstatic communion with his God. Many other mystical sects ad-
vocate turning away from the material world—as did most of the
early Sufis.[3] The Taoist, Buddhist, or Vedantist mystics, for example, held firmly to the belief that the illusory veil of the phenomenal world had to be pierced before enlightenment or
freedom could occur. Yet, the same acceptance of the mundane
world exists in some parts of Mahayana Buddhism. In the
Vimalakirti Sutra, for example, a wealthy layman, Vimalakirti,
is more eloquent and profound in his dialogue than even the
Bodhisattvas who come to argue with him. The text teaches that
one does not have to live the homeless life of the bhikshu monk
in order to attain enlightenment. The householder's life can be,
in Buddhist belief, as good and pure as the religious ascetic's.

The Hindu religion also teaches that a man can be several
things during his lifetime, such as householder, husband, bus-
inessman as well as monk or ascetic. But these roles are lived
out in stages, each in its turn during the Hindu's lifetime. The
Hindu does not normally attempt to be a monk, mystic, and busi-
nessman at the same time.

Even during the first Sufi period the Sufi ascetic was not forbidden conjugal sex. Rabi'a herself, for instance, was asked to
marry several times. The convents during the early period of
Sufism were filled with both men and women living and working
together (as were some of the early Christian monasteries and
retreats). In Sufi convent life, where celibacy was not a require-
ment for membership, the devotees concentrated on simple living, performance of rituals, and recitation of the mystical religious classics. So the pantheism and mystical calling of the Sufis
clearly was not a simple conception of God as existing in all
things, or man's ability to unite with Him, but rather a complicated, multileveled perception of the world and God that
changed frequently over the years as it slowly developed a theology of its own.

After Mohammed's death factionalism set in almost immediately, splitting the Islamic faith into two main groups—Sunnite
and Shiite. The Sufi movement itself emerged from the Shiites
(Arabic for "sectarians" or "followers"). The Sufis were so
named because of the coarse white wool (suf) garments which
they wore as part of their ascetic practices. Sometime after 800

---

[3] Compare this to the Christian approach. Christ did advise, of course, that
one should be in the world but not of it.

A.D., however, the term "Sufi" was applied to Muslim mystics generally, whether or not they were ascetics or wore hair shirts.

Some argue that the Sufis have misrepresented the true tradition of Mohammedanism; others that in the Sufis' constant emphasis on the mystical union of God and man, and on the singular, unitive aspect of God, they are closer to Mohammed's true teachings. The latter argument seems stronger in the sense that Mohammed's essential teachings were in close agreement with the Sufis' mystical monism. Theological disputes did erupt, however, because numerous types of monism developed and the earlier Sufis differed among themselves about the finer points of their beliefs.

While Islamic faith generally emphasized piety, good works, service to Allah, and attention to the inner life, little true religious philosophy existed in the Western sense of the word. Yet, although Islamic theology immediately following Mohammed was of a low order, by the first period of Sufism (750-1050) it had become a high order of mystical poetry. The problem of rationally or philosophically explaining mysticism has always seemed doomed to confusion and failure. Paradox abounds in descriptions by mystics of their experiences. Indeed, in this the Sufis paralleled all other mystical philosophies, but their particularly intense passion and evocation of sensual descriptions added to the problems of developing any rational theology.

The first period of Sufism joined the general asceticism of the time with pantheistic beliefs and mystical meditational and devotional practices. The unitive theme of both Sufi pantheism and mystical union were justified by the Sufis from passages in the Koran such as "Wheresoever you turn is the face of Allah" (II.109). This mystical identification with Allah led to the Sufi doctrine of fana, introduced by the Persian ecstatic Abu Yazid (d. 875), who is also often called Bayazid. Fana had an important and central role in later Sufi theology. Usually translated as "annihilation," it seems quite Buddhistic in the sense that nirvana can also be translated literally as "blown out." In both cases, however, the word should be interpreted as extinguishing the attachments to this world. Many scholars accept the premise that later Sufi mystical theology was profoundly influenced by Buddhism, Hinduism, Neoplatonism, Gnosticism, and Christianity.[4]

Al-Ghazali (1058-1111), one of the greatest figures in Islamic philosophy and Sufi mysticism, lived during the beginning

[4]See, for example, R.C. Zaehner, *Hindu and Muslim Mysticism* (London, 1960); Sidney Spencer, *Mysticism in World Religion*, (Baltimore: Penguin, 1963); and A.J. Arberry, *Sufism, An Account of the Mystics of Islam* (London: Allen & Unwin, 1950).

of the second, or medieval, period of Sufism (c. 1050-1450). In his classical work The Renovation of the Sciences of Religion (Ihya Ulum-id-Din), selections of which are included in this anthology, he analyzed fana as "the effacement of one's individuality in contemplating the unity of God," by which he meant "to live, move, and have our being in Him."[5] This distinction was vitally important for Islamic religion, for earlier Sufis identified so closely with Allah that they began to think of themselves as identical with God. For example, Bayazid said during an ecstatic trance, "Glory to me, how great is My Majesty." Al-Hallaj (854-922), the "Saint of Baghdad," also became so intensely identified with Allah that all distinctions were lost between God and his own personality, and he loudly proclaimed, "I am the Truth." Al-Hallaj in particular represented this branch of Sufi mystical extremism, for he argued that not only was mankind capable of mystical union with God, but that individual men could thus be viewed as God incarnate. To prove his point al-Hallaj took for his example the God/man Jesus, rather than Mohammed as one might assume. The Muslim orthodox, of course, did not consider either Mohammed or Jesus as men in whom God was incarnate, but rather as inspired prophets.

Both al-Hallaj and Bayazid were executed for their unbridled religious enthusiasm and became the first martyrs to a basic conflict between Muslim religious tradition and the wandering, ascetic mystics. This conflict was deepened by a central Sufi teaching, ma'rifa (or obtaining direct knowledge of Allah). The idea of everyone being able to obtain direct knowledge of Allah carried scandalous implications for orthodox Muslims, for they relied totally upon the Prophet's interpretations. But ma'rifa was important to the Sufis, for it was one of the first ideas that began to lay the foundation for the actual practice of a mystical Muslim religion. Ma'rifa strongly differed for the first time from the intellectual or traditional knowledge ('ilm). This new form of insight, a new gnosis, was knowledge given only in ecstasy, and led to the Sufis' answer about how they could be so sure they actually had experienced or "knew" God: "I know Him through Himself." After this point an increasing use of symbolism and poetry developed that described the Sufis' direct and personal relationship with God. A mystical theology was being born. When the orthodox Muslim attacked the Sufi and pointed out his disrespect for the Prophet's interpretions, the Sufi countered that Mohammed's own visions and ecstasies proved

[5]See Some Moral and Religious Teachings of Al-Ghazali, edited by Syed Nawab Ali (Kashmiri Bazar, Lahore: Sh. Muhammad Ashraf, 1920, 1944, 1960), pp. 126ff.

Allah communicated directly (ma'rifa) with mankind. Why, therefore, could not other men have the same experience?

With early Sufis like al-Hallaj, Bayazid, and Rabi'a, we have the supreme example of the "God-intoxicated" Sufi. So complete was their absorption in God that they were utterly reckless in their encounters with the orthodox establishment, disregarding any consequences that might befall them. Al-Hallaj's crucifixion execution was particularly reminiscent of Christ's. A description of his death reveals the depth and passion of his commitment.

When al-Hallaj was brought to be crucified and saw the cross and nails, he turned to the people and uttered a prayer, ending with the words: "And these Thy servants who are gathered to slay me, in zeal for Thy religion and in desire to win Thy favor, forgive them, O Lord, and have mercy upon them; for verily if Thou hadst revealed to them that which Thou hast revealed to me, they would not have done what they have done; and if Thou hadst hidden from me that which Thou hast hidden from them, I should not have suffered this tribulation. Glory unto Thee in whatsoever Thou doest, and Glory unto Thee in whatsoever Thou willest."[6]

The second period of Sufism, aided by outstanding figures like al-Ghazali, Farid ad-Din Attar, Ibn al-Arabi, and Jalal ad-Din Rumi, provided the extra poetic and intellectual dimension needed to escape the apparent blasphemies of the earlier Sufi mystics, such as Bayazid's "How great is My Majesty." Al-Ghazali in particular melded Sufi mysticism with Muslim orthodoxy by building an intellectual rationalization palatable to both sides. He stressed that self-purification was a part of the Sufi path, followed by penitence, which in turn depended upon recognizing the awe, majesty, and holiness of Allah Himself. Such a belief structure did not ignore Allah in exaltation of one's own self. In this way al-Ghazali tried to justify both the contemplative life and the traditional Muslim requirements of worship, which implied a distinction between the worshipper and God. While the Sufi mystic basically rejected the idea of such separation, al-Ghazali's synthesis largely succeeded in healing the schism and helped Sufism achieve an accepted place within the Muslim orthodoxy. Al-Ghazali nevertheless upheld the basic Sufi doctrine of "striving to know how to attain to the Divine Presence and the contemplation of the Divine Majesty and Beauty."

In addition to being a period of synthesis between the mystic and the Muslim orthodoxy, during the second, or medieval, period the great Sufi orders arose, and today over a hundred still

exist involving millions of people. The modern period of Sufi
philosophy (c. 1450-1850) is often referred to as the time of
the poets, although poetry had always been a main form of religious expression throughout Sufi history. Two of the finest poets
in this period, Kabir and Jami, are included in this volume. The
modern period is also associated with the introduction of miracle
legends involving the earlier Sufi saints, occultism, Cabalism,
and magic charms and rituals. In the fourth or contemporary
period (1850 to the present), Sufism underwent little change
with the exception of the contributions of a few outstanding figures. Sir Muhammad Iqbal (1877-1938) is one of the most
exceptional philosophers and poets in Sufism. He has been
properly compared with Rabindranath Tagore in both philosophy and poetry. He wrote difficult, highly subtle philosophical
tracts, and equally subtle symbolic poetry. Iqbal argued that the
mystic passed through four states: belief in the Unseen; searching after the Unseen; gaining knowledge of the Unseen by delving into the depth of one's own soul; and finally, realization. He
rejected total union with the Unseen as inconsistent with monotheism and in this sense agreed with many of the earlier Muslim
critics of Sufism.

THE SUFI QUEST FOR GOD

Few mystics justify their belief in God on faith alone, even
though faith is considered an important stage of awareness. But
the Sufis are so deeply committed to perceiving the "Real" in its
full actuality, which is tantamount to perceiving God, that their
term for God, al-Haqq, encompasses also the words for "real"
and "reality." Here the Sufis are in agreement with other mystical traditions by their emphasis on the necessity for experiencing
the Reality of God, and on the empirical weight that that experience carries. To resolve all spiritual doubt, and to achieve
this goal of experiencing God, the Sufi adopts certain practices
called Mujahidah, or spiritual exercises.[7]

The ultimate experience is direct and immediate perception of
God, which results in Haqq-u'l-Yagin, or literally, something
that is "absolutely certain." But the Islamic mystic achieves
such yagin, or certainty, in three stages, each emphasizing the
growth of belief as one's empirical foundation expands. The first
stage is called 'ilm-u'l-yagin, and means that when one finds
smoke, he is certain there is fire; then there is 'ain-u'l-yagin,
where one sees fire with his own eyes, he is doubly sure it exists;

[7] See B.A. Faruqi, *Mujaddid's Conception of Tawhid* (Kashmiri Bazar, Lahore, Pakistan: Sh. Muhammad Ashraf), p. 52.

and finally, haqq-u'l-yagin, which means that when one puts his hand in the fire and gets burned there is no more doubt. Thus one has realized fully the existence of fire (i.e., of God). This process must begin, however, with an intuition of God or eternity, what the Islamic mystic calls kashf-o-ilham. The validity of kashf-o-ilham, and the capacity of men to experience it, is assumed by Sufis without question. But the important ingredient in Sufi mystical belief is that kashf is qualitatively different from reason, cognition, or normal perception, for it is not grounded in rational processes, or past associations as are many Western descriptions of intuition, but resembles more the Far Eastern view of intuition, like the Taoist tzu-jan.[8] Kashf is considered the "direct" apprehension of ultimate Reality.

According to Sufi belief, the individual's quest of God is not simply one's response to God's universal design, but the workings of God within the being of the spiritual aspirant. This intimate working of God within the spirit of the individual is the basis of the Sufi's personal conduct and his way of life. As Attar described it, the human soul is divine, and "within the heart and soul is the very essence of God." But mankind is separated from God by ignorance and by allowing the power of his mundane self to dominate his attention and behavior.[9] To overcome this ignorance the Sufi needs to progress through seven spiritual stages. But even before this spiritual journey begins there is needed tauba, or conversion. This conversion is the same "change of heart" experience (or metanoia), that one finds in religions all over the world—as varied as Taoism, Zen, and orthodox Christianity. The Sufi tauba involves the conscious resolve to abandon worldly life, and demands that the Muslim devote himself completely to the service of God.[10] Attar describes this pilgrimage of the spiritually thirsting soul and its seven stages in his Conference of the Birds (Mantiq al-tair).

THE SEVEN SPIRITUAL STAGES

1. *Talab* (yearning). Yearning for union with God involves renunciation of worldly things.

[8]See the more detailed description of tzu-jan in the introduction to the Taoist section in Volume 2.

[9]Compare this analysis with the Buddhist view, which is almost identical. Buddha says clearly that the individual's incapacity to attain nirvana is "ignorance" and "attachment" to the mundane world.

[10]See A.J. Arberry, *Sufism, An Account of the Mystics of Islam* (New York: Harper Torchbooks, 1970), pp. 75ff., for a very detailed listing and description of the terms and demands in the Sufi spiritual progression to union with God.

2. *Ishq* (love). This stage demands an overwhelming desire and love for the goal. One must be so in love with God that every other desire must be burned away, including learning or knowledge, hope or even concern with worldly virtue. Total sacrifice.

3. *Marfat* (enlightenment). At this stage the devotee begins to see God in every particle of creation. His mind is afire with the awareness of the Supreme Immanence in all the world around him. The devotee does not sleep but passes his days and nights in bewilderment and absorption.

4. *Istaghrak*, or *fana* (absorption). Fana has already been defined as the annihilation of the mundane, egoic self, which follows the practice of intense spiritual exercises. But fana has come to mean several things. In this case (istaghrak), it implies that state of mind and spirit described by St. John as the "dark night of the soul." Fana, or absorption in the sense of istaghrak, involves a condition of great despondency, similar perhaps to Suso's moan of ecstatic misery, "Come to my help for without Thee I am lost." To realize enlightenment in marfat and to lose sight and experience of it in this passage into the dark night of the soul is an agony common to many mystics, in both the East and West. Even Christ perhaps felt this pain fleetingly while on the cross as he cried out, "My God, my God, why hast Thou forsaken me?"

5. *Tawhid* (unity consciousness). In this state one experiences God as timeless and a permeating Unity amid worldly multiplicity. Tawhid is also sometimes described as ittihad (identity), for in this condition the mystic has made the attributes of God his own. Rumi writes on identity of God and man as one: "His attributes are extinguished in the attributes of God."[11] The Sufi describes this state as similar to having one's identity consumed in the fire of Supreme Consciousness. "Till duality and consciousness of the world is lost this stage is not reached, and when it is reached He alone is left," says Attar. "I am obliterated." The contemporary French mystic Simone Weil touched on this condition when she expressed fear to even pray because it involved self-expression, and that such self-will might interfere with God's will for her. She felt that even in doing goodness one must do nothing more than one is irresistibly compelled to do.

---

[11]See R.A. Nicholson, *Rumi Poet and Mystic* (London: Allen & Unwin, 1950), p. 180. Nicholson translates Rumi to read: "my ego has passed away, He remains alone. . . . Like the flame of a candle in the presence of the sun, he is really non-existent, though he exists in formal calculation." See also Sidney Spencer, *Mysticism in World Religion* (Baltimore: Penguin, 1963), p. 322.

The Taoist has a similar attitude toward the functions of universal action. The individual should conduct himself as if he were a part of the natural forces of life. In this sense the Taoist held to the credo, "Don't interfere" with the natural flow of life. Another parallel with Taoism exists in Ibn Arabi's conception of tawhid: Being is simply "that which exists." Being is One and whole unto Itself. The parallel is not complete, however, for Taoism does not speak of any personal God but an impersonal energy principle, while Ibn Arabi maintains that this "Self-Existent Being is Allah," and "all else is manifestation."

6. *Hairat* (amazement). This stage is when the seeker is struck dumb by the glorious perception of the divine. "I know I am the lover, yet dare not speak it out to anyone." The seeker lives in a dreamy state even though he walks, talks, and feels the life going on around him. This trance condition is supposed to pave the way for further spiritual advance.

7. *Fuqr Wa Fana* (annihilation).[12] This second type fana experience is the final stage of the spiritual pilgrimage. It involves the total loss of the earthly self and body consciousness. It is a rapturous, ecstatic state; not the fleeting experiences of other stages, but a permanent absorption and rebirth into the Godhead that is the goal of all Sufi mystical aspirations. Al-Ghazali describes this type of fana state in his Mathnawi: "In that state man is effaced from self, so that he is conscious neither of his body nor of outward things, nor of inward feelings. He is rapt from all these, journeying first to his Lord and then in his Lord, and if the thought that he is effaced from self occurs to him, that is a defect. This condition is to be effaced from effacement."

THE SELECTIONS AND TRANSLATIONS

Most of the selections included here are by central figures in Sufi poetry and mysticism. The short surah entitled Unity is, according to Mohammed himself, equal to two-thirds of the Koran, for it contains the essence of his message to his people.[13] All of the translations of the Koran are by E.H. Palmer and taken from the *Sacred Books of the East* (vol. 6). The Pearls of Faith is from a translation by Sir Edwin Arnold.

Muhammed al-Ghazali was a practical mystic whose intellect was balanced by insight and common sense. Some have con-

[12]For further discussion of the seven stages see Bankey Behari, *Sufis, Mystics and Yogis of India* (Chaupatty, Bombay: Bhavan's Book University, Bharatiya Vidya Bhavan, 1962, 1971), pp. 45ff.
[13]See E.H. Palmer, *Sacred Books of the East*, vol. 6, p. lxi.

sidered al-Ghazali so remarkable for his learning that he has
been compared with Origen. He has been called the first and
truest of Mohammedan "divines." Al-Ghazali's The Revival of
Religious Sciences is a massive book, and considered by A.J. Arberry to be the greatest religious book by any Muslim.[14] The selections from this book by al-Ghazali included here were translated by Syed Nawab Ali. The selection on fana by al-Ghazali
was translated by E.H. Whinfield.

Muyi'ddin Ibn al-Arabi was probably the most significant
thinker and greatest mystic of Islam, although many would argue
in favor of al-Ghazali or Rumi for this honor. Ibn Arabi is not
widely known except by scholars and specialists in mystical theology. Until recently the only complete work of Ibn Arabi translated into English is A Collection of Mystical Odes (Tarjuman
al-Ashwaq) by R.A. Nicholson. Few mystical writings offer such
a rich variety of insights into the Sufi mystical mentality. In the
selections included here, Ibn Arabi comments upon his own very
obscure symbolism, giving the reader the rare opportunity to
"see" into the workings of a mystic's own perceptions, his translations and analysis of his own mystical experience into the cultural poetry of his time.

Mention should also be made of another exceptional work of
Sufi mysticism included in this section—the Mathnawi of the
Persian Sufi Jalal al-Din Rumi. The Mathnawi is considered
Rumi's greatest writing. It has been called "the Koran of Per-
sia" by Muslims and is respected by both the orthodox Muslims
for its theology and by the Sufis, some of whom consider it their
own Bible. The Mathnawi selections were translated by E.H.
Whinfield, and the writings from Rumi's The Diwan by J.W.
Sweetman.

The remaining Sufi mystics in Section 3 were translated by
the following:

Abdul Qadir: The Revelations of the Unseen, from the book
translated by M. Aftab-ud-din Ahmad. Sana'i of Ghazna: The
Enclosed Garden of the Truth, edited and translated by J. Stephenson. Muhammad Iqbal: The New Rose Garden of Mystery,
translated by M. Hadi Hussain. Omar Khayyam: Quatrains of
Omar Khayyam, translated by E.H. Whinfield. Kabir: The
Songs and Hymns of Kabir, translated by Rabindranath Tagore.
Talib: The Diwan: Si Harfi Dholla, translated by R. Sirajuddin
and H.A. Walter. All the selections from both Attar and Hafiz
were translated by Margaret Smith. Mawlana Nur ad-Din
Jami's selections were all translated by E.H. Whinfield, except
the Yusuf-o-Zulaykha, which was translated by J.W. Sweetman.

---

[14]See A.J. Arberry, Sufism (New York: Harper Torchbooks), pp. 81-82.

1. The Koran

The Unity of Allah Surah (Chapter 112)

> Say, Allah is One!
> The Eternal Allah,
> He begetteth not, nor was begotten
> And there is none like unto Him.

The Opening Chapter (Chapter 1)

In the name of the merciful and compassionate God.

Praise belongs to God, the Lord of the worlds, the merciful, the compassionate, the ruler of the day of judgment! Thee we serve and Thee we ask for aid. Guide us in the right path, the path of those Thou art gracious to; not of those Thou art wroth with; nor of those who err.

The Star Revealed at Mecca (Chapter 53)

In the Name of the Most Merciful God

By the star, when it setteth; your companion Mohammed erreth not, nor is he led astray: neither doth he speak of his own will. It is no other than a revelation, which hath been revealed unto him. One mighty in power, endued with understanding, taught it him: and he appeared[1] in the highest part of the horizon. Afterward he approached the prophet, and drew near unto him; until he was at the distance of two bow's length from him, or yet nearer: and he revealed unto his servant that which

---

[1] It was the angel Gabriel who appeared in the eastern part of the sky. Tradition says that Gabriel did not appear in his proper shape to any of the prophets except Mohammed, and to him only twice: once when he received the first revelation of the Koran, and the second time when Mohammed took his famous night journey to heaven. This is described in the following text.

he revealed. The heart of Mohammed did not falsely represent that which he saw. Will ye therefore dispute with him concerning that which he saw? He also saw him another time, by the lote-tree beyond which there is no passing:[2] near it is the garden of eternal abode. When the lote-tree covered that which it covered,[3] his eyesight turned not aside, neither did it wander: and he really beheld some of the greatest signs of his Lord.[4]

What think ye of Allat, and al Uzza, and Manah, that other third goddess?[5] Have ye male children, and God female? This therefore, is an unjust partition. They are no other than empty names, which ye and your fathers have named goddesses. God hath not revealed concerning them anything to authorize their worship. They follow no other than a vain opinion, and what their souls desire: yet hath the true direction come unto them from their Lord. Shall man have whatever he wisheth for? The life to come and the present life are God's: and how many angels soever there be in the heavens, their intercession shall be of no avail, until after God shall have granted permission unto whom he shall please and shall accept. Verily they who believe not in the life to come give unto the angels a female appellation. But they have no knowledge herein: they follow no other than a bare opinion; and a bare opinion attaineth not anything of truth. Wherefore withdraw from him who turneth away from our admonition, and seeketh only the present life. This is their highest pitch of knowledge. Verily thy Lord well knoweth him who erreth from his way; and he well knoweth him who is rightly directed.

Unto God belongeth whatever is in heaven and earth: that he may reward those who do evil, according to that which they shall have wrought; and may reward those who do well, with the most excellent reward. As to those who avoid great crimes and heinous sins, and are guilty only of lighter faults; verily thy Lord will be extensive in mercy toward them. He well knew you when he produced you out of the earth, and when ye were embryos in your mothers' wombs: wherefore justify not yourselves: he best knoweth the man who feareth him.

What thinkest thou of him who turneth aside from following the truth and giveth little, and covetously stoppeth his hands?

[2]Commentators say that this tree stands in the seventh heaven and on the right hand of the throne of God. It is the utmost bounds beyond which even the angels must not pass. Others say that beyond this point no creature's knowledge can extend; it is therefore an impassable barrier.

[3]This apparently signifies that what was under the tree was beyond all number or description. Some theorize that Mohammed intends to note the whole host of angels worshipping beneath the tree.

[4]That is, perceiving the wonders of both the sensible and intellectual world.

[5]This lists the three idols of the ancient Arabs.

Is the knowledge of futurity with him, so that he seeth the same? Hath he not been informed of that which is contained in the books of Moses, and of Abraham who faithfully performed his engagements? To wit: that a burdened soul shall not bear the burden of another; and that nothing shall be imputed to a man for righteousness, except his own labor; and that his reward shall surely be made manifest hereafter, and that he shall be rewarded for the same with a most abundant reward; and that unto thy Lord will be the end of all things; and that he causeth to laugh, and causeth to weep; and that he putteth to death, and giveth life; and that he created the two sexes, the male and the female, of seed when it is emitted; and that unto him appertaineth another production, namely, the raising of the dead again to life hereafter; and that he enricheth, and causeth to acquire possession; and that he is the Lord of the dog-star;[6] and that he destroyed the ancient tribe of Ad and Thamud, and left not any them alive, and also the people of Noah, before them; for they were most unjust and wicked: and he overthrew the cities[7] which were turned upside down; and that which covered them, covered them. Which, therefore, of thy Lord's benefits, O man, wilt thou call in question? This our apostle is a preacher like the preachers who preceded him. The approaching day of judgment draweth near: there is none who can reveal the exact time of the same, besides God. Do ye, therefore, wonder at this new revelation; and do ye laugh, and not weep, spending your time in idle diversions? But rather worship God, and serve him.

2. *Pearls of Faith, or Islam's Rosary*

Being the Ninety-Nine Beautiful Names of Allah

Al'-Alim! the "All-Knower!" by this word
Praise Him Who sees th' unseen, and hears th' unheard.

[6]The Dog Star is Sirius, which was an object of worship for the ancient Arabs.

[7]That is, Sodom and Gomorrah.

IF ye keep hidden your mind, if ye declare it aloud,
    Equally God hath perceived, equally known is each thought:
If on your housetops ye sin, if in dark chambers ye shroud,
    Equally God hath beheld, equally judgment is wrought.
He, without listing, doth know how many breathings ye make
    Numbereth the hairs of your heads, wotteth the beats of your
        blood:
Heareth the feet of the ant when she wanders by night in the
        brake;
    Counteth the eggs of the snake and the cubs of the wolf in
        the wood.
Mute the Moakkibat[1] sit this side and that side of men,
    One on the right noting good, and one on the left noting ill;
Each hath those Angels beside him who write with invisible pen
    Whatso he doth, or sayeth, or thinketh, recording it still,
Vast is the mercy of God, and when a man doth aright,
Glad is the right-hand Angel, and setteth it quick on the roll;
Ten times he setteth it down in letters of heavenly light.
For one good deed ten deeds, and a hundred for ten on the
        scroll.
But when one doth amiss the right-hand Angel doth lay
His palm on the left-hand Angel and whispers, "Forbear thy
        pen!
Peradventure in seven hours the man may repent him and pray;
At the end of the seventh hour, if it must be, witness it then."[2]

Al-'Alim! Thou Who knowest all,
With hearts unveiled on Thee we call.

Ar-Rafi'! the "Exalter!" laud Him so
Who loves the humble and lifts up the low.

WHOM hath He chosen for His priests and preachers,
    Lord who were eminent, or men or might?
Nay, but consider how He seeks His teachers,
    Hidden, like rubies unaware of light.
Ur of the Chaldees! what chance to discover
    Th' elect of Heaven in Azar's leathern tent?
But Allah saw His child, and friend, and lover,
    And Abraham was born, and sealed, and sent.
The babe committed to th' Egyptian water!
    Knew any that the tide of Nilus laved
The hope of Israel there? Yet Pharaoh's daughter
    Found the frail ark, and so was Moses saved.

[1]These are the Angels of Record who relieve each other in the duty of registering human actions and conduct.
[2]This is a reference to Chapter 13, Of Thunder, in the Koran.

Low lies the Syrian town behind the mountain
  Where Mary, meek and spotless, knelt that morn,
And saw the splended Angel by the fountain,
  And heard his voice, "Lord Isa shall be born!"
Nay, and Muhammad (blessed may he be!),
  Abdallah's and Aminah's Holy son,
Whom black Halimah nursed, the Bedawee,
  Where lived a lonelier or a humbler one?
Think how he led the camels of Khadijah,
  Poor, but illuminated by the light of Heaven;
Mightier than Noah, or Enoch, or Elijah,
  Our holy Prophet, to Arabia given.
Man knew him not, wrapped in his cloth, and weeping
  Lonely on Hira all that wondrous night;
But Allah for His own our Lord was keeping:—
  "Rise thou enwrapped one!" Gabriel spake, "and write."

Save God there is none high at all,
Nor any low whom He doth call.

An-Noor! "The Light" that lightens all who live!
By this great name to Allah glory give.

Of earth and heaven God is the Light.[3]
As when a lamp upon a height
Is set within a niche, and gleams
From forth the glittering glass, and seems
A star,—wide fall the rays of it:—
So shines His glory, and 'tis lit
With holy oil was never pressed
From olive tree in east or west.
It burneth without touch of flame,
A light beyond all light: the same
Guideth the feet of men, and still
He leadeth by it whom He will.
Light of the world! An-Noor! illume
Our darkling pathway to the tomb.

[3]This refers to the Koran, Chapter 25, Of Light.

3. Selections from the Sufi Mystics

AL-GHAZALI

The Unity of God[1]

There are four stages in the belief in the unity of God. The first is to utter the words: "There is no god but God" without experiencing any impression in the heart. This is the creed of the hypocrites. The second is to utter the above words and to believe that their meaning is also true. This is the dogma of ordinary Muslims. The third is to perceive by the inward light of the heart the truth of the above Kalima. Through the multiplicity of causes the mind arrives at the conception of the unity of the final cause. This is the stage of the initiates. The fourth is to gaze at the vision of an all-comprehensive, all-absorbing One, losing sight even of the duality of one's own self. This is the highest stage of the true devotee. It is described by the Sufis as "Fana fit-tauhid."[2]

To use a simile these four stages may be compared with a walnut which is composed of an external hard rind, an internal skin, the kernel, and oil. The hard rind, which is bitter in taste, has no value except that it serves as a covering for some time. When the kernel is extracted the shell is thrown away. Similarly the hypocrite who, uttering the Kalima, is associated with the Muslims and safely enjoys their privileges, but at death is cut off from faithful and falls headlong into perdition. The internal skin is more useful than the external inasmuch as it preserves the kernel and may be used, but is in no way equal to the kernel itself. Similarly the dogmatic belief of the ordinary Muslim is better than the lip service of the hypocrite, but lacks that

[1]From *The Renovation of the Sciences of Religion* (Ihya-al-Ulum-id-Din) Chapter IV.

[2]That is, the effacement of one's individuality in contemplating the unity of God. Fana is an important word in Sufi terminology and usually means something akin to the Hindu nirvana, that is, "annihilation." But Al-Ghazali here implies, "To live, move, and have our being in Him."

broad clear insight which is described as "He whose heart Allah has opened to Islam walks in His light."

The kernel is undoubtedly the desired object, but it contains some substance which is removed when oil is being pressed out. Similarly the conception of an efficient final cause is the aim and object of the devotees, but is inferior to the vision of the all-pervading Holy One, because the conception of causality involves duality. But the objection may be urged: How can we ignore the diversities and multiplicities of the universe? Man has hands and feet, bones and blood, heart and soul, all distinct, yet he is one individual. When we are thinking of a dear old friend and suddenly he stands before us, we do not think of any multiplicity of his bodily organs, but are delighted to see him. The simile, though not quite appropriate is suggestive, especially for beginners. When they reach that stage they will themselves see its truth. Words fail to express the beatitude of that highest stage. It can be enjoyed, but not described.[3]

Let us consider the nature of the third stage. Man finds that God alone is the prime cause of everything. The world, its objects, life, death, happiness, misery, all have their source in His omnipotence. None is associated with Him in this. When man comes to recognise this, he has no fear of anything, but puts his trust in God alone. But Satan tempts him by misrepresenting the agencies of the inorganic and organic worlds as potent factors independent in the shaping of his destiny.

Think first of the inorganic world. Man thinks that crops depend on rain descending from clouds, and that clouds gather together owing to normal climatic conditions. Similarly his sailing on the sea depends on favourable winds. Without doubt, these are immediate causes, but they are not independent. Man who in the hour of need calls for God's mysterious help, forgets Him and turns to external causes as soon as he finds himself safe and sound. "So, when they ride in ships, they call upon Allah, being sincerely obedient to Him, but when He brings them safe to land, they associate others with Him. Thus they become ungrateful for what We have given them, so they might enjoy: but they shall soon know" (Koran, 29, 65-66). If a culprit, whose death sentence is revoked by the king, looks to the pen as his deliverer, will it not be sheer ignorance and ingratitude? Surely, the sun, the moon, the stars, the clouds, in fact, the whole universe is like a pen in the hand of an omnipotent dictator. When this kind of belief takes hold of the mind, Satan is disappointed in covertly tempting man, and uses subtle means,

[3] In Byron's *Childe Harold's Pilgrimage* there is the line "And thou shalt one day, if found worthy, be so defined. See thy God face to face, as thou dost now."

insinuating thus: "Do you not see that the king has full power either to kill or favour you, and though the pen, in the above simile, is not your deliverer, the writer certainly is?" As this sort of reflection led to the vexed question of free will, we have dealt with it already at some length.

At the outset, let us point out that just as an ant, owing to its limited sight, will see the point of the pen blackening a blank sheet of paper and not the fingers and hand of the writer, so the person whose mental sight is not keen will attribute the actions to the immediate doer only. But there are minds, which, with the searchlight of intuition, expose the lurking danger of wrongly attributing power to any except the All-powerful Omniscient Being. To them every atom in the universe speaks out truth of this revelation. They find tongues in trees, books in the running brooks, sermons in stones. The worldling will say: Though we have ears, we do not hear them. But asses also having ears do not hear. Verily there are such ears which hear words that have no sound, that are neither Arabic nor any other language, known to man. These words are drops in the boundless, unfathomable ocean of divine knowledge: "If the sea were ink for the words of my Lord, the sea would surely be consumed before the words of my Lord are exhausted."

The Love of God and Its Signs[4]

Love of God is the highest stage of our soul's progress and her *summum bonum*. Repentance, patience, piety, and other virtues are all preliminary steps. Although rare, these qualities are found in true devotees and the commonality, though devoid of them, at any rate believe in them. Love of God is not only very rare: the possibility of it is doubted, even by some Ulama[5] who call it simply service. For, in their opinion, love exists amongst species of the same kind, but God being ultra-mundane and not of our kind, His love is an impossibility and hence the much talked of ecstatic states of the "true lovers of God" are mere delusions. As this is far from truth and impedes the progress of the soul, by spreading false notions, we shall briefly discuss the

[4]Also from Al-Ghazali's *The Renovation of the Sciences of Religion* (Chapter IV.6 of the Ihya-al-Ulum-id-Din).

[5]The Ulama, or Ulema, is from the Arabic for "learned." They represent the Islamic doctors of divinity and dogma, and comprise the conservative, powerful hierarchy of Mohammedan theology.

subjects. First we shall quote passages from the Quran and the Hadith[6] testifying to the existence of the love of God.

"O you who believe, whosoever from among you turns back from his religion, then Allah will bring a people: He shall love them, and they shall love Him, lowly before the believers, mightily against the unbelievers, they shall strive hard in Allah's way and shall not fear the censure of any censurer: this is Allah's grace, He gives it to whom He pleases and Allah is ample-giving knowing." (Hadith, 5.54.)

The Prophet used to pray thus: "My God! give me Thy love and the love of him who loves Thee and the love of that action which will bring me nearer to Thee and make Thy love sweeter than cold water to the thirsty."

"Verily Allah loves those who repent and those who purify themselves." Say, "If you love Allah, then follow me. Allah will love you and forgive you your faults, and Allah is Forgiving, Merciful."[7] We have said before that love means yearning towards a desired object and that beneficence and beauty, whether perceived or conceived, equally attract our hearts. But in using the word love for God, no such meaning is possible as it implies imperfection. God's love towards men is the love of His own work. Someone read the following verse of the Quran: "He loves them and they love him" in front of Shaikh Abu Said of Mohanna, who interpreted it saying: "He loves Himself because He alone exists." Surely an author who likes himself, his love is limited to his self. God's love means lifting the veil from the heart of His servant, so that he might gaze at Him. It also means drawing him closer to Himself. Let us give an illustration. A king permits some of his slaves to approach his presence, not because he requires them but because the slaves possess or are acquiring certain qualities which are worthy of being displayed before the royal presence. This privilege, this lifting of the veil, brings us nearer to the conception of God's love. But it must be remembered that approaching the divine presence should entirely exclude the idea of space, for then it would imply change in Him, which is absurd. Divine proximity means the attainment of Godly virtues by abstaining from the promptings of the flesh and hence it implies approach from the point of view of quality

[6]The Hadith is an enormous body of writings on the life and teachings of Mohammed, and with the Koran, forms the basis of Mohammedan religion and law.

[7]In the Koran (3.30), keeping God's commandments, as revealed through His holy prophets, constituted love of Him. The same interrelationship between keeping the Lord's commandments and love is found in Christianity: "If ye keep my commandments, ye shall abide in my love; even as I keep my Father's commandments and abide in His love" (John, 15.10).

and not of space. For example, two persons meet together either when both of them proceed towards each other or one is stationary and the other starts and approaches him. Again a pupil strives to come up to the level of his teacher's knowledge, who is resting in his elevated position. His uphill journey towards knowledge keeps him restless and he climbs higher and higher till he catches a glimpse of the halo which surrounds his master's countenance. The nature of divine proximity resembles this inward journey of the pupil; that is, the more a man acquires insight into the nature of things, and by subjugating his passions leads the life of righteousness, the nearer will he be coming to his Lord. But it must be remembered that a pupil may equal his teacher, even be greater than he, but as regards divine proximity, no such equality is possible. God's love means that which purifies the heart of His servant in a manner that he may be worthy of being admitted before His holy Presence.

It may be asked: "How can we know that God loves a certain person?" My answer is that there are signs which bear testimony to it. The Prophet says: When God loves His servant, He sends tribulations, and when He loves him most he severs his connection from everything. Someone said to Jesus: "Why do you not buy a mule for yourself"? Jesus answered: "My God will not tolerate that I should concern myself with a mule." Another saying of Muhammad is reported thus: When God loves any of His servants He sends tribulations. If he patiently bears them, he is favoured, and if he cheerfully faces them, he is singled out as chosen of God. Surely it is this joyous attitude of his mind, whether evil befalls him or good, that is the chief sign of love. Such minds are providentially taken care of in their thoughts and deeds and in all their dealings with men. The veil is lifted and they live in wrapped communion.

As for the signs of a man's love for God, let it be borne in mind that everybody claims His love, but few really love Him. Beware of self-deception; verify your statement by introspection. Love is like a tree rooted in the ground ending its shoots above the starry heaven; its fruit is found in the heart, the tongue and the limbs of the lover—in fact, his whole self is a witness to love just as smoke is a sure sign of fire burning.

Let us, then, trace the signs which are found in the true lover.

Death is a pleasure to him, for it removes the barrier of body and lets the fluttering soul free to soar and sing in the blissful abode of his beloved. Sufyan Thauri[8] used to say: "He who doubts dislikes death, because a friend will never dislike meeting a friend."

A certain Sufi asked a hermit whether he wished for death,

[8] A Sufi of great renown who died at Baghdad in 840 A.D.

but he gave no answer. Then the Sufi said to him: "Had you been a true hermit you would have liked death. The Koran says: If the future abode with Allah is especially for you to the exclusion of the people, then invoke death if you are truthful. They will never wish it on account of what their hands have sent on before, and Allah knows the unjust." (Hadith, 2. 94-95.) The hermit replied: "But the Prophet says: Do not wish for death." "Then you are suffering," said the Sufi, "because acquiescence in divine decree is better than trying to escape it."

It may be asked here: Can he who does not like death be God's lover? Let us consider first the nature of his dislike. It is due to his attachment to the worldly objects, wife, children, and so forth, but it is possible that with this attachment, which no doubt comes in the way of his love of God, there may be some inclination towards His love, because there are degrees of His love. Or it may be that his dislike is due to his feeling of unpreparedness in the path of love. He would like to love more so that he might be able to purify himself just as a lover hearing of his beloved's arrival would like to be given some time for making preparations for a fitting reception. For these reasons if a devotee dislikes death, he can still be His lover, though of inferior type.

He should prefer, both inwardly and outwardly God's pleasure to his desires. For he who follows the dictates of his desires is no true lover, for the true lover's will is his beloved's. But human nature is so constituted that such selfless beings are very rare. Patients would like to be cured but they often eat things which are injurious to their health. Similarly, a person would like to love God but very often follows his own impulses. Noman was a sinner, who being repeatedly excused by the Prophet was at last flogged. While he was being flogged a certain person cursed him for his iniquity. "Do not curse him," said he; "he has a regard for God and His Apostle."

Experience tells us that he who loves, loves the things connected with his beloved. Therefore another sure sign of God's love is the love of His creatures who are created by and are dependent on him; for he who loves an author or poet, will he not love his work or poem? But this stage is reached when the lover's heart is immersed in love and the more he is absorbed in Him, the more will he love His creatures, so much so that even the objects which hurt him will not be disliked by him—in fact the problem of evil is transcended in his love for Him.

In one of the Hadis Qudsi[9] God has said: "My saints are

---

[9]The Hadis Qudsi in Mohammedanism is the tradition in which God Himself is reported to speak.

those who cry like a child for My love, who remember Me like a fearless lion at the sight of iniquities."

A reverent attitude of mind is another sign of his love. Some hold that fear is opposed to love, but the truth is that just as the conception of beauty generates love, the knowledge of His sublime majesty produces the feeling of awe in us. Lovers meet with fears which are unknown to others. There is the fear of being disregarded. There is fear of the veil being drawn down. There is the fear of their being turned away. When the Sura Hud was revealed, in which the awful doom of the wicked nations is narrated: "Away with Samood, away with Midian," the Prophet heaved a sigh and said: "This Sura has turned me into an old man." He who loves His nearness will feel acutely the fear of being thrown away from Him. There is another fear of remaining at a particular stage and not rising higher, for the ascending degrees of His nearness are infinite. A true lover is always trying to draw near and nearer to Him. "A thin veil covers my heart," says the Prophet, "then I ask for His forgiveness seventy times in day and night." This means that the Prophet was always ascending the scales of His nearness, asking for His forgiveness at every stage which was found lower than the next one.

There is another fear of over-confidence which slackens the efforts and mars progress. Hope with fear should be the guide of love. Some Sufis say that he who worships God without fear is liable to err and fall; he who worships Him with fear turns gloomy and is cast off, but he who lovingly worships Him with hope and fear is admitted by Him and favoured. Therefore lovers should fear Him and those who fear Him should love Him. Even excess of His love contains an inkling of fear: it is like salt in food. For human nature cannot bear the white heat of His love, if it is not chastened and tempered by the fear of the Lord.

Keeping love secret and giving no publicity to it is another sign of His love. For love is the beloved's secret: it should not be revealed nor openly professed. However, if he is over-powered by the force of his love, and unwittingly and without the least dissimulation his secret is out, he is not to be blamed. Some Sufis say: He who is very often pointing towards Him is far from Him, because he feigns and makes a show of his love of Him. Zunnun[10] of Egypt once went to pay a visit to one of his brother Sufis, who was in distress, and who used to talk of his love openly. "He who feels the severity of pain inflicted by Him," said Zunnun, "is no lover." "He who finds no pleasure in

[10]Zunnan is considered the "father of Sufism" by some. He died in 860 A.D. and was renowned for founding a sect of Sufis in Egypt.

such pain," returned the Sufi, "is no lover." "True," replied
Zunnun, "but I say to you that he who trumpets his love of
Him is no lover." The Sufi felt the force of Zunnun's words and
fell down prostrate before God and repented and did not talk
again of his love.

The essence of religion is love; some signs of which have been
enumerated above. The love of God may be of two kinds. Some
love Him for His bounties, others for His perfect beauty irre-
spective of bounties. The former love increases according to the
bounties received, but the latter love is the direct result of the
contemplation of His perfect attributes and is constant even in
tribulations. "These are His favoured few," says Junaid of Baghdad.[11] But there are many who pose as his lovers and with much
talk of his love lack the signs of true love. They are deluded by
the devil, slaves of their passions, seeking a hollow reputation,
shameless hypocrites who try to deceive the Omniscient Lord
their Creator. They are all enemies of God, whether they are revered as divines or Sufis. Sahl of Taster who used to address
everyone as "friend," was once asked by a person the reason of
his doing so, as all men could not be his friends. Sahl whispered
in his ear saying: "He will either be a believer or a hypocrite; if
he is a believer, he is God's friend; if a hypocrite, the devil's
friend."

Abu Turab Nakshabi has composed some verses describing the
signs of love. Their translation is as follows:

Do not profess your love. Hearken to me: These are the signs
of his love. The bitterness of tribulations is sweet to him, he is
happy for he believes that everything proceeds from Him; for
praise or censure he cares not, the will of his beloved is his will.
While his heart is burning with love his countenance is radiant
with joy. He guards the secret of love with all his might, and no
thought save of his beloved enters into his mind. Yahya bin
Maaz Razi[12] adds some lines: "Another sign is that he is up and
ready like a diver at the bank of a river; he sighs and sheds
tears in the gloom of night, and day and night he appears as if
fighting for the sacred cause of his love. He entrusts his whole
self to his love and gladly acquiescing abides in his love.

[11]Junaid is a celebrated Sufi (also called Syed Uttaifa: "Chief of the Sect")
who died in Baghdad in 911 A.D.
[12]A theologian and Sufi of Ray, in Persia, who died in 871 A.D.

Fana, Annihilation of Self or Absorption in God

Prayers have three veils, whereof the first is prayers uttered only by the tongue; the second is when the mind, by hard endeavour and by firmest resolve, reaches a point at which, being untroubled by evil suggestions, it is able to concentrate itself on divine matters; the third veil is when the mind can with difficulty be diverted from dwelling on divine matters. But the marrow of prayer is seen when He who is invoked by prayer takes possession of the mind of him who prays, and the mind of the latter is absorbed in God whom he addresses, his prayers ceasing and no self-consciousness abiding in him, even to this extent that a mere thought about his prayers appears to him a veil and a hindrance. This state is called "absorption" by the doctors of mystical lore, when a man is so utterly absorbed that he perceives nothing of his bodily members, nothing of what is passing without, nothing of what occurs to his mind—yea, when he is, as it were, absent from all these things whatsoever, journeying first *to* his Lord, then *in* his Lord. But if the thought occurs to him that he is totally absorbed, that is a blot; for only that absorption is worthy of the name which is unconscious of absorption.

I know these words of mine will be called an insipid discourse by narrow theologians, but they are by no means devoid of sense. Why? The condition of which I speak is similar to the condition of the man who loves many other things, such as wealth, honour, pleasures; and, just as we see some engrossed by love, we see others overpowered by anger so that they do not hear one who speaks, or see one who passes, and are so absorbed by their overwhelming passion that they are not even conscious of being thus absorbed. For so far as you attend to the absorption of your mind, you must necessarily be diverted from Him who is the cause of your absorption. . . .

And now, being well instructed as to the nature of "absorption," and casting aside doubts, do not brand as false what you are unable to comprehend. God most high saith in the Koran: "They brand as false what they do not comprehend." The meaning of "absorption" having been made clear, you must know that the beginning of the path is the journey *to* God and that the journey *in* God is its goal, for in this latter, absorption in God takes place. At the outset this glides by like a flash of light, barely striking the eye; but thereafter, becoming habitual, it lifts the mind into a higher world, wherein the most pure essen-

tial Reality is manifested, and the human mind is imbued with
the form of the spiritual world, whilst the majesty of the Deity
evolves and discloses itself. Now, what first appears is the substance of angels, spirits, prophets, and saints, for a while under
the veil of I know not what beautiful forms, wherefrom certain
particular verities are disclosed; but by degrees, as the way is
opened out, the Divine Verity begins to uncover His face. Can
anyone, I ask, who attains a glimpse of such visions, wherefrom
he returns to the lower world disgusted with the vileness of all
earthly things, fail to marvel at those who, resting content with
the deceits of the world, never strive to ascend to sublimer
heights?

IBN AL-ARABI

Selections from The Bezels of Divine Wisdom
(Fususu 'l-Hikam)

Sublimity ('uluw) belongs to God alone. The essences (a'yan)
of things are in themselves nonexistent, deriving what existence
they possess from God, who is the real substance ('ayn) of all
that exists. Plurality consists of relations (nisab), which are
non-existent things. There is really nothing except the Essence,
and this is sublime (transcendent) for itself, not in relation to
anything, but we predicate of the One Substance a relative sublimity (transcendence) in respect of the modes of being attributed to it: hence we say that God is (huwa) and is not (la
huwa). Kharraz,[1] who is a mode of God and one of His tongues,
declared that God is not known save by His uniting all opposites in the attribution of them to him (Kharraz). He is the
First, the Last, the Outward, the Inward; He is the substance of
what is manifested and the substance of what remains latent at
the time of manifestation; none sees Him but Himself, and
none is hidden from Him, since He is manifested to Himself and
hidden from Himself; and He is the person named Abu Sa'id
al-Kharraz and all the other names of originated things.[2] The
inward says "No" when the outward says "I," and the outward
says "No" when the inward says "I," and so in the case of every
contrary, but the speaker is One, and He is substantially identi-

[1] This is Abu Sa'id al-Kharraz, a renowned Sufi of Baghdad (c. 890).
[2] The Sufi mystic believes that God cannot be known until he becomes a
haqq, or illuminated by all the Divine attributes.

cal with the hearer.... The Substance is One, although its
modes are different. None can be ignorant of this, for every man
knows it of himself, and Man is the image of God.

Thus things became confused and numbers appeared, by
means of the One, in certain degrees.[3] The One brought number
into being, and number analysed the One, and the relation of
number was produced by the object of numeration. ... He that
knows this knows that the Creator who is declared to be incomparable (munazzah) is the creatures which are compared
(mushabbah) with Him—by reason of His manifesting Himself
in their forms—albeit the creatures have been distinguished from
the Creator. The Creator is the creature, and the creature is the
Creator: all of this proceeds from One Essence; nay, He is the
One Essence and the many individualized essences. . . . Who is
Nature and Who is all that is manifested from her?[4] We did not
see her diminished by that which was manifested from her, or
increased by the not-being of aught manifested that was other
than she. That which was manifested is not other than she, and
she is not identical with what was manifested, because the forms
differ in respect of the predication concerning them: this is cold
and dry, and this is hot and dry: they are united by dryness but
separated by cold and heat. Nay, the Essence is in reality
Nature. The world of Nature is many forms in One Mirror;
nay, One Form in diverse mirrors.[5] Bewilderment arises from
the difference of view, but those who perceive the truth of what
I have stated are not bewildered.

When God willed in respect of His Beautiful Names (attributes), which are beyond enumeration, that their essences
(a'yan)—or, if you wish you may say "His essence ('aynuhu)"—
should be seen, He caused them to be seen in a microcosmic
being (kawn jami') which, inasmuch as it is endowed with existence,[6] contains the whole object of vision, and through which
the inmost consciousness (sirr) of God becomes manifested to
him. This He did, because the vision that consists in a thing's
seeing itself by means of itself is not like its vision of itself in

[3]These degrees each comprise complex and simple numbers, just as a species
can encompass both genera and individuals. The gradations are regular and
move from one in the first degree, ten in the second, one hundred in the
third, a thousand in the fourth, and so on.

[4]Nature is Real Being, yet from it multiple manifestations which are par-
ticularized are formed.

[5]Nature may, according to the Sufis, be perceived as all the particular forms
of creation combined, that is, as a universal; or as a universal form of
Reality that reveals itself as individualized or particular aspects.

[6]Where Absolute Being is reflected, this necessarily means "relative" existence.

something else that serves as a mirror for it: therefore God appears to Himself in a form given by the place in which He is seen (i.e. the mirror), and He would not appear thus objectively without the existence of this place and His epiphany to Himself therein. God had already brought the universe into being with an existence resembling that of a fashioned soulless body, and it was like an unpolished mirror.[7] Now, it belongs to the Divine decree of creation that He did not fashion any place but such as must of necessity receive a Divine soul, which God has described as having been breathed into it; and this denotes the acquisition by that fashioned form of capacity to receive the emanation (fayd), i.e., the perpetual self-manifestation (tajalli) which has never ceased and never shall. It remains to speak of the recipient of the emanation. The recipient proceeds from naught but His most hold emanation,[8] for the whole affair of existence begins and ends with Him: to Him it shall return, even as from Him it began.

The Divine will to display His attributes entailed the polishing of the mirror of the universe. Adam (the human essence) was the very polishing of that mirror and the soul of that form, and the angels are some of the faculties of that form, viz., the form of the universe which the Sufis in their technical language describe as the Great Man, for the angels in relation to it are as the spiritual and corporeal faculties in the human organism.[9]. . . The aforesaid microcosmic being is named a Man (insan) and a Vicegerent (khalifa). He is named a Man on account of the universality of his organism and because he comprises all realities. Moreover, he stands to God as the pupil (insan), which is the instrument of vision, to the eye; and for this reason he is named a Man. By means of him God beheld His creatures and had

---

[7] This cosmology is abstruse and difficult to explain. Rom Landau has described it as well as can be expected: "The world of things was brought into existence before the creation of Man, in so far as every Divine attribute (universal) logically implies the existence of its corresponding particular, which is the Essence individualized by that relation, whereas Man alone is the Essence individualized by all relations together. Since the universe could not manifest the unity of Being until Man appeared in it, it was like an unpolished mirror or a body without a soul." (See Rom Lamdau, *The Philosophy of Ibn 'Arabi* (London: Allen & Unwin, 1959.)

[8] To the Sufi the most "holy emanation" is the eternal Essence manifesting to itself. This is a state where no distinctions exist. Man is capable of perceiving this Essence in that God is revealed to modes of Himself (Man), as each mode becomes capable of such capacity.

[9] R.A. Nicholson notes that with the Sufis Man unites all aspects of God—the oneness of the Essence, plurality of the Divine attributes, and the world of nature. Further, this truth cannot be apprehended except through mystical perception.

mercy on them.[10] He is Man, the originated in his body, the
eternal in his spirit; the organism everlasting in his essence, the
Word that divides and unites. The universe was completed by
his existence, for he is to the universe what the bezel is to the
seal—the bezel whereon is graven the signature that the King
seals on his treasures.[11] Therefore He named him a Vicegerent,
because he guards the creatures of God just as the King guards
his treasuries by sealing them; and so long as the King's seal remains on them, none dares to open them save by his leave. God
made him His Vicegerent in the guardianship of the universe,
and it continues to be guarded whilst this Perfect Man is there.
Dost not thou see that when he shall depart to the next world
and his seal shall be removed from the treasury of this world,
there shall no more remain in it that which God stored therein,
but the treasure shall go forth, and every type shall return to its
ideal antitype, and all existence shall be transferred to the next
world and sealed on the treasury of the next world for ever and
ever?

This was the knowledge of Seth, and it is his knowledge that
replenishes every spirit that discourses on such a theme except
the spirit of the Seal (the Perfect Man), to whom replenish-
ment comes from God alone, not from any spirit; nay, his spirit
replenishes all other spirits. And though he does not apprehend
that of himself during the time of his manifestation in the body,
yet in respect of his real nature and rank he knows it all essentially, just as he is ignorant thereof in respect of his being compounded of elements. He is the knowing one and the ignorant,
for as the Origin (God) is capable of endowment with contrary
attributes—the Majestical, the Beautiful, the Inward, the Outward, the First, the Last—so is he capable thereof, since he is
identical ('ayn) with God, not other than He.[12] Therefore he
knows and knows not, perceives and perceives not, beholds and
beholds not.

He praises me by manifesting my perfections and creating me in
   His form,
And I praise Him by manifesting His perfections and obeying
   Him.
How can He be independent when I help and aid Him? (because
   the Divine attributes derive the possibility of manifestation
   from their human correlates).

[10]By creating them.

[11]Within man's heart there are engraved the Divine names of God, including
the greatest name of all—that is, the Essence! This is the treasure.

[12]While man is limited by his individualization, he is still an Absolute Being,
and in that sense his limitations are unreal or illusory.

For that cause God brought me into existence.
And I know Him and bring Him into existence in my knowledge
   and contemplation of Him.

The believer praises the God who is in his form of belief and
with whom he has connected himself. He praises none but himself, for his God is made by himself, and to praise the work is
to praise the maker of it: its excellence or imperfection belongs
to its maker. For this reason he blames the beliefs of others,
which he would not do, if he were just. Beyond doubt, the worshipper of this particular God shows ignorance when he criticizes
others on account of their beliefs. If he understood the saying of
Junayd, "The colour of the water is the colour of the vessel containing it," he would not interfere with the beliefs of others, but
would perceive God in every form and in every belief.[13] He has
opinion, not knowledge: therefore God said, "I am in My servant's opinion of Me," i.e., "I do not manifest Myself to him
save in the form of his belief." God is absolute or restricted, as
He pleases; and the God of religious belief is subject to limitations, for He is the God who is contained in the heart of His
servant. But the absolute God is not contained by anything, for
He is the being of all things and the being of Himself, and a
thing is not said either to contain itself or not to contain itself.

Selections from A Collection of Mystical Odes
(Tarjumanu Al-Ashwaq)

VII

1. As I kissed the Black Stone,[14] friendly women thronged

---

[13]God is perceived according to the believer's own perception and capacity.
The mystic alone sees God as singular in all manifestations, for the mystic's
heart is all-receptive, all-perceiving. He sees God both as multiple and unitive.

[14]The worship of stones is an ancient form of Semitic cults, and can be
found in early Judaism when Jacob used a stone as his pillow, then as a
pillar and as a libation when he poured oil on it. At Mecca a principal object of sacred veneration is a stone, which is inserted in the wall of the holy
Kaabah or house of God. This stone is believed to be one of the stones of
Paradise. It was originally white, but has been blackened by the kisses of
believing yet sinful lips. The Black Stone, which Moslems call "the right
hand of God on earth," was supposed to have been given to Abraham by the
archangel Gabriel.

around me; they came to perform the circumambulation
with veiled faces.

2. They uncovered the (faces like) sunbeams and said to me,
"Beware! for the death of the soul is in thy looking at us.

3. How many aspiring souls have we killed already at al-
Muhassab of Mina, beside the pebble-heaps,

4. And in Sarhat al-Wadi and the mountains of Rama and Jam'
and at the dispersion from 'Arafat!

5. Dost not thou see that beauty robs him who hath modesty,
and therefore it is called the robber of virtues?

6. Our trysting-place after the circumambulation is at Zamzam
beside the midmost tent, beside the rocks.

7. There everyone whom anguish hath emaciated is restored
to health by the love-desire that perfumed women stir in
him.

8. When they are afraid they let fall their hair, so that they
are hidden by their tresses as it were by robes of darkness."

COMMENTARY

1. "As I kissed the Black Stone," i.e. when the Holy Hand
was outstretched to me that I might take upon it the Divine
oath of allegiance, referring to the verse "Those who swear
fealty to thee swear fealty to God; the hand of God is over
their hands" (Koran XLVIII. 10).

"Friendly women," i.e. the angels who go round the throne of
God (Koran XXXIX. 75).

2. "The death of the soul," etc.: these spirits say, "Do not
look at us, lest thou fall passionately in love with us. Thou wert
created for God, not for us, and if thou wilt be veiled by us
from Him, He will cause thee to pass away from thy existence
through Him, and thou wilt perish."

3. "Have we killed," i.e. spirits like unto us, for the above-
mentioned angels who go round the Throne have no relationship
except with pilgrims circumambulating the Ka'ba.

5. "Beauty robs him who hath modesty," since the vision of
Beauty enraptures whosoever beholds it.

"The robber of virtues," i.e. it takes away all delight in the
vision of beauty from him who acts at the bidding of the possessor of this beauty; and sometimes the beauteous one bids
thee to do that which stands between thee and glorious things,
inasmuch as those things are gained by means of hateful actions: the Tradition declares that Paradise is encompassed by
things which thou dislikest.

6. "At Zamzam," i.e. in the station of the life which thou
yearnest for.

"Beside the midmost tent," i.e. the intermediate world which
divides the spiritual from the corporeal world.

"Beside the rocks," i.e. the sensible bodies in which the holy
spiritual beings take their abode. He means that these spirits in
these imaginary forms are metaphorical and transient, for they
vanish from the dreamer as soon as he wakes and from the seer
as soon as he returns to his senses. He warns thee not to be deceived by the manifestations of phenomenal beauty, inasmuch as
all save God is unreal, i.e. not-being like unto thyself; therefore
be His that He may be thine.

7. In the intermediate world whosoever loves these spiritual
beings dwelling in sensible bodies derives refreshment from the
world of breaths and scents because the spirit and the form are
there united, so that the delight is double.

8. When these phantoms are afraid that their absoluteness
will be limited by their confinement in forms, they cause thee to
perceive that they are a veil which hides something more subtle
than what thou seest, and conceal themselves from thee and quit
these forms and once more enjoy infinite freedom.

XVI

1. They (the women) mounted the howdahs on the swift
   camels and placed in them the (damsels like) marble stat-
   ues and full moons,

2. And promised my heart that they should return; but do the
   fair promise anything except deceit?

3. And she saluted with her henna-tipped fingers for the leave-
   taking, and let fall tears that excited the flames (of desire).

4. When she turned her back with the purpose of making for
   al-Khawarnaq and as-Sadir.

5. I cried out after them, "Perdition!" She answered and said,
   "Dost thou invoke perdition?

6. Then invoke it not only once, but cry 'Perdition!' many
   times."

7. O dove of the arak trees, have a little pity on me! for parting only increased thy moans,

8. And thy lamentation, O dove, inflames the longing lover,
   excites the jealous,

9. Melts the heart, drives off sleep, and doubles our desires and
   sighing.

10. Death hovers because of the dove's lamentation, and we beg
    him to spare us a little while,

11. That perchance a breath from the zephyr of Hajir may sweep towards us rain-clouds,

12. By means of which thou wilt satisfy thirsty souls; but thy clouds only flee farther than before.

13. O watcher of the star, be my boon-companion, and O wakeful spy on the lightning, be my nocturnal comrade!

14. O sleeper in the night, thou didst welcome sleep and inhabit the tombs ere thy death.

15. But hadst thou been in love with the fond maiden, thou wouldst have gained, through her, happiness and joy,

16. Giving to the fair (women) the wines of intimacy, conversing secretly with the suns, and flattering the full moons.

COMMENTARY

1. "The camels" are the human faculties, "the howdahs" are the actions which they are charged to perform, "the damsels" in the howdahs are the mystical sciences and the perfect sorts of knowledge.

3. He says, "This Divine subtlety, being acquired and not given directly, is subject to a change produced by contact with phenomena"; this change he indicates by speaking of "her henna-tipped fingers," as though it were the modification of unity by a kind of association. Nevertheless, her staying in the heart is more desirable than her going, for she protects the gnostic as long as she is there.

"And let fall tears," etc.: she let loose in the heart sciences of contemplation which produced an intense yearning.

4. "Al-Khawarnaq and as-Sadir," i.e. the Divine presence.

5. "Perdition!" i.e. death to the phenomenal world now that these sublime mysteries have vanished from it.

"Dost thou invoke perdition?" i.e. why dost thou not see the face of God in everything, in light and darkness, in simple and composite, in subtle and gross, in order that thou mayst not feel the grief of parting.

6. "Cry 'Perdition!' many times" (cf. Koran XXV. 15), i.e. not only in this station but in every station in which thou art placed, for thou must bid farewell to every one of them, and thou canst not fail to be grieved, since, whenever the form of the Truth disappears from thee, thou imaginest that He has left thee; but He has not left thee, and it is only thy remaining with thyself that veils from thee the vision of that which pervades the whole of creation.

7. "O dove of the arak trees": he addresses holy influences of Divine pleasure which have descended upon him.

"Have a little pity on me!" i.e. pity my weakness and inability to attain unto thy purity.

"For parting only increased thy moans": he says, "Inasmuch as thy substance only exists through and in me, and I am diverted from thee by the dark world of phenomena which keeps me in bondage, for this cause thou art lamenting thy separation from me."

8. "And thy lamentation," etc., i.e. we who seek the unbounded freedom of the celestial world should weep more bitterly than thou.

"Excites the jealous": jealousy arises from regarding others, and he who beholds God in everything feels no jealousy, for God is One; but since God manifests Himself in various forms, the term "jealousy" is applicable to Him.

10. "Death," i.e. the station in which the subtle principle of Man is severed from its governance of this dark body for the sake of the Divine subtleties which are conveyed to it by the above-mentioned holy influences.

11. "Hajir" denotes here the most inaccessible veil of the Divine glory. No phenomenal being can attain to the immediate experience thereof, but scents of it blow over the hearts of gnostics in virtue of a kind of amorous affection.

"Rain-clouds," i.e. sciences and diverse sorts of knowledge belonging to the most holy Essence.

13. "O watcher of the star," in reference to keeping in mind that which the sciences offer in their various connexions.

"O wakeful spy on the lightning": the lightning is a *locus* of manifestation of the Essence. The author says, addressing one who seeks it, "Our quest is the same, be my comrade in the night."

14. This verse may be applied either to the heedless or to the unconscious.

15. "The fond maiden," i.e. the Essential subtlety which is the gnostic's object of desire.

"Through her": although She is unattainable, yet through her manifestation to thee all that thou hast is baptized for thee, and thy whole kingdom is displayed to thee by that Essential form.

16. "Conversing secretly with the suns," etc., in reference to the Traditions which declare that God will be seen in the next world like the sun in a cloudless sky or like the moon when she is full.

XXVIII

1. Between al-Naqa and La'la' are the gazelles of Dhat al-Ajra',
2. Grazing there in a dense covert of tangled shrubs, and pasturing.
3. New moons never rose on the horizon of that hill
4. But I wished, from fear, that they had not risen.
5. And never appeared a flash from the lightning of that firestone
6. But I desired, for my feeling's sake, that it had not flashed.
7. O my tears, flow! O mine eye, cease not to shed tears!
8. O my sighs, ascend! O my heart, split!
9. And thou, O camel-driver, go slowly, for the fire is between my ribs.
10. From their copious flow through fear of parting my tears have all been spent,
11. So that, when the time of starting comes, thou wilt not find an eye to weep.
12. Set forth, then, to the valley of the curving sands, their abode and my death-bed——
13. There are those whom I love, beside the waters of al-Ajra'——
14. And call to them, "Who will help a youth burning with desire, one dismissed,
15. Whose sorrows have thrown him into a bewilderment which is the last remnant of ruin?
16. O moon beneath a darkness, take from him something and leave something,
17. And bestow on him a glance from behind yonder veil,
18. Because he is too weak to apprehend the terrible beauty,
19. Or flatter him with hopes, that perchance he may be revived or may understand.
20. He is a dead man between al-Naqa and La'la'.
21. For I am dead of despair and anguish, as though I were fixed in my place.
22. The East Wind did not tell the truth when it brought cheating phantoms.
23. Sometimes the wind deceives when it causes thee to hear what is not (really) heard.

COMMENTARY

1. "Between al-Naqa and La'la'," etc., i.e. between the hill of white musk, on which the vision of God, and the place of frenzied love for Him, are diverse sorts of knowledge connected with the stations of abstraction.

2. "In a dense covert of tangled shrubs," i.e. the world of phenomenal admixture and interdependence.

3. "New moons," i.e. Divine manifestations.

4. "From fear," i.e. from fear that the beholder might pass away in himself from himself, and that his essence might perish, whereas his object is to continue subsistent through God and for God; or from fear that he should imagine the manifestation to be according to the essential nature of God in Himself (which is impossible), and not according to the nature of the recipient. The former belief, which involves the comprehension of God by the person to whom the manifestation is made, agrees with the doctrine of some speculative theologians, who maintain that our knowledge of God and Gabriel's knowledge of Him and His knowledge of Himself are the same. How far is this from the truth!

5. "A flesh from the lightning of that fire-stone," i.e. an inanimate, phenomenal, and earthly manifestation.

9. "O camel-driver," i.e. the voice of God calling the aspirations to Himself.

"The fire," i.e. the fire of Love.

10-11. He says that his eyes have been melted away by the tears which he shed in anticipation of parting.

12. "To the valley of the curving sands," i.e. the station of mercy and tenderness.

"My death," because the Divine mercy causes him to pass away in bewilderment.

13. "Beside the waters of al-Ajra'": because this mercy is the result of painful self-mortification.

14. "One dismissed," i.e. one who has come to himself again after contemplation, according to the tradition that God says, after having shown Himself to His servants in Paradise, "Send them back to their pavilions."

16. "A darkness," i.e. the forms in which the manifestation takes place.

"Take from him something," etc., i.e. take from him whatever is related to himself, and leave whatever is not related to himself, so that only the Divine Spirit may remain in him.

21. "For I am dead of despair and anguish," i.e. I despair of attaining the reality of that which I seek, and I grieve for the time spent in a vain search for it.

"As though I were fixed in my place," i.e. I cannot escape from my present state, inasmuch as it is without place, quantity, and quality, being purely transcendental.

22. "Cheating phantoms," i.e. the similes and images in which God, who has no like, is presented to us by the world of breaths.

XXIX

1. May my father be the ransom of the boughs swaying to and fro as they bend, bending their tresses towards the cheeks!

2. Loosing plaited locks of hair; soft in their joints and bends;

3. Trailing skirts of haughtiness; clad in embroidered garments of beauty;

4. Which from modesty grudge to bestow their loveliness; which give old heirlooms and new gifts;

5. Which charm by their laughing and smiling mouths; whose lips are sweet to kiss;

6. Whose bare limbs are dainty; which have swelling breasts and offer choice presents;

7. Luring ears and souls, when they converse, by their wondrous witchery;

8. Covering their faces for shame, taking captive thereby the devout and fearing heart;

9. Displaying teeth like pearls, healing with their saliva one who is feeble and wasted;

10. Darting from their eyes glances which pierce a heart experienced in the wars and used to combat;

11. Making rise from their bosoms new moons which suffer no eclipse on becoming full;

12. Causing tears to flow as from rain-clouds, causing sighs to be heard like the crash of thunder.

13. O my two comrades, may my life-blood be the ransom of a slender girl who bestowed on me favours and bounties!

14. She established the harmony of union, for she is our principle of harmony: she is both Arab and foreign; she makes the gnostic forget.

15. Whenever she gazes, she draws against thee trenchant swords, and her front teeth show to thee a dazzling levin.

16. O my comrades, halt beside the guarded pasture of Hajir! Halt, halt, O my comrades,

17. That I may ask where their camels have turned, for I have plunged into places of destruction and death,

18. And scenes known to me and unknown, with a swift camel which complains of her worn hoofs and of deserts and wildernesses,

19. A camel whose flanks are lean and whose rapid journeying caused her to lose her strength and the fat of her hump,

20. Until I brought her to a halt in the sandy tract of Hajir and saw she-camels followed by young ones at al-Uthayl.

21. They were led by a moon of awful mien, and I clasped him to my ribs for fear that he should depart,

22. A moon that appeared in the circumambulation, and while he circumambulated me I was not circumambulating any-one except him.

23. He was effacing his footprints with the train of his robe, so that thou wouldst be bewildered even if thou wert the guide tracing out his track.

COMMENTARY

1. "My father," i.e. Universal Reason.

"The boughs," i.e. the Attributes which bear Divine knowledge to gnostics and mercifully incline towards them.

2. "Locks of hair," i.e. hidden sciences and mysteries. They are called "plaited" in allusion to the various degrees of knowledge.

"Soft," in respect of their graciously inclining to us.

"In their joints and bends," in reference to the conjunction of real and phenomenal qualities.

3. "Trailing skirts," etc., because of the loftiness of their rank.

"Clad in embroidered garments," etc., i.e. appearing in diverse beautiful shapes.

4. "Which from modesty," etc., referring to the Tradition, "Do not bestow wisdom except on those who are worthy of it, lest ye do it a wrong," since contemplation is not vouchsafed to everyone.

"Old heirlooms," i.e. knowledge demonstrated by proofs derived from another.

"New gifts," i.e. knowledge of which the proof is bestowed by God and occurs to one's own mind as the result of sound reflec-tion.

8. "Covering their faces for shame," i.e. they are ashamed to reveal themselves to those whose hearts are generally occupied with something other than God, viz. the ordinary believers described in Koran IX.103.

9. "Teeth like pearls," i.e. the sciences of Divine majesty.

10. "Experienced in the wars," etc., i.e. able to distinguish the real from the phenomenal in the similitudes presented to the eye.

11. "From their bosoms," i.e. from the Divine attributes.

"New Moons," i.e. a manifestation in the horizon.

"Which suffer no eclipse," i.e. they are not subject to any natural lust that veils them from the Divine Ideas.

13. "A slender girl," i.e. the single, subtle, and essential knowledge of God.

14. "She established the harmony of union," i.e. this knowledge concentrated me upon myself and united me with my Lord.

"Arab," i.e. it caused me to know myself from myself.

"Foreign," i.e. it caused me to know myself from God, because the Divine knowledge is synthetic and does not admit of analysis except by means of comparison; and since comparison is impossible, therefore analysis is impossible; whence it follows that synthesis also is impossible, and I only use the latter term in order to convey to the reader's intelligence a meaning that is not to be apprehended save by immediate feeling and intuition.

"Forget," i.e. his knowledge and himself.

15. "A dazzling levin," i.e. a manifestation of the Essence in the state of beauty and joy.

16. "O my comrades": he means his understanding and his faith.

17. "Their camels," i.e. the aspirations which carry the sciences and subtle essences of man to their goal.

18. "A swift camel," i.e. an aspiration in himself.

19. "Whose rapid journeying," etc., i.e. this aspiration was connected with many aspects of plurality which disappeared in the course of its journey towards Unity.

20. "In the sandy tract of Hajir," i.e. a state which enabled me to discriminate between phenomena and prevented me from regarding anything except what this state revealed to me.

"She-camels followed by young ones," i.e. original sciences from which other sciences are derived.

21. "A moon of awful mien," i.e. a manifestation of Divine majesty in the heart.

23. "His footprints," i.e. the evidences which He adduced as a clue to Himself.

"The train of his robe," i.e. His uniqueness and incomparability.

"So that thou wouldst be bewildered," i.e. our knowledge of Him is ignorance and bewilderment and helplessness. He says that in order that gnostics may recognize the limits of their knowledge of God.

LVIII

1. Oh, is there any way to the damsels bright and fair?
   And is there anyone who will show me their traces?

2. And can I halt at night beside the tents of the curving sand? And can I rest at noon in the shade of the arak trees?

3. The tongue of inward feeling spoke, informing me that she says, "Wish for that which is attainable."

4. My love for thee is whole, O thou end of my hopes, and because of that love my heart is sick.

5. Thou art exalted, a full moon rising over the heart, a moon that never sets after it hath risen.

6. May I be thy ransom, O thou who art glorious in beauty and pride! for thou hast no equal amongst the fair.

7. Thy gardens are wet with dew and thy roses are blooming, and thy beauty is passionately loved: it is welcome to all.

8. Thy flowers are smiling and thy boughs are fresh: wherever they bend, the winds bend towards them.

9. Thy grace is tempting and thy look piercing: armed with it the knight, affliction, rushes upon me.

COMMENTARY

1. "The damsels bright and fair," i.e. the knowledge derived from the manifestations of His Beautiful Name.

2. "The tents of the curving sand," i.e. the stations of Divine favour.

"The shade of the arak trees," i.e. contemplation of the pure and holy Presence.

3. This station is gained only by striving and sincere application, not by wishing. "Travel that thou mayst attain."

5. "A moon that never sets," etc.: he points out that God never manifests Himself to anything and then becomes veiled from it afterwards.

7. "Thy gardens are wet with dew," i.e. all Thy creatures are replenished by the Divine qualities which are revealed to them.

"Thy roses are blooming," in reference to a particular manifestation which destroys every blameworthy quality.

"It is welcome," i.e. it is loved for its essence.

8. "Thy flowers," etc., i.e. Thy knowledge is welcome to the heart.

"Thy boughs," i.e. the spiritual influences which convey Thy knowledge.

ABDUL QADIR

Selections from The Revelations of the Unseen (Futuh Al-Ghaib)

The Third Discourse

And he said may God be pleased with him.

When the servant of God is in a trial he first tries to escape

from it with his own efforts, and when he fails in this he seeks
the help of others from among men such as the kings and men
of authority, people of the world, men of wealth, and in the case
of illness and physical suffering, from physicians and doctors;
but if the escape is not secured by these he then turns towards
his Creator and Lord the Great and Mighty and applies to Him
with prayer and humility and praise. So long as he finds the
resources in his own self he does not turn towards the people
and so long as he finds resources in the people he does not turn
towards the Creator.

Further, when he does not get any help from God he throws
himself in His presence and continues in this state, begging and
praying and humbly entreating and praising and submitting his
neediness in fear and hope. God the Great and Mighty, however,
tires him out in his prayer and does not accept it until he is
completely disappointed in all the means of the world. The
decree of God and His work then manifest themselves through
him and this servant of God passes away from all the worldly
means and the activities and efforts of the world and retains just
his soul.

At this stage he sees nothing but the work of God the Great
and Mighty and becomes, of necessity, a believer in the unity of
God (Tawhid) to the degree of certainty, that in reality there is
no doer of anything excepting God and no mover and stopper
excepting Him and no good and no evil and no loss and no gain
and no benefit and no conferring and no withholding and no
opening and no closing and no death and no life and no honour
and no dishonour and no affluence and no poverty but in the
hand of God.

He then becomes in the presence of God as a sucking baby in
the hands of its nurse and a dead body in the hands of the person who gives it the funeral bath and a ball is before the stick
of the polo-player,—kept revolving and rolling and changing position after position and condition after condition and he feels no
strength either in his own self or in others besides himself for
any movement. He thus vanishes from his own self out into the
work of his Master.

So he sees nothing but his Master and His work, and hears
and understands nothing excepting Him. If he sees anything it is
His work and if he hears and knows anything, he hears His word
and knows through His knowledge and he becomes gifted with
His gifts and becomes lucky through His nearness and through
his nearness he becomes decorated and honoured and becomes
pleased and comforted and satisfied with His promise and is
drawn towards His word and he feels aversion for and is re-
pelled from those besides Him and he desires and relies on His

remembrance and he becomes established in Him, the Great and Mighty, and relies on Him and obtains guidance from, and clothes and dresses himself with, the light of His knowledge and is apprised of the rare points of His knowledge and of the secrets of His power and he hears and remembers only from Him the Great, the Mighty, and then offers thanks and praise therefor and takes to prayer.

The Sixth Discourse

He (may Allah be pleased with him) said:

Vanish from the people by the command of God, and from your desire by His order, and from your will by His action, so that you may become fit to be the vessel of the knowledge of God. Now the sign of your vanishing from the people is that you should be completely cut off from them and from all social contacts with them and make your mind free from all expectations for what is in their control.

And the sign of your vanishing from your desires is that you should discard all efforts for and contact with worldly means in acquiring any benefit and avoiding any harm and you should not move yourself in your own interest and not rely on yourself in matters concerning yourself and not protect yourself nor help yourself, but leave the whole thing entirely to God because He had the charge of it in the beginning and so will He have it till the end, just as the charge rested on Him when you were hidden in the womb of your mother as also when you were being suckled as a baby in the cradle.

And the sign of your vanishing from your will by the action of God is that you should never entertain any resolve and that you should have no objective, nor should any feeling of need be left in you nor any purpose, because you will not have any objective other than the one of God. Instead, the action of God will be manifested in you, so that at the time of the operation of the will and act of God you will maintain passivity of the organs of your body, calmness of your heart, broadness of your mind, and keep your face shining and your inside flourishing and you will be above the need of things because of your connection with their Creator. The hand of Power will keep you in movement and the tongue of Eternity will be calling you and the Lord of the Universe will be teaching you and will clothe you with light from Himself and with spiritual dress and will install you in the ranks of past men of knowledge.

After this experience you will ever remain broken down so that neither any sensual desire nor any will stays in you, like a

broken vessel which retains neither any water nor any dreg. And
you will be devoid of all human actions so that your inner self
will accept nothing but the will of God. At this stage miracles
and supernatural things will be ascribed to you. These things
will be seen as if proceeding from you whereas in fact they will
be acts of God and His will.

Thus you will be admitted in the company of those whose
hearts have been smashed and their animal passions have vanished, whereafter they have been inspired with Divine will and
new desires of the daily existence. It is in reference to this stage
that the Holy Prophet (peace and blessings of God be upon
him) says: "Three things out of your world have been made
dear to me—perfume, women, and prayer, wherein has been re-
posed the coolness of my eyes." Indeed things have been
ascribed to him after they have first gone out of and vanished
from him, as we have already hinted. God says, "I am with
those who are broken-hearted on account of Me."

So God the Exalted will not be with you unless all your
desires and your will are smashed. And when they are smashed
and nothing is left in you and you are fit for nothing but Him,
God will create you afresh and will give you a new will-power
wherewith to will. And if in the newly-created will there is
found again even the slightest tinge of yourself, God the Exalted
will break this one also, so that you will always remain broken-
hearted. In this way, He will go on creating new wills in you
and on yourself being found in it, He will smash it every time,
till at last the destiny reaches its end and the meeting of the
Lord takes place. And this is the meaning of the Divine words:
"I am with those who are broken-hearted on My account." And
the meaning of our words: "Yourself being found in it" is that
you get fixed up and satisfied in your new desires.

God says in one of His unofficial revelations to the Holy
Prophet (called *Hadith Qudsi*): "My faithful servant constantly
seeks My nearness through optional prayers till I make him my
friend and when I make him my friend, I become his ear with
which he hears, and his eyes with which he sees, and his hands
with which he holds things, and his legs with which he walks, i.e.
he hears through Me, sees through Me, holds through Me and
understands through Me." This is undoubtedly the state of *fana*
(or self-annihilation). And when you are annihilated in respect
of yourself and the creation and since the creation is good or
bad, as you yourself are good or bad, you will be in no expectation of any good from them nor fear any evil from them. All
that will be left will be now of God alone, as it was before He
started creation, and in His ordination lie good and evil.

So He will give you safety from the evil of His creation and will submerge you under the ocean of His good; thus you will become the focusing point of all that is good and the springhead of all blessings and happiness and pleasure and light and peace and tranquillity. So *fana* or self-annihilation is the aim and object and the final end and base of the journey of the saints.

The Seventeenth Discourse

He (God be pleased with him) said:

When you are united with God and you attain to His nearness by His attraction and help; and the meaning of union with God is your going out of the creation and desire and purpose and becoming established in His action and His purpose without there being any movement in you or through you in His creation unless it be with His order and action and command. So this is the state of *Fana* (annihilation) by which is meant union with God. But union with God, the Mighty, the Glorious, is not like union with anything in His creation, in an understandable and appointed manner:

Nothing is like unto a likeness to Him and He is the Hearing, the Seeing.

The Creator is above being similar to His creatures or bearing any resemblance to anything that He has made. Thus union with Him is a thing which is well known to people, having this experience of union, because of their realisation of it. Everyone of them has a different experience in this matter which is peculiar to himself and which cannot be shared by any other person.

With everyone among the Prophets and Messengers and the Saints (*Awliya*) of God is to be found a secret which cannot be known by any other person, so much so that sometimes it so happens that the spiritual pupil (Murid) holds a secret which is not known to the spiritual preceptor (Shaikh); and sometimes the Shaikh holds a secret which is not known to the Murid although the latter may in his spiritual journey have approached the very threshold of the door of the spiritual state of his Shaikh. When the Murid reaches the spiritual state of the Shaikh, he is made to separate himself from the Shaikh and he is cut off from him and God becomes his guardian and He cuts him off from the creation altogether.

Thus the Shaikh becomes like a wet nurse who has stopped suckling the baby after two years. No connection remains with the creation after the disappearance of low desires and human purpose. The Shaikh is needed by him so long as he is infested with low desires and purposes which have to be crushed. But af-

ter the disappearance of these weaknesses of the flesh there remains no need of the Shaikh because there remains no stain and
no defect in the Murid.

Thus when you unite with God as we have described, you will
feel safe for ever from whatsoever is besides Him. You will certainly see no existence at all besides His. Either in profit or in
loss or in gifts or with their withholding, in fear or in hope, you
will only find Him, the Mighty, the Glorious, who is worthy to
be feared and worthy to be sought protection from. So you keep
on looking at His acts for ever and expecting His order and remain engaged in obedience to Him, cut off from the whole of
His creation whether of this world or of the hereafter. Let not
your heart be attached to anything in His creation.

SANA'I OF GHAZNA

Selections from The Enclosed Garden of the Truth (Hadiqatu' L-Haqiqat)

On the Cause of our Maintenance

Seest thou not that before the beginning of thy existence God
the All-wise, the Ineffable, when He had created thee in the
womb gave thee of blood thy sustenance for nine months? Thy
mother nourished thee in her womb, then after nine months
brought thee forth; that door of support He quickly closed on
thee, and bestowed on thee two better doors, for He then acquainted thee with the breast,—two fountains running for thee
day and night; He said, Drink of these both; eat and welcome,
for it is not forbidden thee. When after two years she weaned
thee, all became changed for thee; He gave thee thy sustenance
by means of thy two hands and feet,—"Take it by means of
these, and by those go where thou wilt!" If He closed the two
doors against thee, it is but right, for instead of two, four doors
have appeared,—"Take by means of these, by those go on to victory; go seek thy daily bread throughout the world!"

O seeker of the shell of the pearl of "Unless," lay down clothing and life on the shore of "Not";[1] God's existence inclines

[1] This embraces the affirmation and negation of God. A Sufi saying is "first
enter the world of annihilation, that so thou mayest find the jewel of eternal
life."

only towards him who has ceased to exist; non-existence is the
necessary provision for the journey. Till in annihilation thou lay
aside thy cap thou wilt not set thy face on the road to eternal
life; when thou becomest nothing, thou runnest towards God;
the path of mendicancy leads up to Him. If fortune crushes thee
down, the most excellent of Creators will restore thee. Rise, and
have done with false fables; forsake thy ignoble passions, and
come hither.[2]

In His Magnification

When He shows His Nature to His creation, into what mirror
shall He enter?[3] The burden of proclaiming the Unity not everyone bears; the desire of proclaiming the Unity not everyone
tastes. In every dwelling is God adored; but the Adored cannot
be circumscribed by any dwelling. The earthly man, accompanied by unbelief and anthropomorphism, wanders from the road;
on the road of truth thou must abandon thy passions;—rise, and
forsake this vile sensual nature; when thou hast come forth
from Abode and Life, then, through God, thou wilt see God.

How shall this sluggish body worship Him, or how can Life
and Soul know Him? A ruby of the mine is but a pebble there;
the soul's wisdom talks but folly there. Speechlessness is
praise,—enough of thy speech; babbling will be but sorrow and
harm to thee,—have done!

His Nature, to one who knows Him and is truly learned, is
about "How" and "What" and "Is it not" and "Why." His
creative power is manifest, the justice of His wisdom; His wrath
is secret, the artifice of His Majesty.[4] A form of water and
earth is dazzled by His love, the eye and heart are blinded by
His Nature. Reason in her uncleanness, wishing to see Him,
says, like Moses, "Show me"; when the messenger[5] comes forth
from that glory, she says in its ear, "I turn repentant unto
thee." Discover then the nature of His Being through thy understanding! recite his thousand and one pure names. It is not fitting that His Nature should be covered by our knowledge;
whatever thou hast heard, that is not He. "Point" and "line"
and "surface" in relation to His Nature are as if one should talk

---

[2]This refers to a saying of Mansur Hallaj, who replied when asked by someone to be shown the way to God: "Forsake thy passions, and come hither."
[3]That is, how can God manifest the incomprehensible to be comprehensible.
[4]God's majesty and glory are hidden, but can be seen in His creative power,
in the origin and source of things. His wrath is hidden and is in this case
the artifice of his Majesty.
[5]Reason, the invisible messenger, is meant here.

of His "substance" and "distance" and "six surfaces"; the Author of those three is beyond place; the Creator of these three is not contained in time. No philosopher knows of imperfection in Him, while He knows the secrets of the invisible world; He is acquainted with the recesses of the mind, and the secrets of which as yet there has been formed no sketch upon thy heart.

Kaf and nun are only letters that we write, but what is kun? the hurrying of the agent of the divine decree. If He delays, or acts quickly, it depends not on His weakness; whether He is angry or placable depends not on His hate. His causation is known to neither infidelity nor faith, and neither is acquainted with His Nature. He is pure of those attributes the foolish speak of, purer than the wise can tell.

Reason is made up of confusion and conjecture, both limping over the earth's face. Conjecture and cogitation are no good guides; wherever conjecture and cogitation are, He is not. Conjecture and cogitation are of His creation;[6] man and reason are His newly-ripening plants. Since any affirmation about His Nature is beyond man's province, it is like a statement about his mother by a blind man; the blind man knows he has a mother, but what she is like he cannot imagine; his imagination is without any conception of what things are like, of ugliness and beauty, of inside and outside.

In a world of double aspect such as this, it would be wrong that thou shouldst be He, and He thou.[7] If thou assert Him not, it is not well; if thou assert Him, it is thyself thou assertest, not He. If thou know not (that He is) thou art without religion, and if thou assert Him thou art of those who liken Him. Since He is beyond "where" and "when," how can He become a corner of thy thought? When the wayfarers travel towards Him, they vainly exclaim, "Behold, Behold!"[8] Men of hawk-like boldness are as ringdoves in the street, a collar on their necks, uttering "Where, Where?"

If thou wilt, take hope, or if thou wilt, then fear; the All-wise has created nothing in vain. He knows all that has been done or will be done; thou knowest not,—yet know that He will assuage

---

[6]And therefore must fall immeasurably short of Him.

[7]This is an abstruse phrase explained by the Sufi commentator Abdul Latif as meaning: "In this world of unreality, with two faces and necessary duality, it would be wrong, with your borrowed existence and without discarding self, to claim unity of existence with God and knowledge of Him. If you assert not His Existence and affirm not His Being in its oneness, you are an unbeliever; whereas if you do this, and assert His Existence, whatever you assert is yourself and not He, for He is above and free from anything you imagine and think. He cannot be designated or described by any description, and however you describe Him you fall into the error of 'likening' Him."

[8]"Vainly" because He is not there!

thy pain. In the knowledge of Him is naught better than submission, that so thou mayest learn His wisdom and His clem-
ency.

On Affection and Isolation

The lovers are drunk in His Presence, their reason in their
sleeve and their soul in their hand.[9] Lo, when they urge the
Buraq[10] of their heart on towards Him, they cast all away under
his feet; they throw down life and heart in His path, and make
themselves of His company. In the face of his belief in the
Unity, there exists for him no old or new; all is naught, naught;
He alone is. What worth have reason and life in his eyes? the
heart and the true faith pursue the road together.[11] The veil of
the lovers is very transparent; the tracings on these veils are
very delicate.[12] Love's conqueror is he who is conquered by love;
"love" inverted will itself explain this to thee.[13]

When the clouds fall away from the Sun, the world of love is
filled with light.[14] The cloud is dark and murky as a Magian, but
water may be useful as well as harmful;—a little of it is man's
life, but his life is destroyed by too much of it; so he who believes in the Unity is the beloved of His Presence, though affection, too, is a veil over His glory.[15]

When He admits thee in His court, ask from Him no object
of desire,—ask Himself; when thy Lord has chosen thee for
friendship, thy unabashed eye has seen all there, is to see. The
world of love suffers not duality,—what talk of this of Me and
Thee?

[9] That is, in such a state they are amazed and confounded, reason and soul
escaping from within them.

[10] This is the name of the animal which bore Mohammed on his night journey
to Heaven.

[11] Abdul Latif writes that "according to certain Sufis the heart (mind, dil)
is superior to the spirit (soul, ruh), and religion (din) to life (soul, jan);
for there are unbelieving souls and these, according to the Koran, will die.
The jan aspect of soul then ought to possess religion (din) and faith
(iman)."

[12] The veil is the mystery of the lovers of God; while the tracings are secret
things that are far removed from explanation or interpretation.

[13] The translator writes that the pronoun used here could mean either love or
God. Love in this sense has been interpreted as the essence of God.

[14] The clouds are phenomenal existence, which hides the sun of Truth.

[15] Abdul Latif interprets this as "Though the cloud of mundane existence,
which hides the sun of Reality, be dark and murky (like still water), the end
for which it exists is beneficial though also at times noxious. So with the
unitarian who is the friend of His Presence . . . even though friendship and
affection is a veil which separates us from Him."

When thy Thee-ness leaves thee, fortune will uplift thy state and seat; in a compact of intimacy it is not well to claim to be a friend, and then—still Me and Thee! How shall he that is free become a slave? [16] How canst thou fill a vessel already full? Go thou, all of thee, to His door; for whoso in the world shall present himself there in part only, is wholly naught. [17] When thou hast reached to the kiss and love-glance of the Friend, count poison honey from Him, and the thorn a flower.

On Poverty and Perplexity

He hears the heart's low voice of supplication. He knows when the heart's secret rises up to Him; when supplication opens the door of the heart, its desire comes forward to meet it; the "Here am I" of the Friend goes out to welcome the heart's cry of "O Lord" as it ascends from the high road of acquiescence. One cry of "O Lord" from thee,—from Him two hundred times comes "Here am I"; one "Peace" from thee,—a thousand times He answers "And on thee"; let men do good or ill, His mercy and His bounty still proceed.

Poverty is an ornament in His court,—thou bringest thy worldly stock-in-trade and its profits as a present; but thy long grief is what He will accept, His abundance will receive thy neediness. Bilal[18] whose body's skin was black as a sweetheart's locks, was a friend in His court; his outward garment became as a black mole of amorous allurement upon the face of the maidens of Paradise.

O Thou who marshallest the company of darwishes, O Thou who watchest the sorrow of the sore at heart, heal him who is now like unto a quince,[19] make him like the bowstring who is now bent as the bow.[20] I am utterly helpless in the grasp of poverty; O Thou, who rulest the affairs of men, rule mine. I am solitary in the land of the angels, lonely in the glory of the world of might; the verse of my knowledge has not even a beginning, but the excess of my yearning has no end.

---

[16] Abdul Latif says "How shall he, who deems himself a free man, become a slave or perform God's service? For a vessel already full cannot be filled."

[17] Again Abdul Latif comments on this line: "Go all; that is, in every way be of Him, and in all ways give up thyself to Him; for whoso goes to His court except in completeness, that is, being partly of Him and partly of other than Him, is in every way naught."

[18] One of Mohammed's first converts was a Negro, Bilal.

[19] That is, of yellow color like a quince.

[20] Heal and make him straight again who is now bent with grief.

On Being Glad in God Most High, and Humbling Oneself Before Him

O Life of all the contented, who grantest the desires of the desirous: the acts in me that are right, Thou makest so,—Thou, kinder to me than I am to myself. No bounds are set to Thy mercy, no interruption appears in Thy bounty. Whatever Thou givest, give thy slave piety; accept of him and set him near Thyself. Gladden my heart with the thought of the holiness of religion; make fire of my human body of dust and wind. It is Thine to show mercy and to forgive, mine to stumble and to fall. I am not wise,—receive me, though drunk; I have slipped, take Thou my hand. I know full well that Thou hidest me; Thy screening of me has made me proud. I know not what has been from all eternity condemned to rejection; I know not who will be called at the last. I have no power to anger or to reconcile Thee, nor does my adulation advantage Thee. My straying heart now seeks return to Thee; my uncleanness is drenched by the pupil of my eye.

Show my straying heart a path, open a door before the pupil of my eye, that it [21] may not be proud before Thy works, that it [22] may have no fear before Thy might. O Thou who shepherdest this flock with Thy mercy,—but what speech is all this? they are all Thee.[23] . . . Show Thou mercy on my soul and on my clay, that my soul's sorrow may be assuaged within me. Do Thou cherish me, for others are hard; do Thou receive me, for others themselves are rent asunder.

How can I be intimate with other than Thee? They are dead,—Thou art my sufficient Friend. What is to me the bounty of Theeness and doubleness, so long as I believe that I am I, and Thou art Thou? What to me is all this smoke, in face of Thy fire? Since Thou art, let the existence of all else cease;[24] the world's existence consists in the wind of Thy favour, O Thou, injury from whom is better than the world's gain.

I know not what sort of man he is, who in his folly can ever have sufficiency of Thee. Can a man remain alive without Thy

---

[21] The straying heart is meant here.

[22] The pupil of the eye.

[23] Another commentator, Alau 'd-Din, writes: "What is all this I have been saying about shepherd and sheep? All that is, is Thee, shepherd and Sheep both."

[24] Abdul Latif explains: "Since Thou, who art the permanent root, art, let everyone else, whose existence is contingent, perish; for the perishing branch harms not the root."

succour, or exist apart from Thy favour? How can he grieve who possesses Thee; or how can he prosper who is without Thee? That of which Thou saidst, Eat not, I have eaten; and what Thou forbadest, that have I done; yet if I possess Thee, I am a coin of pure gold, and without Thee, I am a mill-wheel's groaning.[25] I am in an agony for fear of death; be Thou my life, that I die not. Why sendest Thou Thy word and sword to me? Alas for me, who am I apart from Thee?

If Thou receive me, O Thou dependent on no cause,[26] what matters the good or ill of a handful of dust? This is the dust's high honour, that its speech should be in praise of Thee; Thy glory has taken away the dust's dishonour, has exalted its head even to the Throne. Hadst Thou not given the word of permission, who, for that he is so far from Thee, could utter Thy name? Mankind would not have dared to praise Thee in their imperfect speech. What is to be found in our reason or our drunkenness? for we are not, nor have we an existence.

Though we be full of self, purify us from our sins; by some way of deliverance save me from destruction. In presence of Thy decree, though I be wisdom's self, yet who am I that I should count as either good or evil? My evil becomes good when Thou acceptest it; my good, evil when Thou refusest it.

Thou art all, O Lord, both my good and ill; and, wonderful to say, no ill comes from Thee! Only an evil-doer commits evil; Thou canst only be described as altogether good; Thou willest good for Thy servants continually, but the servants themselves know naught of Thee. Within this veil of passion and desire our ignorance can only ask for pardon at the hands of Thy Omniscience. If we have behaved like dogs in our duty, Thou hast found no tigerishness in us,—then pass over our offence.[27] As we stand, awaiting the fulfilment of Thy promised kindness at the bountiful door of the Court of Thy generosity, on Thy side all is abundance; the falling short is in our works.

---

[25]That is, nothing.

[26]Another rendering is "God's essence is independent of cause."

[27]Because tigers are slain or destroyed outright, while dogs are punished more mildly.

MUHAMMAD IQBAL

Selections from The New Rose Garden of Mystery
(Gulishan-i-Raz-i-Jadid)

Question Four

How did the Eternal and the Temporal
Become two things from one,
Dividing all,
The one becoming God,
The other World?
If God is both the knower and the known,
What is this madness curled
Up in the head of man, this mortal clod?

Answer

THE Ego's *raison d'être* is to create
The Other and therefore
It's good that known and know'r
Are not one, but are separate.
The Eternal and the Temporal
Exist because we calculate
And count and measure all;
It is by doing so that we create
The make-believe of Time. We count
Our yesterdays and our tomorrows, and are wont
To think in terms of "is" and "was"
And "may be"; and our nature has
A tendency to drift away
From the Eternal One,
And then, unable to attain again
To Him, pine night and day.
Without Him we are lost;
Without us He can never rest.
Without each other we could never be:
Our separation is duality in unity.
Separation lends eyes to dust
And gives a leaf
Of grass

A mountain's mass
Of grief,
Separation is love's test
And measure and a mirror
Which shows to himself the true lover:
It is by heartache that we live,
And on heartache do lovers thrive.
What is this He-and-I duality,
This great celestial mystery?
An earnest and a guarantee
That we shall always be.
Being's essence shines alike
In multitude and solitude.
The Many and the One;
To live is not to be alone,
But to be in the thick
Of teeming multitude.
Love's vision needs both seer and seen——
Duality in unity;
It even sees itself in company:
Without the loved one it could not have been.
O look at Beauty's revelations
In our assembly-hall:
There is no world, and He is all in all.
The cities, roads and streets we see
Are all hallucinations,
And there are only He and We.
Strange are the ways in which He treats
Us; for at times He turns a stranger's face
To us; at other times He plays
On us as if on lutes.
We sometimes make His images in stone,
And sometimes worship Him as One Unseen.
We tear off Nature's veils
To see the beauty it conceals.
What madness in a mere clod's head
To thirst for Glory's flood!
But blessed is this madness which keeps man alight.
Much as he mourns his severance from God,
In reaching for Him he adds to his height.
Separation has endowed
Him with a vision which has made
His evening bright like dawn.
It is an ordeal of pain
Through which his Self has grown.
Thus he has drawn

A new joy from an ancient grief
By throwing himself into bold relief.
He has strung long pearl-beads of tears
And from a tree of mourning gathered fruit.
    To keep a firm hold on one's self-identity,
    To link mortality and immortality
    Together as compeers——
    O this is great!
What is Love? It is journeying without a break,
Transcending limits, ending ends.
Love knows no ending, no finality;
Its morning has no evening in its wake.
Its path like wisdom's has its turns and bends;
But it goes forward instantaneously, unerringly.
There are a thousand worlds along our way:
How can our journey's course come to a point and stay?
Be ever steadfast, traveller, both in life and death:
Take in your stride all worlds along your path.
To be lost in His sea is not our destiny;
And if you span it, you can never cease to be.
    That Self should be submerged in Self is an impossibility:
    To be the essence of Selfhood is the Self's apogee.

Question Five

O TELL me who I am and then explain
What the exploring of oneself may mean.

Answer

THE Self is all Creation's talisman,
Its all-preserving amulet.
It is as Life that it first emanates.
When Life shakes off its primal dormant state,
Then, big with Self, it procreates
The Many from the One.
If life did not have us to manifest,
Then it could not continue to exist.
If it did not project itself, we could not be.
Life is a boundless sea,
Whose every drop's-heart is a restless wave.
It knows no tranquil state,
Because it must continually create.
It cannot manifest its own Self save

Through individual Selves—through us:
To us it owes its being thus.
Life is a fire; the Selves are all its sparks—
Stars stable and yet always on the move,
Stars shooting in a million arcs.
Enshrined in its retreat above
The teeming multitude,
Life relishes its solitude,
Watching the Others come and go.
Observe its early flutterings and how
It lifts itself from dust to soar.
Concealed from view, it fills
The sky with tumult and uproar,
Intent upon its quest
For ways to manifest
Itself in colours and in smells—
In sensuous phenomena.
The inner ardour of desire
Keeps it excited and afire,
As if against itself at war.
Its war with itself gives to things
A system and a purpose, and it brings
Light to a pinch of dust.
It is its Selfhood that it radiates:
It is an ocean from which emanates
Nothing but pearls. This frame of clay
In nothing but a curtain to be burst
By Selfhood's light, just as at break of day
The sun shines forth,
A glorious birth.
The rising-place of the Self's sun
Is in our inmost breast:
Its essence lights up our dark dust.
You wish to be told who you are
And what exploring of oneself may mean.
I have already told you of the link between
The Body and the Soul. Explore
Your inner world and find your "I".
Exploring oneself is to be reborn
In soul; to cast a lasso on the sky
And seize the Pleiades;
To see without the radiance of the sun;
To wipe out from your heart all hope and fear;
To sunder Moses-like the waters of a river;
To shatter the illusion of sky, earth and sea;
To move a finger and divide the moon;

To issue forth from God's No-Place again,
With Him in you and His world held by you in fee.
But oh! this secret is ineffable;
Communicating it is quite impossible;
For speech is all opaque like clay
And it is only seeing which is crystal-clear:
A hearer cannot be a seer.
What can I say, what can I say
About the "I," its splendour and its might?
It was the "I" that answered the Creator's call[1]
To take up his vicegerency.
Which caused the heavens to quail
And draw back in sheer fright.
The heavens still tremble at its majesty.
It holds in its embrace
Both Time and Space.
It has selected man's heart for its dwelling—
A hut of mud to house a King!
Distinct from Others, yet attached to them;
Absorbed in itself, yet not self-contained.
How is it that Thought is enshrined
Within a pinch of dust,
For its range is so widespread as to burst
All bounds of Space and Time?
It is a prisoner and yet free!
Hunter, quarry, lasso—itself all three!
There is a lamp alight inside your breast,
And bright are the reflections cast
In your mind's mirror by its light.
   Do not forget that you are its trustee.
   How strange you do not care to see
   Your image, your own image, shining bright!

Question Eight

WHAT does the claim, "I am the Truth,"[2] imply?
Was it a mystery or a madman's cry?

[1] The reference is to the Koran (XXXIII. 72): "Verily We proposed to the heavens, to the earth and to the mountains to receive the trust (of responsibility and free will), but they declined the burden; for they were afraid to accept it. Man alone undertook to shoulder it; but even he has proved unequal to it."

[2] "I am the Truth" was the cry of the Muslim mystic Mansur Hallaj. And since Hallaj was living in an orthodox religious world, and the Arabic word for Truth also means God, his ecstatic cry cost him his head.

Answer

LET me explain
To India and Iran again
The meaning of "I am the Truth".
A Magus once, under his breath,
Spoke in the tavern thus:
"Deluded by itself, Life uttered 'I'.
The magic word sent God to sleep
And in His sleep, both long and deep,
He dreamed of us.
It is His dream that we live by.
Whatever we may seem,
We are a dream.
Our 'up and down,' our 'left and right,'
Our motion and our rest,
Our want and quest,
Our wakeful heart,
Our intellect, so keen and bright,
Our speculation and our thought,
Our faith and certainty—
All this is dream,
Whatever it may seem.
You think you are awake, but really
Your eyes are open in deep sleep.
You walk and talk and act
In dream and not in fact.
    When He awakes, there will be no more of
    This strange dream-stuff,
    And you will have to keep
    Your heart's desires as merchandise
    Which no one buys."
It is through thinking that our knowledge grows,
And thinking is determined by
Our sensuous experience.
So when the nature of our senses undergoes
A change, the world is changed for us.
Rest, motion, quality and quantity
Take on a new significance.
It can be said that all this sensuous
World of phenomena, of colour and of smell,
Of earth and sky and house and street,
Is nothing but illusion, dream, deceit,
And hides the face of the Divine One like a veil.
It can be said that all this is mere sorcery
Of sense, delusion of the ear and eye.

True, but the Self does not reside
In the realm of the sensuous,
Nor do our senses intervene
Between the Self and us.
Sight has no access to its shrine.
We see ourselves displayed
Without the mediation of our eyes.
 The Self's day is not measured by
 The revolutions of the sky.
 In your self-observation lies
 No supposition, guess or doubt:
 It is perception out and out.
If you say that the "I"
Is all pure fantasy,
Nothing but an illusory
Thing seen by the mind's eye,
Then tell me whose experience
Is this delusion of the inner sense.
Who is the subject of this fantasy?
Look inward at yourself: are you not he?
Apparent though the world is, yet
You have to prove that it exists;
But doing so resists
A Gabriel's ethereal wit.
The Self is, on the other hand,
Concealed from view, and yet
It is self-evident,
Beyond all argument.
Reflect a little on this and
Endeavour to find out
The meaning of this mystery.
The Self is not Illusion but Reality.
Do not regard it as a barren field;
For it is rich in yield—
The fruit of immortality.
Its separation from the Infinite
Is a true lovers' separation: it
Is union in duality.
A spark can be lent wings to fly
And throbbingly soar to the sky.
The immortality of God
Is not His deeds' reward:
It is an elemental attribute,
Not a sought-after fruit.
Far better is that immortality
Which is won by a borrowed soul

As its love's meed, its frenzy's goal
The being of hill, desert, city, plain
Is nothing and this world is all a vain
Illusion; but the Self enjoys eternity.
Speak no more of a Shankar, a Mansur;
Seek God in your own being's core.
   Lose yourself in your Self to verify
Your being's truth.
   Declare, "I am the Truth," and testify
Your Self and God's Self both.

OMAR KHAYYAM

Selections from The Quatrains of Omar Khayyam

Arise! and come, and of thy courtesy
Resolve my weary heart's perplexity,
   And fill my goblet, so that I may drink,
Or e'er they make their goblets out of me.[1]

In Allah's name, say, wherefore set the wise
Their hearts upon this house of vanities?
   Whene'er they think to rest them from their toils,
Death takes them by the hand, and says, "Arise."

Thus spake an idol to his worshipper,
"Why dost thou worship this dead stone, fair sir?
   'Tis because He who gazeth through thine eyes,
Doth some part of His charms on it confer." [2]

O Thou! to please whose love and wrath as well,
Allah created heaven and likewise hell;
   Thou hast thy court in heaven, and I have naught,
Why not admit me in thy courts to dwell?[3]

What time, my cup in hand, its draughts I drain,
And with rapt heart unconsciousness attain,
   Behold what wondrous miracles are wrought,
Songs flow as water from my burning brain.

[1]To the Sufi, or rather Arabic theology, the heart is the seat of reason.
[2]This means, of course, that all is God, even idols.
[3]The person addressed here is Mohammed. The Sufis, like other mystics and monists, such as the Taoists and Ch'an Buddhists, were fond of dwelling on the opposition between the beautiful and the terrible attributes of Deity. In the case of Taoism and Ch'an Buddhists this tendency translates itself into a fascination with paradox.

There is a mystery I know full well,
Which to all, good and bad, I cannot tell;
   My words are dark, but I cannot unfold
The secrets of the "station" where I dwell.[4]

With outward seeming we can cheat mankind,
But to God's will we can but be resigned;
   The deepest wiles my cunning e'er devised,
To balk resistless fate no way could find.

No heart is there but bleeds when torn from Thee,
No sight so clear but craves Thy face to see;
   And though perchance Thou carest not for them,
No soul is there but pines with care for Thee.

Death's terrors spring from baseless phantasy,
Death yields the tree of immortality;
   Since 'Isa breathed new life into my soul,
Eternal death has washed its hands of me!

In synagogue and cloister, mosque and school,
Hell's terrors and heaven's lures men's bosoms rule,
   But they who master Allah's mysteries,
Sow not this empty chaff their hearts to fool.[5]

You see the world, but all you see is naught,
And all you say, and all you hear is naught,
   Naught the four quarters of the mighty earth,
The secrets treasured in your chamber naught.[6]

What lord is fit to rule but "Truth"? Not one.
What beings disobey His rule? Not one.
   All things that are, are such as He decrees;
And naught is there beside beneath the sun.[7]

To lovers true, what matters dark or fair?
Or if the loved one silk or sackcloth wear,

[4] The "station" here is hale, which in Arabic is a state of ecstasy. More than most Sufis, Khayyam indicates that the ecstatic often achieves his goal in any way he can—hence the overpowering sensuality of some Sufis. The later Taoists also speak lovingly of wine, or any experience that helps them attain that ecstatic insight they yearn for, and which Khayyam is so excellent at expressing.

[5] That is, souls reabsorbed into the Divine Essence have no concern with the material heaven and hell.

[6] Meaning, all is illusion or maya.

[7] The "Truth" is a Sufi name for the Deity.

Or lie on down or dust, or rise to heaven?
Yea though she sink to hell, he'll seek her there.[8]

Wine-houses flourish through this thirst of mine,
Loads of remorse weigh down this back of mine;
   Yet, if I sinned not, what would mercy do?
Mercy depends upon these sins of mine.[9]

Thy being is the being of Another,
Thy passion is the passion of Another.
   Cover thy head, and think, and thou wilt see,
Thy hand is but the cover of Another.[10]

This worldly love of yours is counterfeit,
And, like a half-spent blaze, lacks light and heat;
   True love is his, who for days, months and years,
Rests not, nor sleeps, nor craves for drink or meat.

Why spend life in vainglorious essay
All Being and Not-being to survey?
   Since Death is ever pressing at your heels,
'Tis best to drink or dream your life away.[11]

Oft doth my soul her prisoned state bemoan,
Her earth-born co-mate she would fain disown,
   And quit, did not the stirrup of the law
Upbear her foot from dashing on the stone.[12]

The "Truth" will not be shown to lofty thought,
Nor yet with lavished gold may it be bought;
   But, if you yield your life for fifty years,
From words to "states" you may perchance be brought.[13]

---

[8]It is often difficult to tell whether a mystical poet is using sensual symbolism and speaking of God, or, as can often be the case with Khayyam, speaking of human love, not divine. The translator believes this is probably a mystical quatrain.

[9]Mercy is God's highest attribute regarding men, Khayyam is saying, and sin therefore is required to call it forth.

[10]In the Arabic this means that God is the Fa'il i hakiki, the only real or true agent.

[11]Here the word "payi," Being, or the Deity, is the only real existence, and Not-Being, the nonentity in which His attributes are reflected. This same concept can be found in other Sufi poets and philosophers. See the writings of Ibn 'Arabi in this anthology for example.

[12]This means "I would make away with myself, were it not for the Almighty's canon against self-slaughter."

[13]Literally, this can be rendered "Unless you dig up your soul, and eat blood for fifty years." The "states" mentioned are those of ecstatic union with the Truth or Deity.

KABIR

Selections from The Songs and Hymns of Kabir

Dear friend, I am eager to meet my Beloved! My youth has
flowered, and the pain of separation from Him troubles my
breast.
I am wandering yet in the alleys of knowledge without purpose,
but I have received His news in these alleys of knowledge.
I have a letter from my Beloved: in this letter is an unutterable
message, and now my fear of death is done away.
Kabir says: "O my loving friend! I have got for my gift the
Deathless One."

Within this earthen vessel are bowers and groves, and within it
is the Creator:
Within this vessel are the seven oceans and the unnumbered
stars.
The touchstone and the jewel-appraiser are within;
And within this vessel the Eternal soundeth, and the spring
wells up.
Kabir says: "Listen to me, my friend! My beloved Lord is
within."

O Man, if thou dost not know thine own Lord, whereof art thou
so proud?
Put thy cleverness away: mere words shall never unite thee to
Him.
Do not deceive thyself with the witness of the Scriptures:
Love is something other than this, and he who has sought it
truly has found it.

I played day and night with my comrades, and now I am
greatly afraid.
So high is my Lord's palace, my heart trembles to mount its
stairs: yet I must not be shy, if I would enjoy His love.
My heart must cleave to my Lover; I must withdraw my veil,
and meet Him with all my body:
Mine eyes must perform the ceremony of the lamps of love.
Kabir says: "Listen to me, friend: he understands who loves. If
you feel not love's longing for your Beloved One, it is vain to
adorn your body, vain to put unguent on your eyelids."

I laugh when I hear that the fish in the water is thirsty:
You do not see that the Real is in your home, and you wander
from forest to forest listlessly!

Here is the truth! Go where you will, to Benares or to Mathura; if you do not find your soul, the world is unreal to you.

When I am parted from my Beloved, my heart is full of misery: I have no comfort in the day, I have no sleep in the night. To whom shall I tell my sorrow?
The night is dark; the hours slip by. Because my Lord is absent, I start up and tremble with fear.
Kabir says: "Listen, my friend! there is no other satisfaction, save in the encounter with the Beloved."

How could the love between Thee and me sever?
As the leaf of the lotus abides on the water: so thou art my Lord, and I am Thy servant.
As the night-bird Chakor gazes all night at the moon: so Thou art my Lord and I am Thy servant.
From the beginning until the ending of time, there is love between Thee and me; and how shall such love be extinguished?
Kabir says: "As the river enters into the ocean, so my heart touches Thee."

He who is meek and contented, he who has an equal vision, whose mind is filled with the fullness of acceptance and of rest;
He who has seen Him and touched Him, he is freed from all fear and trouble.
To him the perpetual thought of God is like sandal paste smeared on the body, to him nothing else is delight:
His work and his rest are filled with music: he sheds abroad the radiance of love.
Kabir says: "Touch His feet, who is one and indivisible, immutable and peaceful; who fills all vessels to the brim with joy, and whose form is love."

My Lord hides Himself, and my Lord wonderfully reveals himself:
My Lord has encompassed me with hardness, and my Lord has cast down my limitations.
My Lord brings to me words of sorrow and words of joy, and He Himself heals their strife.
I will offer my body and mind to my Lord: I will give up my life, but never can I forget my Lord!

I do not know what manner of God is mine.[1]

The Mullah cries aloud to Him: and why? Is your Lord deaf? The subtle anklets that ring on the feet of an insect when it moves are heard of Him.

Tell your beads, paint your forehead with the mark of your God, and wear matted locks long and showy: but a deadly weapon is in your heart, and how shall you have God?

Have you not heard the tune which the Unstruck Music is playing? In the midst of the chamber the harp of joy is gently and sweetly played; and where is the need of going without to hear it?

If you have not drunk of the nectar of that One Love, what boots it though you should purge yourself of all stains?

The Kazi is searching the words of the Koran, and instructing others: but if his heart be not steeped in that love, what does it avail, though he be a teacher of men?

The Yogi dyes his garments with red: but if he knows naught of that colour of love, what does it avail though his garments be tinted?

Kabir says: "Whether I be in the temple or the balcony, in the camp or in the flower garden, I tell you truly that every moment my Lord is taking His delight in me."

There is nothing but water at the holy bathing places; and I know that they are useless, for I have bathed in them.

The images are all lifeless, they cannot speak; I know, for I have cried aloud to them.

The Purana and the Koran are mere words; lifting up the curtain, I have seen.

Kabir gives utterance to the words of experience; and he knows very well that all other things are untrue.

It is needless to ask of a saint the caste to which he belongs;

For the priest, the warrior, the tradesman, and all the thirty-six castes, alike are seeking for God.

It is but folly to ask what the caste of a saint may be;

The barber has sought God, the washerwoman, and the carpenter—

[1]This verse and the remaining five have all been included to show the depth of Kabir's conviction that there is only one God, and that all forms of separateness, all differences in creed and dogma are unimportant and even foolish to the mystic who perceives the Supreme as one single Reality and Truth. Kabir is not unique among mystics for this attitude, but he is the most fervent and dedicated in his denunciation of all divisiveness within religion and one's approach to God. For this reason he has been accepted by both Sufis and Sikhs as their own. Guru Nanak even included some of Kabir's hymns in the Sikh sacred book Adi Granth.

Even Raidas was a seeker after God.
The Rishi Swapacha was a tanner by caste.
Hindus and Moslems alike have achieved that End, where remains no mark of distinction.

If God be within the mosque, then to whom does this world belong?
If Ram be within the image which you find upon your pilgrimage, then who is there to know what happens without?
Hari is in the East: Allah is in the West. Look within your heart, for there you will find both Karim and Ram;
All the men and women of the world are His living forms.
Kabir is the child of Allah and of Ram: He is my Guru, He is my Pir.

O servant, where dost thou seek Me?
Lo! I am beside thee.
I am neither in temple nor in mosque:
  I am neither in Kaaba nor in Kailash:
Neither am I in rites and ceremonies, nor in Yoga and renunciation.
If thou art a true seeker, thou shalt at once see Me: thou shalt meet Me in a moment of time.
Kabir says, "O Sadhu! God is the breath of all breath."

JALALU'D-DIN RUMI

Selections from the Diwan of Rumi, (Kulliyat-Shams-i-Tabriz)

Drunk is the Man of God, drunk without wine;
Sated the Man of God, full without meat.
Aghast is the Man of God in utter bewilderment
Knows not the Man of God slumber nor sustenance.
Sprung not from earth nor air, God's Man is not so born;
Nor is his origin, water nor flame of fire.
King is the Man of God, wrapped in a beggar's robe;
Treasure the Man of God, hid in a ruin's heap.
Soul of devotion he—such is the Man of God——
Yet is the Man of God heedless of merit's gain.
Thus is the Man of God Faith and yet Unbelief;
What to the Man of God is sin then and righteousness?
Taught by Creative Truth God's Man is learned;
Not wise in legal lore culled from a book.

In the Abyss's void. God's Man on Chaos rode,
But here he suffered shame from his unbroken steed.

We have lost our heart in the way of the Beloved:
We have sown dissension in the world.
We have struck fire within the hearts of the people:
And have thrown lovers into confusion.
I have washed my hands of all my belongings:
We have set fire to house and home.
I had a heavy load on my back
But thanks be to God we have thrown aside that heavy load.
What is the wealth of the world but carrion?
We have cast the carcase to the dogs.
We have extracted the kernel of the Quran:
And the husk we have cast to the dogs.
We have scattered the seed of eternal felicity and joy
From the earth to the sky.
The patched robe (of the derwish), the prayer carpet and the
    rosary.
We have cast away in the Tavern of Souls.
The pious cloak and turban and the babbling of knowledge
    about jot and tittle,
We have thrown it all into the flowing stream.
From the bow of desire, the arrow of Gnosis,
Taking straight aim, we have shot at the target.
Thou hast well said O Shams-i-Tabriz,
We have cast love glances at the Lord of the Soul.

O Muslim what can I do? For I do not know myself.
I am not a Christian nor a Jew, a fireworshipper nor a Muslim.
I am not the East or the West, nor of Land nor of Sea.
I am not of the Elemental nor of the Circling Spheres.
I am not of earth nor of air, of water nor of fire.
I am not of the Empyrean nor of the outspread carpet of the
    world, indeed I am not in the category of creation at all.
I am not of Hindustan nor of China nor from near-by Bulgaria.
I am not of the land of Iraq nor of the dust of Khurasan.
I am not of the Faith (or the present obligations of religion)
    nor of the hereafter, nor of Heaven nor of Hell.
I am not from Adam nor from the garden of Paradise.
My dwelling is without location, my trail without trace.
There is neither body nor soul for I am the Soul of Souls.
I have expelled duality from myself. I have seen the two worlds
    as one.
Let me seek One, say One, know One and desire One.
He the First, He the Last, He the Manifest. He the Hidden.
Without Him and other than Him nothing else I know.

I am drunk with the Soul of Love and the two worlds have
    passed from my hand.
Except drinking and revelry I have no other aim.
If in my life some day I should draw but one breath without
    Him,
From that time, yes! from that very hour. I would repent me of
    my life.
If in private some day just for a moment my hand might be
    given to the Friend,
I would tread underfoot the two worlds and wave the other
    hand (dancing in exultation).
How wonderful, my friends! what bird am I that I strike wing
    in the egg?
Within this body of water and clay, all is Love and all is Soul.

I died from mineral and plant became;
Died from the plant, and took a sentient frame;
Died from the beast, and donned a human dress;
When by my dying did I e'er grow less?
Another time from manhood I must die
To soar with angel pinions through the sky.
'Midst angels also I must lose my place,
Since "Everything shall perish save His Face."
Let me be Naught! The harp-strings tell me plain
That "unto Him do we return again"!

Selections from the Mathnawi

From Book Five

A loved one said to her lover to try him,
Early one morning, "O such an one, son of such an one,
I marvel whether you hold me more dear,
Or yourself; tell me truly, O ardent suitor!"
    He answered, "I am so entirely absorbed in you,
That I am full of you from head to foot.
Of my own existence nothing but the name remains,
In my being is nothing besides you, O Object of desire!
Therefore am I thus lost in you,
Just as vinegar is absorbed in honey;
Or as a stone, which is changed into a pure ruby,
Is filled with the bright light of the sun.
In that stone its own properties abide not,
It is filled with the sun's properties altogether;
So that, if afterwards it holds itself dear,

'Tis the same as holding the sun dear, O beloved!
And if it hold the sun dear in its heart,
'Tis clearly the same as holding itself dear.
Whether that pure ruby hold itself dear,
Or hold the sun dear,
There is no difference between the two preferences;
On either hand is naught but the light of dawn.
But till that stone becomes a ruby it hates itself,
For till it becomes one 'I,' it is two separate 'I's,'
For 'tis then darkened and purblind,
And darkness is the essential enemy of light.
If it *then* hold itself dear, it is an infidel;
Because that self is an opponent of the mighty Sun.
Wherefore 'tis unlawful for the stone then to say 'I,'
Because it is entirely in darkness and nothingness."

Pharaoh said, "I am the Truth," and was laid low.
Mansur Hallaj said, "I am the Truth," and escaped free.
Pharaoh's "I" was followed by the curse of God;
Mansur's "I" was followed by the mercy of God, O beloved!
Because Pharaoh was a stone, Mansur a ruby;
Pharaoh an enemy of light, Mansur a friend.
O prattler, Mansur's "I am He" was a deep mystic saying,
Expressing union with the light, not mere incarnation.[1]

That wine of God is gained from *that* minstrel,
This bodily wine from *this* minstrel.
Both of these have one and the same name in speech,
But the difference between their worth is great.

Men's bodies are like pitchers with closed mouths;
Beware, till you see what is inside them.
The pitcher of this body holds the water of life,
Whilst that one holds deadly poison.
If you look at the contents you are wise;
If you look only at the vessel you are misguided.
Know words resemble these bodies,
And the meaning resembles the soul.
The body's eyes are ever intent on bodies,
The soul's eyes on the reasonable soul;
Wherefore, in the figures of the words of the Masnavi,
The form misleads, but the inner meaning guides.
In the Koran it is declared that its parables
"Mislead some and guide some." [2]

[1] Incarnation was not looked upon favorably by either Rumi or another famous Sufi, Shabistari. They both rejected the idea of deity descending into man (Halul), or what they considered incarnation, and both favored the doctrine of intimate union with deity (Ittihad or Wahdat).
[2] The Koran, II.24.

O God! when a spiritual man talks of wine,
How can a fellow spiritual man mistake his meaning?

Thus that minstrel began his intoxicating song,
"O give me Thy cup, Thou whom I see not!
Thou art my face; what wonder if I see it not?
Extreme nearness acts as an obscuring veil.[3]
Thou art my reason; what wonder if I see Thee not
Through the multitude of intervening obstacles?
Thou art 'nearer to me than my neck vein,'[4]
How can I call to Thee, 'Ho,' as if thou wert far off?
Nay, but I will mislead some by calling in the desert,
To hide my Beloved from those of whom I am jealous!"

Inquire now, I pray, of each one of your members;
These dumb members have a thousand tongues.
Inquire the detail of the bounties of the All-sustainer,
Which are recorded in the volume of the universe.
Day and night you are eagerly asking for news,
Whilst every member of your body is telling you news.
Since each member of your body issued from Not-being,
How much pleasure has it seen, and how much pain?
For no member grows and flourishes without pleasure,
And each member is weakened by every pain.
The member endures, but that pleasure is forgotten,
Yet not all forgotten, but hidden from the senses.
Like summer wherein cotton is produced,—
The cotton remains, but the summer is forgotten.
Or like ice which is formed in great frost,—
The frost departs, but the ice is still before us.
The ice is mindful of that extreme cold,
And even in winter that crop is mindful of the summer.
In like manner, O son, every member of your body
Tells you tales of God's bounties to your body.
Even as a woman who has borne twenty children,—
Each child tells a tale of pleasure felt by her.
She became not pregnant save after sexual pleasure,
Can a garden bloom without the spring?
Pregnant women and their teeming wombs
Tell tales of love frolics in the spring.
So every tree which nurtures its fruits
Has been, like Mary, impregnated by the Unseen King.

[3]In the Gulshan-i-Raz there is a couplet (number 122) that reads: "When the object looked at is very close to the eye,/The eye is darkened so that it cannot see it." For the mystic this means that when a man is united with God he no longer beholds Him, for he is dwelling in Him.

[4]The Koran, I.15.

Though fire's heat be hidden in the midst of water,
Yet a thousand boiling bubbles prove it present.
Though the heat of the fire be working unseen,
Yet its bubbles signify its presence plainly.
　In like manner, the members of those enjoying "union"
Become big with child, viz., with forms of "states" and "words." [5]
Gazing on the beauty of these forms they stand agape,
And the forms of the world vanish from their sight.
These spiritual progenies are not born of the elements,
And are perforce invisible to the sensual eye.
These progenies are born of divine apparitions,
And are therefore hidden by veils without colour.
I said "born," but in reality they are not born;
I used this expression only by way of indication.
But keep silence till the King bids you speak,
Offer not your nightingale songs to these roses;
For they themselves are saying to you in loud tones,
"O nightingale, hold your peace, and listen to us!"
Those two kinds of fair forms (ecstatic states and words)
Are undeniable proofs of a previous "union;"
Yea, those two kinds of exalted manifestations
Are the evident fruits of a preceding wedlock.

The ecstasy is past, but your members recall it;
Ask them about it, or call it to mind yourself.
　When sorrow seizes you, if you are wise,
You will question that sorrow-fraught moment,
Saying to it, "O sorrow, who now deniest
Thy portion of bounty given thee by the Perfect One,
Even if each moment be not to thee a glad spring,
Yet of what is thy body, like a rose-heap, a storehouse?
Thy body is a heap of roses, thy thought rosewater;
'Twere strange if rosewater ignored the rose-heap!"

From Book Six

Be not intoxicated with these goblets of forms,
Lest you become a maker and worshipper of idols.
Pass by these cups full of forms, linger not;
There is wine in the cups, but it proceeds not from them.
Look to the Giver of the wine with open mouth;
When His wine comes, is not cup too small to hold it?
O Adam, seek the reality of my love,

[5]That is, ecstatic words and states are the offspring of communion with God. Surat, or forms, means pictures, images, outward appearances as opposed to conceptualization or "forms of thought," such as ideas in the Divine Mind.

Quit the mere husk and form of the wheat.
When sand was made meal for "The Friend of God,"
Know, O master, the form of wheat was dispensed with.
Form proceeds from the world that is without form,
Even as smoke arises from fire.

The Divine art without form designs forms (ideals),[6]
Those forms fashion bodies with senses and instruments.
Whatever the form, it fashions in its own likeness
Those bodies either to good or to evil.
If the form be blessing, the man is thankful;
If it be suffering, he is patient;
If it be cherishing, he is cheerful;
If it be bruising, he is full of lamentation!

Since all these forms are slaves of Him without form,
Why do they deny their Lord and Master?
They exist only through Him that is without form;
What, then, means their disavowal of their Sustainer?
This very denial of Him proceeds from Him,
This act is naught but a reflection from Himself!
The forms of the walls and roofs of houses
Know to be shadows of the architect's thought;
Although stones and planks and bricks
Find no entrance into the sanctuary of thought,
Verily the Absolute Agent is without form,
Form is only a tool in His hands.
Sometimes that Formless One of His mercy
Shows His face to His forms from behind the veil of Not-being,
That every form may derive aid therefrom,—
From its perfect beauty and power.
Again, when that Formless One hides His face,
Those forms set forth their needs.
If one form sought perfection from another form,
That would be the height of error.
Why then, O simpleton, do you set forth your needs
To one who is as needy as yourself?
Since forms are slaves, apply them not to God,
Seek not to use a form as a similitude of God.
Seek Him with humbleness and self-abasement,
For thought yields naught but forms of thought.
Still, if you are unable to dispense with forms,
Those occurring independently of your thought are best.

[6]See note 5. These are the archetypes in the Divine Mind, or the "Intellectual Presence" in God, which are set forth in the world of creation and sensible objects.

"Now have we seen what the king saw at the first,
When that Incomparable One adjured us."
   The prophets have many claims to our gratitude,
Because they forewarn us of our ultimate lot,
Saying, "What ye sow will yield only thorns;
If ye fly that way, ye will fly astray.
Take seed of us to yield you a good harvest,
Fly with our wings to hit the mark with your arrow.
Now ye know not the truth and nature of the 'Truth,'[7]
But at the last ye will cry, '*That* was the "Truth."'
The Truth is yourself, but not your mere bodily self,
Your real self is higher than 'you' and 'me.'
This visible 'you' which you fancy to be yourself
Is limited in place, the real 'you' is not limited.
Why, O pearl, linger you trembling in your shell?
Esteem not yourself mere sugar-cane, but real sugar.
This outward 'you' is foreign to your real 'you;'
Cling to your real self, quit this dual self.
Your last self attains to your first (real) self
Only through your attending earnestly to that union.
Your real self lies hid beneath your outward self,
For 'I am the servant of him who looks into himself.' "[8]
   "What a youth sees only when reflected in a glass,
Our wise old fathers saw long ago though hid in stones.
But we disobeyed the advice of our father,
And rebelled against his affectionate counsels.
We made light of the king's exhortations,
And slighted his matchless intimations.
Now we have all fallen into the ditch,
Wounded and crushed in this fatal struggle.
We relied on our own reason and discernment,
And for that cause have fallen into this calamity.
We fancied ourselves free from defects of sight,
Even as those affected by colour-blindness.
Now at last our hidden disease has been revealed,
After we have been involved in these calamities."
"The shadow of a guide is better than directions to God,
To be satisfied is better than a hundred nice dishes.
A seeing eye is better than a hundred walking-sticks,
Eye discerns jewels from mere pebbles."

[7] This is Al Hagg, the Truth as God, the Divine Noumenon. This whole verse by Rumi teaches that the "Truth," which is also our real self, lies hidden within our phenomenal and visible self.

[8] In the Hadith it is written that "Whoso knows himself knows his Lord."

TALIB[1]

Si Harfi Dholla

Come, Love, within the soul Thy dwelling place doth lie,
Thy distant home desert, and to my fond heart fly!
Thou sayst Thou dost bide than the neck vein more nigh,
Yet, vexing one, Thy form is veiled before mine eye.

O, Love, deceive no more! Thy fickle words forsake!
Without us and within Thy dwelling Thou dost take.
My heart, with wiles bewitched, a captive Thou dost make:
Then into words of scorn Thy mocking accents break.

Oh, Love, for all our woes no pity hast Thou shown,
Exiled from Home, to pine in far off realms alone.
Through Thy false deed, Who once had made our souls Thine
    own,
In this strange land, alas, no peace my heart hath known.

Thou only art; all else is unearthly.
Why press this vain debate if one or separate we?
Since, when Thy face is shown, my sighs Thy grief must be,
And in my prayers for death, my tears are tears of Thee.

I sleep, and at my side Love sinks in slumber deep:
When first my eyes unclose, He rouses, too, from sleep.
I laugh, He shouts for joy; His tears fall when I weep:
Yet bargains He, nor cares my plighted hours to keep.

None knows my state save Love; for no one else 'twere meet.
I sacrifice my all, an offering at Love's feet.
Each moment yearns my heart its guileless Love to greet:
Unless Love quickly come, this heart must cease to beat.

'Twas told that the Beloved to holy Mecca came:
That never man should know He chose Muhammad's name.
Medina, now, His home: and Talib's fond lips frame
Prayers for "God's peace" on Him, and His high service claim.

[1]Talib is the name given to the unknown author of this verse. The word
"talib" means a seeker of God. These verses are examples of highly popular
sacred lyrics chanted daily by street singers in the Indian Punjab. It is
typical of much modern Sufi literature in India.

A gift I crave whose sight sweet thoughts of Thee shall start;
With ring from Thy dear hand, or necklace, Thou must part.
In Hindustan, my home; Thou in Medina art.
Slain by Thy love, what sins had soiled my helpless heart?[2]

By telling o'er Thy name each passing hour I grace.
Leave town and vale and make my heart Thy resting place.
Love reigns the Lord of all; His, earth and sky and space.
Since Thou hast made me Thine, whom else should I embrace?

If e'er my lips, unsealed, Thy mystery reveal,[3]
From mighty rivers' depths great flames of fire will steal,
Blood from God's throne will rain, the stars will earthward reel.
Ah, Love, what streams can cool when these hot fires I feel?

My years of youth were spent in doleful tears and sighs,
Now, to my aged heart, Love's winged arrow flies.
Bring hither my Beloved, the darling of mine eyes.
Talib's true love from hearts as well as tongue doth rise. . . .

Thou who my surety art, O Love, stir not away.
Summon me to Thyself, and share my grief, I pray.
Secure my pardon, Love for I have gone astray.
To my dead soul give life, and sinless I shall stay. . . .

Inside and out my Love holds His high Sovereignty:
In every place He dwells, the First and Last is He.
Save only the Beloved, none other can there be.
I live but by His life, Love's own eternally.

From the great Presence sought, Thy bounteous Love I own.
Afar or near, O Love, I see but Thee alone.
All from Thy light have come—no other source have known.
Send pardon from Thyself, nor bid my steps begone. . . .

Stricken to death, I lie, crushed by Thy beauty's wave.
In Thy love's ocean vast my soul hath found its grave.
In every town men's tongue for Thee their tribute save,
To Thee our lives we yield: to see Thy face we crave.

This daily task to do, of old my destiny—
That I His praise proclaim, whenever Love summons me.

[2]From this verse on the seeker speaks of himself as a bride, a wife, and uses the feminine gender to describe himself and the masculine for the Divine Beloved. This symbolic rendering, as was noted earlier, is quite common for mystics the world over.

[3]This line refers to the esoteric secrets of the Sufis, which are supposed to have originated with the prophet Mohammed, and to which a Sufi's lips must forever remain sealed.

O, friends, I am consumed; Love's form I cannot see.
My Love hath learned to work with what strange witchery! . . .

Love, I would die for Thee, most ravishing Thy grace.
Bring news, O friends, from whence come the Beloved's face.
My soul with joy grows faint, and faster, my heart's pace.
What if, this morn, should come Love's step and His embrace.

My necklace is God's praise, wherewith I am arrayed.
My ear-rings are the prayer, "God's peace" my lips have prayed.
Love, on my heart, for gems, longing for God hath laid.
The nuptial bed I mount, invoking Chishti's aid.

The heavenly lightnings flash, and blazing fountains spout.
With Sinai's splendour clothed, my glory shines about.
Love, entering at last, "My follower", calls out.
Beings of lights and fire and earth,[4] "God's blessing" shout.

To meet Love, as He comes, with bended head I go,
"God's benediction" ask, and at Love's feet bow low.
This hand-maid's ministry, unworthy, all must know.
Talib, Thy slave to keep—this boon, O Love, bestow.

ATTAR

Selections from the Writings of Attar

The world is full of Thee and Thou art not in the world.
All are lost in Thee and Thou art not in the midst.
Thy silence is from Thy speech;
Thine hiding from Thine appearing.
I see the way to Thee by means of the smallest atom;
Then I see the two worlds as the face of Allah.
For dualism there is no way into Thy presence.
Thou and Thy power are the whole universe.
A man of eloquent speech has well said in respect to the Essence
That Oneness is the dropping of all adjuncts.
There is no doubt as to the meaning of what I have said.

[4]See the Koran, 15.26,27, and 4.13,14. The beings are angels, jinn, and men,
who the Muslims believe are created out of light, fire, and clay respectively.

Thou art without eyes and there is no Universe ('Alam) or Knower ('Alim) but one.

A Sufi devotee began to weep in the middle of the night and said: "This is what I see the world to be: it is like a closed casket in which we are placed and in which, through our ignorance, we spend our time in folly. When Death opens the lid of the casket, each one who has wings takes his flight to Eternity, but that one who is without wings, remains in the casket, a prey to a thousand afflictions. Then give the wing of the mystic sense to the bird of spiritual desire: give a heart to reason, and ecstasy to the soul. Before the lid is taken away from this casket become a bird of the Way to God and develop your wings and your feathers. Nay, rather, burn your wings and your feathers and destroy yourself by fire, and so will you arrive at the Goal before all others.

The lover thinks nothing of his own life, for he who is a lover, whether he be an ascetic or a libertine, is prepared to sacrifice his life for the sake of love. If your spirit is at enmity with your soul, sacrifice your soul and you will be able to go on your way unhindered. If your soul is a distraction to you on the road, cast it aside, then look straight before you and give yourself to contemplation. If you are bidden to renounce your faith or to give up your life, cast away both: abandon your faith and sacrifice your life. If one who is ignorant of spiritual things should say that it is untrue that Love should be preferred to infidelity or faith, say to him: "What has Love to do with infidelity or faith?" Do lovers concern themselves with their souls? A lover sets fire to the whole harvest: he puts the knife to his own throat and pierces his own body. Torment and affliction are what pertain to Love. He who has his feet set firmly in the abode of Love renounces at once both infidelity and faith.

The Valley of Gnosis has neither beginning nor end. No other road is like the road which is hidden therein, nor any road there like any other road there, but the traveller in the body is other than the traveller in the spirit. Soul and body are for ever in a state of deficiency or perfection according to their strength and weakness. Therefore, of necessity, the road is revealed to each one according to his capacity for that revelation. On this road, trodden by Abraham, the friend of God, how could the feeble spider be a companion to the elephant? The progress of each will be in accordance with his spiritual state. Though the gnat were to fly with all its might, could it ever equal the perfection of the wind? Since, then, there are different ways of making the journey, no two birds will fly alike. Each finds a way of his own, on this road of mystic knowledge, one by means of the *Mihrab* and another through the idols. When the Sun of Gnosis shines forth from the heaven above, on to this most blessed road, each is enlightened according to his capacity and finds his own place in the knowledge of the Truth.

When that sun shines upon him, the dustbin of this world is changed for him into a rose-garden: the kernel is seen beneath the rind. No longer does the lover see any particle of himself, he sees only the Beloved: wheresoever he looks he sees always His Face, in every atom he beholds His dwelling-place. A hundred thousand mysteries are revealed to him from under the veil, as clearly as the sun. Yet thousands of men are lost eternally, for one who perfectly apprehends these mysteries. He must be perfect, who would succeed in this quest, who would plunge into this fathomless sea. If the joy of its secrets be revealed to him, every moment will renew his longing for it.

Even if you should attain to the Throne of Glory, do not cease each moment to say: "Is there more than this?" Plunge yourself into the Sea of Gnosis, or if you cannot do that, sprinkle the dust of the road upon your head. O you who remain asleep—and it is no matter for congratulation—why do you not put on mourning? If you have not attained to the joy of union with the Beloved, at least arise and put on signs of mourning for your separation from Him. If you have not looked upon the Beauty of the Beloved, arouse yourself, do not sit still, but seek out those mysteries destined for you, and if as yet you do not know them, seek them out in shame.

Strive to acquire the mystic gnosis, so that you may learn to know God. He who truly knows God by contemplation, realises that Eternal Life means passing away from the personal self. Without this knowledge man has no real existence: he is not worthy to approach God, nor will he attain to the goal of his desires. If you really know your self and its desires, you will know God Most High and His gifts.

He alone is the true gnostic who knows God, and whoever is without this knowledge is unfit to be counted among human beings. The gnostic has a heart full of sincere and constant love, all his actions are pure and without stain. The one to whom the gift of gnosis has been given finds no place in his heart save for God alone.

To the gnostic, this world is of no concern, nay, more, he gives no thought to himself. Gnosis means that the gnostic passes away from himself into God. How can the one who does not completely pass away from self attain to this perfection?

The gnostic is occupied neither with this world nor the next: he is not concerned with any but his Lord. Because he has died altogether to himself, he is completely absorbed in the attainment of union with God.

HAFIZ

Selections from the Writings of Hafiz

O heedless one, strive thou to heed;
Blind to the Path, how canst thou lead?
A Sire wouldst be? Strive thou O Youth
Before Love's Tutor in the School of Truth.
Self's dross purge out, as saints of old,
And by Love's Alchemy become fine gold.
Eating and sleeping, still of Love bereft—
Spurn sloth and feasting for the Love you left.
I vow the heavenly Sun is not so bright
As heart and soul indwelt by His Love-light.
Lost Thou in God, sans life and limb,
Art head to foot all Light of Him.

O you who are without knowledge, make every effort to attain it. Until you have travelled over the road, how can you be a guide thereon? In the school of Divine Truth, as you learn from the teachers of Love, strive in every way, my son, so that one day you may become a father in wisdom. Your concern with sleep and food have kept you far from the high station of Love. You will attain to the Beloved when you have learnt to do without sleep and food. If the radiance of the love of God falls on your heart and soul, surely you will become fairer than the sun in the firmament. Rid yourself of the copper of your own self, like the warriors of the Path, so that you may find the alchemy of Love and become gold. The light of God will shine on you, enveloping you from head to foot, when you are borne without head and foot along the Path of the All-Glorious. For one moment sink into the ocean of God, and do not suppose that one hair of your head shall be moistened by the water of the seven seas. If the vision you behold is the Face of God, there is no doubt that from this time forward you will see clearly. When the foundations of your own existence are destroyed, have no fear in your heart that you yourself will perish.

O Hafiz, if in thine heart, thou dost crave for union, thou wilt need to become as the dust on the threshold of those who contemplate the Vision of God.

None hath ever seen Thy Face, though thousands are looking in expectation of it. Thou art at rest in the rosebud and even now a thousand nightingales are seeking Thee. If I come by where Thou dwellest, it is not strange, since many are strangers wandering in that land. Far from Thee though I be—and pity it is that any should be far from Thee—nevertheless the hope of union with Thee is always near to me. To those who love Thee, there is no difference between monastery and tavern, for everywhere shines the light of the Face of the Beloved. Wherever glory is given to Thee in a place where Thou art worshipped, the bell which summons men to prayer, and the cloister and the monk and the name of the Cross, all serve one purpose. What lover of God is there whose state is not regarded by the Beloved? O sir, there is no pain for you in this, and if it should be otherwise, there is a Physician, Who can heal you.

Nothing I behold, save the Vision of Thee: all paths I take are the road that leads to Thee. Though sleep falls gratefully upon the eyes of all, when Thou givest it, I pray Thee, O Lord, that my eyes may remain ever wakeful.

Where is the glad news of Union, that I may rise again? A holy bird am I, ascending from the vanities of this low world. If Thy love calls upon me to be Thy bondslave, I shall arise above the claims and the power of being and place. O Lord, give me the rain of guidance from Thy clouds. O Beloved, towards Whom all men move and strive, from life in this world I will arise and live again in Thee.

JAMI

Selections from the Yusuf-o-Zulaykha

Be prisoner of Love; for so may'st thou be free.
Bear in thy breast its grief, so thou may'st blithesome be.
Thousands of learned men and wise have gone their way—
Have passed from ken, for strangers to Love were they.
But now no name or trace of them the world retains;

In the hand of Time nor tale nor fame of them remains.
How many birds there are of exquisite hue and mould!
But never a lip moves *their* story to unfold.
Lo! When the wise in heart, love-taught, take up the tale
They tell the story of the moth and nightingale.
Triest thou in thy life a hundred tasks in vain;
Thou from thyself, by love alone canst freedom gain.
Scorn not that lower love, the symbol of the Real,
Since by its aid thou may'st achieve the ideal.
Till from the Tablet, thou hast conned the Alphabet,
How canst thou from Quran, study the lesson set?
A novice once before his Soul's Director stood,
Who shewed to him the Path of Mystic Brotherhood.
"If thou'st not lost thy footing in Love's way," said he,
"Go! Be a lover! Then return thou here to me.
For shouldst thou still disdain to drink Form's cup of Wine,
To drain the Ideal to the dregs can not be thine.
But yet beware, beware! In Form make no delay,
And let that Bridge be crossed as quickly as it may.
If to the stage's end thy chattels thou wouldst bring,
Rapt at the Bridge's head, why standst thou lingering?"

Selections from the Lawa'ih (Flashes of Light)

Deliver Us From Ourselves

O God, deliver us from preoccupation with worldly vanities, and show us the nature of things "as they really are." Remove from our eyes the veil of ignorance, and show us things as they really are. Show not to us non-existence as existent, nor cast the veil of non-existence over the beauty of existence. Make this phenomenal world the mirror to reflect the manifestations of the beauty, and not a veil to separate and repel us from Thee. Cause these unreal phenomena of the universe to be for us the sources of knowledge and insight, and not the cause of ignorance and blindness. Our alienation and severance from Thy beauty all proceed from ourselves. Deliver us from ourselves, and accord to us intimate knowledge of Thee.

Make My Heart Pure

Make my heart pure, my soul from error free,
Make tears and sighs my daily lot to be,
   And lead me on Thy road away from self,
That lost to self I may approach to Thee!

Set enmity between the world and me,
Make me averse from worldly company:
   From other objects turn away my heart,
So that it is engrossed with love to Thee.

How were it, Lord, if Thou should'st set me free
From error's grasp and cause me truth to see?
   Guebres[1] by scores Thou makest Musulmans,
Why, then, not make a Musulman of me?

My lust for this world and the next efface,
Grant me the crown of poverty and grace
   To be partaker in Thy mysteries,
From paths that lead not towards Thee turn my face.

The Absolute Beauty

The Absolute Beauty is the Divine Majesty endued with the
attributes of power and bounty. Every beauty and perfection
manifested in the theatre of the various grades of beings is a ray
of His perfect beauty reflected therein. It is from these rays
that exalted souls have received their impress of beauty and
their quality of perfection. Whosoever is wise derives his wisdom from Divine wisdom.

My Love Stood By Me At The Dawn Of Day

My love stood me at the dawn of day,
And said, "To grief you make my heart a prey;
   Whilst I am casting looks of love at you,
Have you no shame to turn your eyes away?"

[1]The Magis and Zoroastrians.

All my life long I tread love's path of pain,
If peradventure "Union" I may gain.
　Better to catch one moment's glimpse of Thee
Than earthly beauties' love through life retain.

God The Only Love Eternal

Yesterday this universe neither existed nor appeared to exist,
while to-day it appears to exist but has no real existence: it is a
mere semblance, and to-morrow nothing thereof will be seen.
What does it profit thee to allow thyself to be guided by vain
passions and desires? Why dost thou place reliance on these
transitory objects that glitter with false lustre? Turn thy heart
away from all of them, and firmly attach it to God. Break loose
from all these, and cleave closely to Him. It is only He who always has been and always will continue to be. The countenance
of His eternity is never scarred by the thorn of contingency.

How To Obtain Union With The Divine

In like manner, as it behoves thee to maintain the said relation continuously, so it is of the first importance to develop one
quality thereof by detaching thyself from mundane relations and
by emancipating thyself from attention to contingent forms;
and this is possible only through hard striving and earnest endeavour to expel vain thoughts and imaginations from thy mind.
The more these thoughts are cast out and these suggestions
checked, the stronger and closer this relation becomes. It is,
then, necessary to use every endeavour to force these thoughts
to encamp outside the enclosure of thy breast, and that the
"Truth" most glorious may cast His beams into thy heart, and
deliver thee from thyself, and save thee from the trouble of en-
tertaining His rivals in thy heart. Then there will abide with
thee neither consciousness of thyself, nor even consciousness of
such absence of consciousness—nay, there will abide nothing save
the One God alone.

The Glorious God

The glorious God, whose bounty, mercy, grace,
And loving-kindness all the world embrace,
　At every moment brings a world to naught,
And fashions such another in its place.

All gifts soever unto God are due,
Yet special gifts from special "Names" ensue;
  At every breath one "Name" annihilates,
And one creates all outward things anew.[2]

The God Behind The Veil

"O fairest rose, with rosebud mouth," I sighed,
"Why, like coquettes, thy face for ever hide?"
  He smiled, "Unlike the beauties of the earth,
Even when veiled I still may be described."
Thy face uncovered would be all too bright,
Without a veil none could endure the sight;
  What eye is strong enough to gaze upon
The dazzling splendour of the fount of light?

When the sun's banner blazes in the sky,
Its light gives pain by its intensity,
  But when 'tis tempered by a veil of cloud
That light is soft and pleasant to the eye.

The Divine Self-Sufficiency

Absolute self-sufficiency is a quality involved in Divine Perfection. It signifies this, that in a general and universal manner all the modes, states, and aspects of the One Real Being, with all their adherent properties and qualities, in all their presentations, past, present, or future, manifested in all grades of substances, divine and mundane, are present and realised in the secret thought of that Divine Being, in such wise that the sum of them all is contained in His Unity. From this point of view He is independent of all other existences; as it is said, "God most glorious can do without the world."

---

[2]This is an obscure passage and the translator interprets it to mean that a portion of the material world, through the mercy of God, is capable of receiving the Very Being, and thus the phenomenon becomes the Very Being externalized. But Omnipotence requires the total destruction of all phenomena and all multiplicity of the same substance. The process is repeated *ad infinitum*. The "Names" mentioned in this passage are listed in the Masnavi of Jami. See R.A. Nicholson's *Divani Shamsi Tabriz*, p. 71.

The Universe A Number Of "Accidents"

The universe, together with its parts, is nothing but a number of accidents, even changing and being renewed at every breath, and linked together in a single substance, and at each instant disappearing and being replaced by a similar set. In consequence of this rapid succession, the spectator is deceived into the belief that the universe is a permanent existence.

The Sea Of Being

Being's a sea in constant billows rolled,
'Tis but these billows that we men behold;
   Sped from within, they rest upon the sea,
And like a veil its actual form enfold.

Being's the essence of the Lord of all,
All things exist in Him and He in all;
   This is the meaning of the Gnostic phrase,
"All things are comprehended in the All."

The Revelation Of Truth

The Majesty of the "Truth" most glorious is revealed in two manners—the first the inward, subjective revelation, which the Sufis name "Most Holy Emanation"; it consists in the self-manifestation of the "Truth" to His own consciousness from all eternity under the forms of substances, their characteristics and capacities. The second revelation is the outward objective manifestation, which is called "Holy Emanation"; it consists in the manifestation of the "Truth," with the impress of the properties and marks of the same substances. This second revelation ranks after the first; it is the theatre wherein are manifested to sight the perfections which in the first revelation were contained potentially in the characteristics and capacities of the substances.

Our Need Of The Beloved

O Thou whose sacred precincts none may see,
Unseen Thou makest all things seen to be;
   Thou and we are not separate, yet still
Thou hast no need of us, but we of Thee.
None by endeavour can behold Thy face,
Or access gain without prevenient grace;
   For every man some substitute is found,
Thou hast no peer, and none can take Thy place.
Of accident or substance Thou hast nought,
Without constraint of cause Thy grace is wrought;
   Thou canst replace what's lost, but if Thou'rt lost,
In vain a substitute for Thee is sought.
In me Thy beauty love and longing wrought;
Did I not seek Thee, how wouldst Thou be sought?
   My love is as a mirror in the which
Thy beauty into evidence is brought.
O Lord, none but Thyself can fathom Thee,
Yet every mosque and church doth harbour Thee;
   I know the seekers and what 'tis they seek—
Seekers and sought are all comprised in Thee.

MENTOR Titles of Related Interest

☐ **THE WAY OF LIFE: TAO TÊ CHING by Lao Tzu.** A new translation by R. B. Blakney of a masterpiece of ancient Chinese wisdom. (#MW1459—$1.50)

☐ **THE SAYINGS OF CONFUCIUS translated by James R. Ware.** The wise teachings of the ancient Chinese sage in a new translation. (#MY1557—$1.25)

☐ **THE SERMON ON THE MOUNT According to Vedanta by Swami Prabhavananda.** A fascinating and superbly enlightening Hindu reading of the central gospel of Christianity by the renowned author of books on Indian religious philosophy. (#MW1518—$1.50)

☐ **HOW TO KNOW GOD: THE YOGA APHORISMS OF PATANJALI translated with Commentary by Swami Prabhavananda and Christopher Isherwood.** This classic work on yoga, its goal and methods, is essential to an understanding of Hindu religious practice. For more than fifteen hundred years the writings of Patanjali have been a principal influence on Hindu spiritual exercises. Index. (#MY1382—$1.25)

☐ **THE LIVING TALMUD: THE WISDOM OF THE FATHERS AND ITS CLASSICAL COMMENTARIES, selected and translated by Judah Goldin.** A new translation, with an illuminating essay on the place of the Talmud in Jewish life and religion. (#MW1453—$1.50)

Other MENTOR and SIGNET Books of Interest

☐ **CHINESE FOLK MEDICINE by Heinrich Wallnöfer and Anna von Rottauscher.** Acupuncture, love philters, moxibustion—all of these are explained in this comprehensive book. (#MY1292—$1.25)

☐ **A SHORT HISTORY OF CHINA by Hilda Hookham.** Enlivened by human interest anecdotes and poetry selections, this book traces the world's oldest civilization from its beginnings in pre-history through the major dynasties to the People's Republic of today.
(#ME1566—$2.25)

☐ **A CHINA PASSAGE by John Kenneth Galbraith.** From the author of *Ambassador's Journal*, one of the most readable, witty, wonderfully humane and truly enlightening accounts we have ever had of China—her people, her government, her economy, her culture, and her implications for the modern world. (#W5654—$1.50)

☐ **ASIA IN THE MODERN WORLD, Helen Matthew, editor.** Prominent authorities study the people, culture, and political history of Asia and provide the background needed to understand its decisive role in the shaping of world events today. Illustrated. (#MY1215—$1.25)

☐ **THE NATURE OF THE NON-WESTERN WORLD by Vera Micheles Dean.** A timely, penetrating look into the ancient traditions and modern ideas by which half the world's people live. "Everything she writes in her lucid and persuasive style bears the stamp of a liberal and courageous mind."—**New York Herald Tribune**
(#MW1224—$1.50)

THE NEW AMERICAN LIBRARY, INC.,
P.O. Box 999, Bergenfield, New Jersey 07621

Please send me the MENTOR and SIGNET BOOKS I have checked above. I am enclosing $＿＿＿＿＿＿(check or money order—no currency or C.O.D.'s). Please include the list price plus 35¢ a copy to cover handling and mailing costs. (Prices and numbers are subject to change without notice.)

Name＿＿＿＿＿＿＿＿＿＿＿＿＿＿＿＿＿＿＿

Address＿＿＿＿＿＿＿＿＿＿＿＿＿＿＿＿＿＿

City＿＿＿＿＿＿＿State＿＿＿＿＿Zip Code＿＿＿＿＿
Allow at least 4 weeks for delivery

The MENTOR Philosophers

A distinguished series of six volumes presenting in historical order the basic writings of the outstanding philosophers of the Western world—from the Middle Ages to the present time.

☐ **THE AGE OF BELIEF: THE MEDIEVAL PHILOSOPHERS edited by Anne Fremantle.** Basic writings of St. Augustine, Boethius, Abelard, St. Bernard, St. Thomas Aquinas, Duns Scotus, William of Ockham and others.
(#ME1536—$1.75)

☐ **THE AGE OF ADVENTURE: THE RENAISSANCE PHILOSOPHERS edited by Giorgio de Santillana.** Da Vinci, More, Machiavelli, Michelangelo, Erasmus, Copernicus, Montaigne, Kepler, Galileo, Bruno.   (#ME1342—$1.75)

☐ **THE AGE OF ENLIGHTENMENT: THE 18TH CENTURY PHILOSOPHERS edited by Isaiah Berlin.** Locke, Berkeley, Voltaire, Hume, Reid, Condillac, Hamann.
(#MW1494—$1.50)

☐ **THE AGE OF IDEOLOGY: THE 19TH CENTURY PHILOSOPHERS edited by Henry D. Aiken.** Kant, Fichte, Hegel, Schopenhauer, Comte, Mill, Spencer, Marx, Nietzsche, Kierkegaard.   (#MW1452—$1.50)

☐ **THE AGE OF ANALYSIS: 20TH CENTURY PHILOSOPHERS edited by Morton White.** Peirce, Whitehead, James, Dewey, Bertrand Russell, Wittgenstein, Croce, Bergson, Sartre, Santayana and others.
(#MW1179—$1.50)

Other MENTOR Books of Special Interest

☐ **THE ESSENTIAL DESCARTES, edited and with an Introduction by Margaret Wilson.** Included are the major writings of the great 17th century French philosopher.
(#ME1543—$2.25)

☐ **THE ESSENTIAL ROUSSEAU newly translated by Lowell
Bair; with an Introduction by Matthew Josephson.** The
major contributions of the great 18th-century social
philosopher whose ideals helped spark a revolution that
still has not ended. Included are: The Social Contract,
Discourse on Inequality, Discourse on the Arts and Sciences, and The Creed of a Savoyard Priest (from Emile).
(#MJ1289—$1.95)

☐ **THE ESSENTIAL ERASMUS newly translated and with
an Introduction by John P. Dolan.** The first single volume
in English to show the full range of thought on one of
the great Catholic minds of the Renaissance.
(#MW1358—$1.50)

☐ **THE ESSENTIAL THOMAS PAINE, with an Introduction
by Sidney Hook.** The fascinating and informative work
that will lift the mist which surrounds this important
figure in American political thought. Included are: Common Sense, The Crisis, The Age of Reason (Part I and
II).
(#MW1468—$1.50)